Praise for Christy Ring

'*As long as young people swing their caman for the sheer thrill of the tingle in their fingers of the impact of ash on leather, the story of Christy Ring will be told and that will be forever.*'

Jack Lynch at Christy's graveside

'*Christy Ring a Cork hurler? He's more than a Cork hurler. He's a Cork religion.*'

Dublin supporter to his girlfriend at Croke Park

'*I met hurling men in Antrim who could reel off every record Ring achieved and one of them told me he could die happy now that he had played on Christy in a league match.*'

Justin McCarthy, Cork, Antrim, Clare and Waterford manager

'*I didn't fulfil my greatest ambition to win an All-Ireland hurling medal but I retired with the next best thing – the honour of having played on Christy Ring. To say he is the greatest hurler of all time is a gross understatement. There never was and never will be anyone like him.*'

Des Ferguson, Dublin hurler and footballer

'*No matter how prosaic the occasion Ring always drew the crowds. The bigger the occasion, the greater the crowd. Over 40,000 people turned up annually to see him in the Railway Cup final on St Patrick's Day and Croke Park was crammed with over 80,000 for his last two All-Ireland appearances. Attendances declined dramatically after his retirement.*'

Dermot Crowe, *Irish Independent*

'*One day my father took me to the Athletic Grounds for a big match and we met dozens of people coming against us. "Is the match called off?" my father asked. "No," he was told, "but Ring isn't playing so there's no point in going in."*'

Tony Connolly, Cork hurler

'*I wasn't Christy Ring. I was just a good honest hurler who tried to give his best every time he wore the black and amber.*'

Charlie Carter, Kilkenny hurler

'Tipperary were on holidays in Florida in 1989. We were waiting for a bus to take us sight-seeing. This tall Afro-American was watching us with interest. We told him we were a hurling team from Ireland. "Hurling," he exploded. "Is that guy Christy Ring still playing?" He had shared digs in New York years earlier with the Kilkenny hurler of the 1940s Terry Leahy who never tired of talking about hurling and the greatness of Christy Ring.'

Seamus Leahy, Tipperary mentor

'To us kids Christy was the ultimate. We all modelled ourselves on him. It was a personal honour for me to play against him in the league final of 1962. He was in his forties at the time but he scored seven points and had a grand game.'

Eddie Keher, Kilkenny hurling legend

'Tipperary were first out on the field and then the Cork players came out. One by one they arrived and each one got a mighty cheer. Then Christy Ring came out and the whole place shook. It shook I tell you. I never experienced anything like it.'

Jimmy Doyle, Tipperary legend, on his first Munster final

'Before the 1957 Railway Cup games Christy challenged me to a bet – which of us would score most that day. I was playing well at the time so I took up the challenge. Then Christy went out and scored three goals and five points. How could I follow that?'

Frank Stockwell, Galway football star

'Christy always tried the impossible. Who else would practise sideline cuts from behind the end-line?'

Jim McKeon, biographer of Frank O'Connor

'Ring was hurling's Shakespeare, its Pele, its Mozart. He came as close to perfection as any sportsman can.'

Eamonn Sweeney, *The Pocket History of Gaelic Sports*

'In training he always perfected the hard shots. He showed us how to take a sideline cut from a ball stuck in the mud and still send it over the bar.'

Con O'Leary, colleges captain

'We asked him his technique with 21-yard frees. "I always aim at the funkiest player on the goal line," he said. I watched him in matches afterwards and, sure enough, at the last moment a timorous head would bob sideways as Christy's shot whizzed by to the net.'

Louis Marcus, film director

'His greatest game? Impossible to say, he had so many. The 1946 All-Ireland and that magnificent goal after a lengthy solo run. The three goals he scored in the last six minutes to beat reigning champions Limerick in 1956. The 4–5 he got in the Railway Cup final the day the Hogan Stand was opened in 1959. The six goals and four points he scored against Wexford the same year just months before they won the All-Ireland. And the winning goal against Mick Mackey's men in 1944 just when a draw seemed likely. Someone asked him why he had not taken a point to win the game. "Anyone could do that," he said.'

Din Joe Buckley, Cork hurler

'I have seen them all and he is the greatest hurler ever. Ring is a natural. A pocket Hercules, beautifully built with a powerful frame. And those hands? I have never seen a man with such perfect hands. He had tremendous wrists packed with dynamite.'

P.D. Mehigan, *The Irish Times*

'There is little doubt but there are two – Mick O'Connell in football and Christy Ring in hurling. I remember talking to Jack Lynch about Christy Ring and he was the greatest. In fact, my son played hurling with Christy on Ballyinskelligs beach. Christy believed that hurling was not indigenous and could be learned, so that brings me back to my earlier point that Kerry could win the hurling All-Ireland.'

Hugh O'Flaherty, former Supreme Court Judge

' 'Tis a sin to bury that man.'

Woman at Christy Ring's removal

Come counties all both great and small who boast a hurling king,
Can one tonight hold candlelight to Cork's own Christy Ring?

CHRISTY RING

HURLING'S GREATEST

TIM HORGAN

The Collins Press

Published in 2008 by
The Collins Press
West Link Park
Doughcloyne
Wilton
Cork

© Tim Horgan 2007, 2008
First published in hardcover in 2007 by The Collins Press

British Library Cataloguing in Publication data.

Horgan, Tim, 1946 -
  Christy Ring
  1. Ring, Christy 2. Hurling players - Biography
  I. Title
  796.3'5

ISBN-13: 9781905172740

Book design and typesetting: designmatters
Font: Times New Roman, 11 point
Printed in Malta

Cover photographs:
Front: Christy Ring, watched by Jimmy Doyle (Tipperary, with cap) and
John Nolan (Wexford) in the 1963 Railway Cup Final, courtesy *The Irish
Times*;
Spine: Christy returning from his first tour to America, courtesy *Irish
Examiner*;
Back: Battered but unbowed. Christy typifies Cork's blood-and-bandage
spirit after beating Tipperary in 1952, courtesy *Irish Examiner*.

CONTENTS

Praise for Christy Ring   *i*

1. Boyhood   1
2. A Cork Minor   12
3. The Glen   30
4. Four-In-A-Row   54
5. Brief Hiatus   65
6. 1946 – His Greatest Final   70
7. Lean Years   84
8. The Churches Tournament   99
9. 1950   107
10. Wexford Arrive   123
11. 1953 – Glory And Controversy   147
12. Wave Wildly The Flags   163
13. 1954 – The Goal That Made History   179
14. 1956 – A Year To Remember   208
15. Retirement?   222
16. 1958 – Sitting It Out   230
17. 1959 – Hurler Of The Year   237
18. 1960 – Year Of Miracles   252
19. Ups And Downs Of 1961   260
20. 1962   273
21. Farranferris   282
22. Twilight Time   292
23. Easter 1966   304
24. The Mentor   318
25. Ringey And Keano   326
26. Last Days   337
27. The Statues   347
28. Hurler Of The Century   355

Christy said …   360
Christy Ring's Roll of Honour   362
Picture Credits   363
Acknowledgements   364
Bibliography   366
Index   368

*A young Christy with Donie O'Sullivan (Ballycotton) on left
and a friend in relaxed mood on Patrick's Street.*

CHAPTER ONE

BOYHOOD

'Any sign of them?'

The question was repeated from time to time as the cluster of men in their Sunday best assembled at a corner near the Litton fountain in the centre of Cloyne. Lacking the means to get to the match themselves, they waited impatiently for the first sighting of the bicycle carrying Nicholas Ring and his young son as they returned from the big hurling game at Midleton, Carrigtwohill, Riverstown or even Cork city.

'They're back,' someone would shout and the men would eagerly look down River Street and watch the slender cyclist approach with renewed vigour after the long journey. Passing the school and the terrace of half-door cottages, he would finally draw to a halt as the group gathered around for details of the match. Then, as Nicholas lit a Woodbine and began to narrate the happenings of the game, his fair-haired son would dash off home to regale his mother and family with every detail he could remember.

It was a familiar Sunday for young Christy, a weekly highlight that he looked forward to, with little thought of the discomfort of sitting on a crossbar, as his father's bike traversed a bumpy road that often led the 18 miles to the city and back again.

Hurling was in Nicholas' blood. He himself played with Cloyne in his youth and he longed for the day when the village would make a mark in hurling once again. The vagaries of fortune rendered that hope unlikely to materialise in the late 1920s and early '30s, but nothing would stop Nicholas from travelling to as many hurling games as possible, no matter who was playing. Almost invariably young Christy accompanied him.

'After Cloyne,' said Christy, 'Carrigtwohill was my father's team and Tommy Barry – Paddy's uncle – was his favourite player. He used to talk about them a lot as we travelled to the matches. He spoke about other great teams too and other great hurlers, especially the Dungourney men with Jamesey Kelleher, a hurling legend and a great horseman. I learned all about the great Jamesey on the way to hurling matches. He was well retired by the time I was taken to big games, but I saw some of the great Cork hurlers of the 1926-31 period in action with their clubs – men like Eudie Coughlan, Jim Hurley, Dinny Barry-Murphy, Morgan Madden, the Aherne brothers and Paddy Delea.'

Other great sportsmen would have come to the attention of the wide-eyed youngster in those years – men like Dr Pat O'Callaghan and Bob Tisdall, winning Olympic gold medals for Ireland, Danno Mahony the world wrestling champion from Ballydehob and, above all, the young boxer Jack Doyle from the Holy Ground in nearby Cobh, bringing excitement to the lives of Irish people in those drab days. All four were regally fêted on their return to Cork.

Momentous Times

Christy was born on Saturday, 30 October 1920 at Kilboy, about a mile from Cloyne. His family later moved to the village and Christy grew up at Spittal Street, known to all in Cloyne as Spit Lane and destined to produce many fine hurlers, none greater though than the second son of Mary and Nicholas Ring. Christy had two sisters, Katie and Mary Agnes, and two brothers, Willie John and Paddy Joe.

At the time of his arrival, Ireland was in a state of deadly turbulence – ambushes, reprisals and hunger strikes underlining the gravity of the struggle for independence. The very week he was born, two of the most revered names in Irish history made world headlines. Cork's Lord Mayor, Terence McSwiney, died after a 74-day hunger strike in Brixton Prison and was brought home where he lay in state at the old City Hall on the Saturday of Christy's birth. The following Monday morning, eighteen-year-old Kevin Barry was hanged in Mountjoy Jail for his involvement in the ambush of a troop convoy in Dublin.

Terence McSwiney's funeral drew thousands of mourners to the streets of Cork to watch the procession to St Finbarr's cemetery and convey their sympathy and shock at his painful death. It was a massive outpouring of grief, the likes of which would not be seen again in Cork for almost 60 years.

'Christy had a tremendous love of his country,' said Liam Ó Tuama. 'He learned this at home in Cloyne and later from his great friend Jim Hurley, with whom he constantly re-lived the exploits of the great Irishmen who fought for freedom.' A Clonakilty man, Big Jim had been active with Tom Barry's Flying Column during the War of Independence and later became one of Cork's great hurlers.

'Christy loved singing patriotic ballads,' said Willie John Daly, 'and on the way home in his car after winning matches, we'd be singing all the way. Songs like "The Bould Fenian Men" and other ones that John McCormack made famous. Tough Barry would try and get an operatic aria in from time to time but Christy always went for the rousing patriotic ballads.'

'Tough'

Christy was just six when Jim Barry began his association with the Cork teams, and twelve years later the genial trainer welcomed him to the county senior ranks and a lasting friendship developed between them.

Popularly known as 'Tough', Jim had been a competent amateur boxer in his youth and had been billed as 'champion welterweight of the IRA' when he took on Ireland's top professional heavyweight in an exhibition fight. 'It wasn't so hard to be IRA champion just then,' said Jim, 'because the IRA could not be described as being madly enthusiastic about boxing, but I had a bout with my good friend, Packey Mahony, who was Irish heavyweight champion.'

Jim and Packey were asked to train the Cork hurlers in 1926 and they steered the county to All-Ireland glory that year. They managed a repeat performance in 1928 when Seán Óg Murphy was captain for the second time, and in 1929 when Dinny Barry-Murphy was skipper. In 1931 came the three games against Kilkenny, the second of which is rated as one of the best ever All-Ireland finals. A lean period followed before Cork returned to Croke Park the day the

Fourteen-year old Christy with hurley (front left) and a Cloyne hurling team in 1934. Note the variety of jerseys.

Second World War started. They lost that game, but there were good times ahead and Tough Barry would become synonymous with the great glories of the 1940s and '50s.

Early Games

'Why did I take up hurling in the first place?' a surprised Christy repeated to Limerick hurling scribe and historian, Séamus Ó Ceallaigh. 'The only reason I took up hurling was that there was nothing else to do in Cloyne village in my young days. There was a field where the lads went hurling and I joined them there as soon as I could. I spent many hours practising there with the local lads. Many of them, including my brothers, Willie John and Paddy Joe, were very good hurlers, but they had other interests. I had just one – to learn the game of hurling and play it well.'

'After school we'd go down to the field,' said Paddy Motherway, 'and we'd play with a sponge ball. We'd be after making a chal-lenge at school between two or three classes, but we always made sure that Christy was on our side. We'd play for twenty goals or something like that and it would be dark before we finished. Other times the farmer would chase us out of the field.'

Just behind Christy's home was Spillane's field, later to become the Cloyne hurling pitch, and it was there that Christy and Willie John spent hours training together. 'Christy found no problem coping with four or five hours' training every day,' said Willie John. 'This was not just a puck around the field. It was first-time pulling on the ground, doubling on the ball in the air, sideline cuts and free pucks. Relaxation never entered Christy's mind while training and he practised from both the right and the left. All through his career he firmly believed in training and always keeping fit.'

'Christy told me that he was familiar with the feel of a hurley at an early age and during his childhood and boyhood he never played at anything else,' said Paddy Downey. 'He believed in constant practice.'

Yet Christy himself discarded the word 'practice', when Seamus Hayes, in an interview in Cork's diocesan magazine, *The Fold*, asked him about it years later. 'There is no such thing as practice,' he said. 'There is such a thing as hard work. Hurling is hard work – it's like carrying 100 bricks before you put up one. You must learn to carry them first. Then you'll put them up. You must work step by step. The hardest things that you must do in training will serve you well in the game because you'll never be asked to do them as hard again. The easy way happens in the game but, of course, it only seems easy because you have been doing the hard things in training.'

'I remember quite well when Christy was very young and there was a ruck, he'd always be in the middle of it,' said Paddy Motherway. 'He was very small, he'd be under your feet he was so small, and he'd a man's hurley that his father had cut down to size for him. He'd be inside in the middle of it all and he'd come out with the ball, always. And there was an old man, Pad Aherne, living by the field and he'd be leaning over the garden wall, watching us. I remember well, one day he said to Christy, "You'll play in Croke Park yet, boy!"'

Debut

'I was twelve when I played in my first real match,' said Christy. 'It was for the Cloyne minor team and I was put in goal.'

Jimmy Motherway remembered the occasion well. 'The first time I ever saw Christy playing a proper match was in Midleton against Sarsfields, a minor match. They put him in goals. He wasn't as high as the man's hurley he was given, but he could stop every ball. However, the Sars forwards soon sensed that he was vulnerable. So they rushed in and knocked him and he actually cried inside in goals. His brother Willie John and my brother Paddy were in the full-back line and they made sure the bigger boys didn't rush him a second time.'

In no way daunted by his baptism of fire against the older lads, Christy continued to play whenever he was asked or allowed, and went on to win his first medal two years later.

'The first medal I ever won was on Glenbower Sunday,' he recalled. 'There used to be an annual festival on May Sunday at Glenbower Wood near Killeagh. People used come from all over east Cork by pony and trap, side-cars, horse-drawn floats, bicycles, whatever, and down from Cork city by train. Killeagh was the last stop before Youghal on the railway line in those days. You'd get people coming over from Waterford too, as Waterford teams were often involved in the Glenbower tournament matches. It was at Glenbower that I won my first medal. I was fourteen at the time and I played at right wing-forward.'

School Days

'By all accounts Christy was a very bright, intelligent and diligent pupil,' said Michael O'Brien, a former teacher, school principal and Cloyne hurler. 'He was also very determined and he showed that one year when the principal, Maurice Spillane, made a hurley and a ball available to the pupil with the highest grade in the school. That was a great prize as most youngsters played with old hurleys cut down to size or even improvised sticks we called "crookeens" and ten-year-old Christy was determined to win the hurley. There were 48 pupils altogether and it was Christy who got the highest grade and won the prize.'

'The master called out the name of the pupil with the highest grade,' recalled Jimmy Motherway, 'and we gave a *buala bas* as Christy sat shyly in his seat – proud and delighted but still shy.

Then Mr Spillane called him up to the front of the class and presented the hurley and asked him to test it. He grasped the handle, got the feel of the hurley, swung it gently and hopped the ball on the bas. It was great to watch.'

From an early age Christy took part in school hurling games and was always so intense and focused on winning that occasionally he would disregard authority and vent his annoyance at the referee – the schoolmaster – if a decision went against him. It was a trait that would be associated with him for many years to come.

Winning the prize hurley was one of Christy's fond memories of his schooldays. He always spoke highly of the school and its masters who gave him so much encouragement.

Jerry Moynihan

'Jerry Moynihan was largely responsible for the revival of the Cloyne club in 1934,' wrote Willie John Ring in his history of Cloyne GAA. 'On his appointment to the boys' school in 1933, Jerry was so impressed by the hurling abilities of his charges and the older players that he suggested a meeting to discuss re-affiliation. A first meeting failed, but the second one saw the coming into being once again of the Cloyne hurling club.'

'The Cloyne club is actually one of the oldest in east Cork,' said David Daly, secretary and hurler. 'We can trace our history back to the 1890s and we played in the divisional championships from the beginning except for a two-year gap in the early '30s.'

A native of Ballingeary, Jerry was a regular inter-county footballer who, according to Willie John, brought his own particular blend of courage and tactical skill to hurling. He figured on the great Cloyne sides of the late 1930s and won junior football honours with Midleton.

Christy was once asked to compare the Cloyne county champion sides of 1939 when he played himself, and 1961 when his brother Paddy Joe was in goal, but he declined to say which was the better team. 'I'll say this though,' he added with emphasis, 'I, for one, would hate to have to mark Jerry Moynihan.'

Renowned *Irish Times* journalist, Paddy Downey from Toormore in the Goleen area of west Cork, interviewed Jerry Moynihan during

The youthful Christy.

the course of his research on Ring and he retains a fascinating tape recording of the school teacher's assessment of young Christy. The interview was published for the first time by Denis Walsh in *The Sunday Times* in 2004.

Jerry had started in Cloyne by teaching the junior classes and did not meet Christy until he began organising hurling games after school in a field owned by Mr Creed, a well-known horse breeder.

'On the second evening, I spotted this very slight young fellow. I didn't know him at the time because he was in the senior classes. Even though most of the children of his age group were bigger, they hadn't the art of hurling at all as he had. As well as that, he had grit and determination. Even though it was only a friendly game, he was giving all that was in him. He wasn't the normal type of child. He was rather severe in himself. He wasn't the fine smiling child that you might find at that age. There was fire in him – he was a fiery type of lad. I remember one decision I made during a match which Christy disagreed with. Although his team won well, he came up to me crying with temper.'

Jerry kept a sharp eye on Christy's progress in the years ahead and soon realised he had the makings of a Cork minor. 'I told Seamus Long, who was in charge of the county minors in 1938, to watch Christy and to pay particular attention to his sideline cuts. He could send in a ball 70 yards or more at that stage, and in the Munster championship, when Limerick were leading by four goals, Christy sent in four sideline balls which Ted Sullivan and Kevin McGrath turned into the net. Cork won by a point.'

How young Christy developed his hurling skills would in time give rise to some colourful stories – ringing the parish priest's doorbell by hitting a sliothar from various distances was one of the more fanciful yarns – but his nephew Willie Ring recalled one imaginative method Christy did actually use to improve the accuracy of his striking.

'There was an old house near the playing field,' said Willie in the *Ringy* video. 'It was in a state of disrepair and one window was broken and a board put over it for protection. Christy would wet a ball with water and then hit it at the piece of timber so that the wet ball left a mark on the timber and he'd know exactly the spot that the ball struck. He would then hit the ball again, possibly to a different spot and continue like that to get absolute accuracy with the blow of the ball.'

Some years later when Christy had moved to Cork city and taken up lodgings over the Fountain Café on the Grand Parade, he continued to perfect his wristwork by sitting on a bed and angling a ball from his hurley to the bedroom walls. Finbarr Deane remembered finishing work at Capwell one night and finding a CIÉ colleague, who shared digs with Christy, walking up and down outside the café. 'He's after finding a new spot on the wall that he hasn't hit yet,' the man explained, 'and I'll get no rest until he hits it.'

Work

In those days of high unemployment and emigration it was typical of boys and girls to leave school at fourteen and try to supplement their family income with menial jobs. Christy was luckier than most youngsters, in that he found work as an apprentice mechanic in Midleton. Cycling the four miles to work with the Williams firm was no problem and he enjoyed his stay there. More significantly, he learned to drive, and that qualification would prove to be an invaluable asset in his employment prospects, even more so than his reputation as a hurler.

Working with the Williams family had the side effect of introducing Christy to rugby and he attended many games out of curiosity, interest and above all loyalty to his employers, a great rugby family. Hurling was paramount, of course, but sport in general intrigued him, even the four games excluded by the GAA Ban. He was not foolhardy enough to risk suspension by attending the major rugby games at Musgrave Park, but he knew he was safe at a poorly-attended club match at the Mardyke. The GAA vigilantes, whose job was to catch hurlers or footballers transgressing the Ban and getting them suspended, reserved their activities for the big rugby and soccer fixtures in the city.

Yet Christy's attitude to the Ban was ambiguous. He had a natural interest in the inherent skills of rugby, soccer, hockey and cricket, and he was keen to unravel the playing techniques of the top exponents of those games. He realised from an early age, however, that these garrison games were introduced to Ireland by the British Army as a recruiting device and were anathema to true republicans. Imbued with a strong sense of patriotism, Christy cannot have felt very comfortable at those rugby matches and it is no great surprise that at the height of his playing career Christy asked in a rare interview – 'Where would we be without the Ban?'

Like many families of the time, the Rings were comfortable enough, not poor, although work was long and hard and money was scarce. Nicholas Ring worked for a local landowner as a gardener and his children contributed to the family income as soon as they left school. Nicholas' great weakness was his smoking habit which led to his death at the early age of 45, making it all the more difficult for Mary Ring to sustain the family.

Already in declining health in 1937, when Christy was chosen as a sub on the Cork minor side and in 1938 when he made his playing debut for the county, Nicholas did not live to see his second son winning an All-Ireland medal or any of the glories that followed.

In the City

Having completed his apprenticeship at Midleton, Christy moved to the city and found work as a lorry driver with CIÉ. He took up lodgings in a flat over the Fountain Café next door to Fitzgerald's electrical store on the Grand Parade, just around the corner from St Augustine's church.

'Before Christy went off to work every morning,' said Michael Morey, 'he attended 7.30am Mass at St Augustine's. Then at weekends, he cycled home to Cloyne where he would help his mother with jobs that needed to be done in the house and, of course, when time permitted, he would go hurling in a field with the local lads. About 1953, after he started working with Shell, he bought his first car – a black Consul – and after that he continued the weekly journey in much greater comfort.'

'Christy frequented St Augustine's church over a long period when he was in digs on the Grand Parade,' said Fr Pat Moran OSA, 'and he became friends with the priests here, notably Fr Denis B. Redmond, a Tipperary man with whom he had endless hurling conversations. Fr Redmond always believed that Christy gave him valuable information which he duly fed to his friends in Tipperary. Christy knew this, of course, but he never let on. There was no fear of Christy giving away any tactical secrets, especially to the old enemy.'

The proximity of the church to his new abode and the friendship of members of the Augustinian order obviously helped Christy, a shy young country boy, to settle in the city. He developed lasting friendships with the priests and this was best exemplified when he donated his eighth All-Ireland medal to form part of a special chalice during the Marian year of 1954.

CHAPTER TWO

A CORK MINOR

There was an expectant hush in the boardroom at Cook Street on the Tuesday evening as the names of the Cork minor hurlers to play Kilkenny in the All-Ireland final of 1937 were called out.

Over twenty players were named to travel to Killarney but, to the surprise of all present, Tom Powell, the Midleton delegate, stood up and voiced his disapproval.

'Mr Chairman,' he said in an agitated tone, 'why is Christy Ring only a sub? Christy is one of the best minor hurlers in the county. He should be on the team, not a sub.'

'I liked Tom Powell,' said Jim Hurley who was at the meeting. 'He loved the games and the players and when he spoke about them, he spoke from the heart, but when he made his protest that evening he lost his usual good humour. He was quickly silenced by the big guns at the head of the table, of course, but as he sat down I could hear his last remark – "Time will prove me right."'

'That was the first I ever heard of Christy Ring from Cloyne,' added Jim. 'I attributed Tom's disappointment to local patriotism. Christy was playing minor hurling with St Enda's of Midleton at the time but, like the county selectors, I was wrong. Time would certainly prove good Tom Powell right.'

The Cusack Stand was under construction in Croke Park that September and the All-Ireland senior and minor hurling finals were transferred to Fitzgerald Stadium, Killarney.

'I was chosen as last sub for the 1937 minor final,' said Christy, 'but I continued wearing the Cork jersey every year for 25 years after that.'

Christy was only sixteen throughout the championship and had

Christy, standing second from left, about to play his first minor match with Cork in 1938. Also included are future Cork seniors Ted O'Sullivan (standing extreme right) and Alan Lotty (second from right in front.) Ray Cummins' father, Willie, is third from left, front.

not been included in the earlier selections. His St Enda's team-mate, Bobby Dineen, had been picked from the start, Willie Aherne got chosen for the Munster final, and both travelled to Belfast to play Antrim in the All-Ireland semi-final. Being naturally diffident, Christy was particularly ill-at-ease as a late addition to the panel, when they prepared to travel to the final on the Sunday morning.

'I remember the trip to Killarney very well,' said Tony Slattery, who became the first to score in a hurling final at the famous football venue. 'Christy Ring was a sub that day and he sat next to me in the bus. He didn't open his mouth all the way to Killarney.'

Another sub was Din Joe Buckley. 'I remember sitting next to Christy on the sideline when a Kilkenny senior player, Paddy Dowling, walked past us and turned to Christy and said, "You have the strongest pair of hands I ever saw".'

1938 Cork County Minor Hurling Champions.
*Back row: T. Powell (Official), W. Deasy, S. Murphy, T. Barry, T. O'Sullivan, C.
Donovan, K. O'Keeffe, J. Hennessy, P. Kirby, E. Cleary, E. Hayes, J. Sullivan,
J. Houlihan (Official) (Min). Front row: W. Ahern, C. Ronayne, P. Mulcahy, J.
White, C. Ring, W. Walsh, J. O'Brien, W. Marie O'Connell, P. Barry.*

Looking back at his first appearance on the Cork minor panel,
Christy said: 'I remember very clearly the jersey I was given for the
1937 minor final in Killarney. It was number 26 and when Cork
won the All-Ireland I didn't get a medal. That didn't worry me too
much as I was still eligible for the 1938 minor championship.
Winning an All-Ireland medal that year meant an awful lot to me.'

'I saw Christy playing for the first time with St Enda's against
Sars at the Pond Field in Carrigtwohill,' said Willie John Daly, who
was twelve at the time. 'Christy was outstanding at left half-back

and I remember Christy Duggan, a great Midleton hurler, was very excited on the sideline. Every time Christy would do something good, Christy Duggan would shout: "Come on Christy, come on me little flower."'

'I played with Christy and Ted Sullivan on the St Enda's team for two years,' said Ted Barry. 'St Enda's were mostly Midleton players, but those of us from surrounding areas joined them because there were no minor teams in our own places. I was from Ballinacurra, Willie Aherne came from Aghada, John Joe McCarthy from Cloyne, Maurice Prendeville and Jackie White from Castlemartyr, Killian O'Keeffe from Ballymacoda and Christy, of course, came from Cloyne.

'We beat Sars in the 1937 championship but they later objected because the Carrig pitch wasn't properly lined. Sars lost their appeal but we agreed to play them again and they beat us! Christy was great in the two matches against Sars and the first round against Cobh. We were surprised he didn't make the Cork minors until the final.'

The following year, Ted and Christy were among the heroes of St Enda's great championship run and it was the tall Ballinacurra lad who became Cork minor captain in 1939. 'Sign of the times,' said Ted. 'I did not even have a pair of boots when I went up to play the All-Ireland final. I had to borrow a pair from one of the subs.'

Cork Debut

Christy played in the red and white colours for the first time on Sunday 22 May 1938 and the venue, appropriately, was Thurles, which was to be the setting for so many of his triumphs in the years to come.

Cork won a fantastic game against Limerick by 7-2 to 6-4 and, although defenders rarely got mentioned in newspaper reports of minor matches at that time, Christy was singled out by the *Cork Examiner*: 'Ring was doing very well for Cork in the various challenges and Kelly was equally good for Limerick.'

After two exacting games against Limerick and Tipperary, the Munster final against unlikely opponents, Kerry, was an anti-climax at the Cork Athletic Grounds. Kerry, who had surprised Waterford, failed to score and Cork won by over nine goals. Christy contributed to the victory from an early stage as the *Examiner* reported: 'Ring took the free and placed nicely for McGrath to put up Cork's second goal.'

The All-Ireland semi-final against Galway at Ennis was another riveting encounter. Cork won by 7-4 to 5-3 and, according to the *Connacht Tribune*, the two Sullivans, Ryan, McGrath, Hogan, Ring and Young were best for the winners, with most of the scores coming from Ted Sullivan, Kevin McGrath and Tadhg Ryan from Mitchelstown.

Croke Park

Christy made his first appearance in Croke Park on Sunday 4 September 1938 when he played with the victorious Cork minors. He lined out in defence, yet still contrived to score a crucial goal when the outcome was in the balance. Christy marked Maurice Keane, son and namesake of a Dublin Geraldine's All-Ireland star.

'We played Dublin and it was a very hard game,' recalled Eamonn Young. 'I was in the middle of the field trying to give Jerry Looney of the Glen a hand. Standing at full-back was a tanned, strong-chested lad named Alan Lotty, with Paddy Hogan, short haircut and strong jaw, mounted on his hurling pedestal at centre-back. At right half-back, a slim crew-cutted lad from Cloyne, shouted at you during play – he was called Christy Ring – and the father of the Cummins hurlers, Willie, stroked away beautiful shots from the half-back line up to the other side, where Ted Sullivan of Castlemartyr helped Kevin McGrath of the Glen to get the scores we needed.'

'Christy may have been a quiet, shy country lad who hardly spoke to anyone off the pitch,' said Con Murphy, 'but once the game got going, he became totally focused on winning. And if that meant shouting at his team-mates or taking frees himself, he did it.'

Early goals by Kevin McGrath and Ted Sullivan had Cork two points in front when, according to the *Examiner*, 'A free to Cork, taken by Ring, was nicely placed and Sullivan netted'.

Cork led 3-1 to 1-2 at the break and, despite further goals by McGrath and Sullivan, Dublin hit back, reducing the lead to two points with ten minutes to go. It was then that Christy, on his own initiative, went forward to take a 21-yards free.

1938 All-Ireland Minor Champions.
Back (from left): Tadhg Ryan, Ted Foley, Eamonn Young, George Sadlier, Alan Lotty, Paddy Hogan, Luke O'Sullivan, Ted O'Sullivan. Front: Christy Ring, Killian O'Keeffe, Jerry Looney, Kevin McGrath (captain), John O'Mahony, Willie Cummins, Paddy Quinn.

'Our captain, Kevin McGrath, a prolific scorer, was our free taker in the forwards,' said Eamonn Young. 'We expected him to take the 21 and get the point that would put us three in front but, to our astonishment, Christy arrived up and blasted the ball to the net. There were no questions asked afterwards – it was a crucial goal.'

That was the most significant score of the game, and Ted Sullivan later added another goal to give Cork a 7-2 to 5-4 victory.

'Going for a goal was madness, Christy,' said his mentor, Jerry Moynihan, afterwards. 'Why didn't you take your point? It would have been safer and Cork would have been three points in front. Why did you take the risk?'

'I knew I could do it,' said Christy, expressing the confidence and self-belief that would characterise his free-taking at the highest level for so many years afterwards.

The complete 1938 minor panel was: Pat Joe Quinn (Tracton), Jimmy O'Mahony (Bandon), Alan Lotty (Sars), George Sadlier (Buttevant), Christy Ring (St Enda's), Paddy Hogan (Glen), Willie Cummins (Carrigtwohill), Eamonn Young (Glen), Jerry Looney (Glen), Killian O'Keeffe (O'Neill-Crowleys), Ted Foley (Glen), Luke O'Sullivan (St Colman's), Tadhg Ryan (Sean Clarachs), Ted O'Sullivan (St Enda's), Kevin McGrath (Glen). Subs: Donie O'Sullivan (St Colman's), Danny Murphy (Valley Rovers), Jim Murphy (Glen), Nicholas O'Connor (St Colman's), Willie Aherne (St Enda's), H. Twomey (St Anne's), David O'Driscoll (Rochestown), Tadhg Barry-Murphy (Cloughduv), Con Kelly ('Barrs) and Sean O'Sullivan (Glen).

Four weeks after young Christy's first All-Ireland final one of his favourite singers, the distinguished tenor John McCormack, gave his final concert at the Savoy in Cork as part of his farewell tour of Ireland and Britain. 'Why am I retiring?' he asked. 'It's hard work for a grandfather, you know. I am 54 since June. Better to go with the audience saying "why" instead of "why not?"'

The end of one legend, the beginning of another.

Cloyne Champions

Christy's impressive form with St Enda's and the Cork minors in 1938 was replicated with the Cloyne juniors and he played a big part in helping them reach their first east Cork final. Fittingly, Jerry Moynihan was captain and they met Bride Rovers at Midleton.

The Ring brothers were prominent from the start, Willie John scoring 1-1 and Christy pointing a free to give them an interval lead. During the second half, as the *Examiner* put it, 'Cloyne came on with undaunted energy for Christy Ring to drive a long shot all the way through for a beautiful point.' Paddy Moss Aherne, scorer of the first goal, and Paddy Hoare, who got three in the second half, were also among the heroes of Cloyne's 5-5 to 3-2 victory.

'Suspended,' said Willie John Ring, when I asked him why Christy was not on the Cloyne team in the county championship semi-final that year. 'In fact, we were short three of our best players the day we lost to Brian Dillon's.'

Willie John did not elaborate on why his younger brother had incurred a suspension that possibly cost Cloyne a county junior title, but Christy's first sending-off indicated two things – even at seventeen his hurling prowess had made him a player to be marked in every sense of the word and, secondly, his volatile temperament ensured that he would not accept foul play from anyone, regardless of strength or age difference.

'That team was good enough to win the county,' said Willie John, 'but you can't expect to do well with three top players missing.' Not the least important was Christy who stood perforce on the sideline watching Cloyne lose to Dillon's by two goals just three weeks before his eighteenth birthday. Twelve months later there would be no such handicap. Cloyne would go all the way.

Victories over Ballymacoda, Carrigtwohill and Castlemartyr saw them through to the east Cork final where they defeated Aghada. Then came the county championship and a first-round meeting with Clonakilty.

'For a long time Clonakilty were quite as good as their opponents,' wrote Jerry Beckett in his *Examiner* column, 'but the cleverness of the small Ring on the Cloyne wing turned the scales in favour of his side. What a player he would be if endowed with an inch or two more in stature.'

Cloyne won well and next met Newtownshandrum. Christy scored 2-6 and Cloyne reached their first county junior final against Mayfield at Midleton. Yet for days before the match, there was grave doubt about Christy's chances of playing. He had injured his ankle three days before the final. It troubled him greatly and he agreed to go to a bone-setter with Paddy Motherway, who needed treatment for his knee.

'The bone-setter put in my knee,' said Paddy, 'but he told Christy that a little bone was out in his ankle and that, if he put it in, Christy wouldn't be able to play on the Sunday. "Leave it alone," he said, "it'll be very sore but I'll put it in after the match."'

In the dressing room before the final, Jerry Moynihan stuffed Christy's boot with cotton wool to ease the pain and told him to play in the half-back line where he would not have so much twisting and turning to do. 'Normally Christy would have been up with the forwards,' said Paddy Motherway, 'but he started in the backs.

After a while the match was going against us and Christy gradually moved away up the field. He forgot about his leg and scored five points from play the same day. I don't think any other man would have stuck the pain that he went through.'

The final was played in mid-November 1939 and Cloyne's 6-5 to 3-3 victory brought great delight to the village and surrounding areas. A happy Christmas for all seemed assured but, unfortunately, there were already rumblings that would in time rupture the progress of the club, just when its future seemed so bright. And, through no fault of his own, Christy's name was at the heart of the dissension.

The Cork Juniors

'Christy Ring was an outstanding wing-back on the Cork minor team in 1938,' said Dan Coughlan from Ballydehob who joined the Glen when he was a student at Farranferris, 'but when he was picked for the Cork juniors a year later there was no place for him in defence. I was right half-back when we won the All-Ireland home title and the selectors decided I should retain that position. Christy was too good a hurler to be left off the team so the selectors decided there was only one thing to do and that was to play him in attack. That's how Christy Ring became a Cork forward.'

Eighteen-year old Christy (right) in the parade prior to his first adult game against Tipperary in 1939 and behind in black shorts are Batt Thornhill and Dan Coughlan.

Drumcollogher was the setting for Christy's first junior game with Cork on 18 June 1939. He lined out at wing-forward along with Willie Horgan on the 40 and Tim O'Riordan in the corner, with all three scoring goals in Cork's defeat of Tipperary.

'Christy was the youngest player on the team – very fast, very skilful,' said Willie. 'After we beat Tipp, he was moved to midfield alongside Derry Beckett. We were missing a few players for the semi-final, notably our full-back, Batt Thornhill, who was promoted to the senior team, but we were still fancied to retain the Munster title. We got quite a shock when Waterford beat us. Vincent Baston was their star player that day at Dungarvan.'

The Decies won by 5-6 to 1-8, with the Cork scores coming from Willie Horgan (1-2), Christy Ring (0-2), Derry Beckett (0-2), and a point each from the captain, Paul Humphries, and John Barry-Murphy, whose son Jimmy would in time become a celebrated figure in Cork's sporting history.

The players who took part in Christy's short-lived 1939 Munster junior championship were: Ned Porter (Brian Dillon's), Patsy Corbett (Mayfield), Dan Coughlan (Glen), Sean Hyde (Blarney), Paul Humphreys (Blarney), John Mescall (Blarney), Jeremiah Crowley (Tracton), Derry Beckett (Sars), Tim O'Riordan (Éire Óg),

Christy listens attentively to the referee as Waterford and Cork players hold hurleys before the start of the Munster junior semi-final of 1939.

John Lucey (Éire Óg), Humphrey O'Callaghan (Éire Óg), Willie Horgan (Brian Dillon's), John Barry-Murphy (Aghabullogue), William Twomey (Blackrock), Tim O'Mahoney (Cloyne), Eddie O'Riordan (Brian Dillon's), Tim O'Connell (Kinsale), Paddy Hogan (Glen), Maurice O'Flynn (Fr Matthew Hall), Tim O'Keeffe (Douglas) and, of course, Batt Thornhill, the Buttevant barber who played in the 'thunder and lightning final' (1939) before winning four consecutive All-Ireland medals in the early 1940s.

Senior Debut

Christy made his first appearance in the county senior colours early in 1939, and he remembered the occasion very clearly when asked about it years later.

'I came on as a sub when Cork played Limerick in a league or tournament match in the Gaelic Grounds. The subs and selectors used to sit where the Hogan Stand is now and I was sitting next to Seán Óg Murphy, watching Cork getting well beaten. Towards the end of the match Seán Óg turned to me and said, "Young fella, would you like to go on there for a while?" I said "Yes sir", so he sent me on instead of a Mayfield player, Johnny O'Mahony, who later played for the Lough, I think. Just after I came on, I was watching a Limerick ball going over the bar and trying to judge if it was going inside or outside the post. As I did so, my opponent gave me a lash across the ankle but, if he did, I wasn't long flaking him back. That was my introduction to senior hurling!

'Afterwards as we were leaving the grounds, Seán Óg shouted across at my opponent, "Hey, there was no need for you to hit that young fella."'

Clearly Seán Óg had seen the incident, although play was at the other end of the field. Many others would watch Ring rather than the play itself in years to come.

First League Medal

On 22 October 1939, Cork played the newly installed All-Ireland champions, Kilkenny, in a league match at the old Athletic Grounds. It was a hugely significant day for Cloyne people, with the club having a player on the county senior team. As many supporters as possible made the long journey to the city, most of them placing their bikes at the quay wall in Tivoli before crossing the river by ferry boats manned by the Garrett family and their neighbours near Beale's Hill.

'Whenever he'd talk about that game,' said Din Joe, 'Christy always mentioned that we were put on Kilkenny's two best men that day. I was marking Jim Langton and Christy's man was Paddy Phelan.'

The ground was packed almost to capacity to see the All-Ireland pairing so soon after the 'thunder and lightning' final. Most of the players involved were match-hardened hurlers, but for Christy, still only eighteen, it was a high-pressure occasion lining up with Jack Lynch, John Quirke, Jim Young, Micka Brennan, Jack Barrett and the others, against the likes of Paddy Phelan, Terry Leahy, Paddy Grace, Jim Langton, Jack Mulcahy and Sean O'Brien. A famous picture shows the anxiety clearly on his face as he watches the captains awaiting the toss of the coin.

Yet almost as soon as the game began, Christy overcame his nerves and quickly merged into an impressive Cork forward line dominated by Quirke. Terry Leahy opened the scoring with a point, John Quirke instantly replied, before Micka Brennan, in his trademark black togs

Jack Lynch and Jimmy Walsh (Kilkenny) await the toss of the coin as Christy (behind Billy Campbell) watches anxiously. He was about to play his first full league game for Cork.

and peak cap turned backwards, blasted a free to the net for the first of the nine goals the match would produce.

Twenty minutes into the game, Christy took a pass from Quirke and darted away from Phelan to score a fine point. The sides were level at half-time, 1-4 apiece, and Jim Langton sent a free to the net soon after the restart. Then, according to *The Irish Press*, 'Quirke and Christy Ring took a hand in a dazzling Cork dash, before Ted O'Sullivan shook the net with a grounder'.

Further Cork goals came from 'Bobby' Ryng and Jim Young, with Kilkenny scoring from Terry Leahy, Sean O'Brien and Jim Langton, plus a point from a midfield free by Paddy Phelan. The champions were edging towards another win when 'Bobby' Ryng had a late goal and Micka Brennan sealed matters with a final goal deep into injury time (6-5 to 4-7).

Cork's next game was against Clare on 13 November, the day of Cloyne's county final, and Christy had to miss that outing. He was back in the red jersey a week later against Limerick, although he went off injured in the first half of that match.

Cork gradually progressed to the league final of 1940, the county's first in ten years, and Christy lined out at right half-forward against Tipperary in April at the Park. One of the features of the game in those days was fast, direct ground hurling which often culminated in spectacular goals. No fewer than fourteen were scored on this occasion and Christy, the youngest player on the field, was among the goal scorers.

John Quirke was at his devastating best once again, scoring three goals and four points in the first half to help Cork to a commanding 6-8 to 1-2 interval lead. 'Quirky', who would have been a strong contender for the hurler of the year, outclassed no less a man than the Tipp captain and centre-back John Maher.

In an effort to haul down the seven-goal deficit, Tipperary moved wing-back Billy O'Donnell to full-forward and he managed to score four goals, a great feat in itself, but inconsequential on the day. Ger Looby and Tommy Doyle also got Tipp goals, but Cork finished well in front, 8-9 to 6-4, the other goals coming from O'Sullivan (two), Barrett and Ring.

Christy won his first senior medal with Cork and there was great excitement and pride in Cloyne that evening as the game was recounted stroke by stroke and Christy's performance lauded over and over again. It was a particularly proud occasion for Mary Ring and her family, but in the midst of all the joy and delight there was the sadness that Nicholas Ring was not there to witness another notable milestone on the road to glory for his son.

Munster Final

Although Cork won the league title in April, Limerick beat them in the Thomond Shield in May, so the provincial final in July was even more eagerly awaited than usual. It lived up to its promise.

'The Munster final and replay of 1940 have gone down as two of the best championship games ever seen on the famous Thurles sod,' said Mick Kennedy, the only Tipp man to win three All-Irelands with Limerick. 'I first got a close-up of Christy Ring in those games. His duel with Peter Cregan was a classical one and is still talked about today.' ('Peter came from Croom,' said Eamonn Cregan. 'My father was from Monagea, Newcastlewest, but we all originally came from Ardagh.')

'Our first meeting was a draw,' Mick added. 'On the following Sunday we met again and another epic resulted. Our attack sparkled that afternoon. Jackie Power, Dick Stokes and the Mackeys were simply superb. They had to be to break through a Cork rearguard that included such giants as Willie Murphy, Alan Lotty and Batt Thornhill. We would never have won that game, were it not that Timmy Ryan at midfield gave the greatest exhibition of his life. His overhead striking and ground play were brilliant and in the closing stages he once carried the ball from the back line to the halfway line in a wonderful relieving run.'

Never short of a colourful image, Paddy Mehigan – who wrote as 'Carbery' for the *Cork Weekly Examiner*, as 'Pat O' for *The Irish Times* and was also Irish radio's first great sport's commentator – was at his most lyrical describing the 1940 drawn game, Christy's first Munster final. Listen to his breathless account of the scoring:

'Striding along Din Joe Buckley let fly downhill and Micka gave John Quirke an opening the size of a hen. A sweet smooth swing and the ball was in the net behind Scanlan. The Limerick net-minder stonewalled a few more hot ones before Christy Ring of Cloyne put Cork a goal clear. Timmy Ryan, the stalwart Ahane farmer, placed cleverly for Paddy McMahon, the Kildimo Thrasher who crashed the ball in the webbing. Young Ring's smooth point gave Leeside the razor edge of the scoring.

'Soon we had the irrepressible playboy Mick Mackey dodging his burly way past Buckley to part out to his brother John, whose flaxen hair was bobbing in waves as he goaled. So the great game swung from end to end. Hardly was Stokes' point registered when Cork were surging inshore like a sudden summer hurricane from Inisclere. Dr Jim Young, playing a glorious game, swung on a travelling ball. Deadly was his aim and perfect his timing – the ball sped in low trajectory to the netting. Cork was a point behind. Billy Campbell, a darling striker, hit a beauty from long range. The teams were level.

'Mick Mackey led. Crashing ash held him but I think it was UCD man Stokes that finished the good work. Limerick the odd point ahead in 29. Livid closing minutes like sunset in a lightning storm of vivid flashes and bombing clouds. Cork tearing in eager waves. Ted Sullivan and Brennan through for a goal. A moment of doubt. Crossed flags. Score disallowed. Both protest. On with the dance. John Quirke shaved the sticks. He makes amends. John is masterly in his precision. The ball sails for the levelling flag and whistle.'

The final score: Limerick 4-3 Cork 3-6. 'Just think of it, Mick,' said Jack Lynch to Mick Mackey as they shook hands afterwards, 'we've got to go through this all over again next Sunday. We'll never do it.'

'We will,' said Mick, 'and I'll tell you this. Whoever wins on Sunday will win the All-Ireland.'

Time would prove Mick Mackey right, but not before another frenetic encounter with the Corkmen. 'We served up a repeat performance in Thurles, almost score for score,' said Mick (to Philip Roderick). 'Another classic of hurling and it was the game that really won the All-Ireland for us. We were two points down at half-time but, like the previous Sunday, we began the second half with two goals by Paddy McMahon. Then a third goal by Dick Stokes to put us seven ahead, but Cork fought back and with five minutes to go we were down to two points ahead, but we held out in a desperate finish.'

'Were it not for the unruly scenes that marred the closing stages, it would go down as one of the greatest hurling struggles in the history of the GAA,' wrote the *Youghal Tribune*. 'Lost time was being played when the crowd invaded the pitch as Micka Brennan was carried off injured. It took about ten minutes to clear the field and the match resumed on a high level of excitement. Cork did everything to get the winning goal, but Jack Lynch's great effort went narrowly wide and Limerick won by two points.'

Many years later Christy would recall those two games when he wrote an article in *The Spirit of the Glen*.

'My first big test was in the Munster final of 1940. That game ended in a draw and Limerick won the replay which ranks as one of the toughest Munster finals ever played. I was on Peter Cregan both days, a tough but fair hurler and I must have acquitted myself pretty well as I was selected on the Munster Railway Cup panel early in 1941 at a time when every county had players fighting for their places on the team. The Munster final gave me the extra confidence I needed for my own career. It taught me a lesson I never forgot, that hurling needs courage, heart and a firm belief in one's own ability to stand shoulder to shoulder with the best.'

Although he was among the scorers in both games Christy was bitterly disappointed at losing the replay by a narrow margin. Nevertheless his first season in senior ranks had been good to him. He had helped Cork to win their first league title in ten years and he had shown that he could live comfortably in the high voltage atmosphere of Munster championship hurling.

As the year drew to a close, his brother, Willie John, joined him on the Cork team at Croke Park for an Oireachtas game against Kilkenny. The selectors used the occasion to test a few newcomers including George Sadlier (Buttevant), Eddie O'Riordan (Brian Dillon's), Willie Cummins (Carrigtwohill) and the Glenmen, Paddy Hogan, Charlie Tobin and Dave Creedon. Willie John's display augured well for his prospects of becoming a regular Cork senior hurler but, unfortunately a serious knee injury, sustained the following year when he was 24, ended his hopes of inter-county glory.

It was a cold and wet autumn afternoon as the Ring brothers took the field together, Willie John at right corner-back and Christy at right half-forward. Kilkenny proved too strong, however, and won by a high margin but, according to the *Youghal Tribune*, Cork did well despite the result, adding that 'Christy Ring, one of Cork's best workers, scored three points and placed Ted Sullivan for the goal.'

Sitting together on the train home afterwards, Willie John and Christy were in gloomy mood. For both brothers to play together for Cork at Croke Park should have made it a great day for them, their family and their club, but the 7-11 to 1-6 defeat had cast a shadow on the occasion. Yet it was not the hefty trouncing that weighed heavily on their minds. They had much more to worry about back home, where troubles had reached such a dismal state that there was a real prospect of Willie John or Christy never playing for Cloyne again.

Departure

Brendan Behan once said that in Ireland, when a committee is formed, the first certainty is a split. Conflicting personalities, inflated egos, petty jealousies, the emergence of rival groupings or cliques inevitably lead to frictions which, if left to fester, will ultimately split the group.

It happened in Cloyne just at a time when their hurlers were emerging as a team poised for great things. County junior champions of 1939 and an inspirational young hurler in their ranks, the future should have been bright for the men in red and black. But word went round the village that Christy was leaving the club and, even though there was no truth in the rumour, the matter was raised at an acrimonious meeting where it was sarcastically suggested that his brothers should go too.

The painful upshot was that Willie John went to Ballinacurra and Paddy Joe to Russell Rovers. And Christy went nowhere. He remained 'unattached' for over a year until the summer of 1941 when, at Jack Lynch's suggestion, he put on the Glen Rovers jersey for the first time. He would play for the Glen for 26 years.

'Christy had come to live in the city,' said Jack, 'and he was working for CIÉ driving a lorry and delivering newspapers around Munster and south Leinster. He had a minor accident in Urlingford when he was reversing the truck and knocked the piers off a couple of pillars. He came to me, very upset and fearful of losing his driving licence. I told him it was a trivial matter, that he'd get off with a five shilling fine and, to ease his mind, I promised to ask a friend of mine, a superintendent in Blarney, if that would be the case. He agreed that it would. Christy was actually fined ten shillings in court and the next time I met him he was greatly relieved and thanked me for my help even though I had done nothing and told him so. Anyway, we soon got talking about hurling and he told me about the dispute with the Cloyne club which he said couldn't be resolved. I said being unattached was no advantage to his hurling progress, that he should be playing club hurling. "I know that", he said, "but what can I do?" "Why not join the Glen?" I suggested. "Yes", he said, "I might do that". So he went away, thought about it and the rest, as they say, is history.'

CHAPTER THREE

THE GLEN

'There is a magic quality attached to the name of Glen Rovers. It is a distinctive name, conjuring up visions of wooded slopes reaching down to the floor of a valley through the golden mists of a morning in May. It is a poetic name – a name which would inspire, for example, the genius of such an author as Maurice Walsh to write a novel about. And indeed "the Glen", as it is affectionately known by all Corkonians, was one time a thickly wooded area known as Goulding's Glen. The woods have long since vanished but the name of the locality is perpetuated in the title of this famous club which has played such a great part in the history of Cork hurling.'

So wrote Niall Cahill in a *Gaelic Weekly* tribute to the club in 1959 and, though Maurice Walsh of *The Quiet Man* fame may not have written stories about the Glen, local sons Frank O'Connor and Daniel Corkery certainly did, and sculptor Seamus Murphy, who also grew up in the area, had fond memories of its rugged beauty.

The Glen at one stage had been known as Dodge's Glen and there were several little mills along the Glen River from Ballyvolane to Watercourse Road, the first of these being a flax mill that later became the home of Professor Aloys Fleischman. The woods referred to were cut down to provide timber props for the trenches during the First World War.

The most significant event in the Glen's industrial history was the opening of Goulding's fertiliser factory at Spring Lane in 1856. William Goulding ran a paint shop with Humphrey Manders at 108 Patrick Street, but when he acquired an old distillery building at Spring Lane he began the manufacture of artificial manure.

Goulding, who was knighted for his work, is thought to have been the first in the world to produce artificial fertiliser. The original building burnt down in 1906 and was replaced by a modern structure with its gigantic chimney shaft that became so familiar to locals and to travellers arriving by train at the tunnel entrance to the city. Goulding's provided welcome employment for hundreds of workers from the Glen environs of Blackpool, Ballyvolane and Dillon's Cross, and remained in production until 1962 when the company moved to the Marina.

After leaving the old factory Sir Basil Goulding, grandson of the founder, donated the company's lands in the Glen to Cork Corporation to be developed as an amenity park. Spring Lane residents were provided with a neat people's park across the road from their houses and Glen Rovers were given extensive land on which to develop their hurling pitches.

The Start

Hurling had been played in the Blackpool district long before Glen Rovers were established and areas like the Commons Road and Thomas Davis Street had teams from time to time. In 1910, however, a hurling club honouring the Fenian leader Brian Dillon was established at Dillon's Cross and met with early success. Harry Lyons was the captain.

'Harry was courting a Blackpool girl, Lollie Barry, whom he later married,' said Henry Lyons, his nephew. 'Naturally, he spent a lot of time in and around Blackpool and he encouraged Lollie's brother, Robbie Barry, to play for Brian Dillon's, and also some other fine hurlers who were working in Goulding's at the time.'

With a healthy sprinkling of Goulding workers in their ranks, Brian Dillon's won the county minor – no age limit – title in December 1915, beating Rockmills in the final. With the Great War in progress, the medals were not readily available and when Dillon's lost to Lisgoold in the county junior championship on 17 September 1916, the Blackpool men's patience finally ran out. They still had not received their county medals, so a decision was taken to form their own club at the other side of the Glen.

The new club, which they called Glen Rovers, was established late in 1916 and affiliated the following year. Dick Geaney became the first secretary/treasurer, Johnny Cooke was the first captain and the other Dillon's players who were founder members of the Glen were Mickey Geaney, Dan O'Connor and Robbie Barry. The club's first chairman was Billy Flynn, with Mick Flynn as vice-chairman.

The colours chosen were green, white and orange, but as the Easter Rising and particularly the execution of the 1916 leaders had created such an impression on the minds of Irish people, it was decided to add a black band to honour the recently deceased patriots. And so Glen Rovers and their distinctive hooped jersey came into being.

Paddy O'Connell

Like other clubs, Glen Rovers made little headway in those years of torment, but in 1922 the Thomas Davis club, which catered for sixteen-eighteen year-old hurlers, merged with the Glen, and their clubroom at Bird's Quay became the Glen's new headquarters. More significantly, Paddy O'Connell, who had done so much for the juveniles at his old club, now gave his undivided attention to the Glen.

'Paddy O'Connell had been chief organiser of the Thomas Davis club,' wrote Paddy Deasy in *The Spirit Of The Glen*. 'He had this very rare ability of being able to control, guide and inspire young boys. He imposed a pretty strict discipline which was ruthlessly carried out. A list of the club rules and penalties was pinned on a notice board at Bird's Quay. These included a twopenny fine for talking to girls and a penny fine for missing training, being found beyond Blackpool Bridge at night or being caught smoking. But on a more positive level, Paddy was brilliant at organising parties and, though funds were scarce, he was noted for beating Our Lord in his ability to turn water into "Raza". Everyone was amazed at how far Paddy could stretch the bottle of raspberry cordial to fill so many cups for the boys.'

'Paddy had a very keen eye for a good hurler,' said Jack Lynch, 'and whenever he'd go to big matches, he would bring youngsters with him and tell them to watch particular facets of the style of top players. It was Paddy who took me to Dublin for the first time in

1931 and we saw two of the great Cork-Kilkenny finals that year. He brought me to many another venue and he used to point out some of his favourite players and ask me to watch their individual techniques. I remember one such occasion when he brought me to Charleville and told me to ignore the rest of the game and concentrate on Mickey Cross and how he met and broke up attacks on the Limerick goal.'

'The thing that struck me most about Paddy was his generosity,' said Bishop Michael Murphy. 'Money was scarce in the '30s and '40s and Paddy didn't have much, but whenever he saw a young player in need, he managed to help him out.'

Paddy and a few older boys had played with the Glen juniors prior to the merger and he continued as a player until 1938, but it was his contribution to the minor section of the club that earned him the epithet 'Father of the Glen'.

There was no age limit to minor games when the Glen started and their first success came with a county minor championship in 1922. Another minor title in 1923 was followed by a junior county in 1924 and the intermediate championship the following year. Then in 1926 the Glen became a senior club.

Traditional kingpins, the 'Rockies and the 'Barrs, may have scoffed at the notion of a long run in the premier grade for the newcomers from Blackpool, even after the Glen reached the county final against Blackrock in 1930. But four years later the Glen had a sensational win over the 'Barrs in the final and the cup crossed the bridge to the northside for the first time. It was destined to stay there for eight years.

'Fox' Collins

'A big factor in the Blackpool men's first victory,' wrote one scribe, 'was the magnificent hurling of Paddy "Fox" Collins. Good judges consider him the finest centre half-back in Ireland today and the forwards who found their most frenzied efforts unavailing against his granite defence will not be disposed to challenge that verdict. Cork has produced many notable half-backs and Collins is the latest addition to an illustrious roll which already numbers James Kelleher, Connie Sheehan and Jim Regan.'

Reflecting on the Glen's historic win, the *Cork County Chronicle* wrote: 'Fox Collins was a happy if a tired man on Sunday night. A great hurler and a good sport, he saw the labours of several years crowned with success. For he had worked hard and loyally to build up a great hurling club in Blackpool. Many times his hopes were dashed but he never tired. And his strong heart infused hopes in others who, as time passed, gathered round him – a splendid band – and worked with him towards his high ideal. When the cheers of the big crowd rang round his team on Sunday afternoon, he was the quietest of the throng. The achievement had come and he was satisfied.'

By this time Fox Collins had become the Glen's first All-Ireland medal winner and was club captain up to 1933. 'A change of captain might bring a change of luck,' said Fox, with typical self-deprecation. 'Let someone else be given the job.' So, reluctantly deferring to his wishes, the Glen mentors asked Joe Lee to captain the side for 1934. He was to remain their victorious captain for five of the Glen's eight-in-a-row! Jack Lynch would captain the 1939 and 1940 sides and Connie Buckley completed the sequence in 1941.

First County with the Glen *1941*.
Christy (front) in the parade with Dan 'Cooper' Moylan, Dinny 'King' McDonnell, Paddy O'Donovan etc behind him.

Grand Hurlers

The hurling career of Paddy Collins was remarkable in that it coincided not only with the arrival of Glen Rovers, but also with the beginning of the North Monastery's outstanding record in college hurling. A few years before he first attended the school, the Mon was a rugby college, but, largely due to the influence of dedicated teachers, Jimmy Hayes and Harry Atkins, hurling began to be promoted there. The school entered for the newly-established Dr Harty Cup in 1917 and won the trophy two years later when Paddy was one of the younger players on the team.

'The hurlers I admired most when I was a boy were Eudie Coughlan, Billy Hough and Dinny Lanigan,' said Paddy. 'I played junior with the Glen in 1919 and we won two minor championships in '22 and '23. My first game with Cork was a league match against Galway in 1927 and my last game was against Waterford in the championship at Dungarvan in 1938.'

'The day Nowlan Park was opened in 1928 we played Dublin in the All-Ireland semi-final and, after we arrived at Kilkenny Station, we were escorted to our hotel by two bands and a huge crowd. I was fortunate to play with some grand hurlers in those years, men like Eudie, who had an outstanding style; Jim Hurley, a great centre-field man; Tommy Barry of Carrig, who was big and strong yet very fast; Johnny Kenneally of the 'Barrs, very quick in the forwards; Morgan Madden, tough, hard and strong; and of course Dinny Barry-Murphy, a sweet hurler, very light, very fast, a grand half-back. The Aherne brothers Paddy [Balty] and Michael [Gah] were great too. Balty was more robust than Gah, but Gah was a clever two-handed forward who always got the scores. Mick O'Connell was another great worker, a big man, feared nothing. Paddy Delea, Willie Clancy from Mallow and Peter O'Grady, an army man from Buttevant and our goalkeeper Jeremiah Burke were other great players.'

'Yet when it comes to picking the greatest hurler of all,' said Fox, 'I have to say that the best I ever saw was Christy Ring. He was in a class of his own.'

'Winning the county in 1934 is my sweetest memory,' he said, adding that he played in seven of the eight-in-a-row Glen wins

Christy (third from right, middle row) with players and supporters after Glen Rovers completed the eight-in-a-row in 1941. It was Christy's first county medal with the Glen.

before ending his playing career in 1940. 'A funny thing was that Christy and myself just missed playing together with Cork and the Glen by a matter of months. When I finished with Cork after losing to Waterford in '38, Christy was starting his career, playing a great game for the Cork minors the same day, and he became a Cork senior the following year. And when I finished with the Glen after the 1940 county final Christy arrived for the 1941 championship. In both cases I was on the way out just as Christy was on the way in.'

Christy wore the Glen colours for the first time in July 1941, against the 'Barrs in the county semi-final. Sean Condon made his senior debut for the Blues the same day. The occasion felt a little strange for Christy at first but, encouraged by Jack Lynch, he soon settled and gave a fine display.

'Connie Buckley came well into the game in the last quarter, with Lynch and Ring continuing to do very effective work,' said the *Examiner*. 'Five minutes from the end Jack Lynch got the equaliser. Then came a brilliant piece of play by Ring who raced along the right wing and turned a neat centre over the heads of a number of players. Paddy "Chancer" Barry was just in the right spot and, unmarked, he gave Buttimer no chance of stopping the goal.'

Thus, twenty-year-old Christy Ring began a playing career with Glen Rovers that would last for over a quarter of a century.

Foot-and-Mouth

Long before 'the back door' became a familiar term in hurling and a team, defeated in an earlier round, could win the All-Ireland, Christy had an unusual distinction. He won his first All-Ireland senior medal when he was twenty and his first Munster medal when he was 21. For many years it sounded like a paradox, but such were the curious happenings of 1941, the foot-and-mouth year, that several anomalous occurrences became fact.

'We were due to play Tipp in the Munster semi-final down the Park on the last Sunday in August,' said John Quirke, 'and we were all looking forward to it, when word came through that the match was called off because of a foot-and-mouth outbreak in Tipperary and Kilkenny.'

'The Department of Agriculture contacted the Munster Council to tell us that the match must not go ahead,' said Sean McCarthy, the secretary. 'We had a special meeting at Tralee to discuss the matter and I mentioned that none of the Tipperary team lived within 26 miles of the affected area. Johnny Leahy agreed and said that the Minister's order preventing people from travelling outside Tipperary was a drastic one. However, the chairman, Seamus Gardiner, said farmers in other counties would object strongly to people travelling in to them from infected areas. Nothing could be done about the matter, he said, so we had no choice but to make alternative arrangements.'

It was decided that Limerick, who had already qualified for the Munster final, would play Cork for the right to represent the province in the All-Ireland. Afterwards, the winners of the Cork-Limerick game would play Tipperary for the Munster title. In Leinster, a similar situation applied to Kilkenny.

Limerick, who lined out without the Mackey brothers and Paddy Clohessy, fell behind by three goals from Micka Brennan, Jack Lynch and John Quirke inside the opening ten minutes. Dick Stokes managed to get one back for the Shannon men, but Ted Sullivan and John Quirke retaliated and Cork led by 5-3 to 1-0 at half-time. Christy Ring resumed the scoring spree after the break and further goals from Lynch, Sullivan and Jim Young completed the rout. Jack Lynch's goal from a sideline cut, Billy Murphy's 100-yard drives and Con Cottrell's impressive debut were talking points afterwards.

'To beat Limerick was a wonderful honour even though they were short three great players that day,' said John Quirke, who blamed himself for the 1940 draw when he claimed he wasted a great cross from Dan 'Cooper' Moylan. Although born in Milltown, County Kerry, John was just ten months old when the family moved to Blackrock and during his youth he basked in the glory of the great 'Rockie teams.

All-Ireland

A fortnight after the Munster final, Cork met Dublin in the All-Ireland and, despite the restricted rail services in Munster, a crowd of over 26,000 turned up. Five pipe bands and the Artane boys provided plenty of music and Seán Ó Siocháin led the singing. The match itself, though, was another one-sided affair.

After Harry Gray missed an early Dublin free, Billy Murphy's puck-out landed within 21 yards of the Dublin posts where John Quirke sent in Cork's first goal. It was the start of another barrage of scores by the Cork forwards. Ted Sullivan got the second goal and points came from Christy Ring (three), Jack Barrett (two), Jim Young, Ted Sullivan and Jack Lynch to leave them 2-8 to 0-3 at the break. Further goals by Quirke, Sullivan and Brennan led to a comprehensive 5-11 to 0-6 win.

James 'Bobby' Ryng came on as a substitute late in the game, along with Paddy O'Donovan, when John Quirke and Jack Lynch had gone down, ostensibly injured, but in reality to give their old pals a run in the final. In the dressing room banter afterwards, 'Bobby' Ryng turned to the Cork goalie, Jim Buttimer, and said, 'I was only on for a few minutes, Jim, but I had more to do with the victory than you. You only got one puck, I got two!'

'I expected a much closer call from Dublin,' said Cork captain, Connie 'Sonny' Buckley, 'but I must give them credit for the way they kept pegging away to the end. They showed real good spirit.' Son of a former St Mary's player, Connie became the first Glen Rovers man to lift the McCarthy Cup and, like his brothers Din Joe and Jack, he played Harty Cup hurling with North Mon before making his mark with club and county. 'Sonny' was the only one to take part in all of the Glen's eight consecutive wins but, like so many other young men of his time, he had to emigrate to England to find work shortly after his 1941 glory with Cork. 'Many people left home for good in those days,' he said, 'but I was lucky. I was able to return in 1943.'

Winning the twelfth title – the first in ten years – meant much to the Cork supporters who turned out in droves to welcome the champions. 'Many had come long distances and many had to leave to catch buses before the train arrived an hour and a half late,' wrote the *Examiner*, adding that the delay failed to dampen the heartiness of the welcome. 'There must have been close to 15,000 present along the route as the Killeens Pipers led the parade from the station to Mackesy's restaurant, where a supper was ready for the team, the substitutes, the officials and the trainer, Mr Jim Barry.'

Batt Thornhill, the great full-back, had alighted from the train at his native Buttevant where the local confraternity band had welcomed him home. Then he was borne in triumph from the station towards his house, an ordeal he said that was more strenuous than the match itself!

The day Cork beat Dublin also saw the county minors defeating Galway. 'We had a really good side in 1941, possibly the best Cork minor team of all,' said outstanding defender Michael Murphy from Kilmichael, later to become Bishop of Cork and Ross. 'Tom Mulcahy was in goal and we had Sean Condon, Mick Kenefick, Jim Morrison and Joe Kelly, all destined to win senior All-Ireland medals very soon after. We won all our matches fairly handily, but we almost failed to take part in the final at Croke Park. Just before the game the selectors told us we'd have to go home after the match, due to the war. We wouldn't accept that. If we couldn't stay the night in Dublin, we wouldn't play the All-Ireland. It was down hurleys and all-out strike. Eventually the selectors relented and we played the match, won it and spent the night in Barry's Hotel.'

Tipp Lurking

Meanwhile, Tipperary were lurking in the background waiting for their chance to play Cork. They defeated Waterford in July and now that the mantle of All-Ireland champions had been assumed by the Leesiders, Tipp's incentive to win was greater than ever. By contrast, Cork, having won the league and secured two facile wins in the championship, took their preparations for the deferred Munster decider less seriously.

'If we had met Tipp on the way up that year, I'm sure we'd have beaten them easily,' said John Quirke, 'but after winning the All-Ireland we were a tired team and we couldn't muster any real enthusiasm for the game.' Din Joe Buckley agreed: 'We put our hearts into winning the All-Ireland and after that we relaxed and didn't really bring the same spirit into our approach to the Munster final.'

By accepting the Munster Council's contingency plan in August, Tipperary had forfeited the right to compete in the All-Ireland even if they were to win the Munster championship. Perhaps at that stage they felt they had not a realistic chance against either Limerick, the reigning All-Ireland champions, or Cork, the league winners for the past two seasons. Cork's form in their two championship matches supported that view. The sensational result at the Gaelic Grounds in October, however, brought about a situation that became a source of animated discussion for a long time afterwards.

Cork started well with a Jack Lynch point, but Billy O'Donnell responded with a 70 and added a goal to send Tipperary on their way. Further goals by O'Donnell, Treacy and Heeney had them in front (4-1 to 1-3) at the break, but an early 'Bobby' Ryng goal heralded a Cork comeback. 'They made a great effort in the last quarter,' wrote the *Limerick Leader*, 'but Tipp's goalie Maher and that old quintet Gorman, Cornally, Ryan, Maher and Doyle held up well, while Billy O'Donnell, Tommy Treacy and Peadar Flanagan played dashing games. For Cork, who never got going or were never allowed, Batt Thornhill, Jack Lynch and Christy Ring were up to their usual form but the rest did not seem to get going at all.'

Tipperary won by eight points (5-4 to 2-5) and the big question afterwards was what happened the Cork team, holders of league and championship titles? There was talk about Cork players stopping on the way to the match for a few pints and of some players being slightly intoxicated as they took to the field. Talk led to heated debates, accusations, recriminations, calls for an inquiry and even the suggestion that Cork should send the McCarthy Cup to Tipperary along with the All-Ireland medals.

'To say the mood of Cork people was angry is putting it mildly,' said Michael Murphy, who was centre-back on the minor side that consolidated their All-Ireland status by beating Tipperary in the curtain-raiser. 'The senior result really put a question-mark on Cork's standing as champions, although they trounced Tipperary in subsequent meetings soon after. By then the damage was done.'

For Christy, who had celebrated his twenty-first birthday the previous day, Tipperary's victory was a source of bitter disappointment, mingled with a sickening sense of dismay and disillusionment with some of his senior colleagues. Since he was eleven he had religiously honoured his confirmation pledge by abstaining from alcohol. His coming-of-age meant he had fulfilled his obligations in that regard, but while it never seemed likely that Christy would imbibe

– alcohol did not interest him – the 1941 affair certainly soured his attitude to drink.

'The most disturbing factor,' said Sean McCarthy at the subsequent board meeting, 'was the rumour that two or three players even on the day of the match had not full regard for the issues at stake.' Another speaker, Liam O'Shea, was more blunt. 'I move that the players in question be not again considered to represent Cork.' At the East Cork board one delegate claimed that not alone were some of the players given drink before the match, but even while they were in their togs on the field! A motion that Tipperary and Cork should meet again to decide the All-Ireland championship was passed, although Denis Conroy went even further. 'Cork should send the Cup to Tipperary as they are definitely All-Ireland champions.'

'We have the anomaly of the hurling champions of the country being unable to make that claim in their own province,' wrote the *Southern Star* in Skibbereen, arguing that the All-Ireland championship should have been allowed to lapse for that year. 'Central Council were spared the utter humiliation that a victory by Kilkenny over Dublin would have meant, but nothing can ever clear them of the stigma of having been primarily responsible for the All-Ireland title not being in the keeping of the side that has proved itself most worthy of it. If Kilkenny had beaten Dublin the position would have been rendered even more ridiculous for the All-Ireland test would have been completely vitiated.'

The *Tipperary Star* stated that all hurling counties deserved a fair crack of the whip. 'Neither Tipperary nor Kilkenny can be said to have got it but we hope it is not yet too late to undo the injustice that has been done to both of them.'

Despite the editorials, the situation remained unchanged. Cork were the All-Ireland winners, Tipperary the Munster champions, and as such their Thomond Shield final a few weeks later was vested with unprecedented interest.

Limerick was again the venue and this time Cork won by 4-7 to 3-3 with Paddy O'Donovan captaining the side. 'That result was a fitting answer to some of the critics in the county who asked the board to give up the All-Ireland Cup to Tipperary,' said Tom O'Reilly of the Glen.

Still without a Munster medal after two seasons, Christy had the compensation of winning his first county with Glen Rovers in 1941. Ballincollig, with Billy Murphy as captain, had reached the final but were not strong enough to stop the Glen completing their eight-in-a-row. 'Christy Ring, Jack Lynch, the Buckley brothers and Jim Young were most prominent,' wrote the *Examiner*, adding that the key area was centre-field where Connie Buckley and Christy Ring had mastery of their opponents.

It was the first of thirteen county medals Christy would win with the Glen, yet, for him and many others, memories of 1941 would be overshadowed by the curious happenings of the foot-and-mouth year.

It was ironic that in the midst of the controversy, Guys, the well-known photographers, had the All-Ireland trophy on display in their shop window at Patrick Street. The Liam McCarthy Cup was 'the cynosure of all eyes' according to the *Examiner*, but some of those eyes belonged to Corkmen who wanted to send the trophy to Tipperary, where they felt it rightfully belonged that year!

1942 Cork Senior Hurling Team.
Back (from left): Jack Buckley, Paddy O'Donovan, Charlie Tobin, Jack Lynch, Con Murphy, Jim Barry. Centre: Ned Porter, Mick Kenefick, Billy Murphy, Sean Condon, Jim Young, Din Joe Buckley. Front: John Quirke, Derry Beckett, Christy Ring, Batt Thornhill, Con Cottrell.

Banking on Youth

It was no surprise that some of Cork's old-stagers, who had waited almost a decade for All-Ireland glory, decided to retire after the 1941 success. The captain, Connie Buckley, emigrated to England, adding to the selectors' problem of finding new talent. Promising young players were introduced perforce, but did so well that Cork went on to retain the McCarthy Cup with no fewer than seven changes in personnel from the previous year.

Christy, still smarting from Tipp's foot-and-mouth victory, was more than determined to win a no-strings attached All-Ireland in 1942 and he first demonstrated his resolve in the semi-final against Limerick. 'Ring, Young, Thornhill and Buckley were the pick of the Cork team,' wrote the *Examiner*, 'with the newcomers Ned Porter, Sean Condon, Mick Kenefick and Con Murphy also distinguishing themselves.'

'It was a very tough game,' said Ned Porter. 'The papers called it one long succession of thrills, but I was kept so busy in goal that I didn't notice. I remember Din Joe struck a great one-handed point from about 30 yards and Christy was flying throughout the match. Mick Mackey and Tim Ryan were outstanding for Limerick.'

Cork won by two points (4-8 to 5-3) and then faced Tipperary in the Munster final.

'Tipp Gaels were so anxious to get to the final that they volunteered to cut sufficient wood for a train from Thurles to Cork,' said a railway official. 'Talk about Percy French and "the rest go a gatherin' sticks". Their offer was not accepted, however, so they had to find some other means of getting to Cork.'

'For 45 minutes the final was as grand a game as you could wish to see,' wrote *The Irish Press*. 'It was score for score, a changing lead and thrusts and parries by the old rivals. Tipperary battled with their traditional tenacity, but could not shake off Cork forwards who, ably led by Christy Ring and John Quirke, barraged the Tipp posts from all angles.'

The youthful Cork players were better suited to last the blistering pace and pulled away in the final quarter. 'In the last ten minutes it was a score a minute for Cork, five points coming from Christy Ring, and Tipp had no response,' added the *Press*.

'After two tough matches in Munster, we met Galway in Limerick and had a good win,' said Ned Porter. 'Then it was on to the All-Ireland against Dublin whose best forward was an old neighbour of mine from Dillon's Cross, Mossie McDonnell. His brother Dinny and myself had won a junior county with Brian Dillon's in 1938 and a senior county with the Glen in 1941. In the All-Ireland final though, I had to retire injured and who struck me the accidental blow but Mossie McDonnell!'

'The Cork attack is arousing most discussion,' wrote Green Flag in his *Irish Press* preview of the final. 'It is youthful and fast with Christy Ring and the schoolboys, Sean Condon and Mick Kenefick, in the half-line. Ring is a grand hurler, as we saw in the Railway Cup and Munster finals. He is going to be Dublin's biggest danger and we may see more than one player make an effort to mark this young stylist. Condon and Kenefick, two lovely stylists, may just lack the Croke Park temperament, but John Quirke is another source of danger for he, too, has won matches almost on his own.'

It was Mossie McDonnell who opened the scoring with a Dublin point, but Cork hit back with three from Ring, two from Lynch and one each from Kenefick and Beckett. The hurling was fast and exciting, with little between them as O'Brien and McDonnell had Dublin goals, but John Quirke finished a Condon pass to the net, giving Cork a psychological boost for the second half.

Ned Porter's injury forced him to retire soon after the resumption and he was replaced by the 'Barrs stalwart, Jim Buttimer, who had played in goal in the 1939 and 1941 finals. Meanwhile Cork pressed on with further points by Kenefick, Tobin and Ring, but Dublin stayed in contention and a Dan Davitt goal brought them to within a point of the champions. Cork finished the stronger, however, and a Derry Beckett goal was followed by points by Quirke and Lynch, confirming their superiority. They won by 2-14 to 3-4.

'That was a fine Cork team, a good mixture of young and old, but we gave them a good run,' said Harry Gray. 'You had great men like Jim Young, Billy Murphy, Din Joe Buckley, John Quirke, Christy Ring and Batt Thornhill, but the player I admired most was Jack Lynch. He was a great ball-player, very clean and he had wonderful anticipation. Jack would move into position as soon as the ball was struck and he always picked the right spot to be under it. My gambit was to pull as the ball landed, otherwise I might as well say goodbye to it.'

'It took rare quality to survive the fire and fury of many of those games,' wrote Garry Redmond in his book *Sapient Colloquy*, 'but Jack Lynch was durable for all the lightness of touch. Catching the eye at the same time was a compact little forward named Christy Ring, soon to become the Babe Ruth of hurling. Where Ring was all speed and power and hard grafting, Jack Lynch, whether as a forward or more usually at centrefield, was all grace and style; the proof of his quality that he never seemed to hurry, never was flustered but moved along in a deceptively swift lope.'

1943 All-Ireland Champions.
Back (from left): John Quirke, Jim Young, Tom Mulcahy, Con Murphy, Jack Lynch, Alan Lotty, Ted O'Sullivan. Front: Din Joe Buckley, Batt Thornhill, Sean Condon, Mick Kenefick, Micka Brennan, Christy Ring, Jim Barry (trainer). Seated: Con Cottrell and Billy Murphy.

Jack's imperturbability was a feature of his character on the field and later in politics, although there is a tale that he once tackled Tony Reddan with more vigour than the Tipp goalie appreciated. Jack was newly elected to the Dáil at the time, and after the tackle Reddan warned him, 'Try that again Lynch and there'll be another by-election in Cork!'

Giving it Back

'I have been asked on many occasions what was the secret of our success during the four-in-a-row-years,' said Jack Lynch. 'Firstly our teams were good – very good – and there is no substitute for real merit. We were evenly balanced and there was seldom a weak position. There was also wonderful spirit among the players. Naturally, in such a long run of championship games there would be occasions when some players flagged or the team had an off-day, but it was on those occasions that some individual would raise his game and carry us through. It might be Jim Young one day or John Quirke another day or Christy Ring, but we always had one or two who did that bit extra when it was needed.'

'I started as a Cork minor in 1929,' said John Quirke. 'Seán Óg put me on as a sub for Blackrock against Carrigtwohill the same year, and I didn't know until it was over that it was the famous

1943 Cork Senior Hurling Team.
Back (from left): Bernie Murphy, Ted O'Sullivan, Paddy O'Donovan, Jim Young, Jack Lynch, Alan Lotty, Con Murphy, Micka Brennan. Front: John Quirke, Billy Murphy, Con Cottrell, Mick Kenefick, Christy Ring. Seated: Tom Mulcahy, Batt Thornhill.

Tom Barry I was marking. That was my lucky day and three county championships ('29, '30, '31) came my way. Cork picked me in
1932, but it wasn't until 1941 that I won an All-Ireland at last. That
was the start of the four-in-a-row. They were great years.'

'I always used to train for ball play between two players,' added
John. 'I had to be quick to double each ball or meet it or belt it back.
The men who made the greatest change in modern hurling were Mick
Mackey and Christy Ring, whose solo-running thrilled the crowds. If
Ring saw a ball he could get a goal from, John Landy wouldn't beat
him to it.' (Australian athlete, John Landy was favourite to win the
1500m Olympic final in Melbourne in 1956, but was beaten into third
place by Ronnie Delany and Klaus Richtzenhain.)

'Hurlers nowadays hit more balls while on the run than ever
before, a very difficult feat,' said Jim Young. 'Ring was one of the
first to perfect this art. Speed has now become a *sine qua non* and
the increased tempo of the games means that the players have to
become more accurate.'

'People sometimes say very strange things,' said Christy, 'and
you'd often wonder about their way of thinking. I remember one day
meeting a man I knew after a match, where Sean Barrett had a really good game. He was getting on a bit at the time, but that didn't
stop him having a brilliant game. Anyway, this man was talking to
me about the match, "Hadn't Barrett a great game?" he asked, and
before I could agree, he said, "He should retire now!"'

Kinsale man Sean or Jack Barrett did not retire until he had
achieved his All-Ireland medal in 1941, and, after his playing days
were over, he became prominent in GAA administration. He was
a very popular county chairman in the 1960s. Long before that, he
had made his first championship appearance with Cork, something he remembered in great detail.

'My first championship game was a very tense affair. They put
me left half-back and for a week I was as nervous as a kitten for
fear John Mackey would destroy me. I didn't sleep a lot and when
Jim Regan saw me in Thurles on the morning of the game he
thought I was sick. Maybe he was right.

'We lined up and I fell back to left quarter-back. It was the
jubilee year of the Association and they made a presentation to

Archbishop Harty on the field. This, of course, took some time and then we had "Faith of our Fathers" and the National Anthem. During all this time I was alone and defenceless, standing near the sideline with, as I thought, the eyes of everyone on me and each man saying, "That's one fella who shouldn't be there".

'At last the sliothar went in and I forgot the crowd, for down the wing came John Mackey himself, tapping the ball in front of him and heading straight for me. This was it, I knew, and I was ruined if he passed. Luckily, he went to tap the ball past me and I must have moved at the right time, for John was down and the ball was gone up the field. As it was the first clash of the game, you can imagine how the pent-up feelings of Cork people on the sideline were released in a roar. That told me I had made the grade, but if John Mackey had slipped me – as he was quite capable of doing – you wouldn't have heard much more of Barrett.'

'Small things shape a man's career especially at the start,' observed Jack. 'Mick O'Connell, who won All-Ireland medals in '28, '29 and '31, gave me sound advice when I started. "Never take anything lying down," he said. "If you get it hard, just give it back – fair and honest but *give it back*." That was how Mick himself played. I remember two great Limerick centre-fielders, strong men and fine hurlers. I'll never forget a game in Thurles, when at the end of the hour, Mick O'Connell stood four square in the middle of the field with the two of them, not one, on the ground beside him. He was every inch a man.'

There is no record of anyone giving Ring similar advice, but from his first senior appearance as a teenager when he swung back on a seasoned campaigner trying to soften him up, Christy instinctively adopted Mick O'Connell's shrewd words of wisdom – never take anything lying down, give it back – fair and honest, but give it back. Ringey always gave it back.

Antrim

The Antrim hurlers hit the headlines in 1943. They surprised many people by beating Galway in the championship and they amazed even their own supporters by defeating Kilkenny in the All-Ireland semi-final. In an age when Mackey, Keane, Doyle, Langton and

Ring were among the big names in hurling, Antrim arrived with their own heroes – Jackie Bateson, Noel Campbell, Kevin Armstrong, Sammy Mulholland, Jimmy Walsh, John Hurl, Paddy McGarry and so on – and a huge northern support followed them to Croke Park.

'The weekend found Dublin festooned with the green and gold colours of Antrim,' wrote the *Irish News*. 'There were supporters from Ballymena and Ballymoney and even from Ballyclare, industrial workers from Belfast and big strapping Gaels from the Glens of Antrim. I heard accents from Derry and Tyrone and quite a sprinkling from Fermanagh. Even the Shankill Road of Belfast sent its quota. They swarmed out of Amiens Street station like bees out of a hive and took complete control of Dublin.'

'It was a wonderful achievement for Antrim to reach the final,' said Pádraig Ó Caoimh. 'There were 30 other counties in Ireland who would have given their right hand for the same honour. And all 30 of them were hoping for an Antrim win.' Jim Barry went a bit further. 'Thirty-one and a half counties supported Antrim that day,' he said.

The attendance of 48,843 was the largest to see Cork in an All-Ireland final up to then, and the third highest after the Limerick-Kilkenny games of 1936 and 1940. Not surprisingly, the bulk of support favoured Antrim and a tremendous cheer greeted their arrival on the field but, no matter how sympathetic Cork people may have been towards the opposition, no matter how much they would have liked to see Antrim winning the title at some other county's expense, the fact remained that this was an All-Ireland final and not an occasion for sentiment. Consequently the Cork players gave their all in securing their fourteenth title and scored an easy win.

The *Belfast Telegraph* described the game as the poorest final ever seen. 'Cork were masters in every phase,' it said, 'while Antrim's hitting was good but the blocking was crude. John Curry, Kevin Murphy and William Graham played well, but the star of the team was Noel Campbell.'

'We had no idea what to expect from Antrim,' said Mick Kenefick who, at nineteen, was Cork's youngest All-Ireland captain. 'It transpired that they were quite a good team, as we found out later in the year when we played them in a tournament in Belfast, but the All-Ireland final was too much for them and they

Youngest captain.
Nineteen-year-old Mick Kenefick with the McCarthy Cup at Cork's railway station in 1943. Christy kneels in front, fourth from left, between Billy Murphy (left) and Tom Mulcahy (right).

couldn't really live with Cork.'

Before the game, he and the Antrim captain, Jimmy Walsh, exchanged token gifts. 'I present-ed him with some Cork butter and he gave me a pound of tea – remember it was war time and shortages and rationing were common. It was a small gesture in keeping with the friendly nature of an event that was a bit of a novelty really.'

Cork won by 5-16 to 0-4 and the scorers were: Quirke (2-2), O'Sullivan (1-2), Brennan (1-1), Kenefick (1-0), Ring (0-4), Condon (0-3), Lynch (0-2) and Cottrell (0-2). Antrim had their points from Campbell and Mulholland.

A huge crowd attended a joint reception for the teams at the Gresham Hotel that evening, with Seán Ó Siocháin and Danny Hobbs the leading artists in the hotel's large Aberdeen Hall. 'Everything about the 1943 final was cordial,' said Mick Kenefick, 'and lasting friendships were made.'

CHAPTER FOUR

FOUR-IN-A-ROW

As fifteen Cork hurlers stood to attention for the National Anthem at Croke Park on a damp September afternoon in 1944, they were close to uniqueness. The game that would set them apart from all other hurling teams was about to begin and 80 minutes later, Sean Condon, the captain, would ascend the rostrum to receive the McCarthy cup and bring it home to Cork for the fourth consecutive season. No other county had won four All-Ireland hurling titles in a row. Cork achieved their first treble in 1894, Tipperary in 1900 and Kilkenny in 1913, but on 3 September 1944 the Cork hurlers set out to break all records.

For Christy and Din Joe Buckley, who had effectively begun their senior days together in October 1939, there was an extra bit of history in the making. In their first five championships they won four All-Ireland medals apiece, an achievement that has still to be equalled.

Yet for all the historic connotations, the 1944 final turned out to be an anti-climax, with Dublin failing to match the skill and experience of the star-studded Cork side. It was, however, the only tranquil hour the Corkmen enjoyed in a hectic championship campaign.

Tipperary, who had beaten Waterford, were Cork's first opponents and a gruelling struggle ended in a six-point win. Unfortunately the young 1943 captain, Mick Kenefick, sustained a wrist injury which brought his promising inter-county hurling career to a premature end. He was not yet twenty years of age.

Then came the first of two classic encounters with Limerick. 'This was a game that scintillated and sparkled from the opening clash to the final whistle,' wrote Green Flag in the *Press*, while the

Independent described it as 'an individual triumph for Mick Mackey who led the Limerick rally, weaving his way through the Cork defence to obtain himself, or make for others, the scores that helped his side to share the honours'.

With John Quirke, Joe Kelly and Jim Morrison getting the goals and Condon, Cottrell, Ring, Kelly and Lynch adding the points, the Corkmen went nine points clear at one stage in the second half. A Limerick resurgence, however, changed matters entirely, with scores by the two Mackeys, Dick Stokes, Paddy McCarthy and Dave Clohessy edging them two points in front as the game drew to a close. Then John Quirke got his third goal and Cork looked safe, but in the last minute Dick Stokes levelled with a point from a free. Final score: Cork 6-7, Limerick 4-13.

Replay

The replay aroused enormous interest and, although war clouds still hovered menacingly over Europe, the main concern among sport followers at home was the means of getting to Thurles.

A hardy 65-year-old named Peter Ryan walked the 40 miles from Lisnagree to Thurles, many soldiers walked from Castleconnell and back to see the Mackey brothers and, of course, hundreds of supporters travelled by bicycle.

'I myself met a man and his young sons at Thurles who had cycled from Cork,' wrote an *Irish Press* columnist. 'As all the hotels and guest houses were full, these brave travellers slept the Saturday night in a hay barn. On the way to Thurles the chain of the fifteen-year-old boy's cycle broke. His two companions made *sugán* ropes in a field, tied his bike to their own and towed him the rest of the way to Thurles.'

Mick Kennedy, who won his first All-Ireland in 1934, had retired after winning his third in 1940. He had not played an inter-county game for over three years when Mick Mackey, Timmy Ryan and Paddy O'Reilly invited him to return for the Munster final against Cork. 'Although I was fit, I didn't fancy making a comeback in a Munster final, so I told them if the match was a draw I'd return for the replay. Imagine my surprise when the match did actually finish level, but I kept my word. I lined out in the replay, marking Jim Morrison in what became known as the Bicycle Munster Final.'

Legendary duo.
Rival captains Mick Mackey and Christy Ring await the outcome of the toss in 1946.

The match started at a frantic pace and after early points for Limerick Jim Morrison got a Cork goal. Nine minutes gone and Cork were a point in front. Jim Mulholland, writing in *Gaelic Sport* (1964), takes up the story:

'It was then Mick Mackey moved out. He got the ball, moved right, sidestepped two men and hit low and hard and the net shook. After a Sean Condon point there was not a flag raised for ten minutes. I have rarely seen better hurling. Then it was Mick Mackey, again 35 yards out, and he beat three men and once more crashed the ball into the net. Mick, you were never greater and to prove it, he whipped over a point. At half-time it was Limerick 2-4 Cork 1-4 and we spent the interval talking excitedly about Mackey.'

Limerick went five points clear early in the second half and a goal apiece by Joe Kelly and John Mackey left the margin intact entering the final quarter. A John Quirke point clipped the lead a little but as the game sizzled to a close, Jim Morrison got his second goal to leave just a point between them. Laois referee Carroll was looking at his watch just before John Quirke brought the sides level and extra time beckoned. Or did it?

'There was certainly no more than a minute remaining,' said Jim Mulholland, 'and no more exciting a minute could there have been. Limerick pucked out, Cork cleared, Limerick sent it in again but back out came the ball. Then Ring had it at midfield and he was away.

'I don't know how many Limerick men tried to cut off his passage but at least three or four closed on him only to lose him. He was still coming, the ball glued to his hurley. A side-step, a half-turn and then he hit. We knew it was a score and the winning one but for the life of me I never saw the ball. Neither did anyone near me and by all indications neither did Dinny Malone in the Limerick goal, nor Kennedy, Cooney or Cregan. However, it took the vast crowd but a second to realise where it had gone. It was in the net. Cork were through.

'It was certainly the score of scores in my book. He certainly cut through the Limerick defence and the ball must have flashed from his stick at extraordinary speed. To this day I have wondered why he went for a goal when a point would have done, but then it could have been for a number of reasons. The Limerick net minder Dinny Malone had saved two tremendous efforts of his during the hour – it could be that he wanted the satisfaction of finally beating him – or perhaps he was confused regarding the scores and how much time remained.

'My opinion is that he knew he had a goal. Even then, twenty years ago, Ring had that uncanny judgement which we have long since come to accept. When he got that ball near midfield and rounded and outsped one Limerick man after another he probably knew that nothing between heaven and earth could stop him – and it didn't. It was his only score of the game but, if it had been the only score of his entire career, he would still be remembered for it.'

Cork retained the Munster title and met Galway in the All-Ireland semi-final at Ennis. 'We were confident enough after the two games against Limerick,' said Sean Condon, 'but virtually at the last minute, John Quirke and Jack Lynch cried off because of injury. They were a fierce loss.'

'Sean Condon's accuracy with frees probably meant the difference between victory and defeat for Cork at Ennis where Galway put up a grand display,' wrote Green Flag. 'With a little more accuracy in attack they might have dethroned the champions who were hard set to win by a point in a thrilling and gruelling finish.'

Cork won by 1-10 to 3-3, the goal coming from Joe Kelly and the points from Sean Condon (eight) and Christy (two). It was a relieved Cork party that travelled home that evening.

On to the All-Ireland final and Cork's bid to break all records and complete the four-in-a-row. It was an historic week for the county, and indeed for the world, which watched the progress of the war in Europe. While Jim Barry was exhorting his men to prepare for All-Ireland victory, Dwight D. Eisenhower was encouraging his forces to conquer the Reich. The end of the long struggle, which had begun the day Cork lost to Kilkenny in 1939, was in sight and the people of western Europe would soon sleep easy again. As for the 26,000 spectators who came to Croke Park, their main concern was the outcome of the Cork-Dublin clash for All-Ireland honours.

A Female View

That morning, the *Independent* sent a female columnist, who had
never seen a hurling game, to Barry's Hotel to meet the Cork party:

'From the pall of cigarette haze at Barry's materialised former
GAA president, Sean McCarthy, and trainer, Jim Barry, a master
tailor by profession, his fair wavy hair and deeply sun-tanned face
belying his years. I ran into most of the members of the team – a
railway man and a Dunlop worker, a newly qualified doctor and an
almost B.L., Army men and students – but I did not meet Christy
Ring who was not with the main group. Such was the confined
effect of a hotel full of talking Corkmen that the very walls seemed
to sway with the lilt of the accent. In fact, I have been speaking
Cork since, albeit in a double-Dutch way.

'Handsome young Cork captain Sean Condon was prised loose
from the swarm of followers cluttering around him. He is a nice
lad, fair and rosy, almost reddish eyebrows over deep blue eyes in
a lean face, his twelve stone evenly filling his athlete's figure. He
is not merely proud of being a Cork city man, he is a parishioner
of St Finbarr's West and thus born with a hurley in his cradle. His
quick, argument-packed speech betrays the insurance agent by
profession and his Irish Assurance Company boss, McKeogh, a
devout hurling man, gave him the week off with the blessing of the
entire Parnell Place staff.'

The highlight of the day's assignment was the All-Ireland final
itself:

'There was just a drizzle of rain sailing over the field like a soft
waft of muslin when I got to my high and dry seat on the Hogan
Stand. Then the sun broke out, glowed the tens of thousands of
faces into a cheerful pink and set the city around us aglow from
Howth Hill to the Dublin Mountains. The boys of the Artane Brass
Band swirled by, blue capes lined with red; the saffron kilted pipers
preceded the double line of red-and-white and blue-and-white
players under an applause clattering like hailstones.

'As I already admitted, I am not a follower of the game but the
beauty of the movement, the swiftness and the team-work, a blue
never without a watchful red anywhere, was a thrill to follow in its
fast play mounting and ebbing all over the field. When a score

looks nigh, the roaring crowd stops so suddenly that you can almost hear thousands of people holding their breath for just one split second, then the triumphant roar as a point is scored. The volume of sound shakes the stand but when expectation suddenly dies after a failed effort, the low rumble of disappointment falls like a high cliff collapsing in one dull thud.'

Tough Struggle

'It was not a great game,' wrote the *Independent*, 'but allowing for the heavy sod it was a tough struggle with patches of thrilling play.'

Dublin had their big names in Ned Wade, Charlie Downes, Jim Byrne, Frank White, Harry Gray, Jim Donegan and Terry Leahy, and for the first ten minutes they held Cork scoreless. Then Jack Lynch got the opening point and this was followed by similar scores from Condon (three), Ring (one), Cottrell (one) and Lynch (two more), leaving Cork 0-8 to 0-2 ahead at the break.

On the restart Joe Kelly had a goal and a point before Dublin staged a brief rally prompted by a Charlie Downes goal. Some great saves by Tom Mulcahy proved crucial, however, and the comeback was aborted. At the other end, Joe Kelly continued to break Dublin hearts with sparkling solo runs and some delightful scores. Quirke and Morrison were also on target and Cork went on to win by 2-13 to 1-2.

Joe Kelly and Tom Mulcahy were hailed as Cork's heroes, while Jack Lynch, Con Cottrell, Billy Murphy, Jim Young, Jim Morrison, Christy Ring, Sean Condon and substitute Paddy 'Hitler' Healy were also praised in the papers. (A brilliant goalkeeper, the fair-haired 'Barrsman Tom Mulcahy played in four All-Ireland finals and inadvertently forced into retirement Dave Creedon, who grew weary of sitting on the subs' bench for so long. He would, of course, make an unexpected comeback in 1952 and belatedly collect three All-Ireland medals. By then Tom Mulcahy, a plumber by trade, had retired from hurling, but advertised his business with the fetching phrase: 'He used to stop goals, now he stops leaks'!)

'It was a wonderful experience to play with Cork that day,' said Joe Kelly. 'I played with the Cork minors in 1941 when we won the All-Ireland but because of my studies, I didn't get an outing with the seniors until the Munster semi-final against Tipperary. I was thrown in at the deep end, so to speak, when I was picked for the 1944 championship. In the All-Ireland final I was marked by an old club rival, Jim O'Neill of Sars.'

Tall, slim and lightning fast, Joe Kelly made his name as an athlete and a hurler at St Patrick's national school and Farranferris College, before distinguishing himself with Glen Rovers although, as Liam Ó Tuama pointed out, Joe never played a county final with the Glen. His clerical studies had taken him back to St Patrick's College in Carlow by the time the county final would be played. Joe won countless athletic awards and was runner-up in the Irish sprints championship just before the 1944 All-Ireland final.

'Time and again,' wrote the *Examiner*, 'Kelly thrilled the crowd with his flying solo runs.' 'Joe Kelly, star of a clever set of forwards, scored two goals and three points,' said the *Independent*, while the *Press* described him as 'the darling of the Cork supporters, who danced his way through the Dublin defence'.

Over 400 guests were present when the Cork and Dublin teams were entertained in Clery's restaurant after the 1944 final, but the real victory reception awaited the champions on their return home the following day. The train stopped at Thurles and Mallow, where large crowds waited to greet them and the players broke their journey at Blarney and continued to Cork by horse-drawn coaches. A huge crowd met them at Blackpool Bridge and the Volunteer pipers led the parade to the city where over 20,000 supporters had gathered to welcome the champions. The captain, Sean Condon, the county chairman Bowler Walsh and the trainer Tough Barry addressed the crowd outside Mackesy's restaurant and then the team adjourned to a well-earned meal.

John Power

John P. Power, whose wonderful books *A Story of Champions* and *Honour to Cork* delighted hurling followers at a time when the GAA library was very sparse, had some interesting things to say about the great Cork hurlers of 1944. Of Jack Lynch he wrote, 'His game is ever clean, no shouting, no nerves, no fraying temper. He can give and take hard knocks and being grassed, which isn't often, can pick himself up with as charming a smile as you could wish to see. Jack seems to me to typify the kind of Irishman Cusack, Croke and those others had in mind when they brought back hurling to Ireland.'

'The Buckley brothers played a similar type of hurling,' he contended. 'Both always drew on a ball first time. No dilly-dallying. No wasting time. And no rising of the ball. Only long sweeping ground play in the old Cork tradition. Whenever Mick Mackey proceeded to wreak havoc among the right-wing defenders Din Joe Buckley was invariably brought over from the left to quell the storm. It was that switch that won the game against Limerick this year. Though now out of hurling Connie, playing Fox Collins' position, has given great service to club and country. Hard, fearless tacklers both, it took a mighty man to pass either of the Buckleys.'

He described Joe Kelly as a rare opportunist who can flash from goalmouth to corner flag retrieving impossible balls; Charlie Tobin a swift deadly goal-getter; Paddy O'Donovan an outstanding backman who can rough it with the best; Sean Condon a fast, plucky ballplayer reminiscent of the great Dannix Ring from the Lough; Tom Mulcahy the best goalkeeper in generations; Jim Young not so tall but stocky enough and at his best when his side is in danger of losing; Batt Thornhill, a brilliant full-back, tall, sure and strong; Billy Murphy a magnificent hurler who is never happier than when in the midst of a bunch of forwards and pulling all around them; Alan Lotty a clean, scientific hurler making up in dexterity for what he lacks in brawn; Con Cottrell a fast sweeping midfielder who feeds his forwards with scoring chances; and Con Murphy a defender 'with plenty of muscle and the knowledge of how to use it to the best advantage'.

Not surprisingly John Power reserved his warmest praise for two hurlers who had, with Jack Lynch, arguably done most to help Cork achieve the four-in-a-row – John Quirke and Christy Ring.

Of the Blackrock man he wrote:

'For twelve years Cork has been supplied with a utility hurler who is equally at home at either end of the field and in any position. He is a hurler of quality, skilled in every department of the game and indeed a true representative of the village once reckoned as the home of hurling. That he kept himself going through eight years of defeat and depression and turns out each year as fit as a fiddle and eager to meet the best in the land speaks volumes for the make-up of this splendid hurling man. Indeed, I'd say John Quirke was the most deserving man on the team, though of course he'd be the first to decry this himself.'

'Christy Ring,' wrote Power, 'is a pure, skilful ball-player, indefatigable and a trier all the way. For years to come his goal against Limerick in this year's Munster final will be spoken of with pride by grateful Cork supporters the county over. It was the effort of an athlete who would not accept defeat. An effort the like of which for sheer dramatic intensity occurs only once perhaps in a lifetime. Limerick it seemed were winners all the way. There was brave Mick Mackey dashing from goal to goal playing several men's part to uphold the lead. Then, well back in his own half, this unconquerable Ring snapped up the ball. Tim Ryan went for him, Christy tapped the sliothar with his hurley and sailed round him. Out came Jackie Power, then Cregan, then McCarthy, then Power again. Christy Ring still had the ball. Suddenly he stopped, steadied and swung his hurley. Like a bullet the ball flew, straight and true. Hurleys flashed to meet it but there it was, dead in the back of the net. Tense and dramatic. It was seconds before the crowd realised the truth. A few moments later and the game was over – Limerick defeated. So there he is, gentlemen, Christy Ring, hero of Cork's recordbreaking hurling champions and, in my book anyway, the hurler of 1944.'

Jamesey

In October that year, *The Youghal Tribune* carried a remarkable compliment to Christy who had just turned 24: 'Jimmy Kennedy, the famous Carrigtwohill hurler and captain of the Cork All-Ireland team of 1919 paid a fine tribute to Christy Ring of Cloyne on his exhibition of *camán* craft at Cork on Sunday last. "He is the greatest hurler Cork has produced since Jamesey Kelleher, the Lord have mercy on him", said Jimmy. Surely this is a remarkable appreciation and worthy of record in the Gaelic annals.'

A few months before the legendary Dungourney man's untimely death Carbery had written in his 1942-43 annual:

'Round the firesides and clubs, where hurling stars are discussed, the name of Jamesey Kelleher of Dungourney crops up again and again. For consistent brilliancy over a long number of years Jamesey had no equal in my memory. Standing around 5'7" Kelleher had wide shoulders, a deep chest and beautifully turned limbs. He was as nimble to turn as a native hare of the uplands. As full-back he stood up to the fiercest assaults with cool courage and endless resource. He was fresh at the end of the hardest hour and he was the outstanding man of 30 stars on field after field and year after year until we came to think of him as a charmed personality. He went into the thick of the fray fearlessly and yet was so clever that he was never hit to my knowledge and never left the field of play. On ground or overhead he was a glorious striker off right or left hands. As a dribbler and circling genius he never had an equal. He would twist and turn and circle round a group of opponents. His eye never erred. He was an able leader who saw a weak corner and played on it. He would move upfield on occasion to win a game on his own. His place pucking was a model of accuracy. Kelleher aroused opponents and supporters alike to wild enthusiasm at Croke Park, Cork Park, Dungarvan, Fermoy, Thurles, Limerick and Tralee. He never played a moderate game and drank nothing stronger than lemonade. His peerless hurling from 1900 to 1914 will live in memory at home and overseas. I reckon him the greatest hurler of my time and experience.'

If you substitute Christy Ring's name for Jamesey Kelleher's in Carbery's tribute and make just a few slight changes, the words sound remarkably familiar. Yet, when Jimmy 'Major' Kennedy likened young Ring's hurling to that of the great Jamesey Kelleher, Christy had been playing for Cork for just five years with two decades of greatness ahead of him. In truth the words of Jimmy Kennedy were, as the *Youghal Tribune* stated, a remarkable appreciation of the youthful Christy Ring and worthy of record in Gaelic annals.

CHAPTER FIVE

BRIEF HIATUS

'We'll win two matches today and I want to tell ye we'll win two All-Irelands this year,' said Johnny Leahy, an hour before the Munster hurling semi-finals at Thurles in 1945. It was a big prediction but those who came early and saw the Tipp minors in action realised that the old Boherlahan and Tipperary skipper knew what he was talking about. Outstanding young hurlers with names like Kenny, Bannon, Stakelum, Ryan, Harris and O'Shaughnessy had the home supporters rating them the best minor team they had seen in years.

'We missed the packed rows of motor cars in Liberty Square but we sensed an electric atmosphere of a Big Match day in Thurles,' wrote *The Irish Press*. 'Tipp followers flocked in by bike, trap, outside car, float, dray or shank's mare. They made no secret of their confidence in John Maher and his men from Thurles, Moycarkey, Boherlahan, Cashel, Clonoulty and Carrick. Cork followers were not as numerous as usual. Many of them, we were told, were waiting for the final!'

There was little to suggest that Cork's winning sequence would be broken that summer's day. A few weeks earlier they had beaten Galway in the Thomond Feis Shield, a competition usually regarded as a harbinger of championship tests. 'Dr Young, Din Joe Buckley and Billy Murphy gave a grand exhibition of first time hitting,' wrote Carbery, 'and Christy Ring, that brilliant winger, was irresistible; his pace, his *camán* artistry, his swerve and deadly shooting were a treat to watch.'

It was understandable that a sense of déjà vu should have permeated the minds of Cork supporters after four glorious years at the top. 'The Glen had won eight counties in a row,' said Din Joe Buckley.

'What was to prevent Cork doing the same with the All-Ireland? That was the sort of thinking that had so many Cork supporters avoiding the early games and waiting for the final. They got a land when we lost to Tipp.'

'When a team wins an unprecedented number of All-Ireland championships in a line, the edge wears in any metal of high quality,' wrote Carbery. 'Cork's skill and keenness, which won them 1941, 1942, 1943 and 1944, was as dull as a scythe that has mowed heavy and prolific hay for four consecutive seasons.'

The exuberant Tipp men put it up to the champions from the start and though Cork had a strong wind in the first half, the sides were level at the break. Then, led by Tommy Doyle, outstanding in attack, the home side cantered away to a 2-13 to 3-2 victory.

A significant factor was the tenacious display on Ring by Tommy Purcell, who kept him uncharacteristically subdued for the hour. 'That day Tommy became one of the rare elite of hurlers who outplayed Christy in a championship match and did so by fair means,' said Joe Kelly.

The Moycarkey man earned Christy's great respect as, indeed, did other Tipp hurlers, a respect that lasted long after his playing days were over. 'Christy was a frequent caller to the home of his old opponent Tommy Doyle in Thurles,' recalled Seamus Leahy, 'and roadworkers on the main Cork-Dublin road near Horse and Jockey told of how they once saw a familiar figure kneeling at the grave of the Tipp wing-back Tommy Purcell, at the time dead for nearly 30 years. It was the once dreaded wizard of Cloyne who, on a far off day in 1945, had been held by the fair-haired Purcell when Cork were stopped on their march to five All-Irelands in a row.'

'Whatever about Tipp's chances of winning the All-Ireland,' the *Examiner* wrote after the game, 'there is no doubt that their minors are as good as home and dry and it will be one of the biggest surprises of the season if they fail to bring home the minor title.'

Johnny Leahy's main prediction came true when Tipp collected the McCarthy Cup in September, but lionising youngsters in the papers proved to be an unreliable exercise. Dublin beat Tipperary in the minor final.

Pat Stakelum, who was bitterly disappointed at the minors' defeat, would emerge as one of the stars of the victorious Holycross-Ballycahill team four years later and captain Tipperary to the first of their three-in-a-row in 1949.

'When I was a young lad,' he recalled, 'if there was a big match on in Thurles me and my pals would watch the play intently and afterwards when the crowds were gone, we'd slip into the field with our hurleys. We'd take sideline pucks from where Christy Ring took them and we'd try and score points from where Mick Mackey scored them. We'd copy their every move. When I made the Tipp senior team, centre-back became my favourite position and I played there for many years with Tipp and Munster. I met many great centre-forwards but none of them could touch Christy.'

Thomas Davis

The year 1945 marked the centenary of the death of Thomas Davis and various events were held to honour the occasion. The Mallow poet and patriot was a founder of *The Nation* newspaper and author of the stirring ballads, 'The West's Awake' and 'A Nation Once Again'. A Protestant by birth, Davis was a true United Irishman, and famously remarked: 'What matter that at different shrines we pray unto the one God?'

'No celebrations of the memory of Davis would be complete without a first-class exhibition of the game which he loved so well,' wrote the *Examiner*, 'and such an exhibition was given yesterday. At the conclusion, the Lord Mayor Michael Sheehan presented special souvenir publications of the works of Thomas Davis to members of both sides.'

'Christy Ring on the Mark for Cork Champions' was the *Examiner* headline, after the Glen beat the Army 4-12 to 3-3 in the centennial game. Lieutenant Harry Goldsboro captained the Army side which included the Kennys, Hitler Healy and Jim O'Neill, but the big disappointment was that Corporal Mick Mackey was unable to play. (Although he spent most of his working life as a driver for the ESB at Ardnacrusha, the legendary Limerick man served in the army for five years.)

'Glen Rovers had a good win,' said the *Examiner*, 'but it was only a series of points by Christy Ring that made their superiority so pronounced. Ring, who scored 1-2 in the first half, got a rotation of points near the end which took the sting out of the game.'

While most of the Cork hurlers had to content themselves with club hurling after the 1945 defeat, Jack Lynch was making his mark with the county footballers and won an All-Ireland medal when Cork beat Cavan. In fact, by adding another hurling medal to his collection a year later, Jack would have the unique distinction of winning All-Ireland medals in six consecutive years, an achievement still unequalled.

'Winning the Sam Maguire Cup was a bit of a rarity for Cork in those days,' said Eamonn Young. 'As a matter of fact, we were the first to win it and after us the trophy wouldn't come back to Cork again for 28 years, although we were very unlucky to lose the final to Louth in 1957. In 1945, however, the County Board threw a dinner in our honour and invited all surviving members of the 1890 and 1911 teams that had won the All-Ireland for Cork before us.'

Club Glory

At club level in 1945, Glen Rovers won their tenth county title and for years afterwards Christy rated the final against Carrigdhoun as one of the best ever played.

'In the most thrilling county final for many years,' said the *Examiner*, 'Glen Rovers survived narrowly a determined and plucky Carrigdhoun bid. Indeed, had the game continued for another ten minutes it would have been a different result. The best man on the field was the Glen captain Paddy O'Donovan, who was responsible for thwarting raid after raid by the opposing forwards, while the scores by Christy Ring from all angles again played a great part in the Blackpool men's victory.'

The referee was Christy Duggan of Midleton who had recognised Ring's potential as a minor almost a decade earlier. The Glen won by four points and on receiving the trophy from Bowler Walsh, Paddy O'Donovan called for three cheers for the 'more than gallant losers Carrigdhoun', whose stars included Jack Barrett, Con Murphy, Joe West and Mick Nestor.

In the semi-final the Glen had enjoyed a runaway victory over the 'Barrs, beating them by no less than eight goals and five points

(10-8 to 2-3), surely the biggest margin ever to divide the old rivals. 'It was their well-balanced teamwork, coupled with the brilliance of individual players like Christy Ring, who played one of his finest matches of the year, Dave Creedon in goal, Dr Jim Young left half-back and Paddy O'Donovan that carried the day,' wrote the *Examiner*.

So, in his fifth season with the Glen, Christy collected his third senior county medal, but an even greater honour was to follow. At the club's AGM a few months later, Christy was nominated as Cork captain for 1946. It was an honour he would bear with great pride and distinction.

CHAPTER SIX

1946 – HIS GREATEST FINAL

If you look closely at the picture of Christy Ring leading the Cork team in the parade before the All-Ireland final of 1946, you will see that, along with his hurley, he is carrying an ornamental horseshoe in his right hand. The horseshoe, which was a red and white woollen one, also appears in the team photograph. It was made by my aunt, Bobbie Horgan, and given to Christy for good luck.

Christy leads the 1946 parade followed by Paddy O'Donovan,
Tom Mulcahy and Con Murphy.

'Aunt Bobbie was very good with her hands, knitting, embroidery and all that,' said Willie Buckley. 'She worked in the Sunbeam and she loved making bits and bobs. She knitted that red and white horseshoe for me to give to Christy before the final. I was only a kid at the time and went to all the matches with Bobbie and her husband, Jack Barrett from Blackpool, a great Glenman. Despite the big crowds, things were a lot more informal at Croke Park in those days and kids often got into team photographs or looked for autographs before a match or even at half-time. When the Cork team came on the field that day, my aunt told me to run on and give the horseshoe to Christy, but I was too shy and would not do it. So Jack, her husband, took it instead and got it to Christy. It must have brought him good luck for he went on to have a brilliant game and won the match for Cork.'

'Up to that year, 1946,' said John Quirke, 'Christy had been a very good young hurler on a great team. He fitted in well from the start and was always recognised as an important part of the team during the four-in-a-row years. But in the 1946 final, he gave a performance that marked him out as someone very special. He scored a magical goal that day, but it was not just the goal, it was his overall display at centre-forward. I suppose you could say that 1946 was the start of the real legend of Christy Ring.'

Din Joe Buckley agreed. 'You could say Christy Ring came of age that day. He gave an outstanding performance in a very memorable final, one that was spoken about for years after. I played in six All-Ireland finals, but 1946 is the one I remember best.'

'That day,' said Con Murphy, 'Christy launched himself on to a new greatness that lasted with him for years.'

'Christy Ring – Man of the Match – Bewildering Display Puzzles Kilkenny' ran *The Irish Press* headlines, 'C. Ring's Wonder Goal was Highlight of Cork's Great Win' said the *Examiner*, while the *Independent*'s headline proclaimed 'Ring the Star as Cork Win 16th Title'.

'Thousands of Cork supporters, waving red and white flags, gave vent to their feelings of delight in front of the Hogan Stand,' wrote Green Flag, 'as Christy Ring, the Cork captain, bore away the All-Ireland Hurling Cup which he had done so much to win from Kilkenny whom they defeated 7-5 to 3-8.'

'It was score for score almost to the interval,' wrote Recorder (Jim Bolger of Wexford), 'and then came the turning point with goals for Cork by Jerry O'Riordan and Ring, who brought the ball on his hurley from beyond midfield to drive it to the net.'

'At first Christy Ring seemed to have lost his touch with frees, and his solo runs were generally smothered by Jimmy Kelly or Shem Downey,' wrote Green Flag. 'Then suddenly, just like the sun bursting from behind a cloud, he began to sparkle. He opened up a move that went to the O'Riordan brothers and Jerry, finishing Mossie's centre, gave Cork the lead they would never again surrender. In and out through the Kilkenny defence danced the elusive Christy and when he finished a lengthy solo run again for a goal, he set Cork on the fairway to a new hurling record.'

Cork led by 2-3 to 0-5 at half-time, their points scored by Ring, Billy Murphy from long range and Jack Lynch, with Kilkenny's scores coming from Jim Langton (three), Tom Walton and Sean O'Brien.

1946 Cork Senior Hurling Team.
Back (from left): W. Walsh (chairman), A. Lotty, J. Kelly, C. Murphy. G. O'Riordan, M. O'Riordan, J. Lynch, P. O'Donovan, T. Mulcahy, J. Barry (trainer). Front: C. Cottrell, C. Murphy, W. Murphy, C. Ring, P. Healy, D. J. Buckley, J. Young

The match restarted at a lightning pace with a point by Ring, a goal by Mossie O'Riordan, set up by Ring, and a Kilkenny goal by Terry Leahy – all inside the first three minutes. 'A five-point lead still hung over Kilkenny at the end of the third quarter,' wrote Green Flag, 'but three rapid points had their supporters in happy mood. It was then we saw Christy Ring at his best, roaming from wing to wing and back to centre-field to rally his men. Like a magic wand, his hurley lifted rolling balls or flicked them off an opponent's stick and away he danced towards the Kilkenny posts to shoot or part to his inside men.'

Goals by Connie Murphy (two), Mossie O'Riordan and Joe Kelly ensured victory for Cork, whose heroes included Alan Lotty who gave a superb display, Tom Mulcahy in goal, Billy Murphy, Jim Young, Con Murphy, Din Joe Buckley, Paddy O'Donovan and Con Cottrell, but the centre of attention afterwards, of course, was Christy.

'If ever a captain deserved to be shouldered off the pitch by his team-mates and supporters, Christy certainly merited the honour,' said Green Flag, while Recorder wrote: 'Elusive as ever, Ring was again the leading light of the Cork attack, too speedy and clever for Kilkenny's new centre-back Downey and showing a craft and judgement whether in scoring himself or placing the ball for others.'

'My father was county board chairman at the time and I went to Croke Park with him,' said Billy 'Bowler' Walsh, a fine hurler himself with Brian Dillon's and Sarsfields. 'He told me to mind the Sam Maguire Cup which Cork were returning after the 1945 win. The Lottys lived near us at Dillon's Cross and I was delighted to see Alan playing such a great game, second only to Ringey on the day. I was only sixteen at the time, but when I met Alan after the game he asked me very seriously, "How do you think I played, Billy?" Imagine an All-Ireland star asking a sixteen-year-old that question. It was as if he didn't realise just how good he was and needed reassurance.'

'We got great satisfaction out of winning the 1946 final,' said Joe Kelly. 'You see, one reporter, Green Flag, I think, had written us off completely early in the year and had published something like an epitaph on the Cork team that had won the four-in-a-row.

This annoyed us and made us more determined than ever to win the All-Ireland again. We went out to show that the Cork team was very much alive in 1946 and we succeeded in doing just that.'

Green Flag himself gave a fair account of the game next day, but on Tuesday he alluded to an incident which he claimed might have seen a different outcome. 'With only the net to stop the ball,' he wrote, 'a Kilkenny forward muffed one of the greatest chances presented to a player. If he had scored, it might have changed the whole face of the game. Kilkenny had every bit as much of the play and maybe a little the better of it up to the time Ring daringly went through for the goal that will be long remembered.'

Jack Mulcahy, the Kilkenny captain, had no doubt that Cork were worthy champions. 'The better team won,' he said, 'and Ring's first-half goal was one of the best things in a great match.'

Apart from being Cork's captain for the first time, Christy was also a selector. 'It was an unusual situation for me,' he said, 'but it gave me the chance to suggest to my colleagues that I should play at centre-forward. I felt that was my best position at the time.'

There were no arguments from his co-selectors and Christy wore the No. 11 jersey throughout the championship. Cork played five games altogether, beating Clare by eight points, Waterford by nine, Limerick by eleven, Galway by thirteen and Kilkenny by nine points. 'Not bad going for a team that was supposed to be dead and buried,' quipped Joe Kelly.

Build-Up

Earlier in the year, Christy had shone for Munster in the Railway Cup final against Connacht, an all-Galway team destined to win the celebrated trophy the following year. 'Billy Murphy was hitting haymakers down,' wrote Carbery, who also praised Andy Fleming, Dick Stokes, Jackie Power and Tommy Doyle. 'But it was Ring who saved the day for the holders and set up a record – five wins in a row – as well as scoring 1-7 off his own ash.'

The afternoon was notable for the Young family from Dunmanway. Jim and Eamonn became the first brothers to win Railway Cup hurling and football medals on the same day and watching them doing so was their father, John Young, who had won an All-Ireland football medal in 1911.

The hurling final was a thriller, as Carbery reported: 'On the fiftieth minute the teams were dead level. Ring, elusive as an eel, was slipping Brophy (sound man) and raised three flags, but back came the westerners and Josie Gallagher flashed home a grand goal. The crowd went wild – scores level again, 3-11 to 4-8. Broken time was being played when Munster won a touchline free and Christy Ring got a cut in. He hit it perfectly, judged wind and all, an astonishing ball. It soared and curled high above the bar for the decisive point of 41.'

Surprisingly, the Galwaymen, who had played so well in the Railway Cup final, were quite disappointing in the All-Ireland semi-final against Cork five months later. 'A poor game disappointed the large crowd,' wrote the *Independent*, 'and bore no comparison to the 1944 and 1945 semi-finals.'

Alan Lotty, Jim Young and Paddy O'Donovan were impressive in defence, while Jack Lynch and Con Cottrell were on top at midfield. Although Seanie Duggan had a fine game in the Galway goal, the speedy Joe Kelly managed to get two shots past him. The Cork scores came from Joe Kelly (2-1), Christy Ring (0-4), Jack Lynch (0-3), Paddy 'Hitler' Healy (0-1) and Mossie O'Riordan (0-1). 'Ring was again a good centre-forward,' said the *Independent*, 'getting good support from Healy and Con Murphy of Bride Rovers.' The Rathcormac man would later play for Dublin against Cork in the 1952 final.

The Munster final had also been a disappointment, with Cork scoring an easy win over an ageing Limerick side (3-8 to 1-3). Joe Kelly, Mossie O'Riordan and Connie Murphy got the goals with Ring, Lynch and Young adding the points. It was 37-year-old Mick Mackey's last Munster final and also marked the departure of the great John Quirke, who had intended to retire four years earlier. He had been asked to take the unavailable Din Joe Buckley's place in the semi-final against Waterford and after Cork's victory over Limerick he decided to bring his illustrious career to an end. 'Winning an extra Munster medal in '46,' he said, 'made up for the one I didn't get the foot-and-mouth year.'

For the All-Ireland final Kilkenny had seven of their 'thunder and lightning' side still in action, while Cork had just four – Billy Murphy, Alan Lotty, Jim Young and Jack Lynch. Christy was aware that many shrewd observers, including John Quirke, believed that, had he been playing in the 1939 senior championship, Cork would have won the All-Ireland. Now was his chance to prove how good he could be against Kilkenny at Croke Park. And he did just that.

'Christy Ring, the Cork skipper, excelled himself,' wrote Carbery. 'His tireless elusiveness, his artistry, his rapid unselfish passes to a pal well placed – all made the Glen Rovers man the ideal leader, of whom I have often written in praise. That solo run of his near the end of the first half, following hot on Jerry Riordan's smashing "netter", will live long in hurling memory, for it inspired his men and sent them to the dressing room at half-time with bubbling confidence.'

''Twas at the thirtieth minute of actual play,' he added, 'that Paddy Donovan was struggling strongly, with Reidy on the Cork right half-back line and Christy Ring ever watchful for a chance, sailed down to the halfway line to pick up Donovan's clearance. He had the ball on his hurley in a flash and raced with it at sprinter's pace. As he dodged past man after man without losing speed, he kept the leather in perfect control. The huge crowd were roaring now. Coming to Mulcahy he swerved, cut on inside Walsh and reaching the 21-yards line, drove a smashing shoulder-high shot to the net corner. It proved the key score to the championship golden gate.'

'One of the grandest of the many great goals he has scored in his career,' was how the *Examiner* described it, adding that 'the crowd, which had cheered lustily as he made his 70-yard run, now gave him a tremendous ovation, an ovation that came from friend and foe alike'.

'A funny thing,' said Christy, 'after the game a friend of mine came over to me and said, "You played well, but how in God's holy name did you miss those two early frees?"' Even Ringey could not please everyone.

The champions were accorded the usual warm reception at Mallow and the city when they returned with the Cup, but for Christy the homecoming was of special significance. As captain of the team he would be bringing the All-Ireland trophy to Cloyne for the first time.

By now the ill-feeling caused by the split had dissipated and Paddy Joe Ring was back playing for the club, with Willie John about to serve in his first of many official capacities. When Christy brought the McCarthy Cup to Cloyne a fortnight after the final, the biggest crowd ever to throng the village streets – about 5,000 – turned out to welcome him home. Amid great cheering and excitement, he was presented with a wallet of notes, a popular ceremonial gift in those days. He thanked the organisers and the massive attendance and, though his words were few, it was clear that this was the most important welcome home he ever desired.

First London Trip

Christy was to display his hurling skills to the delight of exiles in the USA and Australia in future years, but one Whit weekend in 1947 he was as excited as a child as he prepared for his first trip outside Ireland. Having played so well as victorious captain in the All-Ireland final, he was the star attraction as the Cork hurlers headed to London to play Tipperary at Mitchum Stadium. He was determined not to disappoint anyone.

The game drew an attendance of over 12,000 and, after the Terence McSwiney Pipers from Manchester had played the teams on to the field, Cork and Tipperary gave a tremendous display of full-blooded hurling, which both Jim Barry and Tom Semple claimed was as good as you would get at home. Tipperary looked like winning until Mossie O'Riordan got a point to equalise on the stroke of full-time, but Christy was the one who commanded most interest and discussion afterwards.

'Ring, who gave a masterly display, was the spearhead of the Cork attack and the inside forwards were well plied with his centres,' wrote the *Independent*. 'One move by Ring was particularly spectacular, intercepting a shot from Connie Murphy, he ran from midfield, hopping the ball on his hurley and finished off with a grand point.'

'A feature of the match,' wrote *The Irish Press*, 'was the solo runs of Christy Ring who time and again weaved his way through a strong defence, drawing tremendous applause from the crowd.' 'Only for Jimmy Maher in goal,' wrote the *Tipperary Star*, 'Ring's performance would have brought Cork victory. The game finished level, so Tipperary, the holders, retained the trophy.'

'For that trip we had to get passports from the British Embassy in Dublin, but only fifteen were allowed,' Sean Condon told Con Hannigan in his *Echo* column. 'So, if someone got injured, we were in trouble. However, when we got to London, two hurlers – Tommy Kelly of Blackrock and Jackie Sullivan of the 'Barrs – came up from Dagenham and togged out as subs. Dave Creedon had a great game at full-forward on Ger Cornally and scored a grand point. It was like coming out of the Park after the match, with all the Cork fans shaking hands and sending messages home to their loved ones. I remember taking a sideline puck during the match and an old schoolmate leaned over the railings and shouted, "Sean, tell me mother I'm all right".'

'On the Monday evening,' said John Lyons, who joined his old Mon colleague, Con Murphy, in the full-back line, 'we were treated to a grand céilí in Holloway – not the prison – and it was a very entertaining end to a great weekend.'

1947 – A Game For The Gods

'Unless you saw the 1947 final, you haven't seen hurling.' That was the put-down older hurling devotees used whenever younger men enthused about subsequent matches that reached a high level of excellence. Nothing could compare in their eyes with the classic Cork-Kilkenny game that ended in victory for the Nore men by what Jack Lynch used to call 'the usual point'.

'Cork won the battles and Kilkenny won the classics,' said Dave O'Brien who rated the 1947 final as the best game of hurling he saw between the counties. But was it really that good?

'It was gripping, glorious and dazzling hurling,' said Séamus Ó Ceallaigh, 'a colourful classic from start to stop, with a finish which completely captivated and enthralled the great crowd, who carried from Croke Park memories of hurling brilliance beyond compare, of men who rose to heights we hardly dared to dream about, and of power-packed minutes with all the lustre and genius hurling has known; paraded before our admiring, if spell-bound eyes.'

Heady words from the great Limerick scribe, who was not given to hyperbole. 'There were 30 heroes in that hurling hour of extraordinary beauty whose dazzling sheen of brilliancy has served to lighten many a heart as hurling days are recalled. I cannot see any game being recalled with greater relish than this supreme hour,' he added.

'That was the game judged by many to have been the classic of all time,' said Laois man, Chris Phelan. 'It was also the game that many said Kilkenny couldn't win because of Cork's proven superiority the year before and because of the threat posed by Christy Ring. A record crowd witnessed a game that is to be remembered for several good reasons. For the first time ever, Christy Ring was held scoreless from play by Peter Prendergast. Then it was the first game to be won by a team not scoring a goal (0-14 to 2-7). Also it'll be remembered as marking the fade-out of such outstanding players as Jack Lynch and Con Cottrell.

Hold tight.
Cork forwards Joe Kelly (15) and Jerry O'Riordan (14) are well held by Kilkenny backs in the 1947 final. In the centre is Mossie O'Riordan.

'Above all, though, the 1947 final will live on as the game that had everything – spectacular scores like Terry Leahy's point from one knee and Christy Ring's point from a sideline cut – drama, as provided by the falling of six Kilkenny backs to the ground for Cork's first goal – and suspense as Kilkenny's Prendergast was carried off in the last quarter and his side only a single point in front. One could go on forever, but I think it could be adequately summed up by describing it as the greatest and saying thanks to Hayden, Grace, Mulcahy, Kennedy, Leahy, Langton, Downey, Walton, Murphy (2), Lotty, Young, Donovan, Lynch, Cottrell, Ring, O'Riordan and Kelly.'

'It was not a final that promised a great deal,' recalled Old-Timer in the *Gaelic Weekly* almost twenty years later. 'In the Munster final Cork got all the lucky breaks, including a ball with wide wrapped all around it, turned into his own net by a Limerick defender, while Kilkenny had been more than fortunate to finish a point ahead of Galway, the Railway Cup champions at Birr in a rip-roaring game.'

Christy, who had amazing recall when asked about his matches, rated the 1947 provincial final as one of his most satisfying wins. In the previous game against Waterford, he had scored 2-5 of Cork's 3-10 and in one of the encomiums heaped on him afterwards, he was described as 'the quicksilver Ring who was the mainspring of a fast-moving attack'. Cork had easily beaten Limerick the previous year, but in the Munster final they were decidedly lucky to retain their title. 'If ever a better team lost it was Limerick,' said one reporter. 'They were magnificent throughout and it was a chastened Cork team that left the arena, winners by 2-6 to 2-3, their goals coming from Christy Ring and Joe Kelly.' That his team had salvaged a win in such circumstances was a source of sweet satisfaction to Christy.

After the Ring-inspired win of 1946, Kilkenny drew heavily on their junior champion side and there were concerns about a new look team in the senior final. Two players were delegated to keep an eye on Christy, and Paddy Grace was instructed to stay close to Joe Kelly for the hour. But Kilkenny had to reshuffle the team almost as they took the field, for at the last moment, Bill Walsh cried off with a blood-poisoned hand. Mark Marnell went in at corner-back, Jack Mulcahy was brought from the forwards to left half-back and Jimmy Heffernan came on to partner Dan Kennedy, the captain, at midfield.

'Yet the Noresiders dominated the exchanges with smooth, stylish hurling for three-quarters of an hour,' said Old-Timer. 'Point after point they picked off while their defence, featuring for the first time the dynamic Pat "Diamond" Hayden, contained the much vaunted Leeside attack. But Cork, hurling with all the craft and confidence of the great champions they were, never let Kilkenny get entirely away and then in the last quarter they struck back.'

Cork's resurgence stemmed from positional switches, which saw Jack Lynch swapping places with Sean Condon and Christy moving to the wing. A five-point deficit was quickly changed to a one-point lead as Cork tore through the hitherto invincible Kilkenny defence for two great goals, but Kilkenny levelled matters as the game drew to a close.

'It looked any money on a draw,' said Old-Timer, 'but Cork had a last shot left. They swept away up the left wing under the Cusack Stand, but Paddy Grace came sweeping out to meet the challenge and drove a stupendous clearance right to the Cork goalmouth. The ball was swept out again, but there was the prowling Terry Leahy who calmly canted the sliothar between the posts for the winning point on the call of time.'

'For thrills, for sportsmanship, for sheer hurling brilliance on both sides, I have yet to see that final surpassed,' he concluded, 'and one memory remains above all. Kilkenny goalman, Jim Donegan, goes out to a high cross, the ball is diverted towards the undefended net and left half-back, Jack Mulcahy, comes from nowhere to bring off an amazing save when all seemed lost. It was that kind of match.'

Kilkenny's match-winner, Terry Leahy, later emigrated to America and played top-class hurling over there in John 'Kerry' O'Donnell's famous Gaelic Grounds. On a return visit home, he gladly described his 1947 point to Paddy Downey. 'How could I forget it?' he said. 'A weak Cork clearance came towards Alan Lotty and myself. I got my hurl under it and was away. "Goodbye Alan", sez I, "This is it!" and it was. The game was over with the puck-out.'

Over 40 years later, when Tipperary won the 1989 All-Ireland final, the players were treated to a fortnight's holiday in Florida. 'One morning,' said Seamus Leahy, 'we were waiting for a bus to take us on a sight-seeing tour and this huge Afro-American was standing nearby, watching the players and the hurleys with keen interest. Noel Morris explained that they were a hurling team from Ireland. "Hurling?" exploded the Afro-American. "Is that guy Christy Ring still playing?" He had worked with Terry Leahy for many years in New York and the great Kilkenny star never tired of telling him of the wonders of hurling and the wizard of Cloyne.'

Joe Kelly Leaves

Joe Kelly, a leading light in the 1944 and '46 wins, had scored Cork's final goal against Kilkenny in 1946 and, like Christy, he was earmarked for special treatment in the '47 final. 'With flier Joe Kelly and Ring tightly held, the Cork attack was very disjointed,' wrote the *Independent*.

'Peter Prendergast and Jack Mulcahy marked Ring very tightly that day,' said Din Joe Buckley. 'Any time the ball would come his way they'd close in on him.'

'Prendergast followed Christy everywhere,' said Joe Kelly, 'and it wasn't until he was switched to wing-forward that he broke loose and helped us to make a recovery. Paddy Grace was doing much the same with me and I couldn't break free. In fact, I have to admit that the only goal I got, according to the papers, was actually scored by Jack Lynch. He should get the credit. As for myself, it was a disappointing end to my hurling days with Cork, but I took many happy memories with me when I made the 12,500 mile journey to the southern hemisphere.'

Joe was ordained a priest in June 1949 and arrived in New Zealand the following October, to spend the rest of his life ministering in Christchurch. Naturally, he kept in contact with home and the progress of the Cork teams and he was always delighted to welcome sportsmen from the northern hemisphere.

On one occasion the *New Zealand Tablet* carried a cover photograph of Fr Joe with Denis Law, Mike Campbell-Lamerton and Noel Murphy. 'The Lions were touring New Zealand and Manchester United were also there on an off-season tour,' he said, 'so the

Auxiliary Bishop of Christchurch, who was a sports fanatic, brought us all together. He got on great with everyone, especially Noel Murphy – the Cork accent, I suppose – and he gave Noel the use of his car for the weekend the Lions were in Christchurch. He was intrigued by hurling and used to ask me about Christy Ring whenever he'd see the hand-painted picture of Christy hanging on a wall in my house. Noel Murphy was able to back me up on Christy's greatness but, sadly, the bishop never got to see Christy in action.'

The portrait of Christy was presented to Fr Joe when he returned home on holiday nine years after he left for New Zealand. It was designed by Donnacha Ó Griobhtha who had a wonderful collection of hurling photographs on display in his popular café, *An Stad*, in Leitrim Street, in Cork.

Reprise

Despite the high quality of the hurling and the fact that the 1947 game would be ranked among the greatest of all finals, Kilkenny's one-point win was a bitter disappointment to Cork players and supporters. The tight two-man marking of Christy Ring rankled with many followers and there was an added sharpness to their interest in the meeting of the two teams in Cork within weeks of the All-Ireland final.

'The weather was so bad in March that year that Kilkenny couldn't travel to Cork for a league match,' said Willie John Daly, 'so it was put back to September, two or three weeks after the All-Ireland. Kilkenny had a full team except for the goalie, but we beat them well. I made my senior debut that day. It was a tough match.'

'With Christy Ring right back into his old form,' wrote *The Irish Press*, 'it was Cork's game from midway through the first half to the very end. Ring was continuously sending his forwards attacking, and they well deserved their 5-7 to 0-5 win.'

Two quick goals by Josie Hartnett late in the first quarter sent Cork on their way to a satisfying victory. 'They never seemed to be in danger with Kilkenny's Leahy and Langton well subdued by Paddy O'Donovan and Michael Nestor,' added the *Press*. 'The game was over-robust and players on both sides were inclined to play the man rather than the ball.'

CHAPTER SEVEN

LEAN YEARS

'If Christy Ring never won an All-Ireland medal,' declared Denis Conroy, 'he would still be regarded as the greatest hurler Cork or anyone else ever produced.' A fanciful assertion, some doubters might suggest, yet a look at Ring's form when Cork were not winning provincial or national titles would seem to substantiate the Carrigtwohill man's opinion.

Even during his veteran days after 1956, Christy was still the most dangerous forward in the game – and Texaco Hurler of the Year when he was 39 – but it was his form during the lean years from 1947 to the start of 1952 that underscored Ring's unique brilliance. Tipperary, as a team, may have dominated the hurling scene, but Christy was far and away the supreme individual hurler.

An *Irish Press* columnist selected Christy as Top Hurler of 1948, although it was not a distinguished year for Cork, and in 1951, Tipperary took the drastic decision at half-time of moving Mick Ryan from centre-forward to midfield to curb the rampant Ring. 'Many thought the decision was born of something in the nature of delirium,' wrote John D. Hickey, 'but, while not beating Ring, Ryan cramped his style to an extent that must have meant the difference between victory and defeat.'

'There are those who claim that Christy's display against Kilkenny in the 1946 All-Ireland was his greatest game ever,' wrote Alan Fitzpatrick in *Gaelic Sport* (1959), 'and I can still vividly recall his wonderful solo run and goal shortly before the interval. Since then he has never, I think, had a poor game at Croke Park, but his greatest game ever? For me it has to be a day against Tipperary early in the '50s. I can't pinpoint the exact year but on that particular day Christy was playing at midfield.

'Now in those Cork-Tipp clashes at the time, Tipperary usually had the whip hand and on the day in question they were, through the field, several goals the better team. But there was only a point or two in it at the end and the reason for this was that Ring played the game of his life for Cork. I have seen him before and since, inspiring Cork teams to victory, but for me his midfield exhibition that day was Ring's finest hour. If ever a man carried a team on his back, Christy carried Cork in that game. He has never played more superb hurling as he did in that hour of defeat. Overhead, on the ground, ranging from one 40-yard mark to the other, he time and again baffled the might of Tipperary and some of his magical moments will surely be remembered for years to come.'

1948

'Who do you regard as the outstanding hurler of 1948?' a reader asked 'Conal' in *The Irish Press*, naming Waterford's John Keane as his own choice.

Conal replied that 1948 would be remembered as the year of the goalkeepers with Kevin Matthews (Dublin), Jim Ware (Waterford), Tom Mulcahy (Cork), Paddy Collopy (Limerick) and Sean Duggan (Galway) all outstanding.

'But,' he added, 'the display of 1948 that will remain in my mind is Christy Ring's exhibition against Waterford at Cork in the National League. This was "tops" and those of us who saw it were agreed that for artistry we had not seen its equal since the 1946 final.'

The year had started well for Christy with another Railway Cup triumph. 'Sean Herbert, Jackie Power and Christy Ring are a trio to test any defence and I couldn't forecast a comfortable hour for their Leinster opposites, Kelly, Brennan and Mulcahy,' wrote Traolach in his *Independent* preview. A week later, Andy Croke commented: 'Ring who is back in match-winning form, and Good, a surprise packet, laid the foundations for Munster's win by 3-5 to 2-5.' Munster had previously beaten the holders Connacht at Ballinasloe, where Ballincollig's Billy 'Long Puck' Murphy had begun his successful captaincy of the province.

'A comedy of errors' was how one reporter described the

Kilkenny-Cork league fixture at St James' Park, Kilkenny in the spring of 1948. And he was not referring to the match.

'The stewarding arrangements could hardly have been worse,' he wrote. 'The crowd completely obscured the view from the press table and when reporters and members of the public stood on the table to see the game, it collapsed under them. After the interval, Paddy Grace, the Kilkenny full-back and county secretary, had to leave the field to clear one of the sidelines almost unaided and the game was held up for about fifteen minutes.'

The omens were bad even before the match started. One of the cars bringing the Cork players to the venue was delayed on the road for nearly two hours, with the result that the Cork team took the field without a single sub. Dave Creedon, who was reserve goalkeeper, fell in at full-forward.

For all that, the game was played with championship fervour. It was obvious that Kilkenny were eager to avenge the previous autumn's result at the Athletic Grounds, and equally clear that Cork were again determined to reverse the one-point All-Ireland defeat.

As in the All-Ireland, two men were delegated to mark Christy but, according to the *Examiner*, 'Ring played one of the best games of his career and came out on top in every duel with the Kilkenny men.' The home side led by two points just before the finish but two late goals by Paddy Barry and Mossie O'Riordan secured a spectacular victory for Cork. 'It was a great way to win at Kilkenny,' said Paddy, 'and we didn't mind that our victory was greeted with a stony silence.'

Destined to become Ring's outstanding adjutant in the Cork and Munster attack, Paddy Barry had made his senior debut a few months earlier. 'I was playing table tennis with one of my brothers when a Cork selector arrived at the front door and asked me to get ready for a league match in Wexford. Naturally, I jumped at the chance of playing with the Cork seniors and I marked my unexpected debut by scoring 3-1.'

Cork went on to win the league and Paddy landed the first of a medal haul that would include three All-Irelands, four Munster championships, two league medals, four Railway Cups and two county senior medals with Sarfields, a club he and his brothers would serve with distinction.

'My hurling developed in Farranferris, but not right away,' said Paddy. 'Canon Jim Kelly and Dr Dan Connolly decided to put me in goal for a Harty game against the Mon. I got ten shots to save and I blocked two. After that, they felt I should play a little further out the field!'

It was quite a coincidence that both Christy Ring and Paddy Barry should begin their careers by playing in goal as youngsters. Remarkable too that Jimmy Doyle should start in the same position, although the Tipperary man made it to Croke Park as a minor goalkeeper.

'I have no doubt that Christy would have been a top-class goalkeeper too,' said film-maker Louis Marcus. 'I remember after we'd finished filming one day, Christy went into goal himself while we fired in shots from all angles. With an expression of amusement he blocked our shots with ease, shifting the hurley from hand to hand while standing rooted in the same spot. Once he shaped to move the wrong way and just as we thought we had him beaten, he whipped around full circle and doubled on the ball before it crossed the line. The entire performance was uncanny. Ring must be the greatest goalman that has ever lived.'

A Drop

Archbishop Kinane of Cashel presented a trophy for inter-club hurling in May and Glen Rovers were invited to represent Cork. They beat Thurles Sars in the semi-final at Waterford before meeting Éire Óg (Kilkenny) in the tournament final.

'The Glen was a very progressive club for the time,' said Paddy O'Donovan. 'Not alone did we play many club games around our own county, but we were often invited to tournaments and challenges in other counties. I remember one evening in Limerick, watching a Glen selection play Clare shortly after I had retired. The match ended in a draw, a great thing for the Glen to do. Anyway during the match, a small fella near me on the line was giving out yards, so I told him over my shoulder to shut up, that he probably never saw a game in his life. Quietly he said, "I might have seen as many as you, Paddy" and I turned only to see it was Larry Blake of Clare who played in six Railway Cup finals in the 1930s. I got a drop.'

'Talking about getting a drop,' said Dave Creedon, 'I remember the day the Glen played Éire Óg in the Dr Kinane Cup in Walsh Park. Charlie Ware was the ref. There was a dispute over an Éire Óg goal and the match had to be abandoned. As we were leaving the ground, a fella standing by a wall kept jeering Ring, who took it for a few moments but no more. Christy went straight over to him and gave him a dig. His knees buckled under him and he went down like a cowboy in the old pictures. I can still see him dropping to the ground.'

Christy had scored 3-2 that day and the sides were level 4-5 to 5-2 near the end when the disputed goal prompted the referee to stop the match.

Championship

A few weeks later Cork beat Limerick in the 1948 championship and met Waterford in the Munster final. Unlike the match in Dungarvan a decade earlier, the final was played on a beautiful August Sunday and many followers opted for a day at the seaside instead. 'We had four trains ready at Glanmire station,' said a CIÉ official, 'but only two were needed, so we ran the other two to Youghal because of the huge holiday crowd. Most people thought little of Waterford's chances.'

Alan Lotty could not play in the final, so Joe West (Carrigaline) came into the defence, with Mattie Fouhy taking Lotty's position. Blackrock's Eddie John O'Sullivan lined out at full-forward between Mossie O'Riordan and Jack Lynch.

Cork started well with points by Willie John Daly and Ring (four) and a goal by Lynch, but Waterford soon hit back with goals by Johnny O'Connor and Christy Moylan. Points by Carew, O'Connor and Keane stretched the Decies' tally and they led 2-3 to 1-5 at the break. A further goal by Tom Curran fired them up and Cork began to realise their Munster title was in jeopardy. With John Keane and Vin Baston outstanding, the Decies looked set to cause another sensation.

'Waterford were playing like champions,' wrote Moltóir in the *Independent*, 'and every stroke was cheered to the echo. But out came trainer Jim Barry and positional switches were made. A goal from a 60-yards free by Billy Murphy showed the way and two more points brought them closer. Then Christy Ring scored a goal and when Willie John Daly added a point, Waterford were left hanging on to a one-point lead.'

'Lost time was being played,' said the *Examiner*, 'when Christy Ring put in a great solo run and, having carried the ball on his hurley for 30 or 40 yards, his shot was only a couple of inches wide.' The game ended with the puck-out by Jim Ware.

'Christy was furious with himself that his last shot didn't go over to make it a draw,' said Mattie Fouhy. 'He had a fine game and scored a goal and four points, but he hated losing and that last shot was so close it made losing even harder to bear. I suppose it was the only time he didn't pull the game out of the fire for us in a Munster final. He was only human after all!'

While Waterford's win was greeted with national acclaim and would lead to a celebrated All-Ireland victory over Dublin in September, nobody realised that it also signalled the end of a glorious reign for Cork. The previous seven years had seen them winning five All-Ireland titles, but now they would give way to Waterford and later Tipperary as kingpins of hurling. It would be four long years before Cork would come out of Munster again.

County Final

At club level in 1948 the 'Rockies met the Glen in the county final and with John Quirke, Jerry and Mossie O'Riordan, Derry Hayes, Eddie John O'Sullivan and football star 'Moll' O'Driscoll in their ranks, they had high hopes of regaining a title not won since Eudie Coughlan's time almost two decades earlier. 'They had weight, they had strength, they had speed and stamina and they lacked nothing in pluck and enthusiasm,' wrote *The Irish Press*, 'but those attributes availed Blackrock nothing in their bid to wrest the county title from Glen Rovers.'

Blackrock started well with a Derry Hayes goal, but with Ring in great form the Glen soon took over. Then at the end of the first quarter came a shock decision. 'Glen Rovers suffered a serious set-back when their star sharpshooter Christy Ring, who up to then had dominated at midfield, was ordered off by the referee, Johnny Vaughan of Lismore,' said the *Press*.

Christy had figured in the scoring before his dismissal, but his early departure served to rouse his colleagues to greater endeavour and the Glen went on to win by 5-7 to 3-2. It was their eleventh county title.

Christy's dismissal meant missing the league semi-final against Dublin a week later, and the final itself against Tipperary at Croke Park. 'Cork never needed motivation to beat Tipp in a big game,' said Jim Young, the captain, 'but in the dressing room beforehand I pleaded with the players to win this one for Christy who was devastated at missing a Croke Park final against Tipp. The match was played with all the fervour of a Cork-Tipp Munster final and I believe the players made that extra effort. We won by seven points.'

Sean Twomey (Carrigtwohill), Bernie Murphy ('Barrs), Mick O'Toole (Charleville) and Donie Twomey (Glen) were the newcomers joining Cork's tried and trusted hurlers who captured the 1948 league title. It was the only final Cork ever won without Ringey during his long career.

1949

Christy began the year in typical style, helping Munster to win the Railway Cup. 'Ring's Two Brilliant Goals Swung the Day' was the *Examiner* headline after the semi-final win over Leinster (2-8 to 1-8) and in the final 40,609 spectators saw Munster beating Connacht.

'When I was in secondary school,' said Galway hurler Frank Duignan, 'I used to read newspaper reports with sentences such as "then Ring added four points in a row" or "Christy Ring accounted for all but four points of Cork's tally of 3-8". He was my hero and I visualised him as a Tarzan-type figure. When I finally met him face to face in the 1949 Railway Cup final, I felt rather disappointed on seeing that Christy looked mortal after all. But looks can be deceiving as I soon found out, for it was Ring who sealed our fate that day. Apart from Tom Boyle of Roscommon, it was an all-Galway team and we were about to spring a major surprise. In the event we lost by a goal (5-3 to 2-9) and if memory serves me rightly, it was a side-line puck by Christy which either went all the way to the net or was boosted in during a goalmouth scramble, that beat us. My direct opponent that day was the great Tommy Purcell of Tipp, and also playing were two other brilliant hurlers I admired, Waterford's Vin Baston, who used to play with An Chéad Chath in Galway, and that other hurling giant, John Keane.'

John Keane was one of the hurlers Christy greatly admired and the admiration was mutual. The Waterford man introduced Christy to a young hurler one day and added, 'Son, there's only one Christy Ring', to which Ring replied, 'And there'll never be another John Keane'.

Cork were again doing well in the league in 1949 with Bernie Murphy, Sean Twomey and Donie Twomey enhancing their reputations as the county advanced to the closing stages.

'Christy Ring, as is customary in matches against Kilkenny, found two or three men marking him in the league semi-final at Croke Park,' wrote Walter McGrath in the *Examiner*, 'but nevertheless he succeeded in eluding them on several occasions and scored a great goal after a characteristic run. Donie Twomey also notched a brilliant goal in Cork's six-point win.'

Three weeks later Cork went to Thurles for the league final against Tipperary and the home supporters were impressed by some fine young hurlers, notably Pat Stakelum and Phil Shanahan. 'The stylish ground play and excellent stamina of the fifteen was a pleasant surprise,' wrote the *Examiner*, adding that 'Tony Reddan stopped some amazing shots from Ring and Lynch. If he can get over his dangerous habit of running out too far, he may develop into the finest goalkeeper in the country.' In time Tony would be selected as Goalkeeper of the Millennium.

A low-scoring first half ended with Cork 1-2 to 0-1 in front, the goal coming from Jack Lynch and the points by Lynch and Bernie Murphy. Play remained even enough afterwards, but the home side pulled away in the last quarter with a goal by Sonny Maher and two by the young captain, Pat Stakelum. Tipperary won by two points.

A feature of the match was another tight-marking performance by Tommy Purcell on Ring, and the fair-haired wing-back was

1949 League finalists.
Back (from left): Seamus O Seaghdna (chairman), Mattie Fouhy, John Quirke, Sean Twomey, Tom Mulcahy, Bernie Murphy, Jack Lynch, Paddy O'Donovan, Sean McCarthy, Jerry O'Riordan. Front: Willie John Daly, Christy Ring, Donie Twomey, Jim Young, Con Murphy, Billy Murphy, Josie Hartnett, Mossie O'Riordan.

justifiably rated as one of the heroes of the hour. He had also played well with Christy in the Railway Cup final on Patrick's Day, but few guessed then that 28-year-old Tommy would never play in Croke Park again, nor indeed in his beloved Thurles after the league final. A fatal illness, known only to his family and close friends, took its toll in October when the hurling fraternity was stunned to hear of his death in the very prime of life.

'Who can forget Tommy's magnificent display for Munster on his last appearance at Croke Park,' asked *The Sunday Press*, 'or his superb display in the National League final, just a few short months ago? On that occasion he had the distinction of holding scoreless Ireland's greatest forward, Christy Ring. That in itself speaks volumes for his worth. As a left half-back in Tipp's All-Ireland success of 1945 and Munster's monopoly in the Railway Cup for some years Tommy Purcell was a true hurling star.'

Drawn Final

When the counties next met in a championship game at Limerick, the match was played in blistering heat, with temperatures in the eighties. 'It was a fierce weekend of heat and lightning storms,' said a Fermoy shopkeeper. 'On Friday a wynd of hay was destroyed by lightning and a bullock was killed in a field outside the town. The lightning also wrecked the belfry of the church at Coolagown.'

The match itself was only marginally less dramatic and finished level at 3-10 apiece. In a pulsating finish, Tipp were denied a Sonny Maher point when a Cork player threw his hurley and the resultant free was cleared.

'Cork followers looking for a label for the game might well call it the solo-run hour,' wrote *The Irish Press*. 'Three of their vital scores in the nerve-tingling second half came from individual efforts that are usually rationed to one per match. Christy Ring, Jack Lynch and Bernie Murphy were the respective scorers. There were some drab spots in the opening half, some first-class Munster hurling mingled with patches of mediocre play, but the second half was terrifically exciting. On the whole, the game can be written down as hard rather than brilliant, with Tipp's Jimmy Kennedy of UCD giving a superb exhibition of clever and accurate hurling.'

'Ring, Murphy and Daly earned the constant care and attention of the entire Tipp defence,' said the *Examiner*, 'and with Tommy Doyle, Paddy Furlong and Mickey Byrne in great form, the Cork trio got little chance of shining although all three did succeed in shooting spectacular points.'

Jack Lynch, who was at his brilliant best, scored 1-6, the other goals coming from Gerard Murphy who finished a Ring sideline puck to the net, and Bernie Murphy who drove a long ball home after a Ring free had been batted down.

The match, which drew a record attendance for a first round – 34,702 – saw Ignatius O'Flynn (Carrigaline) starting in attack and Gerard Murphy replacing the absent Paddy Barry. The young Midleton man, destined to become one of Cork's more stylish midfielders, was back on the subs' bench for the replay, but replaced an injured Alan Lotty in what became the great Sars man's last championship appearance with the county.

The replay was a disappointing, bad-tempered game, marred by injuries, stoppages and spectator encroachments. 'The sun which blistered the Gaelic Grounds was not as hot as the tempers of the players,' wrote the *Independent*, 'and I don't think any one of the players escaped unscathed. From the word go, it was pull first and ask questions afterwards and we saw some regrettable incidents which culminated in Young of Cork and Maher of Tipp getting marching orders in the closing minutes.'

Jimmy Kennedy was the hero of the hour for Tipperary, scoring the equalising goal in the last minute to add to his five points from frees. Yet, despite Kennedy's great display, the day is best remembered for the fact that Tommy Doyle held Ring scoreless for 90 minutes.

'It was a unique experience for Ring, prolific scorer that he is, to find himself so effectively policed that he did not even get a solitary point,' wrote the *Independent*, adding that Jack Lynch found himself facing a stone wall in Flor Coffey, though he did elude him on a few occasions.' 'With Ring and Lynch well held,' said *The Irish Press*, 'Cork's supremacy was never translated into goals and points.'

'At the end of normal time both teams were prepared to go for a second replay,' said Pat Stakelum, 'but a decision had to be agreed between our spokesmen, Johnny Leahy and Jim Barry. So Leahy and myself walked over to Jim Barry and Jack Lynch. "Begod lads," Leahy said, "'tis wonderful stuff, we can't be separated. What's going to happen at all?" "I don't know," says Jack, "but I've had enough of it anyway." Leahy gave me a nudge: "We're playing extra-time."'

Stakelum and Leahy then followed the rest of the Tipperary team to the dressing room to convey the outcome and, more importantly, to gain some respite from the unrelenting heat. An athletic family, the Blakes of Coolquill, had had the foresight to bring a little churn of water with them and they applied the welcome balm to the players during the break. 'They doused us behind the neck, behind the knees, down the back and it helped to revitalise us,' said Pat Stakelum. 'While all that was going on the Cork players stayed out on the field in the scorching heat.'

The extended period provided the best hurling of the afternoon with Mick Ryan creating a big impression. The Nenagh man, who later won county medals with Dicksboro (Kilkenny) and the

'Barrs, got the crucial goal when he slammed a shot past Mulcahy from 20 yards. Cork fought hard to the finish, only to lose by two points (2-8 to 1-9).

'An incident in the second half is still disputed,' said Seamus King. 'Cork claimed that Mossie O'Riordan scored a second goal that rebounded from the stanchion supporting the wire netting with such speed that the umpire failed to see it before it was cleared. The Tipperary view is that the ball struck the crossbar, bounced down and rebounded outfield from the goalkeeper's boot. It was the first of a series of such incidents that were to be associated with Tipp-Cork games. As a result of the episode, corded netting was introduced the following year.'

Christy, who was convinced it was a goal, was furious and vented his outrage at both the umpire and referee – to no avail. Tipperary went on to beat Clare and Limerick in Munster before taking the first of three consecutive All-Ireland titles.

At the end of the year *Sunday Press* readers voted on the best hurling team of 1949. The fifteen players chosen were:

Seanie Duggan
(Galway)

Andy Fleming	Con Murphy	Mark Marnell
(Waterford)	(Cork)	(Kilkenny)

Jimmy Murray	Vin Baston	Tommy Doyle
(Laois)	(Waterford)	(Tipperary)

Joe Styles   Phil Shanahan
(Laois)   (Tipperary)

Paddy Fitzgerald	Christy Ring	Jimmy Kennedy
(Limerick)	(Cork)	(Tipperary)

Shem Downey	Jackie Power	Josie Gallagher
(Kilkenny)	(Limerick)	(Galway)

The presence of two Laois hurlers on the team reflects the fact that the O'Moore county reached the All-Ireland final that year, only to lose to Tipperary. Laois or Leix, as they were better known at the time, previously appeared in the 1915 final and scored a sensational win over a Cork team that included Connie Sheehan, Bowler Walsh, Sean Hyde, Larry Flaherty, Major Kennedy and a young Seán Óg Murphy. Asked to explain the defeat, a Cork player said, 'The pitch was muddy,' to which an opponent replied, 'It was muddy for Leix too!'

The Footballer

'Christy Ring was the spearhead of their attack and he scored a goal and two points at a crucial stage and so paved the way for the victory of his side. Even when the other forwards scored, Christy had a say in leading up to the scores and there could be no doubt that his dashing solo-runs and well-timed passes caused consternation to the defence.'

At first glance this 1949 extract from an *Examiner* report of a club game seems to be a routine account of another fine display by Ring for the Glen. What makes it unusual and rather intriguing is that it is not part of a hurling report at all. Christy, in fact, was playing football for St Nick's and helping them to a championship victory over far-famed Clonakilty.

For a Cork hurling star to be proficient at football comes as no surprise. Ever since Billy Mackesy and Jerry Beckett played on both county teams in the early 1900s, Cork hurlers have taken to football with ease whenever it suited them to do so. Jim Regan, Jim Hurley, Jack Lynch, Alan Lotty, Jim Young, Pat 'Hitler' Healy, Sean Condon, Derry Beckett, Paddy O'Donovan, John Lyons, Dave Creedon, Josie Hartnett, Jimmy Lynam, Tom Furlong, Eamonn Goulding, Jimmy Brohan, Jerry O'Sullivan, Charlie McCarthy, Teddy O'Brien, Jimmy Barrett, Dave Moore, Patsy Harte, Tom Corbett, Johnny Crowley, Dinny Allen and Denis Coughlan all wore the Cork football colours in their hurling heyday, and three of Cork's all-time greats in hurling, Ray Cummins, Brian Murphy and Jimmy Barry-Murphy, played a big part in helping the county to win the Sam Maguire Cup in 1973. Others including Teddy McCarthy, John Allen, Denis Walsh, Tomás Mulcahy, Brian Corcoran, Diarmuid O'Sullivan, Tom Kenny and Seán Óg Ó hAilpín continued the trend.

But Christy Ring, a football star? It certainly is a curiosity, seeing that he once declared with some venom in his voice, 'Football should be abolished.' Dave O'Brien remembers Christy stopping his car on the way home from a hurling match one evening and asking him to climb a ditch and point out roughly where Kinsale was located on the panorama beneath. 'Dava,' said Christy, when Dave had hazarded a guess, 'a line should be drawn from Kingsale to Charleville and every football east of that line should be destroyed.'

Despite the dual-code success of some players, traditionally, there has been an antipathy towards football in hurling strong-holds, none more so than in Cork, where football is seen as a game for bad hurlers. 'An hour spent at football is an hour lost to hurl-ing,' Kevin Cashman once declared.

Even at club level, old die-hards would prefer to see their 'sister' football teams fail rather than weaken the power and prestige of their hurling counterparts. Yet, somewhat ironically, when hurling clubs like the 'Barrs, the Glen, the 'Rockies, Na Piarsaigh and Midleton have been at their strongest, their football teams have thrived as well. 'A rising tide lifts all boats,' the old cliché runs, yet many old-time hurlers would prefer to see the smaller football-laden boats sink without trace.

How then did Christy Ring become a footballer? He had been playing hurling with the Glen for eight years before deciding to wear the black and white hooped jersey of sister club, St Nicholas. Val Dorgan suggested that he did so to prove to Kerry footballer James (Jas) Murphy that any good hurler could do well at football. A tall, determined footballer, Jas played with St Nick's when he moved to Cork as a garda and he captained Kerry to All-Ireland glory in 1953. He smiled at the memory when we spoke about Ring's footballing days at his Capwell home. 'Christy was a knacky enough footballer,' he conceded.

Dave O'Brien agreed. 'Ring was very determined and won pos-session very often. He scored many goals and points when he played for St Nick's, but a funny thing was that he preferred to use his fist to score or pass a ball, rather than his feet. He had very strong wrists.'

Christy's first senior football game was in May 1949 against St

Patrick's, a team from the Lower Road-Tivoli area, whose players from time to time included fine hurlers like Alan Lotty, Derry Hayes, Sean 'Roundy' Horgan and Mossie O'Riordan, as well as the great Beara footballer, Neally Duggan.

'Christy Ring made his debut on a senior football side,' wrote the *Examiner*, 'and he displayed many of the moves which have made him such a force on the hurling field. Playing at right corner-forward he "worked" many of the St Nick's scores, showing on several occasions that he can control the larger ball almost as well as the hurling ball.'

Playing football on and off after that first outing, Christy had more club success than many dedicated footballers and he climaxed a notable, if disjointed, career by winning a county senior medal with St Nick's in 1954, an achievement greatly overshadowed by his eighth All-Ireland and also his eighth county hurling medal the same year. He was even asked to wear the Cork colours in football but he dismissed the suggestion out of hand. 'Ye must be really desperate to ask me to play football for the county', he told the selectors.

Yet when he had helped the Blackpool men to win the double in 1954, he remarked with satisfaction and no small degree of pride, 'We're the best in everything now'.

CHAPTER EIGHT

THE CHURCHES
TOURNAMENT

'The GAA is unashamedly Catholic and unashamedly national,' declared Bishop Cornelius Lucey in a speech delivered in Dublin late in 1953. He was speaking at the presentation of church tournament hurling trophies to the St Vincent's club at the Catholic Young Men's Society Hall in Fairview.

Nobody saw anything unusual or amiss with those comments and there were no letters to the editors after his words appeared in the newspapers. In effect, Bishop Lucey was voicing the perceived notion of the GAA at the time – Catholic and national. At that time, the Catholic Church exercised a huge influence on Irish society and its role in the affairs of the country's largest sporting organisation seemed natural and right.

Before the start of major hurling and football games, a Catholic bishop was officially escorted on to the pitch and had his ring kissed by the rival captains before he threw in the ball. The huge attendance usually sang 'Faith of Our Fathers' with as much heartfelt gusto as '*Amhrán na bhFiann*' that followed. I once attended a game in Thurles where the crowd was enjoined to say a decade of the rosary for two men who had died in the attendance. Even the popular GAA newspaper, the *Gaelic Sportsman*, was not averse to carrying a large photograph of Pope Pius XII on its front page.

The bond between Church and GAA went further than mere ceremonial trappings, however, and many tournaments were organised to help raise funds for church building and other church-related activities.

The most successful and memorable of the fund-raising competitions was the Cork Churches Tournament which involved top clubs from Munster and Leinster. It was hugely popular with Cork sportsmen and women and provided a rare opportunity of seeing at close quarters most of the great hurlers of the day in action at the Dyke or in the Park.

'The Churches Tournament was organised in 1953 by Glen Rovers,' said Liam Ó Tuama, 'with the assistance of Rev Dr Connolly, president of Farranferris and Rev Dr McCarthy, who became president later. Dr McCarthy was vice-chairman of the Glen at the time and he was the main man behind the very successful tournament.'

It was during the autumn of 1953 that Dr Carthach McCarthy suggested to Bishop Lucey that a challenge between Glen Rovers and the new Dublin champions, St Vincent's, would be a very attractive fixture. This would feature Christy Ring and the other household names on the Glen team, pitted against Kevin Heffernan, Des 'Snitchy' Ferguson, Noel Drumgoole, Norman Allen, Marcus Wilson and their clubmates. Proceeds would go towards 'The Rosary of Churches' being built in the newly-developing housing estates at Churchfield, Spangle Hill (later Farranree), Ballyphehane, Dennehy's Cross and Mayfield.

Dr Lucey, a great hurling man himself, was impressed with the idea and invited Pádraig Ó Caoimh to his residence, the Bishop's Palace near Farranferris, where arrangements were made to play the match at Croke Park. As a result, the first significant inter-county club game was held in Croke Park on 6 December 1953.

'Christy was always a man for the big occasion and for a good cause,' said Dr Carthach McCarthy, 'and the idea of playing for the Glen in Croke Park really appealed to him. He was very excited about it and it was no surprise that on the day he gave an exhibition.'

'There was an attendance of about 15,000 spectators at the game,' said Liam Ó Tuama, who was in goal for the Glen that day. 'The game should really not have been played because it was impossible to see out to the halfway line due to the heavy fog over the pitch.'

'A dull grey December afternoon was lit at Croke Park by some thrilling hurling,' said the *Examiner*, 'with St Vincent's, the Dublin champions, proving worthy winners over Glen Rovers, the Cork title-holders, by 3-11 to 2-11. Even the strong contingent of visiting supporters would agree that the winners showed all-round superiority.'

True to form Christy revelled in the occasion and scored 2-7, his goals coming from 21-yard frees. 'Ring gave a typical display of skilful opportunism, added the *Examiner*, 'but even he could not win the game on his own.'

'Glen Rovers are synonymous with skilful teamwork, fast accurate ground passes, bewildering pattern-weaving combinations, hard first-time pulling on the ball and an experience and confidence born of long years as Cork champions,' wrote Tommy McQuaid in *The Gael*. 'How would Vincent's fare against them? That was the question that sent Dublinmen thronging to Croke Park to find out. But they needn't have worried, for fifteen men from Dublin town stood the shock of Glen Rovers in full cry and hurled them into defeat. Not all the wizardry and artistry of the legendary Christy Ring could save the Glen nor the 2-7 he scored. What a success it was for St Vincent's.'

Des Ferguson was a member of St Vincent's, the first all-Dublin team to win the Dublin county championship. 'That meant an awful lot to us,' he said, 'but it was nothing compared to playing and beating the famous Glen Rovers at Croke Park. That was one of the highlights of my career and I still cherish the miniature trophy I received from Bishop Lucey that evening in Fairview.'

Despite the result, the Glen supporters were delighted with the novelty of seeing their club in action at Croke Park. The organisers had reason to be pleased as well – the venture was a great success – and it was decided to have a re-match between the clubs three months later, again at Croke Park.

News of the game was conveyed far afield and in New York *The Advocate* gave a detailed account of the match and another magisterial display by Ring: 'Without doubt these are two evenly matched sides and in the final summing-up the essential difference between them was the undimmed genius of Christy Ring. The Cork maestro was at his brilliant best and his deft flicks were beautiful to watch. Des Ferguson kept a tight rein on him for most of the hour but, despite all his attention, the Cork captain got in many telling strokes with split-second timing and lightning bursts of speed.

'Two typical Ring mastermoves in the second half drove St Vincent's to the wall. The first was a ball he collected around the 50-yards mark and, having raced through the entire defence, he sent over a truly magnificent point. Better still was to follow. Christy coolly moved up to take a 21-yards free, gazed coolly over the bar, bent in a leisurely fashion to lift the ball and then, in the flick of an eyelash, he galvanised into action, put the accumulated force of his weight and speed behind the puck and the ball was in the net. That was the beginning of the end for St Vincent's.'

'Such was the splendour of Christy Ring in fashioning the 4-8 to 2-7 victory that it was sheer hurling sorcery,' wrote John D. Hickey. 'Innumerable the great games the Cork wizard has played but, most assuredly, none better. Never have I so much enjoyed the enchantment of his hurling. On his day there is no doubt that Ring is a man apart on the hurling field. The St Vincent's captain, Snitchie Ferguson, tried valiantly to cope with his wiles, but it was for the most part labour in vain and on his form of yesterday I doubt if there is or ever was a hurler who would have held the Corkman. I think that Ring's point midway through the second half was the greatest I have ever seen. Getting the ball about 45 yards out when there seemed as much chance of his gaining possession as there was of the ground swallowing the ball, he careered through a battalion of Vincent's men to send the ball sweetly between the posts. What a pity that great effort was not filmed so that posterity could see hurling at its very greatest.'

Corpus Christi

After the success of the Glen-Vincent's games at Croke Park, it was not surprising that Dr Carthach McCarthy and others began to consider expanding the idea by pitting county champions from other counties against Cork's top hurling clubs.

The Croke Park matches had shown clearly the appeal inter-county club games had for supporters and there was further proof at home of the huge interest in summer tournament games between star-studded hurling clubs, none more so than the annual Eucharistic Sunday meeting of the Glen and the 'Barrs.

Since the 1920s the Corpus Christi feast day had been honoured by a Eucharistic procession through the streets of Cork with prayers and hymn-singing by the men as they marched from their local churches to the Grand Parade, where a devotional service was held at a specially erected altar at Daunt's Square. It was a Sunday afternoon when all GAA games in the city were cancelled to enable the men to take part in the procession and for decades thousands did so. It also became the Sunday when the Glen and the 'Barrs played an annual evening challenge match at the 'Dyke.

Christy took part in many of those games over the years and scored many a goal, but in 1953 it was the one he did not score that had people talking. 'Ring was robbed of a certain goal by a most unusual incident,' wrote the *Examiner*. 'At one stage in the first half he was in possession on the 21, he shot well but the ball burst and curled wide.'

In those rather frugal days overused footballs were known to burst on occasion. It happened with the Clonakilty football in a championship game, when Jack Lynch had to dive into a raging stream to retrieve the St Nick's ball and ensure that the match ran its course. It even happened during a Cup final at Wembley and there was also the soccer match at the old Camp Field when Sunday's Well, a team of republicans, were in danger of losing to Barrackton, mainly British soldiers. A supporter, to avoid defeat, produced a revolver and shot the ball.

For a sliothar to burst in mid-flight, however, was unusual in the extreme. Was it overused and worn-out leather that encased the ball? Unlikely, seeing that the incident occurred early in the match and no referee would throw in a defective ball. It is more probable that the sheer power of Ring's stroke from a scoring position was too much for the sliothar and it gave.

Rivalry

During the first decade or more of Christy's association with the Glen, the 'Rockies were going through a long trough (1931-1956), and rivalry between the clubs was not as intense as that of the

'Barrs-Glen encounters. George Hook, the broadcaster, remembers as a boy idolising Ring in the Cork colours and hating him when he wore the Glen jersey against the 'Barrs – a situation familiar to countless southsiders.

Another 'Barrs supporter, Paddy O'Callaghan, conductor of the Barrack Street Band, explained the dichotomy to his *Examiner* colleague, Val Dorgan. 'When Ring played with Cork, I'd think, "Oh God, I hope he gets the ball". When he played with the Glen against the 'Barrs, I'd say, "Oh Jesus, he has it".'

'I remember the year the Augustinians put up a set of bicycles for their tournament,' said Jim Young. 'Fr Cummins was the organiser

Christy in full flight against Sarsfields in 1949 with Alan Lotty in pursuit. On the left is Donie O'Donovan.

and we were due to play the 'Barrs in the final. They were so cocky they didn't bring their bikes to the match – they walked it – but they were in for a big land. Christy had a blinder, we won the game and we took the bicycles home. At the time there was a notorious murderer in England by the name of Christie and he had just been given the death penalty. Anyway, the next morning I met a 'Barrs supporter coming down Barrack Street and, even though I could see he was *go brónach* after their defeat, I asked him how he was. "You know, Youngie," he said, ignoring my question, "they hung the wrong Christy!"'

The two Croke Park games between Vincent's and the Glen led to a third in Cork, and by 1955 Jim Langton was playing for Éire Óg against the 'Barrs and Mickey Byrne, Tony Wall, Ray Reidy, Larry Keane and Tommy Ryan were in action for Thurles Sars against UCC.

'The Churches tournament really struck a chord with Cork supporters,' said John Lyons, 'and thousands looked forward to Easter Sunday when the games began.' Among the visiting clubs were Mount Sion (Waterford), Bennettsbridge (Kilkenny), St Vincent's (Dublin), Rathnure and St Aidan's (Wexford) and Thurles Sarsfields. Local clubs, the Glen, the 'Barrs, the 'Rockies, Sars and the College ensured that the visitors met formidable opposition.

A programme for a double bill in 1958 has a picture of Ring with Bishop Lucey on the cover, features on Willie John Daly, Pat Philpott, Jimmy Doyle and Joe Salmon, who had come to live in Cork and joined the Glen, and photographs of 'Barrs goalkeeper, Jim Cotter, in action the previous year, and Nicky Rackard and Christy chatting before the Rathnure-Glen game.

A random selection of the hurlers involved in that day's matches gives some idea of the attractiveness of the tournament: Kevin Heffernan, Noel Drumgoole, Des Ferguson, John Lyons, Vincie Twomey, Jackie Daly, Pat Healy, Gerald Mulcahy, Jimmy Brohan. Bernie Hackett, Joe Twomey, Sean Kenefick, Mick Cashman, Martin Thompson, John Redmond, Tom Furlong, Patsy Lyons, Sean 'Roundy' Horgan, Larry Keane, Sean McLoughlin, Mickey Byrne, Jimmy Doyle and, of course, Ringey. No wonder the people came in their droves.

Christy was in typical form that afternoon, but it was a Dublin youngster who drew most attention at the Mardyke. 'If St Vincent's had brought schoolboy Des Foley into the game earlier, there would be no replay,' said the *Examiner*. 'Foley is every inch a hurler and if he improves as he promises, Dublin have a match winner of the future.' How prophetic those words would prove!

Memories

Des Ferguson and his wife Maura reared ten children in Kells. Sadly, their eldest son, Ronan, died of a brain tumour at the age of sixteen. 'Ronan loved hurling,' said Des, 'and he was a fine hurler. He was delighted when Christy Ring came up to see him in hospital, as indeed we all were. It was a typical gesture by Ringey.'

After one of the early club games in Croke Park the *Gaelic Sportsman* carried the following item:

We had occasion to visit the Glen Rovers dressing room after the game between the Cork champions and Dublin's St Vincent's a couple of Sundays ago and there we witnessed a scene so simple and yet so grand that it shall remain in our memory for many a long day. Through the packed room an aged priest approached the corner where Christy Ring was getting dressed. He shook the Cork captain's hand. 'My eyesight is not what it used to be for watching a hurling game,' he said, 'but your play has given me more pleasure than I have ever had from any hurler. Will you accept this?' he said, extending a valuable fountain pen to Ring. 'Will you accept this as a small appreciation of what your hurling has meant to me through the years?' And with that he was gone through the crowd and the smoke haze. On enquiry, we found that he was completely unknown to Ring, nor was he a Corkman.

CHAPTER NINE

1950

Jerry O'Riordan, the tall, fair-haired Blackrock man, came to prominence beside his younger brother, Mossie, in the Cork attack during the mid-1940s and both played in the Munster forward line of 1947. After an impressive career in the North Monastery, Jerry went to Shannon Airport as a customs officer and continued his hurling career with the Limerick club, Claughaun. In 1951 he married Noreen O'Carroll from Castleconnell, the hurling stronghold that produced the Mackeys, Jackie Power, Timmy Ryan, Paddy Scanlan and the Herberts, and he later joined the Ahane club.

By 1950 Jerry had reverted to defence for both Cork and Munster and would, with John Lyons and Tony O'Shaughnessy, form the brilliant full-back line that conceded just one goal in three All-Ireland finals. Mossie was still in the Munster forward line in 1950, but brought a very promising career to a premature end when he emigrated to England some time later.

The O'Riordan brothers, along with Christy and Mattie Fouhy, were Cork's representatives on a Tipperary-dominated Munster team that defeated Leinster in the 1950 Railway Cup final. Waterford's Andy Fleming and Vin Baston, Clare's Willie McAllister and Limerick's Jim Sadlier were the other non-Tippmen on the Munster team.

After the Railway Cup win, Christy was absent for some time due to injury, but he came back for a Beamish tournament game against Tipperary, played well and accepted the trophy from Richard Beamish. 'The outstanding feature of the Cork display was the marvellous exhibition of Christy Ring who returned in great style at midfield,' wrote the *Examiner*.

Shortly afterwards Christy accepted another trophy, this time from popular entertainer, Danny Hobbs, after the Glen had beaten the 'Barrs in the annual Eucharistic tournament. The match was notable for three great goals Ring scored within two minutes during the first half and for the return of Paddy O'Donovan, who was back to his best in defence.

'During his heyday Paddy Donovan blossomed into a powerful centre-back,' said Eamonn Young. 'The feature of his play was the ability to catch a falling ball amid a forest of hurleys with what appeared to be a complete disregard for personal safety. Time and again I saw him carve his way with powerful hips and shoulders out through a bunch of frantically struggling players to clear away downfield with an energy that discouraged opponents and set us cheering wildly.'

By 1950 Paddy's impressive career in the Cork colours was coming to an end and when he left the inter-county scene, Christy became the sole survivor of the famous nine men who had played in all four-in-a-row wins. The others were Jack Lynch, John Quirke, Billy Murphy, Alan Lotty, Batt Thornhill, Din Joe Buckley and the oldest of the nine, Dr Jim Young.

Born at Ballabuidhe, Dunmanway in 1915, Jim was the eldest of a family of fifteen and was the first of many Farranferris students to be recruited to the ranks of the Glen. He studied for the priesthood in Maynooth but, according to himself, he forestalled a likely schism in the church by leaving and becoming a doctor. He was Christy's personal physician for many years. Jim was a versatile sportsman, excelling at lawn tennis, golf, football and squash, besides the magnificent hurling career he enjoyed. After his playing days, he immersed himself enthusiastically in the administrative side of Glen Rovers and was ultimately granted the club's highest honour – the presidency.

Championships

Towards the end of 1950 the County Board decided to honour the nine four-in-a-row men by presenting each with a miniature replica of the McCarthy Cup. By then, Batt Thornhill had become a noted referee and he took charge of that year's county final in which John Lyons led the Glen to their thirteenth title.

'Splendid goalkeeping by Dave Creedon, who saved shot after shot from all angles, denied the 'Barrs,' wrote Carbery, who also spoke highly of Paddy O'Donovan and Jack Lynch. 'Christy Ring was in his element and his solo runs were thrilling at times,' he added, crediting intense club spirit as the secret of the Glen's continued success. The game was also memorable for a 'Barrs puck-out sent 160 yards over the Glen end-line by former soccer star, Miah Lynch.

The Munster championship pitted Cork against Waterford in the semi-final and a dismal game ended in Cork's favour (1-4 to 0-5). 'Tom Mulcahy in goal and the three full-backs, Jerry O'Riordan, Con Murphy and John Thornhill (Oldcastletown) were excellent,' said the *Examiner*, adding that Vincent Baston and Andy Fleming were Waterford's best. Willie John Daly, who got two points, was the only Cork forward to score.

The paucity of scores from the Cork attack reflected a good overall display by the Waterford backs and goalkeeper Johnny O'Regan. At midfield, however, Mattie Fouhy, who got the only goal, and Christy (two points) were outstanding as Carbery reported: 'Christy Ring again stood head and shoulders above every player on the field. He was tireless and inspiring, every shot was clean and skilful, some of his moves were artistic. And in Matt Fouhy he had an unsparing partner who got through an immense amount of work and hit more solid ground balls than I have seen for some time.'

'Only for Mattie and Christy at centre-field, we wouldn't have won that game,' said Willie John, 'and there were a lot of people who thought we hadn't a hope against Tipperary, who were All-Ireland champions, remember. But a Cork-Tipp Munster final is something special, it brings out the best in both sides and you never can tell the outcome till the final whistle is blown. That's the way it was in 1950, a day I'll never forget in Killarney.'

Killarney

'All the best traditions of Munster hurling were upheld at Killarney when Tipperary defeated Cork by 2-17 to 3-11 in a thrilling final. From the first minute to the last the exchanges were fast, fierce and skilful but no matter how hard bodies or sticks clashed there was never an unsporting incident to mar the hour. Cork were only once ahead with an early point by Christy Ring, but they were always in the hunt, and in beating them, Tipperary showed themselves a team of champions.'

That was how Moltóir began his *Independent* report of the 1950 game but, unfortunately, it was not the quality of the hurling itself that would be remembered, but the regrettable incidents that forced a complete stoppage of play near the end, and the risk of injury to referee and hurlers afterwards.

'The Cork trains arrived early in Killarney that morning and many of the supporters had imbibed a little too much,' said Jack Lynch. 'That was a contributory factor to the disruption near the finish.'

'What most people remember about that game,' said Willie Buckley, a supporter, 'was Jack Lynch appealing to the Cork follow-ers to get off the pitch and let them finish the match and Christy Ring protecting the referee from some drunken supporters as he left the field after full-time.'

'The attendance surpassed all expectations,' said *The Irish Times*, 'and it cannot be properly estimated, for thousands came in over the walls and barriers. There must have been more than 50,000 within the park.'

'There were periodic outbursts of fisticuffs among sections of the crowd,' said *The Irish Press*, 'and Sean Kenny of Tipperary was attacked by a spectator in the first half. Then, as Cork staged a tremendous closing rally, their supporters ran into the field with every score, not realising that this enthusiasm was hindering their team who were fighting from behind.'

Ten minutes from the end the game was stopped for some time, as referee Bill O'Donoghue (Limerick), assisted by Jack Lynch, tried to clear the spectators off the field. 'As the oldest player on the field I felt I should try to do something,' said Jack. 'We were making a good comeback, we had the stiff breeze and I thought we could win if the match wasn't abandoned. I pleaded with the Cork supporters to let us get on with the game. They gradually went back to the sideline but when the game resumed, the referee, understandably enough, was anxious to get it over as quickly as possible and I believe he did not play sufficient time.'

1950 Cork Senior Hurling Team.
*Back (from left): Sean Twomey, Tom Mulcahy, Paddy O'Donovan, Jerry
O'Riordan, Mossie O'Riordan, Jack Lynch, John Thornhill, Mattie Fouhy, Jim
Barry. Front: Con Murphy, Willie John Daly, Sean Condon, Christy Ring, Josie
Hartnett, J.J. O'Brien, Seanie O'Brien.*

Only three points separated the sides when the referee blew full-
time, just as an umpire signalled a 70 for Cork. That sparked a pitch
invasion, with livid supporters heading for the referee with intent.
Christy instantly sensed the danger and rushed to his protection and
with the help of some gardaí, he escorted the referee to safety.
Drunk or sober, no Cork supporter would defy Christy Ring.

Tipperary goalie, Tony Reddan, had the longest distance to travel
through the crowd. 'There was great tension in the air – hostility
even – and I had to borrow a long coat from a Tipp supporter and
keep my head down as I slipped out of the crowd. I didn't stop till I
got back to Sixmilebridge,' he said.

Such shameful scenes, deplorable at any time, were even more
lamentable in that they blemished the memory of one of the truly
great Cork-Tipperary Munster finals. The setting was unusual, the
venue inappropriate and the arrangements faulty in the extreme,
but the quality of the hurling was rarely as good.

'I rate this the best ever display by this Tipp team,' said Moltóir, 'and it had to be against a Cork team which played with rare *élan*. The veterans in the Leeside ranks were rejuvenated and one and all stayed the gruelling hour like youngsters.'

Against the breeze, Christy had opened the scoring with a free and when he was fouled again moments later, the first incursion of spectators took place. Paddy Kenny had Tipperary's first goal before Ring added his second point and Jimmy Kennedy started another impressive scoring tally from frees. Superior throughout the first half, Tipperary stretched their lead with points by Kennedy, Mick Ryan and Paddy Kenny, but Cork stayed in contention with a fine goal by Mattie Fouhy and points by Sean Condon and Jack Lynch. Half-time left them in a reasonable position: 1-13 to 1-6.

On the resumption, Ring and Kenny exchanged points. 'Then,' said the *Independent*, 'we saw Ring at his best as he side-stepped several opponents before scoring a splendid goal.' Tipperary were quick to re-assert themselves, however, and after some brilliant passages of play they went into an eight-point lead.

Cork were already rallying in the last quarter before the long hold-up and, after Jack Lynch's remonstrances had helped to get the intruders off the field, the comeback continued with a goal by Lynch himself, and points by Ring and Willie John Daly. It was not enough, however, to stop the Tipp men who retained the Munster title.

'The outstanding player without a doubt was Christy Ring,' wrote the *Independent*. 'Had Cork managed to snatch a win, it would have been due to his magnificent generalship. For a period he switched to midfield to keep a watch on the elusive Shanahan but, when he returned to the half-forward line, the Cork attack regained its potency.'

A few days after the Killarney match, the referee, Bill O'Donoghue, submitted his report at a Munster Council meeting in Limerick. 'The game was played in a fine sporting spirit,' he said, 'and I wish to congratulate both teams. Towards the end of the game spectators encroached on the field and I had difficulty in leaving. I wish to thank especially the captain of the Cork team, Mr Christy Ring, for his help and support.'

A rare instance of a player being complimented in a referee's report.

Christy Ring, hurler of the year, 1951.

1951

'Superman Ring Turned the Tide' was the *Sunday Press* headline after Munster defeated Leinster in the 1951 final, a Railway Cup series that was also memorable for the trial of the Bogue clock at Croke Park. The clock, designed by Martin Bogue from Youghal, was an early attempt by the GAA to ensure accurate time-keeping in games.

Munster, with Tony Reddan, Dave Walsh, Matt Nugent, Mick Ryan and Paddy Kenny in great form, had a six-point win but Ring, as so often before and after, was the man who stole the show on St Patrick's Day.

'There was brilliance in plenty on both teams,' wrote Paddy Flynn, 'but the stars on the winners' side had an infinitely brighter glint. And who was the meteor among the stars? Well, all the adjectives in the book could be used to describe the artistry of Cork's own superman, Christy Ring, but all the superlatives in the world couldn't do justice to his display yesterday. In the best tradition of a Pimpernel he was everywhere a forward should be and the final score – the goal which really sealed the issue – was a classic of anticipation and execution.'

'When the high ball came to his area – that term could cover half the field generally – Ring, the supreme schemer, took on a sniping commission while the other forwards and backs engaged in heavy artillery warfare. But when the ball came clear, Ring was on it like a hawk and without raising it from the ground, wove a pattern through the defence like an ice-hockey player. Then with a flick of the hurley, he had the net shaking before Dowling in the Leinster goal knew what had happened. And all this brilliance from a man who a minute or two earlier was limping with a leg injury!'

'Most of my group headed for Croke Park after an early lunch,' wrote Carbery, 'and there we joined a very fine hosting, approaching the 40,000 mark. Munster stole away near the end and that consummate master of the hurler's art, Mr Christy Ring of Glen Rovers, gave a display rarely equalled at Croke Park or any other park. Christy Ring is an artist and at one stage the field looked to me as Christy Ring and 29 other men.'

So another good start to the year for Christy and, although he was not to enjoy similar success with club or county, his displays throughout 1951 would earn him hurling's pre-eminent position once again.

Another Classic

Incredible though it may seem, the breathtaking nature of the Cork-Tipperary clash of 1950 was surpassed a year later at Limerick. This time Tipperary won by two points, one less than the Killarney match. 'We were getting closer all the time,' said Willie John.

'Words sometimes fail to describe a match of the highest excellence,' confessed the *Sunday Press*, but the *Examiner* decided to have a go nonetheless: 'The hurling and all-round striking was superb, the pace a cracker from start to finish, the clashes in the best tradition and to the 42,000 spectators it will be ever cherished as one of the most memorable games they are ever likely to witness.'

Before the start, Christy joined Willie Griffin, a fine hurler from Shanballymore, at midfield, with Sean Condon reverting to the 40. 'Ring was the star of the Cork side,' said *The Irish Press*, 'and when he took on a roving commission in the second half, he was devastating.' John D. Hickey agreed in the *Independent*: 'Ring was to the end the hope and pride of Cork. For the first five minutes he was astonishingly quiet but when he opened his shoulders to leave his opponent utterly helpless, it looked as if this was to be Tipperary's swan song.'

Early points by Bannon and Kenny (two) got Tipp off to a good start before Ring opened Cork's account and Condon and Lynam brought the sides level. Then Willie John Daly gave Cork the lead for the first time and, though Tipp had further points by Kenny, Shanahan and Stakelum, Tom Crotty heartened the Cork supporters with a great goal from a scorching drive. Half-time: 0-9 to 1-4.

The second half started in a dream-like fashion for Cork, with Christy burying a 21 in the net and adding a point, before Willie John stretched the lead to three points. Alarm bells sounded for Phil Purcell and his co-selectors who had already moved Mick Ryan from centre-forward to midfield in a vain attempt to curb Ring. Now, with their charges in dire danger of losing, they began a series of switches in attack designed to bamboozle the Cork backs.

'Five of the six forwards – only Tim Ryan was a fixture – swapped places almost every minute,' said John D. Hickey, 'and there was much to substantiate the view that all the roaming caught Cork out for two golden goals.'

The goals came from Ned Ryan and Sonny Maher, restoring the Tipperary lead, but Cork were not finished. A point by Willie John and two more by Christy left just a single score between them as the match drew to a close, but in the third minute of lost time, Paddy

Kenny made assurance doubly sure with the last point. Final score: 2-11 to 2-9.

Apart from Ring, Seanie O'Brien, Mattie Fouhy, Willie John Daly, Jimmy Lynam, Con Murphy and Tom Crotty earned praise in the papers.

Con's playing career was coming to an end at that stage, but young Tom Crotty's promising future with the Cork hurlers was aborted in an unusual manner. 'I played in '49, '50 and '51 without being fortunate to win a Munster medal,' he recalled. 'It has always been a bitter memory for me that having turned out in fair and foul weather for virtually every game that Cork played over the best part of three seasons, I was thrown off the team for allegedly playing

Christy leaves Blackpool for Shannon airport prior to his first visit to the USA in 1951.

rugby with Bandon in the spring of 1951. Since I never did actually play rugby with Bandon, but only used their facilities for training purposes, I refused in principle to ask the board to lift my suspension. I am, I believe, utterly unique in being the only one to have been banned from the Cork team.'

'I was always opposed to the Ban,' said Jack Lynch. 'I failed to see the point and I did actually fall foul of the Ban early in my career. I was studying law at UCC at the time, and one evening I went to the Mardyke to watch an Irish rugby trial. I wanted to see all the great rugby names of the time playing together. The following week I heard that I had lost my place on the county team because, as I was told, I had suspended myself. Believing, as my studies dictated, that the accused has a right to defend himself, I wrote a learned defence on Irish water-marked paper to the board, defending myself, and I included the three-guinea appeal fee. Later I got a phone call from a Dáil member asking me to withdraw the appeal. When pressed to explain why, he told me I had overlooked a slight but important detail – the appeal was signed in English. I then asked for my three guineas back.'

Tops

'Who is Tops in Hurling for 1951?' asked Fear Ciúin in the *Sunday Press* as the year drew to a close and, regardless of the fact that Cork had failed to come out of Munster yet again, he had no hesitation in opting for Christy Ring as hurler of the year.

'A general consensus of public opinion would, I feel sure, place the little Corkman at the head of any popular poll,' he contended. 'Nor does he show any indication of losing that appraisement within measurable time. He is still the great artist, the resourceful strategist, the deadly sharpshooter. Tipperary, leading champions at the moment, have more uniform ability and a few star performers, but they have no man comparable to Ring.'

Sars Win

Tears flowed freely at the Park and bonfires blazed in Riverstown and Glanmire, when Sarsfields ended 62 years of striving by winning the county title. It was the first time the cup left the city since

Brothers in arms.
Christy, Paddy Joe and Willie John Ring on the tender at Cobh after Christy's first visit to America in 1951.

Dinny Barry-Murphy's team, Éire Óg, won it in 1928 and it was a fitting reward for Dinny's old Cork colleague, Micka Brennan, who finally collected his county medal.

Pat Barry, destined to become famous as Paddy Barry, thanks to Michael O'Hehir's slightly incorrect use of his name, along with his brothers and Micka, Seanie Carroll, Bomber Coleman, Jim O'Neill, Mossie O'Connor, Tom Bowman and the captain, Pat O'Leary, were among the Sars heroes and the victory was all the more creditable in that they beat a Glen team with Ring in top form.

'Glen Rovers rallied again and again,' wrote the *Examiner*, 'and with such star forwards as Christy Ring, who was playing at the peak of his form, and young Johnny Clifford, the Sars defence was kept well alerted. Some of Ring and Clifford's scores were extraordinary, skilful feats.'

Though never fond of losing, Christy was pleased for Sars, especially for Micka, the Barry family and even Pat Leary, a Blackpool man playing against the Glen and denying them a county title.

'Ringey always teased me about that,' said Pat, 'but when I was a young man I fell in love with Kitty who was the sister of Alan Lotty. So I had no choice but to play for Sars. That's what love will do!'

Christy had no answer to that.

In America

'It was the night before the Railway Cup final in March 1945 and a bunch of the boys were discussing great players and great games in the lobby of Barry's Hotel in Gardiner's Row, Dublin, when I asked Jim Barry to name the six best hurling forwards he ever saw.'

So began Bill Carlos in the New York paper for Irish exiles, *The Advocate*, in October 1951. Bill was from Ballintubber and, having captained the successful Roscommon minors in 1941, he added two All-Ireland senior medals before emigrating in 1949. In New York he played for the Cork hurling team.

Home from the Bronx.
A dapper Christy on his return from America after his first trip to the States in 1951.

'With a twinkle in his eye, Jim, an encyclopaedia of sport, quickly replied, "Sure I can name the six best forwards, but there may not be another man in Ireland who will agree with my selection. The ash trail is milestoned with the achievements of great forwards but the six greatest, in my opinion, were Mick King and Barney Gibbs of Galway, Martin Kennedy of Tipperary, Mick Mackey of Limerick, Christy Ring of Cork and Lory Meagher of Kilkenny."'

'That was six years ago,' added Bill, 'when Mick Mackey was still a force and Christy Ring was at the peak of his career. The years that have elapsed have done little to distract from the magnetism of the name of Christy Ring and today, after a decade in the major leagues, he is as good if not better than the first day he donned the red and white of Cork. What a treat is in store for New York Gaels next Sunday when none other than the phenomenon of Leeside hurling will turn out against Tipperary in the 1951 Knockout Final. Two of his former Cloyne schoolmates, Michael Dorgan and Willie Walsh, will join him on the Cork side.'

Christy had been invited to play for the Cork team of New York against the championship holders, Tipperary, and he was also to give exhibitions in Boston and Philadelphia. It was his first visit to the States and Bill Carlos could not conceal his excitement at the prospect of seeing Ring hurling on American soil.

'Hero of a hundred classics, the prolific Glen Rovers man has for ten years been thrilling Gaelic followers from the Mardyke to Belfast. "Come on Christy" has been the victory cry of Cork followers for many a Sunday afternoon as the diminutive man in the red sweater teased and bewildered opposing defences with slick work and skilful scores from every conceivable angle.

'You have read a lot about the hands of Bobby Feller, ace Indian sportsman, Ben Hogan the golfer and Ted Atkinson the jockey but, in my opinion, the hands with the greatest athletic prowess of all are those of Christy Ring. A hurley in his hands is like a magic wand in the hands of a magician or a violin in the hands of Menuhin.

'While his cleated boots dug divots in the playing fields of Ireland, he was dodging and sidestepping his way to stardom. His zigzag solo runs have made millions of hearts beat faster and his sideline cuts broke the hearts of many a great team yet his peerless sportsmanship throughout has dimmed the eyes of many stern-eyed opponents.

'His fantastic athletic career has made him the idol and hope of Cork followers everywhere and his uncanny artistry has carved for Christy Ring a permanent notch on the goalposts of fame.

'Sports fans have their heroes but so, too, do the players themselves and Christy has long been mine. So it is with great pleasure that I welcome him to these shores. I, for one, am deeply grateful for the privilege of seeing him wave his magic wand once more. Sunday's game should be a real thriller and, even if it is not, you will still have it to say that you saw the great Christy Ring in action.'

Sean Maxwell in the *Gaelic American* was also excited. 'Christy Ring is reckoned as one of the greatest hurlers of all time and has behind him an outstanding record in the hurling field and in this year's Munster final he gave the greatest display ever witnessed, a display that thrilled the thousands present. Many lovers of hurling have been waiting anxiously to see Christy in action and their wish will be gratified on Sunday October 21st.'

After such a build-up it was hardly surprising that much was expected of Christy and that Cork's chances of dethroning Tipperary soared but, in the event, neither hope materialised. After a bright opening Christy was well 'policed' and Cork were out-played, outstayed and outscored.

'A full house awaited his appearance,' wrote *The Advocate*. 'After a shaky start the maestro appeared to have his Stradivarius in tune when he sent the ball straight between the uprights before the game was a minute old and when he shook the Tipp net with a left-handed cut off the ground, the audience held their breath. After that, the greatest name in hurling did little out of the ordinary, which was not so surprising in view of the manner the Tipp men kept tag on him. There were times when he would have been every bit as safe with an atomic bomb in his hand. Spectators saw little of the real Christy except for spasmodic flashes of greatness. The blond mercury-footed Corkonian, who in Croke Park or Thurles is as hard to pin down as a ju-jitsu instructor, was an easy prey for the half-nelsons and body tackles which he encountered in the narrow confines of John "Kerry" O'Donnell's Gaelic Park.'

Despite the rough treatment meted out to him on the hurling field during his initial appearance in New York, Christy enjoyed his first visit to America and promised his countless well-wishers that he would return. He was, in fact, to go back on several occasions and, even when his playing days with Cork were over, he acceded to requests to return for exhibition games.

Yet, on the liner back to Cobh, one thing was foremost in Christy's mind – stopping Tipperary from equalling Cork's four-in-a-row, 'the record of the nine' as he put it. Nine hurlers had participated in the four All-Irelands and Christy did not want to see that achievement equalled by men in blue and gold. He never needed motivation to beat the premier county but, if anything, his treatment by the Tipp hurlers in New York sharpened his resolve to end their reign in Munster.

Rival captains.
Christy (left), Paddy Barry (right) and referee Paddy Cronin ('Barrs') watch the toss of the coin before a Glen-Sars championship encounter.

CHAPTER TEN

WEXFORD ARRIVE

'Bobby Rackard completely subduing Christy Ring, Padge Kehoe popping up all over the field to send in deadly accurate points and Nick Rackard roaming outfield to make scores for the other forwards – these were some of the factors contributing to Wexford's splendid victory over Cork.'

That was how Mick Dunne began his *Irish Press* report of the league match at New Ross in February 1952. It was a highly significant result for the Slaneysiders who had yet to begin their golden era of the mid-1950s. It also brought Bobby Rackard's name to the attention of hurling people outside Leinster.

Bobby – or Bobbeen as Christy would call him in later years – was to become Ring's most respected opponent and a mutual admiration for their hurling skills would develop between them. Christy could be scathing in his criticism of inferior or unsporting players but, when he met genuine class, his praise bordered on the effusive. 'I can't adequately describe the man I marked,' he would say in 1956, 'but I'll say this – I never expected to meet a better sportsman or a cleaner hurler than Bobby Rackard.'

Before he met Bobby, Des Ferguson, Pat Stakelum and other defenders whose play impressed him during the 1950s, Christy was asked by Paddy Downey to name the best back he had encountered up to then. 'Christy singled out no one in particular, but mentioned many great opponents, amongst them Paddy Phelan of Kilkenny, Tommy Purcell and Tommy Doyle of Tipperary and Jimmy Brophy of Galway.'

It was typical of Ring that he should quote a litany of great hurlers he had opposed and refrain from selecting the most accomplished.

Yet one feels that, were he pushed in later years to reach a decision, Bobby Rackard would probably be his choice.

For all that, Christy did not relish the fact that he was held scoreless by the tall, stylish Wexford man in New Ross. 'With Bobbeen beside you, you wouldn't need a cap to keep the sun out of your eyes,' he said of Rackard's height. Being the student of hurling he always claimed to be, Ring immediately studied ways to ensure that a repeat of the New Ross display would not occur. He had only a week to plan his campaign.

'Main topic in Munster is how Christy Ring will show after his performance against Wexford,' wrote Tony Myles in *The Irish Press*. 'The hero of a hundred Cork battles had to admit a lack of pace in that league test, but he is far from being in danger of eclipse. In fact, I shouldn't be surprised if the game against Wexford will prove eventually to have been a pipe-opener for the great Cork forward and I expect to see him on his home ground next Sunday still the idol of Munster with his flying shots at goal.'

Tony was right. The Leinster hurlers came to Cork to play Munster in the Railway Cup semi-final and Christy was a transformed man. The headline in the *Press* said it all: 'Ring Ran Rings Around Leinster.'

'When Christy Ring intercepted a long clearance by Pat Stakelum ten minutes into the second half and dashed away to ram the ball into the back of the net, he wrote *finis* to Leinster's hopes,' said Mick Dunne. The fixture, a novel one for Cork fans, brought a big attendance to the Park to see the cream of Munster and Leinster hurling in action but, as on so many occasions before, Ring was the man who stole the limelight.

'At New Ross a week ago, Ring was completely mastered by Bobby Rackard,' wrote John D. Hickey, 'but yesterday he accepted the opportunity to show in no uncertain manner that he is still the hurling host supreme. We saw sufficient flashes of the real Cork wizard to prove that he must have been at loggerheads with his hurley against Wexford.'

'Mark Marnell did more than one man's share for Leinster,' added Mick Dunne, 'but it was all in vain while Bobby Rackard never struck his New Ross form of the previous week.' Apart from Ring,

Munster had outstanding hurlers in Tipperary's Phil Shanahan and Seamus Bannon, and Waterford's John Kiely, while Padge Kehoe was a tireless trier in the Leinster attack but failed to get the upper hand of Matt Fouhy. 'Nick Rackard also worked hard,' said Mick Dunne, 'but was well covered by Waterford's Dave Walsh, while John Doyle was much too strong for Leinster's Tim Flood.'

Carbery, agreeing that the fair-haired Mark Marnell stood head and shoulders over his colleagues, began to wax lyrical when it came to what he called the high point of the game. 'Against the wind and the run of play the south-men worked upfield and Christy Ring got his stick in contact. Like a kingfisher over a stream the Glen Rovers man streaked away. He shot off Cronin

Action in the Leinster goalmouth as Munster attack during the Railway Cup semi-final of 1952. From left – Nick O'Donnell (L), Sean Cronin (L), Christy Ring (M), Willie Walsh (L), Derry McCarthy (M) and Mark Marnell (L). This was the first Railway Cup to be played in Cork.

with a nimble swerve and waltzed goalwards to shoot with the speed of an arrow and cling the ball in the net. That Ring master-piece was the beginning of the end for Leinster.'

Christy was again at his best in the Railway Cup final when Connacht exceeded all expectations and came close to repeating their 1947 success. 'The all-Galway side might have won, had it not been for the brilliant display of stickwork and fieldcraft by Christy Ring,' said the *Examiner*. 'He accounted for a total of 3-3, all in copybook style, and the fact that he was three times down injured appeared only to rouse him to greater effort. He also had the distinction of having three different men marking him, but not one of them made the slightest impression.'

'I never tired of talking about the harm that has been done to hurling by the likes of Christy Ring, Jim Langton, Josie Gallagher and their host of lesser imitators in the pick and duck methods that all too often pass for hurling in the present codology of an age,' declared Old-Timer in the *Gaelic Sportsman*, 'but after St Patrick's Day I'm afraid I have to haul down my flag. Christy Ring is, on his day, as good a hurler as ever I saw – and I'm not given to handing out compliments. Two or three touches that day were worth the price of admission. Sure, apart from Ring's display, what else was there to remember beyond the lively start Phil Shanahan made in those white boots or the way Seamus Bannon ran to shake Christy's hand after a particularly magnificent score by Ringey?'

Rest of Ireland

A novel exhibition match between fifteen of the nation's finest hurlers and a university selection was played for the first time in March 1952. At Pádraig Ó Caoimh's suggestion the colleges were allowed to include graduates and were given a free hand to make their selection before the Rest of Ireland team was drafted. As a result top hurlers like Nicky Rackard, Joe Salmon, Dick Stokes, Des Dillon, Gerard Murphy, Tom Crotty and goalkeeper John O'Grady wore the intervarsity jerseys, but the Rest selection proved much too strong in the inaugural encounter.

The original 'Ireland' or 'Rest of Ireland' team was:

Tony Reddan
(Tipperary)

Jackie Goode	Pat Hayden	Colm Corless
(Waterford)	(Kilkenny)	(Galway)

Seamus Bannon	Pat Stakelum	Willie Walsh
(Tipperary)	(Tipperary)	(Kilkenny)
	captain	

Phil Shanahan   Christy Ring
(Tipperary)   (Cork)

Padge Kehoe	Mick Ryan	Josie Gallagher
(Wexford)	(Tipperary)	(Galway)

Paddy Kenny	Derry McCarthy	Willie John Daly
(Tipperary)	(Limerick)	(Cork)

Subs: Matt Nugent (Clare), Nick O'Donnell (Wexford),
Kevin Armstrong (Antrim), Billy Rackard (Wexford) and
Seanie Duggan (Galway)

Bobby Rackard, who had been chosen on the initial fifteen, was unable to play and followers were thus denied a chance to see Nicky and Bobby in almost direct opposition. Not surprisingly, Nicky was the colleges' top forward.

'The college hurlers were rather stage-struck against the Ireland experts in the first half,' wrote Carbery, 'and their only scores, two points and a specialty goal from a free, came from the Wexford giant, Nick Rackard of Killane. The picture that stood out in my mind among the Rest craft-masters was that of the tall, slim form of auburn-haired Phil Shanahan at midfield. Seven points separated the sides at the short whistle, but the students lost heart afterwards when the Rest crashed in a goal and a brace of points, where Christy Ring was the primary architect.'

Brewery Visit

One afternoon in the summer of 1952 Paddy 'Fox' Collins called to Beamish's brewery and asked if he could speak to David Creedon. He was directed to the cooperage where he found his friend working away at a barrel. Dave, who had replaced Mick Casey as Glen goalie back in the late 1930s and had been Cork understudy to Tom Mulcahy in the '40s, had retired from inter-county hurling and was surprised to see Fox approaching.

'David,' he said, 'will you come to Thurles with us on Sunday? We need a goalkeeper.'

'No Paddy,' he replied. 'I've had enough of being a sub on the Cork team. I'm retired. You know that.'

'Yes, but we want you in goal. We need you. Mick Cashman has tonsillitis, Seanie Carroll is suspended and Jim Cotter has a bad rash. You're our only hope.'

David was not convinced. Being fourth-choice goalkeeper did not bother him – he would love to play for Cork in the championship – but sitting on the sideline once again certainly did. Suppose one of the others would be available at the last minute. Would it be back to the subs' bench for Dave Creedon yet again?

'David, if you give me your word you'll play,' said his old friend, 'I guarantee you'll be in goal for Cork against Limerick.'

With some thought and much reluctance, the great Glen custodian finally gave the desired answer. As a relieved and happy Fox Collins left the brewery to convey the news to his fellow selectors, and the somewhat bemused cooper got on with his work, neither man realised that Dave Creedon was about to win the first of three consecutive All-Ireland medals.

When Cork faced Limerick a few days later, the selectors had to find more than a goalkeeper to replace their first-choice selections. Vincie Twomey had been injured in a Thomond Cup game and was replaced by Tony O'Shaughnessy, while Mossie O'Riordan's wrist injury earned a call-up for Tom Furlong, a promising Blackrock (and later Ballinure) hurler, destined to become somewhat more famous as a Cork footballer.

Thanks mainly to a marvellous display by Willie John Daly in defence, Cork won well (6-6 to 2-4). 'Daly's anticipation at times was uncanny and his lengthy drives won the admiration of the large crowd,' wrote the *Examiner*. Carbery agreed and added that the duels between Ireland's most prolific scorer, Christy Ring, and Limerick's Thomas O'Brien, a fast, experienced and skilful hurler, were notable highlights of the game.

'Christy was very close to his mother,' said Tony O'Shaughnessy, 'and he used to travel down to Cloyne on the Monday evening after every Munster championship game to tell her all about the match. She'd be after listening to it on the wireless the previous day. The evening after my first match she said to him, "That fella Shaughnessy, would he be a guard from Galway?" "He would," said Christy, "if he was two feet taller!"'

Con O'Donovan (Midleton) drives the ball towards Ring at the edge of the square in the All-Ireland semi-final against Galway in 1952. The Galway goalkeeper is Sean Duggan.

'This Cork team will win the All-Ireland,' proclaimed Jim Barry after the Limerick match, a prediction that surprised even those familiar with Tough's ever optimistic outlook on the county's hurling fortunes. 'Jim Barry is a man who could almost pick a good hurler from the cradle,' said Tony Myles, but even his fellow-countymen were sceptical of his confidence of victory against Tipperary, especially now that the Anner men were out to equal Cork's four-in-a-row.

There was massive interest in the game as the final approached, but Dave Creedon had one big worry: would it be back to the subs' bench again for him now that the others would be available for the Tipp game? 'After we beat Limerick I asked Fox not to call me for the final if I wasn't in goal,' said Dave. 'I told him I'd rather be a spectator than a substitute.'

'Perish the thought,' said Fox.

For The Nine

''Tis a queer thing to see a Cork team coming out in a Munster final and we not to know the half of them, nor even to have heard tell of them,' said a Tipperary supporter to a Dublin journalist just before the 1952 game.

'I'll wager he knew those fellows and had heard enough about them before the hour was out,' wrote the Dubliner in *Gaelic Sportsman* a week later. 'There was Tony Shaughnessy of the 'Barrs, a slashing quarter-back in the best Fox Collins style. There was Gerard Murphy, an awkward looking, but terribly effective hurler from Midleton who lorded it at centrefield. There was the lad by the name of Liam Dowling from Castlemartyr, the best full-forward since Jim Kelly, the scoring machine, was Kilkenny's toast 40 long years ago. Add to those some very solid hurlers in the Twomeys, the Riordans, Lyons, O'Brien and Hartnett, the fire of Willie John Daly and the genius of Christy Ring and you have your new Munster champions.'

'Naturally, we were very tense and nervous in the dressing room beforehand,' said Paddy Barry, 'and being captain I suppose I was the most tense and nervous of the lot. But when Seán Óg Murphy made a passionate speech about Cork and Tipp rivalry and drilled into us how important it was to preserve Cork's four-in-a-row record, he really put fire in our bellies. And I think there was greater fire in Ringey's belly than anyone else's because he went out and gave a masterly display.'

Tipperary's seventeen-point win over Waterford in their semi-final had been described as 'the massacre of the innocents', with Philly Grimes, 'the boy home from New York,' listed as the only Decies man to stand up to such adversity. Now, as established All-Ireland stars like Pat Stakelum, Phil Shanahan, Tommy Doyle, Tony Brennan, Mickey Byrne, John Doyle, Seamus Bannon and Paddy Kenny took on a Cork team featuring more than its share of neophytes, some followers may have wondered if another annihilation was in store.

The last-minute defection of Mattie Fouhy through injury added to their apprehension and, when Cork failed to score in the first quarter as Tipp totted up four points, the situation looked even more bleak. Ring eventually opened the account on the eighteenth minute. Liam Dowling, a revelation at full-forward, added two points and Paddy Barry and Ring two more to leave it 2-5 to 0-5 at the break. Tipperary, whose goals had come from Paddy Kenny and Seamus Bannon, were looking comfortable and the spectre of Cork's record evaporating began to haunt Christy even more than before. A huge effort was needed in the second half and he was determined to provide it.

'Hero of so many victories,' wrote the *Examiner*, 'Christy's second-half display was second to none in his colourful career. It started when his great solo run culminated in an equally great save by Reddan, only to be followed minutes later by another fine save, this time from a point-blank shot by Ring.' Christy settled for a point after that and, as he hurled like a man possessed, his example lifted his team-mates and Cork soon had Tipperary on the rack.

A long-range point by Gerard Murphy was followed by another great solo run by Ring, who shipped a few hefty blows en route before setting up Liam Dowling for a nifty goal.

'For some reason the umpire was a bit slow in raising the green flag,' said Paddy Barry, 'and Christy, who always ran into the square after a score and then wheeled back out, couldn't believe it.

He stopped his run, grabbed the green flag and waved it himself. I must admit I thought Christy would be in trouble for that and I even feared for an instant that the goal might be cancelled, but the referee said nothing, just noted the score in his book. Only Christy could get away with something like that.' (Tipperary disputed the goal, claiming that the whistle had gone before Dowling scored.)

Just one point separated the sides after the goal and a rampant Ring added a point to equalise before further delighting the Cork throng with another point to take the lead.

There was to be no stopping Cork now. With the supporters almost delirious, Dowling stretched the lead and Seanie O'Brien found the range with a free almost 80 yards from the Tipperary goal. Three points in front, the wind in their favour and the Cork players 'flying' was the happy situation as the game sizzled to a close. Tipperary were not finished yet, though, and nobody knew better than they did that just one score could save the day.

In the hectic last few minutes, Tipp continued to storm the Cork goal and forced a 70. Pat Stakelum took the shot and landed the ball in the parallelogram. Another 70 and Stakelum struck again. This time the ball was batted out a short distance towards the waiting Gerry Doyle who got hold of it and let fly. For one brief moment, every Corkman feared the worst, but the ball went over the bar and the lead was still standing.

Seconds later the full-time whistle sounded and Cork were the new Munster champions. 'We all simply went wild,' recalled Eamonn Young. 'Christy Ring was carried shoulder-high through the crowd, blood streaming down his face, blood he never felt, for all he knew was that Tipperary were stopped. "For the Doc … For the Doc …!" he shouted at me as he nearly tore my arm away. I got the meaning. My brother Jim, a doctor, was one of the nine four-in-a-row men along with Ringey. Their record – the record of the nine – was still intact whatever about the All-Ireland of '52.'

Galway Clash

A fortnight later, Cork were back in Limerick to take on Galway in the All-Ireland semi-final. 'It was non-stop ground hurling for the first twenty minutes with no frees and no scores,' said Billy O'Neill, the former Carrigtwohill and Cork player who was now at full-back for Galway. 'By half-time it was two points apiece and, as we had the breeze in the second half, things were looking very good.'

Galway did, in fact, put the new Munster champions to the test and for a time a western victory seemed likely, but a ten-minute flurry near the end saw the spirit that tumbled Tipperary from the All-Ireland throne infuse the Corkmen. They won by 1-5 to 0-6, with Josie Hartnett getting the crucial goal, Ring three points and Gerard Murphy and Joe Twomey a point each. Galway's points came from Joe Salmon (two), John Killeen (two), Hubert Gordon and Padraig Nolan.

'The Leesiders were completely taken off their feet by Galway's fast, hard, confident hitting,' wrote the *Connacht Tribune*. 'Bewitched, bothered and bewildered by Mickey Burke, their sharp-shooter Christy Ring had to be satisfied with a mediocre display in which he had three points to his credit, two from frees.' According to the *Tuam Herald*, 'Ring never got away for those lightning thrusts

1952 All-Ireland Champions.
Back (from left) – Bertie Murphy (selector), Gerard Murphy, John Lyons, Dave Creedon, Liam Dowling, Joe Twomey, Paddy Barry, Mattie Fouhy, Jim Barry (trainer). Front – Jerry O'Riordan, Willie John Daly, Christy Ring, Tony O'Shaughnessy, Billy Abernethy, Willie Griffin, Sean O'Brien, Vincie Twomey.

that have made his name synonymous with classic hurling and in Burke he really met his master.'

'Although he scored three points – half Galway's total – and had a fourth point called back for a free, Cork's inside men failed to turn Christy's many centres to good account,' said the *Examiner*. The Ring-Burke rivalry, so controversial a year later, was already evoking conflicting reports in the western and southern papers.

An incident late in the game involving Hartnett, Burke and Ring would also condition Galway followers to their antipathy towards Christy in future matches. As Josie Hartnett explained in Val Dorgan's book, Ring was blameless for the blow that forced Burke to retire ten minutes from the end of the semi-final:

'I remember a ball coming shoulder high between Christy and myself. We both pulled on it but Mickey Burke stepped between the two of us from behind. I never saw him. I hit him in the hand but it was a complete accident. It would have been difficult for anyone to see what happened, but they blamed Ring and the Galway players went for him. Afterwards it was a bitter game and the Galway supporters in the crowd were very hostile.'

Meanwhile, in Leinster, the Wexford hurlers were hotly fancied to beat Dublin. The metropolitans had disposed of lowly Meath and Laois on their way to the final and would face the Slaneyside dethroners of Kilkenny and do so without three of their top players: Norman Allen, Mick Hassett and Des Dillon. Perhaps Wexford succumbed to over-confidence, but Dublin's victory by 7-2 to 3-6 provided hurling's major surprise of the year.

So it was to be a Cork-Dublin final, the first in eight years, with Christy the sole survivor of the hurlers who played in the 1944 decider.

The Cork team included a complete newcomer, Billy Abernethy of Castlemartyr, a former county minor and Harty Cup star with St Colman's. His display with Imokilly prompted the selectors to draft him into the forward line, where Josie Hartnett's enforced absence through appendicitis would be negated.

'On the morning of the match, Seán Óg Ó Ceallacháin arrived at Barry's Hotel in his new car,' said Tony O'Shaughnessy, 'and Christy suggested he drive the two of us to Richmond Hospital to see Paddy Downey who was laid up. Seán Óg's car was a tiny two-seater Fiat with a canvass roof – it was like a sewing machine on wheels. Anyway, Christy took the passenger seat and I struggled into the bucket seat at the back. Christy wasn't long telling Seán Óg off for not buying a decent car with all his Raidió Éireann earnings, but I reminded him that he had no car himself – decent or otherwise. When we got to the hospital, we weren't allowed in, but, as we walked back to the car, Paddy appeared at a window calling us over. Then all of a sudden he was pulled in by a matron who gave us hell for calling at that time. "What a battle-axe," said Christy, "I'd hate to have her looking after me." Then we drove back to Barry's and had about an hour to spare before we went to Croke Park. That was how I spent the morning of my first All-Ireland final.'

Dull All-Ireland

After Cork's unforgettable defeat of Tipperary, and Dublin's equally exciting victory over Wexford, the All-Ireland promised much to excite hurling enthusiasts. Yet, apart from the first quarter, the game developed into a fairly drab, one-sided affair. 'Melancholy' was the only word John D. Hickey could find to describe it.

Christy Ring in action against Dublin, with Jimmy Lynam behind.

A more sanguine Tony Myles found the entire first half entertaining, but agreed that Cork had the game won by half-time. 'Time and time again Norman Allen and Con Murphy sent the ball high and low into the forwards to little avail. We saw the sliothar in and out of the Cork goalmouth, never in the net.' While blaming the Dublin forwards for this failure, both reporters gave due credit to Jerry O'Riordan, John Lyons, Tony Shaughnessy, Mattie Fouhy and outstanding goalkeeper, Dave Creedon. All five would occupy the first five positions in three consecutive All-Ireland final wins.

'Christy Ring, naturally, was the centre of attention for the Dublin backs,' added Tony, 'but he came through with flying colours. From the throw-in he was off on a solo run but a foul held him up. He made no mistake from the free and Cork were a point ahead in the opening minute.' It was an encouraging start to Christy's quest for his sixth medal.

Although Con Murphy equalised from a 70 and Gerry Kelly pointed a free, Dublin had little to show for their territorial dominance midway through the first half, when Christy set up Liam Dowling for a cracking goal. McCarthy, Allen and Kelly responded with points for the wind-assisted metropolitans, but further points by Ring, Paddy Barry, Willie Griffin and Joe Twomey had Cork in front, 1-5 to 0-5 at the break.

'Dublin's failure to register a score commensurate with their early superiority prompted misgivings,' wrote John D. Hickey, 'and I doubt if there was a Dublin supporter who had the effrontery to proclaim that they were still there with a chance after the change-over. In the first half Des Ferguson did well against Ring, but the ball did not often run their way. In the second half, when the strain was more constant, the Dublin man had to bow the knee.'

Christy was quickly in the picture after the restart, but this time the shouts of acclaim for his shot at goal came from the Dublin supporters, delighted with a brilliant save by Kevin Matthews. It was to be their last moment of joy, however, as Cork took control with a succession of points by Ring (four), Willie John Daly (two), Paddy Barry (two) and Joe Twomey, before Liam Dowling settled the issue with his second goal. Dublin managed just two points from Con Murphy and Norman Allen in the second half. Result: 2-14 to 0-7.

'When one turns to particularise about the achievements of the victors,' said John D. Hickey, 'Creedon, Ring, Daly, Twomey, O'Shaughnessy and Fouhy step forward from their fellows and after due consideration I hand the major portion of the laurel wreath to Creedon. The save he made from Tony Herbert in the fifth minute will be immortal in Cork.'

'The Ferguson-Ring duels were the delight and highlight of the game,' said Tony Myles. 'Ferguson stuck to his man like a leech, but Christy waited and watched his opportunity and, inspired hurler that he is, got away for vital scores. One of these was a peach – a direct cut on a ball when he was on his knees, to put it clean between the uprights. Jim Prior's display must rank with Ferguson's as both were pitted against Cork's most dangerous men. It was paradoxical that while the Corkmen got through for the scores that mattered, Prior and Ferguson covered themselves with glory but, like Ring on Ferguson, Willie John Daly eluded Prior sufficiently enough to keep adding to the Cork tally.'

Des Ferguson

Des Ferguson had been a ten-year-old when he first saw Christy in an All-Ireland final against Dublin in 1942. Now, ten years later, he was back in Croke Park playing for Dublin himself and marking the redoubtable Ring.

'Naturally I was tense. It was my first All-Ireland final. We were complete outsiders and I had to try to curb a hurling genius. I tried hard – my only gambit was to stay with him and pull. The fact that I was young and very fit helped somewhat – but how I learned that day! He rarely did the same thing twice. You might think that you had him figured every now and then, but the illusion lasted only until the next ball arrived. He was like an eel. Even when you were right there with him, he could somehow glide out of reach to send the ball soaring.

'His concentration was the most striking thing about him during a game. Even when the ball was at the other end of the field, his steel-blue eyes were on it and you felt that that nimble brain of his knew exactly what was going to happen. He could analyse a situation in a flash and his ability to assess players was even more

Christy, in typical style, careers into the goalmouth as his shot goes over the bar during a league game against Dublin at the Mardyke in 1952.

uncanny. I remember a league match in which a certain newcomer on the Dublin team was then very much in the news and being hailed as a future star. That afternoon he was having a great game. Ring asked me if that was so-and-so. I said it was. I well remember his remark, 'He'll never make it.' And he was right. A few months later that young player was dropped from the Dublin team and never returned.'

An outstanding dual-player Des, or 'Snitchy' as he was popularly called, would go on to win two All-Ireland senior football medals but, despite Dublin's commendable performance against Tipperary in the 1961 All-Ireland, his dream of winning a hurling medal never materialised.

Pioneers

'I remember some scribe calling us the youngest and probably the lightest team ever to win an All-Ireland,' said one of the 1952 players. 'He could have added that we were also the most sober. Thirteen of us were Pioneers and four of the five subs also didn't drink. Neither, for that matter, did "Tough" Barry, our trainer. So Fr Mathew, the apostle of temperance, must have been very proud on his perch in Pana when we brought the McCarthy Cup home that Monday evening.'

A far cry indeed from the day of a Munster final when a kindly priest offered a Cork hurler a cup of tea in the dressing shed before the match. 'Tay, Father!' he exclaimed aghast. 'Is it tay, Father, an' we playin' Tipperary?'

'Well David,' said Fox Collins, as they enjoyed their pints in Molly Howe's public house a few nights after the homecoming, 'I suppose you'll be going back into retirement now?' 'Yes, Paddy, I will,' said Dave Creedon, 'just as sure as the King of England will referee next year's Munster final.'

'Not satisfied with one All-Ireland medal, eh?' asked Fox, smiling. 'Keep playing the way you did this year and you'll have more All-Irelands than me when you retire again, whenever that will be.'

'You could be right, Paddy, you could be right.'

Christy's Views 1952

Not long after its inception the *Sunday Press* ran a popular series of opinion pieces by top hurlers like Mick Mackey, Tony Reddan, Kevin Matthews and Paddy Scanlan. Although he was later to develop a deep distrust of the media, Christy had no hesitation in presenting his views on the state of the game in 1952 and offering suggestions on its improvement.

Sport Star of the Year 1952.

'I would like to start with a suggestion I've had in mind for a long time. I say, do away with the full-back and full-forward and I, for one, would be very surprised if we didn't get brighter and more open play around the goals. This, of course, would mean thirteen players a side, but remember that at one time we had 21 players on a team. We hear the cry "Give the goalkeeper a chance." Well, give him a chance this way. With an open space in front of goal, the goalie would have a clearer view of movements outfield and I believe that more spectacular play would result.'

Christy's suggestion would be taken up by the colleges twenty years later and for some time the famous Dr Harty Cup and other competitions were contested by thirteen-a-side teams. Club and county games retained the standard format, however, and the colleges reverted to fifteen-a-side teams after a few years.

'The referee should have nothing to do with time,' was Christy's second point.

'We should have the official clock. Nor should the referee be concerned with the actual scores except to note them in his book. His sole job should be the play. The matter of the scores should be the sole concern of the umpires. I would like to see a third umpire appointed to stand directly behind the goal. He would have the casting vote in cases of indecision on the part of the other two umpires. However, I believe it is essential that after every game a referee should be required to appear in person before a select authority to account for his handling of the game and to answer all relevant questions relating to the game.'

Christy contended that deliberate delaying tactics by a goalkeeper or defender pucking out a ball should be punished by awarding their opponents a 70-yards free. 'And I would limit the number of substitutes in any game to three. I would insist that an injured player on his return to the field be regarded as one of the three substitutes. Whatever the position, no substitutes should be allowed for the last ten minutes of the game. This is the most important period of any game, when both teams have battled it out for 50 minutes. Now let them hurl it out as they are to the finish.'

Although he was 32 when he voiced in public these views, Christy was in favour of longer hurling matches. 'In fairness to the spectators who come long distances, I feel that the All-Ireland finals, at least, should have a playing period of 40 minutes in each half. The half-time interval should be fixed at ten minutes – no longer, no shorter.' Christy's idea of 80-minute finals was implemented about twenty years later, but the extra twenty minutes seemed too strenuous for amateur sportsmen and a compromise was finally reached: 70 minute major games.

Christy felt strongly about the importance of promoting hurling in schools. 'I am of the opinion that in every boys' national school at least half-an-hour each day should be devoted to the practice of our national game under the personal supervision of one of the teachers.'

1953 Ireland Team.
Back (from left): John 'Jobber' McGrath (Westmeath), Jim Fives (Galway), Bobby Rackard (Wexford), Liam Dowling (Cork), John Doyle (Tipperary), Pat Stakelum (Tipperary), Paddy Kenny (Tipperary), Connie Murphy (Dublin). Front: Tim Flood (Wexford), Christy Ring (Cork) captain, Willie Walsh (Kilkenny), Billy O'Neill (Galway), Tony O'Shaughnessy (Cork), Willie John Daly (Cork), Seanie Duggan (Galway).

He was not in favour of the open draw in hurling. 'Where would we be without a Munster final – or for that matter a Leinster, a Connacht or an Ulster final? It is natural to have provincial championships.'

A deeply religious man himself, Christy liked the close association of the Church and the GAA. 'Where would we be without a Dr Kinane to throw in the ball?' he asked.

And his final comment in 1952 – where would we be without the Ban?

Billy O'Neill

Billy O'Neill had been a successful Carrigtwohill and Cork junior captain before his army career took him to An Chéad Cath in Galway where he became a notable dual performer. He was also an outstanding athlete and won five Western Command athletic titles, including the long jump. Billy was also related to his well-known namesake and founder of Sarsfields. 'In his own playing days, my uncle used to carry a surgical needle in his coat pocket and actually stitched up hurlers who got injured during a match when no doctor was available.'

The younger O'Neill went on to play for both Galway teams in the All-Ireland against his native Cork, losing the hurling in 1953 and winning the football in 1956. 'It was my great ambition to win an All-Ireland medal and I was thrilled to do so in '56 but, oh, how I wished it was against some other county.'

'When I played senior hurling with Galway I always enjoyed league matches against Cork when Christy would fill me in on the latest news from home. One day I was marking him and we were chatting away while the ball was at the other end. Suddenly Christy said, "Did you hear Willie John is getting married?" I was thunder struck. If ever there was a confirmed bachelor, it was Willie John. As I reeled back, trying to absorb the shock, Ring was off, collecting an incoming ball and charging goalwards. Fortunately, our keeper, Tom Boland, saved a rasper and, as Christy came back, I said, "Is Willie John really getting married?" "Ah, he's thinking about it anyway," snarled Ring, annoyed that his trick had not brought a goal!'

Top Twenty

Towards the close of 1952 the *Gaelic Sportsman* invited its readers to select the Sportsman of the Year and the Cavan footballer, Mick Higgins, won the title with 1,203 votes. Christy Ring was second with 940 and Galway's Seanie Duggan was third with 785 votes. Eamonn Young, who had captained the Cork footballers to a league title, was fourth followed by John Ryan, the Wexford handballer, Bobby Rackard, Tony Reddan, Pat Stakelum, Paddy O'Brien (Meath footballer) and Tommy Doyle.

The top twenty hurlers nominated for Sportsman of the Year in 1952 were:

1. Christy Ring (Cork)
2. Seanie Duggan (Galway)
3. Bobby Rackard (Wexford)
4. Tony Reddan (Tipperary)
5. Pat Stakelum (Tipperary)
6. Tommy Doyle (Tipperary)
7. Nicky Rackard (Wexford)
8. Willie Walsh (Kilkenny)
9. Billy Duffy (Galway)
10. Billy O'Neill (Galway)
11. Tony O'Shaughnessy (Cork)
12. Willie John Daly (Cork)
13. Kevin Matthews (Dublin)
14. Dave Creedon (Cork)
15. Paddy Barry (Cork)
16. Josie Gallagher (Galway)
17. Harry Gray (Dublin)
18. Dick Stokes (Limerick)
19. Norman Allen (Dublin)
20. Mattie Fouhy (Cork)

Twelve months later, Christy would still hold second place in the overall poll, with dual-star Norman Allen taking top position, but in 1954, Christy would be voted the country's number one sportsman. 'Probably my last chance,' he said on receipt of the accolade, little knowing that he would still be receiving playing awards ten years later.

'Somewhere in the archives there is a glossy black and white picture that tells us more about Ring than a thousand words,' wrote Owen McCrohan in *The Corkman*. 'He is shown in the embrace of Cork supporters after a Munster final, his forehead swathed in a white bandage, his face spattered with blood. He seemed to carry those wounds like a badge of honour and undoubtedly that was not the first nor the only time that he had run the gauntlet of flying timber to win a game for Cork.'

'Christy's career was often embroiled in controversy,' he added. 'This was perhaps inevitable seeing that he was a marked man in every game and the orders usually went out to stop him at any cost. Some of the methods to achieve this aim were not always within the rules and Ring's volatile temperament was such that he would sometimes react unwisely but understandably. If he was hit a foul blow, he was not one to turn the other cheek.'

Battered but unbowed.
Christy typifies Cork's blood-and-bandage spirit after beating Tipperary in 1952.

CHAPTER ELEVEN

1953 – GLORY AND CONTROVERSY

'The clouds were low over Castlereagh Hills when Christy Ring stepped out on the taut, smooth ground and pranced on it, testing a new field as he'd test a new hurling stick. Red-jerseyed Corkmen and Galwaymen in white followed him and Casement Park was away to a flying start.'

That was how the distinguished writer Benedict Kiely described the opening of Roger Casement Park at Andersonstown, Belfast, early in the summer of 1953. Cork and Galway met in the initial hurling game, with Kerry and Antrim playing the first football match. For Cork it was a useful pre-championship outing but for Galway, who would have only one match before the All-Ireland final, it was a much more important test. Both counties sent strong teams to Antrim for the fixture.

Christy, who loved displaying his skills in exhibition games, lined out at left corner-forward and delighted the large attendance with a superb performance, scoring three goals and two points in the process. Mickey Burke played well at centre-forward for Galway and scored a fine goal, but when the counties would meet three months later in the championship Burke would be moved from attack to defence to mark Ring.

'I was on the Cork panel,' said John Quinlan, who played with the Glen before moving to Waterford and winning five county medals with Mount Sion. 'We went up by train on Saturday and came back on Monday. We stayed at the Kensington Hotel and I shared a room with Joe Twomey. There was a Union Jack suspended out of our window and, naturally, Joe and I decided to remove it. Fox Collins, who was like a father figure to us, suspected we'd do that, so he told us, after we'd finished taking in the flag, to fold it neatly and place it in a cupboard. There was only one repercussion afterwards – we were moved to another room by the hotel management for our second night there.'

'There was more than one repercussion,' said Tony O'Shaughnessy. 'The hotel reported a missing flag to the RUC and they came in, fully armed, on Sunday morning with all sorts of threats if the flag wasn't returned. We thought we'd all be shot. Anyway, the flag soon returned undamaged and then there were no more repercussions.'

The players brought hurleys to leave with the Antrim people as proper hurleys were so difficult to get in Belfast. 'We also brought several parcels of meat from Tony, who was a butcher by trade,' said John. 'There were shortages and restrictions – and rationing I think – so our northern friends were glad of the meat. I remember Tony giving me one of the bags of meat to bring through customs when we crossed the border.'

Denis Hurley of Sars remembered that trip to Belfast very well. 'It was a volatile period in the North, with people welcoming Cardinal D'Alton and honouring Roger Casement, during what was also the year of the coronation of the Queen. Tensions were high.'

Grand Affair

The ceremonial opening of Casement Park on 14 June 1953 was a grand affair. A trumpeter announced the arrival of the relay runner, Frank O'Gara, the Ulster sprint champion, who carried a silver urn containing soil from Thurles and Croke Park, and completed the last lap of the historic 190-mile journey by running around the perimeter of the field before bringing the urn to the centre. There Cardinal John D'Alton mingled the soil with that of the new pitch as the De La Salle Boys' Band played a salute. Then the vast concourse sang 'Faith Of Our Fathers' and '*Amhrán na bhFiann*'.

'Before the formalities started,' said Ben Kiely, 'my feet on the gravel banking around the new playing field went moving to the marching time that goes with the stirring song about Roddy McCorley.'

When the match began, a Cork newcomer, Jimmy Ring of the 'Barrs, made a big impression beside Gerard Murphy at midfield, but it was Cork's older Ring that captured the crowd's attention.

'The man of the match was once again the inimitable Christy Ring who was in one of his brightest moods,' wrote the *Irish Independent*. 'He teamed to perfection in the front line with Liam Dowling and Paddy Barry and this trio gave the Galway defence a gruelling. Galway full-back, Billy O'Neill, however, kept the Cork scoring down by his dogged marking of Dowling.'

'Ring was the genius behind many successful raids,' said Jim Davey in *The Irish Press*, 'and the large attendance roared its approval as Sean Duggan brought off some grand saves, but Christy topped the scoring with 3-2. His three goals – all of them gems of opportunism – were well worth the admission money.'

Josie Hartnett, Tony O'Shaughnessy, Joe Twomey and Derry Hayes also shone with Galway's John Molloy, John Killeen, Joe Salmon, Miko McInerney and Mickey Burke earning praise as well. 'Ring and Cork Defeat Galway' was the heading in the *Connacht Tribune* a few days later.

Cork won by 5-7 to 4-3 with the scores coming from Ring (3-2), Hartnett (1-3), Paddy Barry (1-1) and Denis Hurley (0-1).

The team that won the first hurling game at Casement Park was John O'Grady (UCC), Dave 'Cody' O'Leary, Tony O'Shaughnessy, Derry Hayes, Denis Maher ('Barrs), Vincie Twomey, Mossie O'Connor, Gerard Murphy, Jimmy Ring, Jimmy Lynam, Josie Hartnett, Denis Hurley, Paddy Barry, Liam Dowling and Christy Ring. The subs included Joe Twomey, John Quinlan (Glen), Seamus O'Callaghan ('Barrs) and Vincent Flanagan (Midleton).

'At that time, games such as this – especially one 250 miles away – would always show many defections,' said Denis Hurley. 'Some players simply couldn't afford to get off work, but only Mick Cashman from the original selection couldn't travel. That shows how seriously Cork treated the game and at the same time we were paying special tribute to the Antrim County Board on the opening of Casement Park.'

'Going back down the Falls,' added Ben Kiely, 'I found that the queue habit had not tampered with the fighting spirit of Belfast people who want to board a bus. So lacking the swerve and agility of Christy Ring, I thought it more prudent to walk. But at every corner I stopped to look, blinking at the radiant houses welcoming the cardinal, honouring Casement. At the corner of Raglan Street we hummed a victory tune while home-going people talked in Belfast accents about the prowess of John Killeen and Christy Ring. I began the day with a sad song about young Roddy who bravely died for Ireland at the bridge of Toome, and ended with a rattling song about victory in Raglan Street. Up above Raglan Street, Casement Park is, to say the least, a bit of a victory.'

'We were given a wonderful reception that evening,' said John Quinlan, 'and I particularly remember walking back to our hotel afterwards with Ringey and the lads. Christy had the cup on his head and we were all in great form singing, and when we met a couple of RUC men they took it in good stead and let us pass. I also remember the train journey home the next day. Ringey was playing cards and I was drinking a bottle of stout, but somehow he knocked it over, spilling the stout. He apologised, of course, but Christy hated drink – and cigarettes too.'

Cardinal D'Alton was also bound for Cork after the pitch opening, not by train like the hurlers, but by limousine. He was met at Watergrasshill by Dean Joe Scannell, former president of Farranferris, who must have been pleased to hear from the cardinal how Christy and Cork had done at the new pitch. They duly arrived on the Lower Road and stopped near the railway station where the cardinal stepped on to a red carpet and walked through a triumphal arch, to be met by the Lord Mayor, Pa McGrath, and large numbers of the Corporation and Harbour Board, all of whom lined up to kiss his ring. Then they all proceeded to the City Hall where Cardinal D'Alton was conferred with the Freedom of Cork.

'I wonder,' asked an onlooker, 'did they give Ringey a reception like that up in the Six Counties?'

League Success

'This year's league final has resolved itself into a virtual Munster final, the epitome of hurling,' wrote Tony Myles after Cork and Tipperary had beaten Dublin and Clare in the semi-finals.

1953 League Champions.
Back (from left): Paddy Collins, Jack Barrett, Jerry O'Riordan, Joe Twomey,
Christy Ring, Dave O'Leary (capt), Dave Creedon, Liam Dowling, Mattie Fouhy,
Jim Barry. Front: Gerard Murphy, Willie John Daly, Tony O'Shaughnessy, Vincie
Twomey, Josie Hartnett, Jimmy Lynam, Paddy Barry, John Lyons.

'Yesterday's encounter between Cork and Dublin put their All-Ireland
meeting in the shade but the heat of the battle got too hot at times.'

'Jimmy O'Callaghan, cool and capable, held Christy Ring well
without subduing that irrepressible man, the greatest artist with a
camán in recent hurling history,' wrote Carbery. 'And in passing I
must say I cannot condone the unsporting barracking by a small
section of the crowd on Christy, as decent and clean a hurler as ever
swung ash. Ring is on a plane apart. His swerves and lightning lifts,
his ball control and consummate accuracy are a delight to watch.
Jim O'Callaghan's close and honest marking rather subdued the
Munster captain in the second half, but he got his moiety of scores
and shaved the whiskers off the uprights on three occasions.'

The league final saw Dave 'Cody' O'Leary (Castletownroche)
representing county champions, Avondhu, and captaining Cork
against Tipperary before a record league crowd of over 38,000 at
Croke Park. 'For most of the game Tipp supporters watched their
team miss glorious scoring chances,' said Mick Dunne, 'and then,

ironically, saw the same team score two grand goals far too late to stop Cork.'

'It was that kind of a day for us,' said Tony Wall. 'Even when Ned Ryan got a point early in the match, the referee called back the play and gave us a free in, which was missed. We had about fifteen wides in the first half.'

In between the wides Tony and the Ryans (Tim, Mick and Ned) scored points for Tipperary, but a great goal by Paddy Barry and points by Willie John and Christy left Cork in front 1-2 to 0-4 at the end of a low-scoring first half.

'After the change-over the Cork team tore into the Tippmen relentlessly,' added Mick Dunne. 'Then out of the blue came the go-ahead signal as Christy Ring, surrounded by a cluster of backs, slipped the ball to Jimmy Lynam who sent a thundering shot into the Tipperary net. From there on Cork were rampant.'

Points by Ring (three), Daly (two), Hartnett (two) and Gerard Murphy had Cork 2-10 to 0-7 ahead near the finish, when Paddy Kenny sent two close-in frees to the net in the dying minutes. One of Christy's points, according to Mick Dunne, was scored 'from a seemingly impossible spot out in the right corner'.

'Ring was watched with an eagle eye by John Doyle,' added Mick, 'but he was there at all-important moments to snatch vital scores. Willie John Daly outpaced Seamus Bannon, while Mickey Byrne had a hard job looking after Paddy Barry.' 'I was a quiet type of hurler and took a lot of stick,' said Paddy in later years, 'but you had to take it. It was part of the game and there was no real animosity behind it. I had a few scraps in my day, usually with Mickey Byrne who was like a terrier, with amazing reflexes.'

Dave Creedon, John Lyons and Tony Shaughnessy were also praised, as was substitute Mick Cashman, who shone in the half-back line where his sons, Tom and Jim, would also become out-standing hurlers in years to come. 'Tipp's best line was their half-back row,' added Dunne, 'and full marks to Tommy Doyle for a display which belied his years. Pat Stakelum, as ever, was a stal-wart defender and Tony Reddan in goal provided the invariable thrills with his delightful saves.'

Juvenile Delight

'That day in 1953 was a very special one for the Cork under-fifteen boys,' said Derry Maher. 'Due to the kindness of Pádraig Ó Caoimh we were able to arrange an inter-county challenge with Dublin before the league final at Croke Park. It was a great success and spectators were amazed at the high standard of hurling by the youth of both cities. Sunbeam Wolsey provided the Cork team with a beautiful set of jerseys and stockings and we used them for many years afterwards in similar challenges with Waterford.'

'It was a fantastic experience to play in Croke Park in front of the biggest crowd of my life,' recalled Sean O'Riordan. 'It was a lovely sunny afternoon and I thought Ned Kearney was outstanding that day.'

The other young hurlers included Mick McCarthy, Willie Walsh and Pat Healy, who later played senior with Cork, Denis Keating, Joseph McCarthy, Kevin Murphy, Pat O'Neill, John Buckley, Ron Tuckey, Pat O'Sullivan, Victor O'Neill, Richard Long and Dinny Pa Foley.

The men responsible for bringing the Cork boys to Croke Park for the curtain-raiser were Fr Nessan, Brother Mel, J.A. Aherne, Mick Barrett and Derry Maher, all officers of the under-fifteen board, which later amalgamated with the juvenile board to form Bord na nÓg.

'It was a very cordial occasion,' said Derry, 'and I remember the Dublin goalkeeper giving his cap to our goalie, Denis Keating, to keep the sun out of his eyes in the second half. We won the under-fifteen match and then we sat back to enjoy watching Ringey and his men beating Tipp and winning the league. Certainly a day no Cork supporter could forget and for our under-fifteen hurlers it was the experience of a lifetime.'

Captain Again

Avondhu, as county champions of 1952, had a right to the captaincy of the Cork team the following year but the North Cork Board took the unprecedented decision of nominating Christy Ring as captain for the 1953 championship. It was to prove both a popular and successful move.

'In theory I like the idea of county champions captaining the county team,' said Eamonn Young, 'but in practice it is too haphazard. Paper captains are no use. They must be leaders on the field. If they are exceptionally good players, all the better. Christy Ring is a great hurler at any time but, when he is captain, he is much more dangerous to opponents. Ring is a natural leader because of his own playing ability. The team becomes Ring. The whole fifteen follow his example.'

Eamonn, like many others, was delighted when Christy was awarded the captaincy and, true to form, Ring brought all his reserves of dynamism, expertise and motivation to the task. On the field of play Christy invariably gave it his all and he did not spare anyone he suspected of not trying hard enough or doing the right thing. As captain, his reaction to the efforts of his team-mates intensified even more, as Johnny Clifford recalled: 'I remember one day pulling on a ground ball and driving it a few inches wide. I thought it was a good effort and that I was a bit unlucky not to get a goal but Christy blew me out of it. "Why the hell didn't you pick it up?" he roared, his face full of fury – and me only a few inches wide!'

Training was always an imperative with Christy and woe betide any hurler who missed a session when he was captain or, worse still, any outsider who interrupted training.

'When Christy was living in the Grand Parade, I used to walk to training with him at the Glen Field,' said John Quinlan. 'One evening after training, we were walking back along Pana when Vincie Twomey came towards us on the other side of the street. "Ignore him," said Christy, "he missed training." Poor Vincie could see he was being snubbed but he crossed over anyway to talk to us. "Why weren't you at training?" snapped Ringey. "I was at the triduum," Vincie explained. Being very good-living himself, that took the wind out of Christy's sails. "You should have been training," he said weakly.' A triduum is a three-day adoration in church.

'I remember travelling down to Cork when I was a young reporter to do some interviews for the 1953 final,' recalled Mick Dunne. 'The Cork hurlers were training in the old Athletic Grounds and a leading photographer asked Christy if he could take some pictures for one of the Dublin daily newspapers. Christy was furious that he should dare interrupt his participation in the training puck-about and he nearly took the head off the cameraman, who only wanted a few special pictures in the lead-up to the All-Ireland final. Yet, over a cup of tea on the very same night, Ring promised me, a young and relatively unknown sportswriter, the hurley he would use in the following Sunday's final. True to his word, he delivered the stick when he travelled to Dublin the following St Patrick's Day for the Railway Cup final.'

'In training he was just fantastic,' said Jackie Daly. 'There was nothing he couldn't do with a ball. Sometimes when we finished training at the Glen Field he'd have a kind of challenge game with Patsy Harte. The two of them would hit balls at the crossbar from the 21 and I'd say Christy would strike the bar eight times out of ten. Other times he'd go in goal and stop shots from all angles. Then after we were finished he'd call a few youngsters who were watching and tell them to have a go, one by one. He'd save all the shots and then, to each lad's amazement and delight, he'd let in one, knowing that each young fella would go home all excited and tell everyone he scored a goal against Christy Ring. What a boast that was for a young fella and what a psychologist Ring was!'

Championship Campaign

The 1953 championship began with a difficult victory over Clare at Limerick. 'No reputations were made,' wrote the *Examiner*, 'and the only man to win unanimous admiration was Christy Ring. He had three points from play in the first half and every time he got possession a quiver of excitement ran through the crowd. He roved about in the attack, demonstrating his unique artistry and when he resumed with a bandaged head after being "downed", his performance assumed heroic proportions.'

'It was a tremendously keen game, fast, robust and at times really tough,' said Oliver Weldon, sports editor of *The Irish Press*. 'Clare looked good from the throw-in, but Christy Ring needed only one ball to show that there would be no holding him when opportunity knocked. Three minutes of play had him opening the scoring for Cork and positional changes, designed to foil this hurling genius, had no effect.'

Others credited with good performances were Mattie Fouhy, Gerard Murphy, Mossie O'Connor of Sars, Dave Creedon, Jerry O'Riordan, John Lyons and Tony O'Shaughnessy.

'Shaughnessy was a great backman,' said Jimmy Smyth. 'He had tremendous acceleration, sharp reflexes and keen anticipation. He didn't stay long in the game, but he was one of the finest defenders in hurling during the early '50s. Mattie Fouhy was another outstanding backman. He had a style similar to that of Jimmy Finn of Tipperary, a style which made it very difficult for a player to get past.'

'Ring, of course, was always the fox,' added Oliver Weldon, 'while Josie Hartnett was always thrustful at centre half-forward. Willie John Daly and Jimmy Lynam were excellent wingers.'

Cork won by three points (2-11 to 4-2) and met Tipperary in the Munster final. Although Tipp's four-in-a-row aspirations had been shattered the previous year by Cork, who subsequently beat them in a league final, they were highly confident of making amends in 1953. 'There wasn't a Tipp man from the Devil's Bit to Slievenamon expected Cork to win this game,' wrote the *Clonmel Nationalist*.

Christy had different ideas, of course, and within a minute of the throw-in he had the ball in the Tipperary net from a 25-yards free. It marked the beginning of another marvellous display by the Cloyne man.

'Ring figured in a captain's role if ever anybody did,' wrote the *Examiner*, 'and his wizardry on the ground and in the air made him the idol of the crowd. His total of 1-8 was the well-earned reward for one of the best games of his spectacular career.'

'Towards the end Tipp got a 21-yards free,' said Eamonn Young, 'and Christy immediately rushed down to the Cork goal, stood as he had often stood in the little pitch at the back of his house, faced a bullet, caught it in the clawing fist and hit it the length of the field. That was the save that won it.'

Others on the Cork team remembered the incident too. According to Tony O'Shaughnessy: 'We lined the goal to stop the shot as we knew Paddy Kenny would go for a goal. Then Christy suddenly arrived and took his place on the line. "What's he doing here?" I said to Jerry Riordan. "Search me," said Jerry.'

'When the whistle went for the free,' said Josie Hartnett, 'Ring made a dash downfield and, as he passed me, he shouted, "You stay right there. I'll clear it to you." And, incredibly, he stopped the shot and drove the sliothar right up to where I was standing.'

Cork won by 3-10 to 1-11 and Tipperary-born John D. Hickey in the *Irish Independent* was prompted to ask, what manner of man is this Ring? 'Yearly he becomes even more a prodigy and I have not the slightest doubt that Tipp would have won as readily as Cork, had he been wearing a blue and gold jersey. He may have had his quiet moments yesterday, being beaten now and again, but the superlative quality of what he achieved must be enjoyable in retrospect to disappointed Tipperary people. One could exhaust a store of adjectives and yet fail to distinguish the Christy Ring wizard adequately from his fellows, team-mates and opponents. A year from now the only vivid recollection of this game will be the almost incredible artistry of the greatest hurler of them all, the one and only Christy Ring.'

The *Tipperary Star* singled out several Cork heroes. 'At midfield Joe Twomey and Gerard Murphy were masters in the art of overhead striking. Shaughnessy, Lyons and Riordan formed a magnificent full-back line. Daly was as fiery as ever with Sean O'Brien equally sound on the opposite flank. Liam Dowling's display at full-forward came as an agreeable surprise for the Cork men as this strapping player hurls with a junior club. Ring was his old ubiquitous self while strong, bustling Josie Hartnett was always a thorn in the side of the Premier county's defence.'

Others to earn acclaim included Derry Hayes of Blackrock, who started at right-wing and moved to centre-back. 'Repeatedly Cork's saviour, he hurled with such élan that it was difficult to believe that this was his first Munster final,' wrote Mick Dunne in the *Press*, while John D. Hickey rated Paddy Barry as Cork's best forward, after Ring.

Bereavement

With players and supporters eagerly looking forward to another All-Ireland final, news spread that Christy had suffered a grievous loss. On 8 August his mother, Mary, passed away at the family home in Spittal Street. It was a devastating blow to the Ring family, and many of their friends wondered if Christy could bring himself to play in the All-Ireland. It was not an easy decision for Christy to make but, after much agonising and encouragement from his brothers and sisters, he re-joined the Cork team in training. Jim Barry extended a discreet welcome on his return, the other players breathed a silent sigh of relief and the papers next day proclaimed that Christy would play in the All-Ireland final.

Prior to the final, Jim Skinner of the *Sunday Independent* visited the Cork team in training and found Christy more accommodating than usual. Asked about Avondhu's decision to nominate him as captain Christy said, 'It was a nice gesture but I do not like the job at all. I wish somebody else had it. I took it only because of the spirit behind the gesture'. Jim continued:

'For the benefit of the youth of Ireland, I asked Christy how a boy could become a hurler of class. Here is his answer, unexpected but down to earth, sensible:

1. Develop the greatest possible strength in your arms
2. Practise swift pucking and striking
3. Never hit the ball for the sake of hitting it – deliver it to the right place.

'When I asked him how a great player like himself, always given special attention by the opposing team, managed to live up to his reputation, Christy said, simply, "Never play on another man's name. Go out and play your own game. And," he added with emphasis, "you'll never be any good unless you play the ball every time, no matter what." He paused for a moment and added, "That's the secret of being – and remaining – a good hurler".'

Rare Recording

Over half-a-century after the 1953 final, Michael Moynihan of the *Examiner* unravelled a fascinating tale of a tape recording made in Barry's Hotel on the morning of the All-Ireland. It was a collector's item par excellence.

Joe Aherne and Ger Murphy told Michael how as young men they decided to cycle to Dublin that weekend for the Cork and Galway final and stay with a friend, Sean O'Connor. Sean had recently started work with Dictaphone and was in the capital for training. When they came together on Saturday, the lads decided to take Sean's new-fangled recording apparatus to Barry's Hotel and see if they could record the voices of Christy and other players for posterity.

'There was no problem getting into the hotel,' said Ger Murphy. 'All the players were in there and we went in among them. At that time, very few people in Ireland had ever heard themselves on a tape. It was a huge novelty and the players got a great kick out of it. We stayed there well past midnight recording the players and letting them hear their own voices.'

The Cork captain was beyond their reach, however. Two men stood guard at the entrance to a separate part of the hotel, where Christy was staying in a room down the corridor. There was no way past the wardens and the boys thought Christy was getting special treatment because of who he was. That was not the case.

'Christy had requested permission to drive to Dublin in his own car that Saturday and not travel by train with the rest of the team,' said Tony O'Shaughnessy. 'He was still greatly upset by his mother's death and some time after we met him at the hotel a few of us went for a walk down to O'Connell Street. It was only after we'd been strolling along for a while that somebody asked, "Where's Christy?" So we went back to the hotel and were told he was in his room. We went up to see him and found him in a distressed state in bed saying the rosary. His mother's death had a terrible effect on him.'

Unaware of Christy's personal turmoil the previous night, the boys tried again on Sunday morning. Joe Aherne's father knew Christy from work, so they tried 'Jim Aherne' as a password and this time they were admitted to the inner sanctum. Inside they found Jack Lynch, Tough Barry, Andy Scannell – and Ring.

'Christy had just finished shaving when we came in,' said Ger, 'and I remember distinctly that he had a gold-plated razor. When I asked him about it, he told us he got it in America at one of the Cardinal Cushing games.'

'When I started the recording, Christy was a bit slow to get going,' said Sean O'Connor, 'but once he got started, he was brilliant.'

'We have battled through a very hard campaign to reach the All-Ireland,' said Christy in answer to the lads' opening question.

Christy with the Liam McCarthy Cup in 1953 accompanied by Jim Barry, Andy Scannell and jubilant Cork supporters.

'We beat Tipperary, when no one else thought we would. We beat them well and we're in this final and we're confident of doing the same to Galway. From the throw-in they'll make it hard for us, but our craft should tell in the end. Our backs should come out and play the ball as it should be played. If the forwards get the breaks, each one of them in turn will do their bit.

'The hardest games we ever played were against Limerick in the '40s. They were fabulous games. Maybe I was a little younger then but they were the hardest games we ever played. The greatest win we ever **had** was against Tipperary in last year's Munster final. That even surpassed the 1947 final. We went into Limerick and we had trained hard. We had ten changes from the year before. We said we were going out there to play for Cork and, when you play for Cork, there's no looking back.

'We played that day in Limerick, but it was with a heavy heart we came to Carrigtwohill that morning, when Mattie Fouhy said he wasn't playing. Mattie, I reckon, is the best man on our team. No doubt about it, Mattie is the man. We threw Willie John back in the back line and we were short a forward but, when the full-time whistle blew in Limerick, there were two points in it. I think that was a great achievement for this Cork team. There were some of them new and some of them never hit a ball in a Munster final, but that day they hit them better than any Cork team that came before.'

When the boys drew up the subject of his toughest opponent Christy was typically forthright and honest:

'When you're playing hurling as long as I am, they're all the same. I never take them as individuals. I play the game for the team, for the fella alongside me. I make the openings for them and do the best I can. I often played on the worst man and he was the most troublesome. Often I played on the best man and I thought he was the easy one. I tell you when a Tipperary man or a Kilkenny man or a Limerick man goes out there in a Munster final or an All-Ireland final, there's nothing soft about it.'

Christy had been both captain and selector in 1946 and had had a say in where he lined out on the team. This time he was captain again, but not a selector, and he told the boys of his dissatisfaction with his positioning in attack.

'The Galway teams I've played against – I've been on the 40 or on the wing which I didn't like. If I had my way I'd be top of the right. The way it is, I'm out too far. Goals will beat Galway and nothing else. We'll have to get goals to beat them. All-Ireland finals are never soft. With the excitement, the swing of the play and the fitness of each man, anything can happen.'

The three young men finally asked him for tips on how to improve their hurling.

'To be a good hurler you have to be fairly strong. No doubt about it, you have to have the arms and one way you can get the arms is to play the ball on the ground. One day you might hit the ball 10 yards, then 20, but the day will come when you'll drive it 80 yards and you'll drive it that length consistently, but you can't do it without making your arms good and strong. You should try to hit the ball in training at all times, but hit it in the right way, on the ground. Never do anything in training that you can't do in a match – that's no use. Always take a dead ball, what I mean is a soft ball. That's a hard ball to hit, but drive it 10 yards because each time that'll strengthen your arms and next time it'll be easier. Without the arms you can't play.'

Up to that point Christy had never heard his voice on tape and he was quite intrigued when the recording was played back. Fifty-two years later, Ger Murphy recalled the scene for Michael Moynihan. 'Ringey got a great kick out of listening to the tape. "That's you," he would say picking out the voices. All the while we were talking – and this was just a few hours before the All-Ireland, remember – Ring had a roll of black tarry-tape in his hands and he was using it to wrap the handle of his hurley, which he was holding between his knees. He was wrapping it and unwrapping it the whole time and eventually I asked him, "Christy, are you going to leave the tape on the hurley or off?" He gave me a look and said, "I'm transferring the adhesive from the tape to the handle of the hurley." He was actually working away all the while he was talking to us.'

1953 All-Ireland Champions.
Back (from left) – Andy Scannell (chairman), Jack Barrett (selector), Derry Hayes, Joe Twomey, Dave Creedon, Liam Dowling, Gerard Murphy, John Lyons, Jerry O'Riordan, Paddy 'Fox' Collins (Selector), Jim Barry (trainer).Front – Paddy Barry, Tony O'Shaughnessy, Willie John Daly, Josie Hartnett, Christy Ring, Tom O'Sullivan, Vincie Twomey, Mattie Fouhy.

CHAPTER TWELVE

WAVE WILDLY THE FLAGS

'Wave wildly the flags, you Corkmen, and let your cheers re-echo around the valleys and hills. Rejoice not just because another victory was won at Croke Park but because yours is the only county that has ever won eighteen All-Ireland titles. That alone gives you the right to be proud today. And do not be amazed if we "outsiders" stand and wonder how one county can continue to produce hurling stars who maintain the high standards of their predecessors. Rightly, you can celebrate today but, in your glee, spare a thought for luckless Galway. You, yourselves, have at times – though not often – tasted defeat but think of a county whose lot it is year after year to drink from the bitter cup.'

Thus, in biblical style, Mick Dunne commenced his *Irish Press* report of the 1953 final and, no doubt, Cork readers enjoyed the feel-good effect of those warm words of acclaim. Indeed, all the Dublin papers conveyed the impression that the match was an entertaining spectacle played in brilliant sunshine before a record attendance of 71,195 and won by Cork by 3-3 to 0-8. What they failed to report was that it was one of the most unsporting finals ever played.

A more detailed picture was painted by Limerick man, Tom Higgins from Bruff in the *Cork Examiner* the following day:

'This final must unfortunately, be ranked as the most unsporting final ever witnessed in Croke Park and there were many neutrals and even followers of Galway, who were disgusted by the attitude of certain large contingents of the crowd. A particular "set" was made from the start on Cork's captain, Christy Ring, who is not only regarded as the great idol of the game by Cork followers, but is also regarded by every true lover of hurling as the ornament of it. No one would find fault with Galway's "policing" tactics, were the rules of fair play followed. But far from it, the unruly element in the crowd continued their unsporting tactics and boohed Christy in the most unrelenting manner, more especially when he went to take frees.'

Tom went on to claim that Christy was not the first player to be ill-treated by the Galway supporters and referred to a similar "set" on Jimmy Kennedy of Tipperary some years earlier at Tuam.

'There are many who always longed to see Galway win an All-Ireland final, for the simple reason that Galway had long been "ploughing the lonely furrow" in the west, but, if their display is to be like yesterday's, whenever they come to Croke Park, then there will be many who must wish that it will be at least another 24 years before Galway will again be seen in an All-Ireland final.'

Despite the non-reference by the national papers to unsavoury aspects of the game, much was said and repeated by spectators immediately afterwards, and indeed for years and decades to come.

The Match Itself

Facing the sun and playing towards the Canal End, Galway had the opening point from Jimmy Duggan. Their supporters were further heartened when Mickey Burke, in his first clash with Ring, out-manoeuvred the Cork captain and cleared. Moments later Christy's uncharacteristic miss from a free added to the hopes of the Galway fans, who had seen Seanie Duggan in goal fumble a Willie John Daly shot and still manage to clear the ball. Then, when he stopped two fine efforts from Ring, things were really looking good for Galway.

Paddy Barry, latching on to a Ring pass, equalised in the ninth minute, but Billy Duffy, already outstanding at midfield with Joe Salmon, soon put Galway in front again. 'Two Galwaymen were often around Ring when the ball came his way,' wrote *The Irish Times*, 'especially Burke, who was covering him capably, but this gave room to Hartnett, Daly and Barry to drive home winners.'

'How the better-placed Joe Hartnett was facilitated by Paddy Barry in scoring Cork's first goal was an education in the art of unselfish play,' wrote the *Evening Herald*.

m. De búrca
Saillim

c. ó Rinn
Concaiġ

The rival captains as they appeared in the 1953 match programme.

Galway's early luck was turning now and, after a forward elected to cut a 30-yards free off the ground and mis-hit a great chance
of a point, play moved downfield, where Christy Ring lobbed a
high ball all the way past the momentarily sun-blinded Duggan.

'Shocked into sharp retaliation and with Joe Salmon in top gear
at midfield, Galway stormed into a series of all-out attacks, but
missed a barrel-full of scoring chances,' wrote the *Connacht
Tribune*. John Molloy did manage to score their third point just
before the break, leaving Cork 2-1 to 0-3 in front at half-time.

'Although we were after missing many chances, we were pretty
confident at half-time,' said Joe Salmon. 'We knew we had the
measure of Cork and we knew, if we held our heads, we'd win. We
were all in a positive mood facing the second half.'

That confidence was soon to be seen, when Joe tested the Cork
defence with a couple of great drives and Josie Gallagher sent a

sideline ball over the bar. 'That was the signal for a period of action rarely equalled at Croke Park,' added the *Tribune*. 'Duffy started it with another point and then, with all Ireland roaring their heads off, Miko McInerney struck the upright from 40 yards. It was all Galway now and Molloy sent over a beautifully struck 70. Try as they might, Cork could not break the challenger's grip and hearts pounded in fevered excitement as Hubert Gordon blazed over the balancing point from 50 yards.'

'From that glorious moment onwards it was anti-climax for Galway,' sighed the *Tribune* reporter.

It would appear that Mickey Burke's object was to stay very close to Ring for the hour, upset his form and thereby eliminate Cork's greatest threat. Christy was never one to accept meekly, what he considered obstructive tactics, and his patience eventually ran out. Burke went down with a mouth injury and had to receive medical attention on the field before resuming play.

The Cork selectors instructed Ring to move to centre-field where Joe Salmon and Billy Duffy were lording it over their opponents. Burke immediately followed him and conceded a free that Ring pointed.

'Those astute strategists, the Cork selectors, traded instantly on the knowledge that the Ring complex had got to the challengers, good and hard,' wrote P.F. in the *Evening Herald*. 'They knew how Galway would react to the shifting of the Glen Rovers man to centre-field and, quick as a flash, events proved them right.'

'Two motives obviously dictated this change,' he added. 'Firstly, a state of something approaching stalemate had been reached between Ring and Burke and, secondly but of infinitely greater importance, some ruse had to be employed to disrupt the flow of danger from the Salmon-Duffy midfield partnership. That much accomplished, the danger gradually receded.'

'Burke's injury didn't seem to hamper him too much in his subsequent hurling,' wrote the *Gaelic Sportsman*, 'but while the stoppage was on, Cork moved Ring out to the middle of the field. Burke moved out after him and that would have been a reasonable decision if Mickey had as much experience of midfield play as Christy has. In any case Burke still "looked after" Ring even at midfield, but something more than that was wanted by the Galway lads up front at that stage. They had been badly in need of someone to hit them in the long ball and that was what the Duffy-Salmon pair had been doing from the start of the second half. But once Ring and Burke came out into the middle, the play became very much of the spoiling kind and the long ball striking was all over. It was Galway who were the losers in this respect and the ultimate losers of the game as a result.'

The dogged nature of the play and the many stoppages for injuries meant that the match would go into nine minutes of 'lost' time. Cork seemed to last the pace better and, after Ring's point had restored the lead, Willie John Daly, having discarded his boots in the heat, scored a left-handed point and then forced Duggan to bring off two great saves. Cork were now dominant and, when a late point by John Killeen clipped the lead to the minimum, Tommy O'Sullivan rushed through for an immediate and unanswerable retort, the crowning goal that gave Cork a four-point win.

'For Galway it was a bitter disappointment,' wrote John D. Hickey, 'but they had the solace that they put up a worthy battle and, for the first eleven minutes of the second half, they enjoyed the most marked superiority of the game. Salmon and Duffy were lords of the midfield domain, Billy O'Neill was brilliant at full-back, while Colm Corless and Jimmy Brophy in defence and Gordon and Killeen in attack were also effective. Mick Burke did very little hurling, but he brilliantly performed his main function of holding Ring.'

'Victory was well within our reach that day,' said Joe Salmon, who played in three All-Ireland finals with Galway and later won county honours with Glen Rovers in Cork. 'If we had held our heads and calmly assessed the situation in the closing stages we might have won. But it was lack of experience more than anything else that beat us.'

'Few will rate the 1953 final as one of the greatest,' concluded the *Connacht Tribune*, 'but none can deny it the honour of being bracketed with the most memorable.' If only the writer J.B.D. could have guessed how prophetic those words would be! Memorable indeed, for all the wrong reasons.

At the time, players usually headed straight to their dressing rooms after the final and did not stay to see the presentation of the trophy. As was his wont Tough Barry accompanied Christy to the podium where he accepted the McCarthy Cup from the GAA president and there was predictable delight afterwards when they brought the trophy into the Cork dressing room. That should have marked the beginning of victory celebrations, but subsequent hotel incidents cast a deep shadow over the weekend. The trouble began at the post-match reception in the Gresham and erupted again at Barry's Hotel the following morning.

Hotel Scenes

Terry Kelly, the Tracton hurler, who had done so well with the Cork juniors earlier in the season and was promoted to senior ranks, had vivid memories of the post-match incidents:

'In the Gresham, the teams stayed at their own particular tables during the meal. Albert Healy and his son provided very pleasant music on their piano accordions. As the meal ended, some members of both teams left to meet relations and friends waiting outside, so they were not present when the hotel incident happened. Around this time, a message was given to Christy that some friend wanted to see him in the foyer of the hotel. Now there were steps in the dining-room leading up to the double doors that led to the foyer and the street outside. There were ornamental columns on the top steps. As Christy bounded up the steps to meet this "friend" a man stepped from behind a column and struck him. I don't think he fell, but he overbalanced backwards and sideways. Some people thought he had tripped and fallen, but those close to the steps saw what happened.

'There was a general rising of bodies from the tables. The music stopped and the waiters hurriedly cleared the tables of breakables. Tough removed his false teeth and prepared for action. It was decided that we [Cork] would not leave by the front door, in case of some trouble outside, so most of us came out through the store-room on to a back street. On the way, one of the Cork lads took some of the empty bottles stored there and handed them out in case we might need them. Nothing further happened that evening.'

Momentarily stunned by the assault on Ring some of the Cork players went for the Galway man who made his escape via the doors to the foyer. Looking on, speechless at first, was GAA president, Vincent O'Donoghue, unable to respond to the repeated question – 'Did you see that?' – and then doing his best to calm the situation.

To compound matters, both teams were staying in Barry's Hotel for the weekend, a fairly common occurrence at the time and one nobody expected to create problems. This time, however, the presence of Cork and Galway hurlers under the one roof was a sure recipe for conflict.

On Monday morning Christy and some other players went to early Mass at the nearby Jesuit chapel and, on returning to the hotel, took their places for breakfast in the small dining room reserved for the Cork team. The players who had left early the night before were being filled in on the happenings at the Gresham. There was an air of disbelief all around.

A group of players, mainly Glenmen and Tony O'Shaughnessy, sat at Ring's table and hardly noticed some Galway players outside the door looking in. One of them made his way towards Christy, who had his back turned.

'Ringey was seated at one of the farthest away tables,' said Terry Kelly, 'so your man had to walk between two rows of tables to reach him. He leant in to strike him but I don't think he landed a full blow as he was impeded by the guy sitting outside Ring. He immediately turned away and ran out.'

'I remember the Galway man making his way towards our table,' said Tony O'Shaughnessy. 'We had no idea why he had come into our room, but when he got behind Ring, he struck him a blow downwards on the face. It wasn't a hard blow and Christy wasn't hurt, but we were all shocked.'

'When the lads realised what had happened,' added Terry Kelly, 'they got up from their tables to have a go at the Galway man, but actually they got in one another's way because of the narrow passage between the seats. A chase ensued out the door of Barry's and up Denmark Street but your man had disappeared.'

'All hell broke loose,' said another player, 'but the uproar ended quickly enough as the Galway players were ushered out to another part of the hotel and the door was locked behind them. By then,

Tough Barry, who usually dined alone on Monday reading the papers in a separate room, came charging in. I never saw him so furious – it certainly explained why he was called Tough.'

'Later on, some of the Galway players gathered across the road outside the hotel and were waiting to continue the fight,' said John Lyons, 'but somebody in authority told them to cop themselves on, that the best thing to do would be to go away altogether. They eventually moved on.'

'I missed all the excitement,' said Willie John Daly. 'I was upstairs in bed fast asleep. I slept through it all.'

It should be pointed out that Mickey Burke was not one of the players who struck Ring in the hotel incidents, but the 1953 final will always remain synonymous with the rival captains. 'Obviously something happened between them during the game,' said Johnny Clifford, a young sub on the day, 'but I didn't see it. In fact, I believe that very few people saw what happened. You must remember that at that time, hurling was much more physical than it is today. That's not saying that anything should happen, but the 1953 final was a particularly dour, physical game.'

As someone who always believed that matters in a match ended with the final whistle and differences between players should be left on the field, Christy was both stunned and shocked by the hotel attacks. The Gresham incident was short-lived and quickly dealt with, but the Barry's assault left him stunned and incredulous. It was uncharacteristic of Ring not to respond to provocation or attack but throughout the mêlée that morning he remained in his place – seated and shocked.

'The whole episode was so unsavoury,' said Terry Kelly, 'that the Cork management were anxious to get away from Dublin as soon as possible that morning. In fact, we got an earlier train than usual and stopped at Blarney to while away the time before the official homecoming.'

Reaction

The game and its aftermath evoked angry reactions in hurling circles throughout the country – the letters page of various newspapers providing the main outlet for strongly-held opinions. Naturally, letters to the editors of Cork and Galway papers were predictably partisan, but the Dublin papers devoted many column inches to the equally passionate views of some of their readers.

'I was amazed to read the accounts of the game in the daily papers,' wrote 'Rara Avis' in the *Evening Mail*. 'They all agreed that Christy Ring had one of his worst games ever when, in fact, he scored one-third of his team's scores and the highest individual score of either team. It would be interesting to know how many times the Galway captain struck the ball or, in fact, how many times he tried to play the ball. The Galway captain's chief aim was to prevent Ring from getting near the ball and all forms of obstruction were used to this end.'

'Is a player who feels he hasn't got justice on the field free to take revenge by assaulting one of his opponents off the field?' asked a Baldoyle reader in the *Herald*. 'The answer is obvious and I believe Central Council should act against any player found guilty of such behaviour. Such incidents besmirch the good name of the GAA much more than unseemly acts perpetrated in the extenuating heat of play. The latter arise from a momentary loss of self-control, while the former is cold-blooded and despicable. Whether Galway got fair play from the referee is beside the point. Anyway, I say they did.'

Another Dublin reader wondered if events surrounding the All-Ireland and other recent games were symptomatic of a growing problem caused by the silence and inaction of GAA authorities. 'Outspoken criticism and full public condemnation of the disgraceful and unsportsmanlike incidents would have long since helped to clean the Augean stables of the GAA,' he contended.

As Others See Us

As it transpired, no action was taken after the hotel incidents, even though GAA president, Vincent O'Donoghue, had witnessed one of them. In hindsight, it may seem very odd that the subject of front-page news in several papers should be swept under the carpet, as Val Dorgan put it, but it is important to put matters into the context of the time.

In 1953 the State was still a growing nation, just over 30 years in existence, and there was an almost paranoiac attitude to the image of Ireland as perceived by outsiders. One politician asked the BBC not to persistently mention 'rain approaching from Ireland' in their weather forecasts as it reflected badly on our climate. Another told John Hinde, the postcard maker, to replace the turf-cutter's donkey with pictures of Dublin Airport and Shannon Industrial Estate. The world was no longer to see Ireland as a rain-soaked land of sham-rocks and shillelaghs, paddy-whackery and stage Irishism, but as a vibrant, enterprising, modern industrial nation. Unemployment and emigration were not to be mentioned, of course.

Rain stops play, as (from left) Dave Creedon, Gerard Murphy, Liam Dowling, Willie John Daly and selectors Dinny Barry-Murphy and Paddy 'Fox' Collins seek shelter.

The GAA reflected this attitude in microcosm. Ever conscious of the ridicule and contempt of advocates of other codes, notably rugby and soccer, any public criticism of occasional hurling or football 'barbarism' was dreaded by GAA officials. If something untoward happened on a GAA field it should be kept quiet if possible and not provide ammunition for enemies of the association, hence, the wall of silence Eamonn Young complained about at board meetings. For a GAA man to publicise unsavoury incidents in matches was tantamount to treachery. The good image of the association had to be preserved at all costs.

Michael O'Hehir devised the word 'schemozzle' to cover incidents in games and he routinely refrained from naming players involved in the fracas, even if they were sent off. When Seán Óg Ó Ceallacháin took over his father's popular GAA results programme on Raidió Éireann, he broke with tradition and named transgressors, only to be taken to task by no less a figure than Pádraig Ó Caoimh.

In the light of this attitude to adverse publicity, it is hardly surprising that the GAA, instead of reviewing the match, the incidents and the aftermath, rounded on journalist Tom Higgins and his report. A supplied statement from GAA headquarters said that the Executive Committee had asked Central Council to take action in connection with the report which appeared in the *Cork Examiner*. 'We take a very serious view of the distorted report of the All-Ireland senior hurling final which created a very wrong impression and misled people into believing that the match was something that it was not,' said the communique.

'I don't remember what action, if any, Central Council took against us,' said Walter McGrath, 'but I do recall that the timing of our All-Ireland report wasn't exactly the best. We had just launched a sales drive in Galway, but after Tom's report appeared, we were told they were burning our paper publicly in the town.'

Special Medal

Apoplectic is probably the best word to describe the feelings of Galway delegates at a specially-convened board meeting in Loughrea to discuss Tom Higgins' match report after it had been reprinted in full in the *Connacht Tribune*.

Far from voicing their sorrow and sadness at losing an All-Ireland they might well have won, the board members were united in their fury at the *Examiner* report and the scornful words expressed by Andy Scannell, the Cork chairman, at a subsequent board meeting when Christy was formally presented with the McCarthy Cup.

True, a Galway official admitted and regretted, Christy Ring had been struck in separate hotel incidents, but he added that the attacks had been grossly exaggerated. 'The Cork captain suffered no serious injury,' he told the board, 'as the steps where the incidents occurred were well carpeted ones.'

The heated debate drew comments from many speakers rebuking Christy, the *Examiner*, the county chairman and indeed all things Cork, and various suggestions were made as to how best to respond to the matter. The one that appealed most, however, was proposed by Canon O'Dea who suggested that a special gold medal be presented to Mickey Burke. The medal would carry an inscription commending him for 'the courage, endurance of pain, chivalry and outstanding self-restraint' which he displayed in the All-Ireland final.

'My own feeling is that the Galway county board made a meal out of it,' wrote Breandán Ó hEithir in his masterly memoir, *Over The Bar*. 'In the first place, if Burke followed Ring to midfield without instruction from the sideline, as he told Raymond Smith years later, the selectors should have sent him back to his place immediately. Secondly, they should have exercised some control over the players who engaged in fair day behaviour in Barry's Hotel and the Gresham. They should certainly have resisted the temptation to strike a special medal for Burke, which was like setting up a Provisional Central Council instead of pressing the real Central Council for a full inquiry into the circumstances of Burke's injuries.'

The gold medal was duly presented to Mickey Burke the following January at Galway's annual convention, while in Cork the yearly gathering heard some delegates voicing their disapproval of the GAA president's handling of the off-field incidents. Most vociferous was Jim Barry, still seething at the assaults on Christy.

'The best way to show our resentment is to nominate another candidate for the presidency,' he said. Others argued that Cork would lose caste if another candidate were nominated but, nevertheless, a Mayo man, P. Munnelly, was proposed. After a lively debate, the proposed nomination was defeated by just two votes.

Homecoming

A large contingent of Cork people domiciled in Dublin were present at Kingsbridge to send the champions on their way and, as ever, Mallow Station was packed with well-wishers to greet them when the train made its customary stop there. It was to be a momentous homecoming for goal-scoring hero, Tommy O'Sullivan, who left his colleagues at Mallow and travelled in triumph by road to his native Buttevant.

The Thomas Davis Pipe Band headed the parade from Ballydaheen Bridge and bonfires blazed in and around his home town, where Tommy was welcomed to the Buttevant ranks of All-Ireland hurlers, Billy Mackesy, Peter Grady and Batt Thornhill. Meanwhile, the rest of the team continued by train to stop for a while at Blarney before the evening ceremonial homecoming.

After the Blarney sojourn, the All-Ireland party set off on the four-mile journey to the city, some of them wondering how the supporters would react to the events in Dublin. They need not have worried. A huge crowd greeted them at Blackpool Bridge and it seemed all of Cork had come out to welcome them home, as the bus carrying the players inched its way into town. It took an hour and five minutes to cover the distance from Blackpool to the Grand Parade. Then, at the junction between the Parade and Oliver Plunkett Street, the bus stopped and the champions were formally introduced to the teeming throngs.

Andy Scannell, the county chairman, made an appropriate speech and, to enormous cheering, he ended with the comment: 'It is our policy to send out teams to play the game – win, lose or draw – and I am glad that we have always carried out that policy.'

Others spoke too, but Christy was the one the crowds wanted to hear and cheer. He said little but thanked the people present for their marvellous reception and their loyal support throughout the championship. 'It is a great honour for me to captain the team that won the eighteenth All-Ireland for Cork,' he said. 'Have no doubt about it, this is the greatest reception ever given to a team.'

Afterwards the players attended a meal in Billy Mackesy's restaurant and in one of the post-prandial speeches, Sean McCarthy, president of the county board, drew a respectful silence followed by heartfelt applause when he said: 'We all know the recent sad bereavement that Christy has suffered on the death of his mother. It was only because of his attachment to every member of the team and his love for the game that he agreed to take his place on the team and to inspire the side to bring further honour to the county. We thank you Christy most sincerely.'

'It was an unforgettable few days for Cobh people,' recalled camogie star, Anna Crotty. 'We had Cork winning the All-Ireland on the Sunday, Christy bringing home the Cup on Monday evening, and Laurel and Hardy arriving in Cobh on Tuesday. They got a massive reception and were mobbed by kids of all ages. The bells of St Colman's played their signature tune and they seemed to enjoy every moment of their visit. Afterwards they went up to Cork to meet the Lord Mayor, Pa McGrath, and then they all went out to Blarney Castle to kiss the stone. The skinny one kissed it alright but the fat fella was too heavy to be held for the kissing!'

Milestone

The opening by Bishop Lucey of the Glen Rovers clubrooms in Thomas Davis Street in October marked another milestone in the club's impressive 37-year history. The timing was felicitous as the Glen, having contributed eight players to the All-Ireland panel, were just about to win their fourteenth county title.

The Glen beat Sars in the county final by a remarkable scoreline: 8-5 to 4-3. 'Centre-back, Mossie O'Connor, moved out to mark Ring,' wrote the *Examiner*, 'but where he succeeded two years ago, he failed yesterday as the Glen genius continually lobbed balls into the square. Although Sarsfields conceded eight goals, Seanie Carroll, who made some fine saves, cannot be faulted for the shots that beat him.'

The diminutive Seanie Carroll, who later played with Ballymartle and Carrigdhoun, was an eagle-eyed, energetic custodian and hurled with the Cork seniors in league games, but missed out on the championship for playing a soccer match. 'I'll always remember a game against Kilkenny in the Park,' said Seanie. 'I got a belt from the big Kilkenny full-forward and Christy Ring ran all the way up the field to me and said, "Next time the ball comes in, Seanie, hit him, never mind the ball." "But they might get a goal, Christy," I said. "Never mind that," he said, "I'll get one at my end to make up for it."'

Review Of 1953

Towards the close of the year, Christy was disappointed once again to finish second in 'The Sportsman of the Year' competition, but he did have the gleeful satisfaction of beating his St Nick's colleague and friendly rival, Jas Murphy, the Kerry captain, who came third in the poll.

Dublin's outstanding dual star, Norman Allen, was the *Gaelic Sportsman's* No. 1 performer of 1953 with 380 votes, Christy received 329 and Jas Murphy got 161. Mickey Burke came fourth with 140. The contest was open to hurlers, footballers, athletes and handball players and the Top Ten selected were:

1. Norman Allen
2. Christy Ring
3. James Murphy
4. Mickey Burke
5. Mal McEvoy (Armagh)
6. Pat 'Diamond' Hayden
7. John Sutton (Kilkenny)
8. Victor Sherlock (Cavan)
9. Sean Quinn (Armagh)
10. Jim Langton

Other recipients of readers' votes included Nicky Rackard, Jerry O'Riordan, Mick O'Hanlon (Wexford) and Maurice Fives (Waterford).

In reviewing the games and players of 1953 the *Gaelic Echo* wrote: 'The year's outstanding personality, of course, was the spectacular

Christy Ring, the Cork captain. He was Mr Hurling of 1953, as he had been in 1952 and many another memorable year back along the line. Irishmen of all counties recognise and applaud unselfishly whenever a great star comes amongst them and there is not a follower of Gaelic games who does not thrill to the flashing solo runs of Christy Ring down the field, 40, 50 yards like a streak of lightning and then sinking the ball in the enemy net or slipping it over the bar as only a great master of the ash can.'

'What thrilling moments Christy can look back on. What other man, for example, stepped up to take a 21-yards free under the hushed silence of a Munster final crowd, eyed the goal in front of him, lined from side to side by strong Tipperary stars with hardly an inch showing as they stood shoulder to shoulder, and then bent, lifted and like a flash blasted the ball to the back of the net. No more need be said of that occasion or the ear-splitting roar of appreciation and delirious delight that rent the air of the historic arena. Like good wine the years only seem to improve the Glen Rovers star for 1953 was Christy's greatest year to date although we had thought his previous best was so brilliant it could not be equalled, let alone exceeded.'

CHAPTER THIRTEEN

1954 – THE GOAL THAT MADE HISTORY

'We hear that some of the Glen supporters were disappointed with former minor flyer Johnny Clifford's showing against Carrigtwohill,' wrote Rambling Rory in the *Gaelic Sportsman* (1952). 'Yerrah, can't ye give the lad a chance? He'll have his day yet and, unless we're greatly mistaken, a good day 'twill be.'

Rory had no idea how prophetic those words would be. Just over two years later Johnny's day would come, a day in the sun that would see him making hurling history. In the closing stages of the All-Ireland final he would score the goal that gave Cork victory over Wexford and Christy his record eighth medal. A good day indeed.

After the goal Josie Hartnett scored a fine point and then came the moment of real triumph with Ring putting the finishing touch to a grand display by scoring the final point.

It was a fitting climax to another wonderful championship for Christy whose general play and final score at Croke Park were almost a mirror-image of his form in the Munster final. On that occasion against Tipperary the *Examiner* reported: 'Were the match to be recorded stroke by stroke, no name would be printed more often than that of the Cork captain because he won the game for his county. All the superlatives of the dictionary have from time to time been used to describe the hurling wizard of the age, so much so that when one endeavours to find adequate praise for his performance, words fail. Perhaps it can all be summed up in one phrase – it was Ring's game.'

Hogan's Glory

Earlier in the year Jim Hogan from Tullaroan gained lasting fame by subduing Christy and helping Leinster to a rare win over Munster in the Railway Cup final. 'With Ring Held, Munster Were Seldom Dangerous' ran the *Independent* headline after Leinster's 0-9 to 0-5 win, their first in more than a decade.

'Hogan watched Ring like a hawk and hurled him ball for ball,' said the *Gaelic Sportsman*, 'and it was well for Leinster that the Kilkenny man did such a fine job, as the Munster captain, on the few occasions that he did slip clear, scored a beauty of a point and let fly two scorchers at goal.' John D. Hickey agreed that Christy was not entirely ineffective, despite Jim Hogan's tight marking. 'He scored three points, one of which was the best score of the game and he was denied a goal when Kevin Matthews made an almost incredible first-half save.'

For all that, Jim Hogan was the undisputed hero of the hour, although Paddy Buggy, Johnny McGovern and newcomer Ned Wheeler at centre-back were also very impressive in the memorable, if low-scoring, win for Leinster. Jim Langton won his second Railway Cup medal that day after a wait of thirteen years.

The all-Galway Connacht side had matched Munster for 50 minutes of the semi-final at Croke Park. 'Then,' said *The Irish Press*, 'Christy Ring, who had already scored a goal and a point, came roving out from his corner-forward position and took charge of the game. Four glorious points in a row he sent sailing over the bar and one in particular from the 14-yard flag on the right-hand touchline was as brilliant a score as even Christy has ever landed. Connacht never recovered from Ring's scoring spree.'

The game brought Ring and Burke in opposition for the first time since the All-Ireland final, Christy at left corner-forward, a position he favoured and Mickey at right half-back. 'Though exchanges were hard and keen,' said Pádraig Puirséal, 'we saw no sign of "needle" and Jack Mulcahy (Kilkenny), a very efficient referee who kept a tight rein on the game, had no trouble from two earnest teams.'

Mission Begins

Gregory Peck came to Cork the day the champions began their mission to complete the three-in-a-row, and there seemed to be more interest in his arrival for the filming of *Moby Dick* than in the Munster championship game against Waterford. Understandably so. Cork, who were never extended by the Decies, won by twelve points and Mick Cashman, playing at midfield, set up the best score of the game when he directed a 70 towards Ring whose centre was doubled to the net by Josie Hartnett.

The Munster final was a different story, of course, with Cork and Tipp battling for supremacy in the usual fashion and Christy's hopes of an eighth All-Ireland medal in jeopardy, as a dominant Tipperary led by a point just as the game entered 'lost' time.

'It was looking like Tipp for the All-Ireland semi-final,' wrote Mick Dunne, 'but then Christy Ring whipped the ball into the square from 20 yards. Tony Reddan jumped to save it, but the ball bounced from his cupped hands. In a flash Paddy Barry pounced on this gift chance and rattled the net. It was a winning goal that made Tipp supporters almost weep, it came so late there could be no adequate fight back.'

'Cork are never beaten,' said Tony Reddan, 'until you are putting on your clothes in the dressing room after a match.'

Although Cork fans were overjoyed by such a delightful finish, neutrals regarded the match as the least impressive of the Cork-Tipperary series of championship clashes since 1949. 'It was only in the last quarter that the hurling rose to a high standard,' wrote *The Irish Times*.

Tipperary, with wind advantage, found the Cork backs in rare form, but a Mick Seymour goal helped them to a 1-6 to 0-4 lead at half-time. On the resumption Christy showed a determination that seemed keener than ever and Tipp were forced to bring John Doyle out to mark him. It was Tony Reddan, however, who kept Ring at bay with two fantastic saves from play, before Christy drove a 21 to the net.

After that Seamus Bannon had a goal called back for a free which Paddy Kenny pointed and Tipp stayed ahead right into 'lost' time when Barry's goal and Ring's final point gave Cork a 2-8 to 1-8 win.

Bannon, Kenny, Jimmy Finn, Theo English and young Tony Wall were rated as the Premier's outstanding performers, while the Cork backs en masse earned the plaudits but, apart from Ring, only one forward, Johnny Clifford, was acclaimed in the papers.

'Once again Cork can thank the fate that made Christy Ring a Corkman,' wrote Mick Dunne. 'Yet again the man from Cloyne pulled his county through. His 1-4 was exactly half of Cork's total. He outwitted Mickey Byrne who had been specially placed on him. Tipp called out John Doyle to mark him, yet Ring was able to make the winning goal.'

In the All-Ireland semi-final, Cork again came face to face with Galway and this time the match passed off quietly enough. 'Ring's display was faultless,' wrote the *Weekly Examiner*. 'In the air, on the ground and from frees he was the personification of the complete hurler. He had the best score of the hour, Cork's first point which followed a lightning pick and overhead stroke that sent the ball soaring high over the bar and this despite the close attention of Billy Duffy.'

Watching the match was a leading British sports writer, David Jack, who had never seen a hurling game before. It was the year of the World Cup and Roger Bannister breaking the four-minute mile, but when asked to select his personal sporting highlight of 1954, Jack must have raised a few eyebrows with his *Empire News* headline: 'Give Me Hurling Every Time.'

'My sports thrill of the year was at a hurling match,' wrote David Jack in the popular English Sunday newspaper. 'Ever been to one? I hadn't until I went to Croke Park. The match was Cork v Galway in the All-Ireland semi-final. Right from the first whistle it was dominated by a balding, stocky Cork hurler who looked the double of Sailor Brown of Charlton Athletic and England inside-forward fame.

'Christy Ring was his name and I soon realised he was the idol of Cork. Every time this genius with the bent hockey stick had possession Galway were in trouble. From all angles and all distances he gathered the ball and with nonchalant flicks slammed it home for a goal or a point. Genius Ring scored plenty of Cork's points. I can't remember how many. But those he did not score he made for his colleagues.

'I read after the match that Galway were thankful Christy Ring was not as devastating as usual. Well, if that was only half a Ring, I must be at Croke Park when the bell really tolls. That would be a sporting thrill to beat the lot.'

In the other semi-final, Wexford beat Antrim comfortably, having defeated Dublin in the Leinster final, a game in which Nicky Rackard accumulated a grand total of five goals and four points.

Victory over Galway meant that Christy was just one game away from a record eighth All-Ireland medal. Fermoy-born Danno Keeffe had won seven football medals with Kerry and Kilkenny's Jack Rochford, Dick 'Drug' Walsh, Sim Walton and Dick Doyle had done so in hurling, but now Christy stood on the verge of uniqueness. Not surprisingly, interest in the All-Ireland reached an all-time peak and over 80,000 people would throng Croke Park on the first Sunday in September.

Fever Pitch

'This meeting of Cork and Wexford has aroused astonishing interest,' wrote John D. Hickey. 'I cannot recall a final that quite caused the fever of Sunday's test. Believe me, the situation in the Croke Park offices these days and nights is just impossible. Had they ten times more tickets at headquarters, they would not have half enough.'

Because of the unprecedented interest, the final brought a greater headache than usual to GAA secretary, Pádraig Ó Caoimh. At that stage Pádraig was still popularly known as Paddy O'Keeffe and requests for tickets took many forms, none more original perhaps than one from a Limerick man, desperate to attend the game.

'Dear Paddy O'Keeffe,' he wrote, 'I once saved a person of your name from drowning and I am hoping it was you and that you'll be able to send me a ticket. If it wasn't you I saved, I suppose there is nothing we can do.'

The final was the main topic of discussion for weeks and John D. Hickey made an interesting point when he wrote: 'For long I have felt that the answer to Ring is not a back that can hold him, but a forward of greater scoring potential and on recent performances there is no doubt Wexford have such a man in Nicky Rackard.' The Rathnure man's scoring blitz against Dublin prompted other

1954 All-Ireland Champions.
Back (from left) – Jack Barrett (selector), Andy Scannell (chairman), Dave Creedon, Jerry O'Riordan, John Lyons, Derry Hayes, Mattie Fouhy, Gerard Murphy, Paddy 'Fox' Collins, Jim Barry (trainer). Front – Sean Nolan (boy), Eamonn Goulding, Willie John Daly, Tony O'Shaughnessy, Johnny Clifford, Josie Hartnett, Christy Ring, Paddy Barry, Vincie Twomey, Willie Moore.

reporters, as well as John D., to suggest that either Ring or Rackard's performance would be the decisive factor in the outcome. Nicky found that sort of pressure hard to take.

'It was my first All-Ireland final,' he said, 'and people were talking about how much I'd score and how much Christy would score in what was his ninth All-Ireland. All the talk and all the build-up didn't do me any good at all.'

Twenty-Ones

The 6d match programme carried pictures of the teams and the captains, Padge Kehoe and Christy, plus details of the individual players. The oldest hurlers were Christy and Nicky Rackard, both 33, while Johnny Clifford at twenty was the youngest. Ned Wheeler, Jim English and Seamus Hearne, each 22, were Wexford's youngest. There were nine Glen hurlers on the Cork panel (seven playing), four from Blackrock, three from Carrigtwohill and one each from Midleton, Sars, the 'Barrs and Buttevant. The Wexford players came mainly from St Aidan's (Enniscorthy), Rathnure, Piercetown-St Martin's, Horeswood and Cloughbawn, with one each from Ardcolm, Cushenstown and Geraldine O'Hanrahan's.

'It is doubtful if there is a moment of greater suspense in hurling with all its thrills than when a player of the astonishing striking power of Christy Ring or Nicky Rackard bends to lift a ball for a 21-yards free,' wrote Réitoir in the programme. 'When a Ring or a Rackard is about to strike it seems an age of intense agony for supporters of the opposite camp and a split-second of glorious expectation for those hoping for a goal.

'Ring and Rackard, and for that matter Jim Langton and Paddy Kenny, have brought the striking of such frees to a fine art. Lifting the ball with a forward motion, they gain a couple of yards and then with quite legitimate venom, strike groundwards in an attempt to record a goal. Three years ago the Referees Committee agreed that such spectacular and accomplished taking of a free should not be vetoed. They unanimously decided not to interfere with a development that has brought such colour to hurling. In doing so, they unquestionably met the wishes of the overwhelming majority of followers, even those in counties who have no Ring, no Rackard, no Langton and no Kenny.'

Contrary to Réiteoir's view, Paddy Tyers contended that Ring's technique was different from the others. 'To score a goal most hurlers would strike the sliothar low but not Christy. He would blast the ball a foot or two under the crossbar. Why? Because it takes more time to raise the hurley than move it down towards the feet and, secondly, there is the possibility that a player will stop a low shot with his leg. Naturally, Christy would always avoid directing the ball towards the man best suited to stop the shot – the goalkeeper. Instead, he'd blast it towards one of the backs who would naturally move his head as the sliothar came speeding towards him.'

Christy admitted as much to film-maker Louis Marcus. 'He showed us his technique for the 21-yard free, racing in on the lifted ball to crash it up into the net. "But how do you decide where to aim?" someone asked. "I aim at the funkiest player on the line," he snapped. I watched carefully in later games and, sure enough, a timorous head would bob sideways as Christy's shot whistled past.'

Lights, Camera, Action!

'The director – Jim Barry. The set – Athletic Grounds. The plot – same as previous years. The actors – almost unchanged with Christy Ring as usual taking the principal role. Yes, Cork's training camp resembles a reissue of a familiar film.' So wrote an unnamed scribe in the *Independent*.

'On arrival at the Park every evening, each player receives a rub-down from the experienced hands of Jim Barry who has probably rubbed more embrocation into All-Ireland medal winners than anybody else in the country. This over, they take to the field for sprinting, trotting, stick work and physical exercises. Special emphasis is placed on wristwork and when their training is over the players gather round for a pep talk, usually given by Barry.

In the city these days one hears more about Ring's eighth medal than Cork's All-Ireland and his comrades are extremely anxious that Christy, who has served his county so wonderfully over the years, will make history. He looks a picture of fitness at the moment and is the centre of attraction each evening as he prepares for the big event.'

Tuesday's county board delegates and the general public next day heard that the selectors had made two changes from the side that

Jim Barry supervises a sprint.
From left – Josie Hartnett, John Lyons, Tony O'Shaughnessy, Jimmy Lynam,
Liam Dowling, Dave O'Leary, Vincie Twomey, Derry Hayes and Dave Creedon.

beat Galway. Tony O'Shaughnessy was recalled at left corner-back and there was one positional switch in attack – Johnny Clifford crossing from left corner to right and Paddy Barry from right to left.

On the morning of the final Seán Óg Ó Ceallacháin dropped into Barry's Hotel to see Christy. 'Christy,' he said politely, 'if ye win today, would you mind coming into Raidió Éireann this evening to discuss the match with me?' Christy gave him a withering look. 'What do you mean, if we win today? Of course we'll win and you'd better be here to collect me.'

Making History

A tremendous cheer greeted the 33-year-old Cloyne man as he led the Cork team out from the dressing room under the Cusack Stand. It was clear even before the game began that this was Christy's final. The Wexford players got a great reception too and many Cork supporters gazed in astonishment at the sheer size of men like Ned

Wheeler, Jim Morrissey, Nick O'Donnell, Padge Kehoe and the three Rackard brothers. How could Cork, with players as light as Vincie Twomey and Johnny Clifford, stand up to such a powerfully-built Wexford team? But what Cork lacked in inches and pounds, they made up for in grit and determination.

'More classical All-Ireland finals there may have been,' wrote John D. Hickey, 'but never can there have been a decider of more tense and electric an atmosphere than the 1954 hurling final. My hand is still a little tremulous after it all, but I enjoyed it so much I would have wished it had continued to midnight.'

Eamonn Goulding, destined to play for Cork in both All-Ireland finals two years later, got off to a dream start with a deftly taken point after three minutes. Then the stadium erupted as Christy scored his first point from a 40-yards free. Wexford, unnerved perhaps by the big occasion and the massive attendance (84,856) failed to score until Nicky Rackard, moving outfield, landed a point and added a free to equalise after twenty minutes.

Re-enter Ring within a minute, side-stepping three men and striking smartly to restore the lead. He quickly added a point from a free and then passed to Willie John Daly for Cork's final score of the first half.

Wexford, meanwhile, had a pointed free by Nicky Rackard before Tom Ryan tapped to the net a cut-in by Paddy Kehoe. 'It was the only goal scored against Dave Creedon in three All-Ireland finals and it was my man who got it,' said Tony O'Shaughnessy ruefully, 50 years later. Yet the courageous 'Barrs man had declined to retire with a bandaged head early in the game and stayed on to hurl brilliantly.

Wexford, whose outstanding player had been Bobby Rackard at centre-back, led by 1-3 to 0-5 at the break and restarted in style with Tim Flood making jinking solo runs and stretching the lead. Then, six minutes into the second half, disaster struck for the Slaneysiders. Gaining possession from a long drive by Gerard Murphy, Christy weaved his way through a bunch of opponents until he came within 30 yards of the Wexford goal. He let fly and the ball whizzed through the air for what looked like a certain goal.

'Some of us had already jumped for joy at the "goal",' said Mattie

Fouhy, 'when we realised that the umpire had his finger raised for a 70. The ball had struck the Wexford full-back Nick O'Donnell and shot out over the end-line. O'Donnell's collar bone was broken by the impact of Christy's shot and he was taken to the sideline. The accident was a severe blow to Wexford, especially since his departure came at a time when we were already on the way back.'

'In the emergency Loc Garman mentors deputed Bobby Rackard to full-back,' wrote John D. Hickey, 'and although he still continued to perform in that majestic manner, I believe that his transfer was a tactical error. The Rathnure star continued to lord it over all rivals in his new position, but not unnaturally his clearances – still great efforts – did not go as deeply into enemy ground and in consequence the Wexford forwards were not fed to such advantage as in the earlier stages.'

Ring sent over his fourth point in the forty-second minute and then Vincie Twomey, who was having a splendid game in the half-back line, moved outfield with the ball and enhanced his performance with a superb point. Only two points then divided the sides and Wexford were grimly holding on with just four minutes to go, when Clifford's shot caught Foley slightly out of position. 'When I went for the ball Art Foley moved out from the goal and stopped in his tracks as I hit it,' said Johnny. 'It's quite possible that if he had stayed on the goal-line, he'd have stopped the shot.'

Clifford's goal did not quite mark the end of the game though. A few minutes still remained and there was only one point between the teams. Wexford, shattered though they may have been by O'Donnell's departure and Cork's late goal, did not go down without a fight. However, with the large Cork contingent of supporters now rising to their team, nothing could halt Christy and his men. As the game drew to a finish Josie Hartnett sent over another point and then, true to form, Christy brought the scoring to a close with a majestic point.

Cork won by 1-9 to 1-6 and history was made. The shy young hurler from Cloyne who had won his first senior medal in 1941 now became the first man to win eight All-Ireland medals.

The 1954 final was the first All-Ireland between Cork and Wexford in over 50 years and it was imbued with a spirit of sportsmanship that was a credit to both counties. 'If it wasn't for my natural desire to win the eighth medal,' said Christy, 'I can truthfully say that I would like to have seen Wexford winning. We had never beaten a cleaner team than Wexford and after that match I expressed the sincere hope that Wexford would win the All-Ireland in 1955. I was very glad when they did.'

On his return with the McCarthy Cup, Christy was duly fêted and thoroughly enjoyed not merely the wonderful reception in Cork on Monday night but the warm greetings the players received on the rounds of their home towns and villages afterwards.

Cloyne folk turned out in force again to welcome Christy when he returned with the trophy for the third time, and in Carrigtwohill, a smiling and proud Christy was delighted to be congratulated by his father's great hero, Tommy Barry.

As the ecstatic crowd gloried in the presence of local heroes Willie John, Mattie Fouhy and Willie Moore standing beside Christy and Paddy Barry outside the parochial hall, all five were called on to speak and each one did so to rapturous acclaim. When Christy approached the microphone, it was the signal for a tremendous outburst of cheering and excitement and, when he finally started his short few words of thanks and appreciation, it was not the 1954 game or any of his other triumphs that he mentioned. 'If I were asked what was the greatest All-Ireland final of all,' he said, 'I would say it was the first replay in 1931 and one great man on the team was Tom Barry himself.'

The Carrig crowd went wild with delight at such a tribute to their stalwart clubman. Tommy smiled at the unexpected, honourable mention, his nephew Paddy reflected in his uncle's glory and up above Nicholas Ring must have been smiling too.

Tributes

Paddy Mehigan could not resist comparing the 1954 team with Steve Riordan's side that had brought honour to Cork over half a century earlier. 'Every man on the 1903 team was a master hurler,' he wrote in his Carbery column. 'The backs, Tom Coughlan, Steve Riordan, Gerry Desmond and Pat O'Sullivan were powerfully built. Jamesey Kelleher was not tall but his shoulders were broad

Throughout his career Christy was always in front for the throw-in. Here (above) we see him in 1952 against Norman Allen (Dublin) with Joe Twomey behind and 1960 against Theo English (Tipperary) (above right). Right: Dr Kinane starts the 1956 final with Christy and Tom Ryan in for the clash. The Cork players behind are Pat Dowling, Paddy Barry, Terry Kelly and Eamonn Goulding. The Wexford men are Seamus Hearne, Padge Kehoe, Martin Codd, Tim Flood, Nicky Rackard and Tom Dixon.

and his skill was a joy to watch. Billy O'Neill was a dynamo of energy and clever too. I rank Billy Mackesy, Andy Buckley and Bill Hennessy among the greatest forwards I have known. I agree that Christy Ring is perhaps the most complete hurling artist that ever handled ash and graced the game, and I must accept that recent Cork teams were swifter to hit and their speed to the ball was better than the 1903 men who had seventeen players against the present fifteen in the same-sized pitch and didn't need to run a lot. It is difficult to weigh up two commanding sides but I think the genius of Ring would force a draw.'

The Holly Bough, Cork's popular Christmas journal, paid tribute to Christy and even essayed an interview with the reticent star. 'It was to Christy himself that the hearts of most of the assembled thousands went out,' the editor wrote, 'for he had done something which no hurler had ever before achieved. Croke Park crowds have not always been overkind to Christy, but on that fine autumn afternoon everyone in the vast arena seemed to be sharing in his joy and giving him the credit which was undoubtedly his due.'

The interview consisted of three questions: What did Christy regard as his most memorable All-Ireland, Munster and county finals? 'I regard our victory over Kilkenny in 1946 as the most satisfying,' he said. 'I think the 1952 Munster final victory over Tipperary was the greatest. Of the county finals, I recall with pleasure the great game Carrigdhoun gave us in 1945 when the south-east men were the first divisional side ever to contest a county final and they actually scored more goals than the Glen.'

There was a further, if not unexpected, honour awaiting Christy at the end of 1954, when *Gaelic Sportsman* readers voted him Sportsman of the Year. Christy topped the poll with 1,045 votes, Bobby Rackard (150) was second and Meath footballer Paddy O'Brien (125) was third, followed by Dr Padraig Carney, Jim English, Peter McDermott (Meath), Nicky Rackard, Ignatius 'Nace' O'Dowd (Sligo), Sean Purcell, Norman Allen, John Doyle, Billy O'Neill, Tom Crotty (Cavan), Jim Hogan (Kilkenny), Shay Elliot (cycling), Phil Clark (athletics), Michael Grace (Meath) and future Olympic champion Ronnie Delany.

Dagenham

Five days after winning the McCarthy Cup the Cork hurlers, accompanied by Lord Mayor, Pa McGrath, set sail in the *Innisfallen* to play an exhibition match at Dagenham, the home of countless Corkmen working in the huge Ford motor plant. The event was organised by the Tomas McCurtain hurling club.

'Like all Corkmen here in Little Cork, as this part of Dagenham is known to the 20,000 working here,' said Michael Ronayne, 'I'm very proud to see Christy and the lads here as reigning All-Ireland champions. The red jersey makes us all so proud, but for me there is another significance in Cork's red colours. You see, my brother Jack Ronayne was an engineer in charge of the building of the Gurranabraher and Spangle Hill houses, which are now known as The Red City because of the colour of the roofs. That colour wasn't chosen by chance.'

Over 10,000 enthusiastic spectators came to see Cork playing a McCurtain selection and, particularly, to watch Christy in action. He did not disappoint them, scoring four goals and three points, and displaying all the craft and skill that had made him so great.

After the game there was a special moment of pride and poignancy for Christy. After all the handshakes, back-patting and autograph signing, he was introduced to one of the heroes of his youth, a man whose name had been mentioned so often by his late father.

Morgan Madden, smiling and proud, a trace of a tear in his eye, told Christy how much he had been looking forward to meeting him. This was the same Morgan Madden of the old Redmonds club who had won three All-Ireland medals with Cork in 1928, 1929 and 1931; Morgan Madden, a staunch hurler who played alongside Sean Óg, Eudie Coughlan, Jim Hurley, Dinny Barry-Murphy, the Ahernes, Jim Regan and Fox Collins; Morgan Madden the only man who was ever successful in neutralising the efforts of Kilkenny's great Mattie Power. Christy and the others were saddened to find that Morgan had lost a limb at work.

New York, New York

In November 1954, the Cork hurlers set off for New York to play two games against the Irish hurling exiles.

Over 30,000 would cram into the Polo Grounds to see Christy
Ring and his team in action but, before that, his arrival generated
great interest among New York's sports writers.

'Christy Ring is the only man to win eight All-Ireland medals,'
wrote Red Smith in the *New York Times*. 'It's like being picked that
often on an All-Star major league baseball team, except that it's more
difficult. He is to his game what Ruth was to baseball, what
Dempsey was to boxing, Bobby Jones to golf, Jim Thorpe to football. Newspapermen waited in the Times Square Hotel to meet Ring.
He would, they assumed, look like a man suited to pound a beat in
Hell's Kitchen. Then they met him. Christy Ring is slightly bigger
than a "scrupper" of Guinness. He has small compact features,
bright blue eyes and thinning blond hair. He does not talk much and,
when he does, it's well to listen sharply for County Cork softens and
broadens his accent, blurring it for American ears.'

'Nicholas Christopher Michael Ring,' wrote *Sports Illustrated*,
'is a balding 33-year-old Irishman with a broad back, strong legs
and hands that could choke a bear. He is also the greatest practising exponent of the ancient Irish game of hurling and, according
to some, the greatest ever. What Ring does so well is play a game
that at first glance looks like field hockey, but which resembles
field hockey as much as a Mercedes-Benz resembles a Baker
Electric. Hurling is more like lacrosse played with axe handles or
ice hockey with the puck continually in mid-air. It is a game of
bruising body contact, constant running and perfect eye and hand
co-ordination. Christy Ring is by far the best of an exceptional
group of fine athletes because he possesses to an extraordinary
degree the physical attributes of a great athlete, plus a competitive
urge that after sixteen years of championship play makes him leap
in the air in glee when his team scores.'

The other players who travelled to New York were Dave Creedon,
John Lyons, Jerry O'Riordan, Tony O'Shaughnessy, Mattie Fouhy,
Vincie Twomey, Sean O'Brien, Joe Twomey, Gerard Murphy, Willie
John Daly, Josie Hartnett, Paddy Barry, Liam Dowling, Tom
O'Sullivan, Owenie McAuliffe, Mick Cashman, Mossie O'Connor,
Dave 'Cody' O'Leary and Jimmy Lynam.

Their opponents, the New York All-Stars, included former

Galway hurlers, Colm Corless and Stephen Gallagher; the Kilkenny star, Terry Leahy, who had scored the winning point against Cork in 1947; and former Glen and St Nick's county medallist, Josie Looney.

'I was the proudest man in New York when Christy and the other players came on to the pitch in the red and white colours,' said Josie. 'It was strange playing against Cork and my old Glen clubmates, but it was a tremendous occasion and the huge crowd loved it.'

The trip to New York, a first for Cork's hurlers, came as a result of winning the National League in 1953. Mayo's footballers were similarly rewarded for their league success and both counties defeated the exiles at the Polo Grounds.

Cork beat New York by 7-8 to 3-10 with the goals coming from Paddy Barry (3), Josie Hartnett, Liam Dowling, Willie John Daly and Christy Ring, who also scored five points. Josie Hartnett and Willie John got the others.

A week later Cork went to 240th Street and Broadway in the Bronx to play a second game against New York at Gaelic Park. They won 8-8 to 3-6 with the goals coming from Tom O'Sullivan (3), Paddy Barry (3), Jimmy Lynam and Liam Dowling. Christy scored seven points and Willie John got the eighth.

After the New York games the players travelled to Boston where their arrival was eagerly awaited as well. 'Gaelic sports followers of Greater Boston will be in for a rare treat this afternoon when Christy Ring – the Babe Ruth of Irish sports – leads the Cork team into action against a team of New England hurling stars at Fenway Park,' wrote the *Herald*.

'We got the train up to Boston and we had a grand time there,' said Willie John Daly. 'It was strange playing hurling in a baseball stadium, but the crowd loved it. There's a famous photograph of Christy togged out as a baseball player. As a matter of fact, Christy, Liam Dowling, myself and a few others were asked to deck out in the Red Sox outfit and try our hand at baseball. We did quite well and Liam Dowling actually drove the baseball out of the stadium, to the astonishment of the famous Red Sox striker Ted Williams. After our stay in Boston we flew back to New York.'

The visit of the Cork hurlers prompted an interesting spread – an article and ten pictures – in the 22 November edition of *Life* magazine! 'Hurling, the Irish national game, is a sport in which teams of strong young men line up to fifteen-a-side with spoon-shaped shillelaghs called camáns and try to bat a hard leather-covered ball into each other's goal. A blend of field hockey and lacrosse, the game is played regularly by enthusiastic Irish-American emigrées in New York from early spring to winter.'

'The big event of the 1954 season,' *Life* added, 'took place when County Cork, the All-Ireland champions, came over to play an all-star team of New York at the Polo Grounds. Although the rules forbid swinging at an opponent with a stick or fist, there were some injuries during the game. This, said Christy Ring, who led the Irish team to a 29-19 triumph, was routine. "It was nothing," he remarked, "compared to when we play at home."'

Nicky's Views

When the great Nicky Rackard won his first and long overdue All-Ireland medal in 1955, Christy Ring and John Lyons conveyed their good wishes. 'I needn't tell you how pleased I was that Christy and John wired their congratulations,' said Nicky.

A few months later the Rathnure man told his hurling story to Pádraig Puirséal, who asked him to rate the best players he had seen. Of the defenders he rated Pat Stakelum as the best centre-back and Paddy Phelan as the quickest thinking player of his era. The forwards he admired most were Mackey, Langton and Ring.

'Mick Mackey had strength, glorious hurling ability, a heart as big as his body. There was character and dash and devil about his hurling and, if he was not perhaps the supreme stylist that Ring or Langton could be, he was the best man I have ever seen to rally a team. Jimmy Langton's anticipation was uncanny and he wanted only one thing to make him the greatest hurler of my time – physical strength. Lacking the wiry build of Ring or the physique of Mackey, Langton could be held out of a game by a stronger man, but what a hurler he was for all that.

'Christy was and is a wonder on a field and consistently successful in baffling all or any opposition. Mackey could be held, Langton blotted out of a game, but Ringey was always the maestro, winning matches off his own stick no matter how closely marked or making match-winning openings for others when he was baulked himself. Bobby and Billy have had ample opportunity to study Christy in action at close quarters and they can never say enough in praise of his wizardry.'

The Banner Rises And Falls

As Cork set out to retain their championship title in 1955 and, possibly, achieve a second four-in-a-row, there were concerns at the injuries that prevented Christy and Josie Hartnett from training with the team. There was concern, too, that Paddy Barry would miss the Clare game due to suspension. For all that, few people in Cork expected the Banner men to cause an upset at Thurles.

Before the game the Clare players were pleasantly surprised to receive a miniature hurley signed by the Rackard brothers and wishing them well in the championship. Little did Nicky, Bobby or Billy realise what giant-killing acts Clare were about to perform. Still less did they envisage Clare's progress helping indirectly to make 1955 Wexford's year.

Over 25,000 people came to Thurles and saw an exuberant Clare side getting three goals in the first half and leading by ten points approaching the break. Then Willie John Daly, who had scored Cork's first goal, set up Josie Hartnett for the second just before half-time. With the wind behind them afterwards, Cork fought back with points by Ring, Daly and substitute Owenie McAuliffe from Glanworth, before Gerard Murphy brought the sides level twelve minutes from time. 'Then Christy Ring put Cork in the lead for the first time,' said the *Examiner*, 'when he scored the best point of the game from 65-yards range.'

The last five minutes were spellbinding. Cork had three wides and Clare one before Jackie Greene levelled scores. Then, with about a minute to go, Jimmy Smyth stepped up to take a crucial free and Clare supporters went delirious with joy as the ball floated over the bar.

There was still one moment of high drama to come, however, as Josie Hartnett sent a sideline ball into the square where Christy grabbed it amidst a mêlée of players. He appeared to slip and as he lay on the ground surrounded by Clare backs, he tried to palm the ball to the net. The referee, who was standing nearby, blew his whistle and thousands of eyes lighted on him awaiting his verdict – a free out. Clare supporters greeted the decision like a score and, indeed, it meant the winning of the game.

'It was hard luck on Christy not getting the vital score,' said the *Examiner*. 'Had he done so, it would have been a superhuman effort on his part. Considering the handicap of his leg injury, it will be generally agreed that he played one of the best games of his career and he was easily the most stylish player on the field and went within an ace of winning the game on his own.'

For all that, it was Clare's great day and, having beaten Cork's three-in-a-row side, there was a buzz of excitement in the county as they faced Tipperary in the Munster semi-final a fortnight later. This time over 38,000 turned up at the Gaelic Grounds.

The game, refereed by Charlie Conway from Blarney, was another thriller, with points by Jimmy Smyth and Des Dillon putting Clare two ahead in the dying moments. Liam Devaney hit back with a Tipp point and Clare supporters were made to endure another agonising moment as Theo English's shot for the equaliser grazed the outside of the left upright.

Having beaten star-studded Cork and Tipperary, who had shared the previous six All-Irelands between them, Clare were supremely confident in the lead-up to the final against lowly Limerick, whose great days had ended when Mick Mackey retired several years earlier.

Many Clare followers thought they had only to go down to the Gaelic Grounds to see their heroes collecting the Munster Cup. It was a glorious day of beautiful sunshine and the conditions reflected the confident, expectant and feel-good mood of the Banner supporters. When the ball was thrown in and Jimmy Smyth surged away to score the opening point it did, indeed, seem that the gods were about to smile on Clare. Then, the dream began to fall apart.

Mick Mackey, now the trainer, had primed his young charges well and an outstanding display by Dermot Kelly, who scored 1-12, was a big factor in the win, but not the only one. 'Speed and more

***1955* Cork Senior Hurling Team.**
Back: Jack Barrett, Gerard Murphy, Joe Twomey, Derry Hayes, John Lyons, Liam McGrath, Dave Creedon, Mattie Fouhy, Jim Barry. Front: Josie Hartnett, Christy Ring, Tony O'Shaughnessy, Johnny Clifford, Vincie Twomey, Willie John Daly, Seanie O'Brien, Mattie McAuliffe.

speed was the secret of Limerick's victory,' wrote the *Examiner* and Clare were thrown off guard by the lightning-fast hurling of Kelly, Seamus and Liam Ryan, Ralph Prendergast, Donal Broderick, Jim and Jack Quaid, Vivian Cobbe and their team-mates, all of whom became known as 'Mackey's Greyhounds'. When Charlie Conway blew the final whistle, Limerick were 2-15 to 2-6 in front and Clare hurlers and supporters stood in disbelief.

Railway Cup

While there was no trip to Croke Park for Cork in 1955, Christy Ring celebrated St Patrick's Day in the usual manner, helping Munster to victory at GAA headquarters.

The same day, legendary road-bowler, Mick Barry, made history by lofting the Chetwynd Viaduct with a sixteen-ounce bowl. 'Christy Ring is one of my idols,' said Barry. The *Examiner*, the following day, recorded both sporting achievements.

'It was a miracle of quick-thinking by Christy Ring that put Munster on the road to victory,' the hurling report went. 'A southern raid brought the ball to the Leinster square, a shoulder upended the maestro, but the sliothar rolled near him and he beat it past goalkeeper Matthews with his cupped hand. The holders came back to terms with a point, but Ring slipped over three successive points and a late goal by Hartnett clinched the issue.'

Munster won by 3-10 to 2-9 with Ring collecting his twelfth medal. The team was: Tony Reddan, Jerry O'Riordan, John Lyons, John Doyle, Johnny O'Connor (Waterford), Donal O'Grady (Clare), Vincie Twomey, Pat Stakelum, John Hough (Tipperary), Willie John Daly, Des Dillon (Clare), Jimmy Smyth, Josie Hartnett, Jackie Greene (Clare) and Christy Ring, with subs Mickey Byrne, Dermot Kelly, Jimmy Finn, Seamus Power and Matt Nugent.

Togging Out

'The Glen always began training after Good Friday,' said Dave Creedon, 'and though training was always taken very seriously, it used to be good fun a lot of the time.'

T.P. O'Mahony, in his biography of Jack Lynch, recalls an incident when Jack, who had retired from hurling, called up to watch the Glen training at the old Glen Field on the edge of Kilbarry. 'The dressing room in those days was nothing more than a corrugated iron shed, measuring perhaps twenty by eight feet and situated in one corner of the ground. It had no conventional windows, that is to say, no glass, but it had two open frames to let in air and light, each measuring perhaps four feet square.'

When the training session ended and the players headed for the dressing room, Ring and Lynch stayed on the far side of the field chatting away, directly opposite the shed. Unexpectedly, Lynch set Ring a challenge. 'A half-crown if you get three sliothars through one of those windows.' Christy, who had plenty of window practise back home in Cloyne as a youth, took up the challenge and, unerringly, sent three balls through one of the windows. Jack immediately handed him a half-crown.

'The only problem,' said T.P. O'Mahony, 'was that the players inside suddenly found themselves bombarded by mini-missiles. As the balls rattled against the corrugated sheeting at the back of the dressing room, creating an almighty din, one of the players, Josie Hartnett, still half-naked, ran out of the place in a fury. With fist raised and eyes blazing, he informed two of the greatest hurlers of all time that they were "madmen" – a descriptive term greeted by the future Taoiseach and the Cloyne man with hoots of laughter.'

Cow-Shed

Early in May, Cork and Dublin played a high-scoring draw to mark the opening by Monsignor Sheedy of the Bishop Casey Memorial Park in Mallow. Old reliables Ring, Barry, Clifford, Hartnett, Hayes, Lyons and Creedon all shone, but the newcomer who created the greatest impression was Brendan O'Shea of St Vincent's, whose brother, Christy, would make his mark a year later. The O'Shea family ran a farm near the old Mon field when Knocknaheeny was still a country area and they were often delighted to let Christy Ring and his team-mates tog out in their cow-shed, near the boreen between the farm and the hurling field.

A week after the Mallow match Christy sustained a leg injury in a football game with St Nick's and was unable to play in the opening hurling match at Markievicz Park in Sligo. The injury also prevented him from training with the Cork hurlers for the championship outing against Clare. In the meantime, he did not want to disappoint the people of Sligo and, despite his handicap, he made the journey to Yeats' country for their big occasion.

Sligo Bound

'Christy Ring will Fly to Sligo' was the blaring headline in the *Gaelic Sportsman* in May 1955. The occasion was the official opening of Markievicz Park and, according to the journal, Christy would be brought by 'air lift' from the southern capital.

Where the *Gaelic Sportsman* got its story is unknown at this remove – perhaps some enterprising member of the Sligo grounds committee genuinely thought it might be possible to fly Christy in for the big occasion. In the event, Christy and the rest of the Cork hurling team arrived in the town by car. To make matters worse, Christy was unable to play due to his leg injury.

Nonetheless, thousands of Sligo people turned out to welcome the Cork team when they arrived on Saturday evening. The first Cork cars to appear at Carraroe were two sleek Hudson saloons, which were soon followed by the black Consul driven by Christy himself. When all motors had assembled, the procession headed towards the new pitch where the huge gathering welcomed the hurlers and then the parade re-formed with the Cork players walking behind the Connolly Pipe Band down Pearse Road to the post office.

At the post office the official speeches were made and Jim Barry, who introduced Christy and the other players to the crowd, raised a great cheer when he said: 'We have travelled to many counties in Ireland, but nowhere in the country has the reception given us here tonight been surpassed.'

'The Cork boys were certainly impressed and surprised by the welcome,' said the *Sligo Champion*. 'Autograph hunters had a busy time and the celebrities were kept very busy. The daddy of them all, Christy Ring, had a particularly heavy evening recording his signature on the pastel coloured pages.'

The following day the grounds honouring the patriot, Countess Markievicz, were opened by GAA president, Séamus Mac Fearain, and two matches entertained the crowd, Cork and Galway in hurling; Sligo and Mayo in football.

'Fielding only eight of the side which won the All-Ireland last September the men of the Lee often looked disjointed and hesitant,' wrote the *Champion*. 'Biggest disappointment of all to the big crowd was the inability of Ring to take the field. Injured when playing for his football club, Christy had travelled to Sligo in the hope of being able to line out, but was forced to sit in a Cork car with a swollen left leg while his comrades took the field.'

Galway won a high-scoring game 7-8 to 3-12 with the Duggan brothers, Seanie and Jamesey, Joe Young, Joe Salmon, Hubert Gordon, Johnny Molloy, Tommy Boland, Mickey Burke and Billy O'Neill in top form.

Another Come-Back

In August 1955, Cork and Tipperary met in a tournament game to mark the opening of the Newmarket grounds in north-west Cork.

The ball was thrown in by Canon Hayes of Bansha, founder of Muintir na Tíre, and Christy got the first point. It was the start of a scoring deluge, with Cork winning by 7-11 to 0-6, probably the highest score ever recorded against Tipp.

Dave Creedon was still between the posts and Derry Hayes lined out at full-forward where he scored a goal. The newcomers included Sean French, later to become Lord Mayor of Cork. Christy, who was captain and top scorer (2-6), accepted a fine trophy afterwards. Dave Creedon, who had been sub goalkeeper for so long in the 1940s before winning three-in-a-row in the '50s, decided to make his second departure after that game. Subsequently, however, he made another comeback and won junior championship medals with Nemo Rangers.

A record crowd of 31,019 had the old Park 'bursting at the seams' when the 'Barrs and the Glen met in the county final replay of 1955, and the man responsible for the second meeting was Dave Creedon. 'Not only did he stop rasping shots,' said the *Examiner*, 'but on at least two occasions, he brought down balls which were going over the bar for certain points and cleared them successfully.'

Two early points by Ring proved to be a false dawning the second day as the 'Barrs soon settled and went on to record a seventeen point win. Mick Ryan, Jimmy O'Grady, Mossie Finn, Tony O'Shaughnessy, Jimmy MacKenzie and Mick Driscoll were listed as the main heroes.

An Tostal

Around this time a festival known as An Tostal – Ireland At Home – was introduced to promote tourism and encourage exiles to return for a few weeks. Dermot Breen was one of the chief organisers in Cork and he came up with the idea of an international film festival based at the Savoy. It proved to be very popular and St Patrick's Street used to be thronged with people eager to catch a glimpse of the film stars. Most of them were British like Dawn Adams, Ronald Shiner, John Gregson, Hattie Jacques and Bernard Bresslaw, quite a few came from the continent and occasionally a Hollywood star would come to Cork.

One of the most famous was Virginia Mayo, a ravishing beauty who starred with Danny Kaye in *The Secret Life Of Walter Mitty*. She was given a great reception when she arrived, but she did not

Christy with film star, Jean Seberg, during the Cork Film Fesitval. The Hollywood actress greeted him in the Cage of the old Athletic Grounds just before he lined out with the Glen in the county championship.

endear herself to the people of Cork when she described the city as 'a cemetery with lights'. She was not invited back.

Another beautiful actress to come to the festival was Jean Seberg, star of the Otto Preminger film, *St Joan*. Publicity stunts at the time included photographs of the stars kissing the Blarney Stone, driving a donkey and cart, ringing the Shandon bells or fishing in the South Channel for a 'catch' bought in the nearby English Market. When Jean Seberg came to Cork, however, it was decided to go one better and get her to be photographed with Christy Ring. She was duly driven down to the Athletic Grounds and seated in the official enclosure called the Cage to await the Glen team as they approached the pitch. Christy obligingly agreed to shake the star's hand and be photographed. The picture appeared in the *Examiner* next day and in quite a few places around the city, the question was asked – 'Who's the aul' doll with Ringey?'

CHAPTER FOURTEEN

1956 – A YEAR TO REMEMBER

'In sweltering heat 18,500 coatless spectators saw Cork defeat Waterford by 5-9 to 2-12 in the first meeting of the counties at Fermoy since 1939,' wrote Mick Dunne in *The Irish Press*. 'This was a changed Cork team with five hurlers new to the Munster senior championship and in the end it had to rely on its experienced, time-hardened campaigners, Gerard Murphy, Willie John Daly and Christy Ring to win a July 1st date with Tipperary. And, ironically, Murphy, one of the men who did most to beat Waterford, spent half an hour watching the game from the sideline.'

With Phil Grimes and John Kiely on top in the centre, Waterford dominated the first half, but wasted many chances. 'The umpires' continuous arm-waving at the wides must have broken the hearts of Waterford supporters who saw them doing everything but score,' added Dunne.

The Deise led by 2-8 to 3-3 at half-time, but the introduction of Gerard Murphy and the switching of Willie John from attack to centre-back on Tom Cheasty had a big bearing on the game afterwards.

'Just what would they do in Cork without the remarkable, triumphant touches of Christy Ring?' asked Mick Dunne. 'Certainly they would never win so many games. For long spells he may be held subdued and scoreless, but then when least expected, he swoops to leave his mark on the match. Just like yesterday when he scooped up a free 30 yards out on the left wing and goaled eight minutes from time.'

Newcomer Mick Ryan from Ballyhea had scored Cork's first goal, Paddy Barry the second and Christy the third just before half-time, but Waterford were still in front twelve minutes from the end of the match. Then Mick Ryan pulled on a centre from Terry Kelly and buried it in the net to add to the goal and two points he had already scored. Christy stretched the lead with his late goal and the captain, Mossie Finn, completed the scoring with a point.

'Cork's first-half display left a lot to be desired,' wrote the *Examiner*, 'with John Kiely, Tom Cheasty and Mick Flannelly hitting peak form and Mick O'Connor effecting some brilliant clearances for the Decies. It is no use dwelling on the weak links on the side, but again it must be recorded that the team will probably never fully appreciate the psychological value of Ring's goals. Things were not looking good nearing the interval when he grabbed a pass from Joe Twomey and slipped a ground shot past a sea of legs, and the last goal, direct from a free near the sideline, finally wrote *finis* to the Decies' effort.'

The Munster semi-final against Tipperary was unusual, in that Cork failed to score in the first half until Christy's pointed free just before half-time saved the Leesiders' blushes. At that stage Tipperary, having enjoyed a strong wind advantage, had 2-6 on the board.

'It was Willie John Daly more than any other who held the Cork team together in the first half when he broke up wave after wave of Tipperary attacks,' wrote the *Examiner*. 'How can one forget the fire and dash of the Carrigtwohill man at centre-back in those early and most dangerous moments? At half-time it did seem that the task might be a little too much for the Corkmen, but the genius of Ring had yet to be reckoned with.'

'Inexorably Cork nibbled at the eleven-point margin,' wrote John D. Hickey, 'and eight minutes from the end a superb point by Ring gave the winners the lead for the first time. Four minutes later Ring put on another Cork point, but this score seemed only to incense Tipperary. Back they came in desperate assaults but their only reward was a point by Gerry Doyle a matter of seconds from the end.'

'Mickey Byrne could never fathom Ring,' said John D. Hickey, 'and the Rattler had a most unhappy game.' Afterwards, Mickey remarked as they shook hands, 'You know Christy, we'll have to shoot you.' 'Well Mickey,' said Ring, 'ye've tried everything else.'

Cork won by a point, 1-11 to 2-7, their scores coming from Christy

Ring (0-6), Paddy Barry (1-0), Terry Kelly, Jim Rodgers, Christy O'Shea, Pat Healy and Mattie Fouhy a point each. Limerick, meanwhile, had beaten Clare and set out to defend their Munster title. Mick Mackey was again the brain behind the fleet-footed Shannonsiders and after 50 minutes of play he and his charges had the trophy in sight. Then Christy struck with deadly force and Limerick were not to be heard from again for another seventeen years.

Christy genuflects and kisses Bishop Lucey's ring watched by Limerick captain, Tommy Casey and referee Bob Stakelum prior to the 1956 Munster final.

Three Goals In Five Minutes

'Isn't Donal Broderick doing a great job on Ring?' John D. Hickey overheard a spectator remark as the Munster final entered its closing stages. 'Then,' said John D., 'just as surely as if he had overheard the remark himself and considered it a reflection on his escutcheon, Christy flashed his new wand, the replacement hurley he had been given, and as surely as night follows day Limerick were dethroned.'

'Five minutes of the inimitable Christy Ring at his greatest have given another Munster title to Cork,' wrote Val Dorgan in the *Examiner*. 'With a quarter of an hour left, Limerick, the holders, led by a goal and three points and looked a winning team. But the brilliance of Ring has still to fade. He took a pass from Joe Hartnett, fought his way through the despairing tackles of two Limerick men and from a kneeling position palmed the ball to the net. A minute later he did it again, solo-running down the left-wing for his second goal. Shaken but undaunted, Limerick hit back with Vivian Cobbe slamming home what seemed to be the winning score. But Limerick cheers quickly died as Ring grabbed the sliothar from between the hurleys of two defenders and crashed home the goal that ended the Shannonside hopes.'

'A few years ago I had occasion to describe Ring's display as sheer hurling sorcery,' added John D. 'Now I can state without any

1956 Cork Senior Hurling Team.
Back (from left): Jim Rodgers, Willie John Daly, Gerard Murphy, Paddy Barry, Terry Kelly, Vincie Twomey, John Lyons, Jim Barry. Front: Jack Barrett, Jimmy Brohan, Paddy Philpott, Mick Cashman, Christy Ring, Josie Hartnett, Christy O'Shea, Mick Ryan.

reservation that there is not a forward playing who would have recorded two of his goals of yesterday. The peerless Christy has played many great games but never did a Cork championship triumph more surely belong to the hurling wizard of the age than this 5-5 to 3-5 victory. I doubt if there ever has been a hurling brain which would have thought quickly enough to obtain those three golden goals.'

'It should be remembered,' said John Lyons, 'that at that stage of his career Christy was pacing himself and picking the right moment to strike. He was 35 and he knew he couldn't last a complete hour in top gear. So he played his matches in spurts and, when the time came for him to strike, he'd take on a tank if he had to.'

'Although the 'Barrs were reigning county champions, Christy Ring was captain that day,' said Paddy Tyers. 'It was a curious situation as the 'Barrs had trounced the Glen in the 1955 county final and had no player on the Cork team, while the Glen had four men playing. Of course Tony Shaughnessy, who was out with a knee injury, would have been captain and did, in fact, return as such for the All-Ireland, but for the Munster final Ringey was assigned the captaincy. And a mighty fine job he made of it too.'

Limerick View

'Christy Ring's Munster final,' was how the *Limerick Leader* described it, noting that Ring's courage was not admired half enough. 'At the receiving end of the most desperate of hard knocks, as almost every defender had a swipe at him, he concentrated completely on the ball and went through a barrage of ash that was almost impenetrable without as much as batting an eyelid. He has everything that makes a great hurler, but without that wild abandon that makes light of flying hurleys, tripping feet and vigorous body charges, he could never be the inspiration and the toast of every team to which he has lent his invaluable aid in seventeen years of inter-county hurling grace and glamour.

'Any hurler that wishes to curb Ring must first of all be certain he can match up in some degree to the Cloyne lad's indomitable spirit. That is the most essential of all the attributes. He must be prepared to put his hand and head where a sensible man wouldn't put a crowbar. That's the secret of hurling success against a team like Cork or Tipperary in a Munster championship tie. I'm afraid a few of our lads were too "sensible" to do that on Sunday.'

Young Observer

A young Limerick supporter, Neil O'Donoghue, was enjoying his first Munster final from a vantage point behind the Limerick goal: 'Only ten minutes were left and we were in front by two goals. Christy Ring had been completely dominated by Donal Broderick up to that point. Things were going according to plan. We were repeating the previous year's great feat when Dermot Kelly's magic had destroyed a much fancied Clare team. The begrudgers in 1955 had said the Clare team were drunk on that day in the Gaelic Grounds, but here we were dominating Cork in another final. Then Christy struck – not once, not twice, but three times and sent me bewildered back to Cappamore to wonder and wonder at what I had just seen. There were no help lines or counsellors in those days but, if there were, they'd have been busy in Limerick that week.'

1956 Munster Senior Hurling Champions.
Back (from left) – John Lyons, Mick Regan, Josie Hartnett, Paddy Barry, Christy Ring, Paddy Philpott, Vincie Twomey, Gerard Murphy, Jim Barry (trainer). Front – Pat Dowling, Willie John Daly, Florrie O'Mahony, Mick Cashman, Christy O'Shea, Terry Kelly, Jimmy Brohan.

'Years later,' added Neil, 'when I had moved to Cork and was teaching in Farranferris, I had Christy Junior in class and got to know his father as a proud and concerned parent and as a gentleman. I reminded him once of that far-off day in Thurles. With a glint in his eye, he said, "That was a good day".'

From time to time Christy had been branded a magician, a wizard and a sorcerer for his hurling skills, but the 1956 exhibition had one pedant sending us all to the dictionary when he wrote: 'Ring has given many spell-binding performances over the years but his coup de grace against hapless Limerick really showed what a "thaumaturge" the Cloyne man truly is in hurling.'

Finals Deferred

'Looking back on 1956,' said Anna Crotty, 'I suppose you'd think that it was a great year for us with Cork reaching three All-Ireland finals – hurling, football and camogie – but it was a dreadful year really, not just because we lost all three finals, but because of the polio epidemic in the city.'

Poliomyelitis, an infectious viral disease causing temporary or permanent paralysis, hit Cork city in the summer of 1956 and over 100 cases were confirmed. The young were particularly vulnerable, and schools scheduled to re-open in early September were ordered to remain closed for at least two weeks. By then the polio epidemic appeared to be lessening in virulence, although by August several deaths had been recorded and there were 137 confirmed cases in the city. Cork had qualified for both the hurling and football finals and there was a great dread in Dublin that the influx of supporters would bring the disease to the capital. As a result the Central Council, on the advice of the health authorities, deferred both games from the customary dates.

Rockies Return

With the All-Ireland now postponed, the first Sunday in September saw the Glen and the 'Barrs play in the county semi-final. The match catapulted three young hurlers on to the All-Ireland panel: Jackie Daly, Pat Healy and Willie Walsh. For Daly, who scored 2-2, one point more than Ring, it was a personal *tour de force*.

John Lyons, Sean Kenefick, Vincie Twomey, Seanie O'Riordan, Josie Hartnett and Ring also shone for the Glen, while, apart from Willie Walsh, the 'Barrs had top notch hurlers in Jimmy Ring, Timmy Cronin, Seamus O'Callaghan and Tony O'Shaughnessy.

'We beat the 'Barrs that day by a big margin – four or five goals – and it gave us sweet revenge for the '55 final,' recalled John Lyons.

The county final was against Blackrock, who had not won the title since 1931. It was to be a happy day for the Rockies, even though according to captain, Mick Cashman, 'We weren't given much of a chance. But we had a great team, especially with players like Pat Philpott, Jimmy Brohan, Martin Thompson, John Redmond, Seamus Hearne, Florrie Mahony, John Bennett, Michael Murphy and Sean "Roundy" Horgan.'

Great Final

Wexford's progress to the All-Ireland was mirrored in Leinster's win over Munster on St Patrick's Day, when Nicky Rackard and Tim Flood ran riot with the southern backs. Des Ferguson held Christy Ring to two points that day, although the maestro also set up Jimmy Smyth for Munster's only goal.

Leinster won by 5-11 to 1-7, the biggest defeat Munster sustained from their old rivals during the golden age of interprovincial hurling. There were nine Wexford men on the team, along with Dublin's Des Ferguson and Liam Cashin, Kilkenny's Willie Walsh, Sean Clohessy and Dick Rockett, and Westmeath's 'Jobber' McGrath.

The 1956 final itself, so redolent of memorable moments, produced its share of 'happenings' that never occurred, but grew in people's imaginations as time went by. Art Foley's late save in particular, a decisive factor in the outcome, quickly became shrouded in mystique and raised many an argument.

The hurling final was held on the unusual date of 23 September and, though the attendance was marginally smaller than 1954 – over 83,000 this time – interest was just as great. Christy was going for his ninth title, and Wexford were seeking the essential imprimatur of their greatness: victory over Cork in the All-Ireland.

'This was a game that had everything,' wrote Pádraig Puirséal. 'Fierce hip to hip clashes, dazzling solo runs, glorious goals,

Believe it or not but Christy is in the thick of this tussle with Nick O'Donnell and Bobby Rackard, showing how closely the Wexford men marked him in the 1956 final.

unbelievable saves, swaying fortunes, flashes of dazzling stickwork that might have been equalled but could hardly have been surpassed by Cúchulainn or Fionn MacCumhaill; and to crown it all, the ever-exciting exchanges, hard, fast and fair, were leavened by a spirit of sportsmanship that set the true seal of greatness on victors and vanquished alike.'

The game started badly for Cork, a point by Tim Flood and a goal by Padge Kehoe shooting Wexford into a strong position within three minutes of play. Then, to make matters worse, Tony O'Shaughnessy was forced to retire with a head injury and his place was taken by Vincie Twomey.

Three points by Ring and one each by Mick Regan and Eamonn Goulding kept Cork within striking distance at the interval, although quick-thinking Mick Morrissey denied them a goal when he swept away a ball from the goal line as the forwards bore down on it. Wexford led by 1-6 to 0-5 at the break, their other points coming from Flood, Rackard, Martin Codd and Tom Dixon.

'In the dressing room at half-time,' said one of the Cork selectors, 'we were toying with the notion of bringing Tony Shaughnessy back into the game, moving Vincie Twomey, who was having a great game, to centre-back and sending Willie John Daly up to the attack where some of our men weren't playing well at all. We didn't carry out that plan I'm afraid, but had we done so, it could have won the game for Cork.'

Points from close and long range frees by Nicky and Billy Rackard and one from play after a lively solo run by Martin Codd had Wexford seven in front eight minutes into the second half. But just as it looked as if the game was slipping away from Cork, Christy Ring suddenly transformed what had been a top-rate final into an unforgettable one. He slammed a close-in free to the net and then raced through the defence to send a left-handed shot over the bar.

Those scores set Cork ablaze and, after Padge Kehoe had slipped over a fine point for Wexford, Paddy Barry hit back with an even better one for Cork. Then, snapping up a well-placed pass from Terry Kelly, the Sars man dashed through again to record a great goal. The sides were level, the Cork fans jubilant and the stadium emblazoned with red and white colours as Ring went through again

*Christy and Bobby Rackard tussle for possession watched by
Ted Bolger and Willie John Daly.*

Christy gives Cork a temporary lead despite Bobby's attention.

*Bobby effects a clearance despite Christy's attempted hand-block.
Josie Hartnett and Billy Rackard look on.*

and, though hindered by Bobby Rackard, palmed the ball over the crossbar. With just ten minutes to go Cork were in front.

If the Wexford supporters were despondent at that stage, their gloom was not reflected in the spirit of the players. A relentless determination not to allow a repeat of the 1954 result fired the Wexford team. They brought play back towards the Cork goal and a point by Nicky Rackard levelled the scores again within a minute. In the pulsating moments that followed, the beleaguered Cork backs gave away two frees which Nicky promptly converted into vital points. They were the two scores that had Wexford ahead in those dramatic closing minutes when Christy made his last determined bid to save the day. He was foiled by Art Foley whose save has since become part of Wexford folk history.

'I was quite close to the play on that occasion,' said Mick Regan. 'Most people, I believe, thought Foley had caught Ring's shot and then cleared the ball. My memory of it is completely different. As I saw it, Ring got the ball in the left full-forward position, beat his man and ran across the goal. Unfortunately, Paddy Barry was in his way, but he did not hesitate, but continued on and knocked Paddy out of his path with his left shoulder, continuing past the square which, unfortunately, narrowed the angle. I think Foley moved forward in anticipation of the shot. Ring did hit a very good shot about knee high. The ball hit Foley's hurley which killed the force and the ball moved upwards towards his face. It was then he caught the ball and cleared it automatically and the rest is history.'

'I think it was a 70 or a free that came in,' said Christy, speaking to Donncha Ó Dulaing on RTÉ radio twenty years later. 'Nick O'Donnell had a habit of batting the ball out and Bobby Rackard was breathing down my neck for the hour. I waited till the last minute and when Nicko batted the ball out, I went out and collected it. There were a lot of things happened between that and the [shot at] goal, but I was kind of hampered a small bit, you know. Foley brought off a great save. I thought I had it, but he thought differently.'

'And then you ran in to shake hands with him?' asked Donnacha. 'No, I was coming out from behind him actually and I tapped him on the back and said, "Well done".' 'What was his reaction at the time?' 'I don't think he saw me really, to be perfectly honest.'

The save led to a clearance by Jim Morrissey and a decisive late goal by Nicky Rackard from a pass by Ryan and with only 30 seconds remaining, Tom Dixon crowned Wexford's greatest hour with the last point. Result: Wexford 2-14 Cork 2-8.

When the final whistle brought the magnificent struggle to an end, the sporting gestures which had begun with Ring's congratulatory pat on Foley's back, continued for another few minutes. An exuberant Nick O'Donnell planted a kiss on the Corkman's cheek and then helped Bobby Rackard and Art Foley to carry Christy shoulder-high off the pitch.

'Martin Codd was our best man today,' said Nicky Rackard afterwards and his opinion was shared by many people. 'Codd made a very big contribution to the victory,' wrote John D. Hickey, who also spoke highly of Seamus Hearne, Mick Morrissey, Nick O'Donnell and Padge Kehoe. 'Until the closing minutes Nicky Rackard was well held by John Lyons. His brother Bobby also had Ring's measure until the closing stages. Although the Cork wizard out-foxed him on a few occasions, the Rathnure man, like Jim English, Jim Morrissey, Ned Wheeler, Tom Ryan and Tom Dixon subscribed generously to the winning endeavour.'

As the shadows lengthened across the pitch that evening, few people could have imagined that ten years would elapse before Cork would be back in a senior final at Croke Park. And nobody at all could have envisaged a 45-year-old maestro being asked to wear the red jersey again in that distant year.

At the close of 1956, a *Gaelic Echo* writer, 'MacLughadha', selected his top ten hurlers. It was no surprise that Wexford dominated his selection with five nominations, but it was not the All-Ireland champions who garnered the No. 1 position. MacLughadha's hurling stars of 1956 were:

1. Christy Ring (Cork)
2. Nicky Rackard (Wexford)
3. Billy Rackard (Wexford)
4. Art Foley (Wexford)
5. Seamus Ryan (Limerick)
6. Jim English (Wexford)
7. Paddy Kenny (Tipperary)
8. Paddy Philpott (Cork)
9. Johnny McGovern (Kilkenny)
10. Nick O'Donnell (Wexford)

CHAPTER FIFTEEN

RETIREMENT?

After the All-Ireland final there was much speculation about Christy's future. At 36 and with so many medals and memories to cherish, it seemed he must retire.

Christy, of course, said nothing about retiring. It was only years later when he was still hurling at the highest level, that he declared he would continue playing as long as he got enjoyment out of it. In fact, Christy would never formally retire. When his playing days with the Glen ended in 1967, he continued to take part in exhibition matches all over the country, as well as in America and Australia.

'Every game had an importance for me,' said Christy, 'and I looked forward eagerly to every outing whether it was challenge, tournament or championship. I entered every game with enthusiasm. There was no such thing as an unimportant match. There are times when the opposition is very poor, but to go into a game with this frame of mind is inviting trouble. I never had time for players who adopt a half-hearted approach and to my mind such players are a liability on a team.'

Christy made his first appearance of 1957 in the Railway Cup semi-final and denied Connacht a deserved win with a late goal. 'Not, mark you, one of those brilliant efforts which usually come from the stick of the Cloyne man,' said the *Examiner*, 'but one of those freak goals seldom seen in first-class hurling. Mike Sweeney in goal saved well, but in attempting to clear, dropped the ball and Paddy Burke lifted the sliothar and as he tried to clear, Ring blocked the shot and the ball rolled over the line for the equaliser.'

If Christy's goal in the drawn match was a lucky one, there was nothing fortuitous about his form in the replay. 'Ring's Great Goal

Put Munster on Road to Victory' was the *Examiner* headline. 'Ring was great as ever,' went the report. 'Even if he had done nothing but score that first great goal, in which he controlled a hopping ball, sold his opponent a beautiful dummy and finished with a great shot, it would have been worthwhile travelling a long way to see.'

Connacht made a brave bid to recover in the second half but then came what the *Examiner* described as one of the most beautifully worked goals ever to be scored in Limerick: 'It was Paddy Kenny who scored it, but it was the irresistible Ring who made it. He took the ball from Walsh on the left wing, literally waved the Tipperary man into position and then he swept a beautiful 30-yard pass straight in front of the right corner-forward who obliged by connecting it first time to the net.'

'Brilliant Display by Ring in Railway Cup Win' blared the *Examiner* after 43,805 saw Munster beat Leinster 5-7 to 2-5. 'Christy Ring drew sparingly on his extensive hurling repertoire for a performance which ensured another Munster triumph,' the report said. 'His first point was a masterly cut from the ground, his first goal came after he grabbed a ball some 40 yards out and drove it home past Foley and O'Donnell with vicious force. His second goal was a ground snap shot from Kenny's cross and his hat-trick, a cut which he took on the turn when Foley had lost the ball. His point from play in the second half might have been a goal if he had not been held up by three defenders.'

'Munster had a captain and full-forward whose long sustained hurling has pauperised our journalists in the search for descriptive adjectives,' said Carbery. 'Christy Ring did not have to run or forage as much as usual for his scores, but every one of his 3-5 was scored with the master's touch.'

So much for talk about Ring's retirement. In April he was back in Croke Park hurling with his usual brio against Dublin and another league game saw him in top form against Wexford. 'Ring, despite the fact that he was always dogged by Mick Morrissey, was the master craftsman,' wrote the *Examiner*. 'One of his points in the second half was hurling wizardry while the incident which preceded his goal underlined his remarkable power and strength. He fairly crashed his way through six-foot Wexford backs and Foley had to be on his toes to pick off the palmed ball.'

'I doubt if the thought of retiring from hurling even entered Christy's mind after the '56 final,' said Terry Kelly. 'He was still in great shape, he didn't drink or smoke, he simply loved playing hurling and even at that stage, he was still learning new tricks to improve his game and baffle his opponents even more. He got injured in the Munster championship of 1957 and missed the final against Waterford, but even that had no effect on his resolve to play on while he enjoyed it.'

'I was delighted to meet Christy Ring after Cork's game with Wexford at New Ross a couple of weeks ago,' said Nicky Rackard shortly after he had brought his own illustrious career to an end in 1957. 'He was very pleased with Cork's display and I saw that his sights are already fixed on next year's Munster championship. This fabulous hurler amazes me. His enthusiasm for the game never wanes. He still bubbles with the spirit of a youngster setting out on his hurling career. This is the spirit which keeps him going after so many gruelling hurling years. And it will continue to do so, for I can tell you now that Christy has no thought of retiring for a long time yet.'

A Cork Religion

Walter Hagen, the colourful and self-confident golfer of the 1920s, used to preface every tournament by teasingly asking his fellow competitors, 'Well, guys, which of you is gonna be second today?'

Christy was also known at times to make dispiriting remarks to his opponents, usually before a game. Lining up at midfield for the start one day, his Tipperary marker, a much younger and faster man said, 'Well Christy, I won't be seeing much of you today.' 'That's all right,' said Ring,'I'll be watching the ball and you won't be seeing much of that either.'

Another well-known story tells of a young Cork hurler who had the misfortune to suffer an appendicitis a few days before his first All-Ireland final. Christy visited him in hospital and, having endured much wailing and lamenting, finally silenced the unlucky player. 'Ah, will ya give over,' he said, 'it could be a lot worse.' 'How could it be a lot worse?' moaned the player. 'It could be me in that bed,' said Christy.

'I remember sitting behind a couple at Croke Park for a Railway Cup game one year,' said Pádraig Puirséal, 'when the man nudged his female companion and said "There's Christy Ring". She must have been a stranger to Croke Park for she said, "He's a Corkman, isn't he?" "A Corkman," her friend replied. "He's more than a Corkman. He's a Cork religion."

'Every man has his favourite picture of Christy in action,' wrote Patrick Conn (real name Terry Connealy) in *Scene* magazine. 'For my money it was when he scored one of three goals in a Railway Cup final against Leinster. Then, a head high ball bulleted towards Christy leaning on his hurley with the nonchalant air of a golfer waiting to tee up. He leaped 2 yards, chopped the hurley against the flight, then reverse hit the spinning ball between his legs as he dummy swerved to the left to leave the Leinster defence flat footed. It was a goal in a million and on Croke Park's Hill 16 that afternoon Clonakilty farmers sobbed like children with the unexpected delight, a savouring of skill to flavour years of pub memories, a priceless, unforgettable dish for the hurling gourmet. Yet, when I spoke to him, Christy scarcely recalled the occasion. "You can call me a gambler," he said. "I try a move a hundred times and, when it comes off in a big match, the crowd goes wild and I say to myself – it worked."'

'Every admirer carries away his own special gem from Ring's many classic performances,' agreed Fr Bernie Cotter, a Youghal man who played with Christy on the Cork team. 'Such was his resilience – he could be prostrate at one moment on the grass at Thurles, Limerick or Croke Park and seconds later he'd produce a palpable ripple of excitement from the crowd when emerging from nowhere to perform some feat that could scarcely be imagined, much less attempted, like the incident in the Railway Cup final of 1955 when, stretched full length on the ground, he met a centre from the wing with a drop-shot that shook the net for a never-to-be-forgotten goal.'

Fr Cotter also recalled the simple modesty and humility of the man. 'Strolling along a street in Limerick before lunch on the day of the Cork-Clare Munster championship match in 1958 when Christy was trying to calm my jittery nerves, I foolishly asked him, "How many goals are you going to score today, Christy?" His reply was one I shall always remember. "It is not easy to score goals, Father."'

What Did Ring Say?

What did Ring say to Mackey as he walked past him the day Justin Nelson, the Clonmel photographer, captured the moment for posterity? 'I wouldn't tell that to the Bishop of Limerick,' quipped the legendary Ahane hurler when the question was put to him on television years later.

The incident occurred during the 1957 championship semi-final against Tipperary, when Mick Mackey was doing umpire duty and Christy retired with a broken wrist. He passed Mackey as he walked to the subs' bench and their verbal exchange most likely related to something that had happened in the Cork goalmouth during the first half.

It started when Mick Cashman on the goal-line got under a lobbing ball. As he made the save, two Tipperary forwards charged into the goalmouth with the obvious intention of bundling him into the net. Before they reached him, however, Cashman threw the ball clear and then the referee faced a dilemma. Should he award a free out to Cork because the forwards had charged the goalie or should he award a free in to Tipperary because Cashman had thrown the ball clear? Before he could make up his mind, Mick Mackey picked up the green flag and signalled a Tipperary goal. As Cashman and the Tipp forwards were embroiled in the net, he may have thought the ball was in there too but, thanks to the quick-thinking Blackrock man, the sliothar was resting safely a yard or so beyond the end-line. So the referee, exercising Solomon-like wisdom, extricated himself from a tricky situation by awarding a 70!

Twelve minutes into the second half, Christy went down with a hand injury and while medical assistance was provided the large crowd waited anxiously to see if he would remain in the game. But even the maestro, a man who probably incurred and endured more injuries on the field than any other hurler, could not continue playing with a broken wrist.

'After Ringey's departure I thought we were doomed to defeat,' said Terry Kelly, 'but Paddy Barry sent in a shot which Roger Mounsey batted out. Luckily enough, I was already on the way in and the ball came directly to me in transit. So without stopping, I had no trouble in handpassing it to the net. No sooner had I done so than a woman, reeking of drink, ran on to the field and gave me an almighty hug.'

After the match Christy was taken to Barrington's hospital for treatment and on his return to Cork he entered the Bons Secours where his wrist was encased in plaster. It was clear that the injury would keep him out of the Munster final against Waterford. His absence would be an immeasurable loss to the county and indeed the Rebels went down to the Deise, 1-11 to 1-6.

Ring, leaving the pitch injured, has words with Mick Mackey, an umpire.

Christy was out of action for some time with his wrist in plaster and many believed that the injury would force the 36-year-old veteran to end his career. They were wrong. He was back again in October, seemingly as good if not better than ever.

Great Return

'One man never made a team, except perhaps, the amazing Christy Ring,' wrote Tom Cryan in *The Irish Press* in October 1957. 'The Cloyne maestro returned to the Cork hurling scene yesterday and nearly 20,000 people saw him almost beat the All-Ireland finalists on his own. Three goals from his flashing stick had Waterford in dire trouble near the end and, when he looked like sinking their hopes, it was perseverence, speed and good team-work that saved them.'

'What a fantastic return it was,' added Cryan. 'Plainly the majority of the crowd came to see him in action for the first time since he fractured his wrist against Tipperary in the championship – and they got more than they bargained for. He struck first with an opportunistic goal, following a shot by Terry Kelly. Then, with his team-mates inexplicably starving him, he was forced into his shell but not for good. All he wanted was the glimmer of a chance and he got it six minutes after the interval. A rasping shot then left Waterford goalie Frank O'Donoghue powerless. Two minutes later the genius that has lifted Ring up among the immortals was there for all to see when he doubled on a dropping ball that appeared to end Waterford's hopes. But Paddy Barry retired with an eye injury and his exit meant that the Waterford backs could devote most of their attention to Ring.'

Frankie Walsh scored the last three points that decided the game, but Tom Cryan asserted: 'If there were a couple more men like Paddy Barry and Mick Regan in the Cork attack, Ring would have got the chances he wanted.'

Railway Cup

'The Railway Cup was a great event in the 1950s,' said Frank Stockwell, the Galway football star. 'It usually attracted over 40,000 spectators on St Patrick's Day and gave us a great opportunity of meeting hurlers and footballers from other counties. I became very friendly with Christy Ring and Jimmy Brohan thanks to the Railway Cup. In 1957, just before the first match, Christy challenged me to a bet – which of us would score most that afternoon? I was playing well at the time and I put my money down, thinking I had a chance of winning the bet, but Ringey, the rogue, went out and scored 3-5. How could I follow that?'

'Christy Ring, the Cloyne maestro, aided in varying degrees by fourteen other Munster men, humbled the holders Leinster,' wrote *The Irish Press* after the 1957 game. 'Seldom can any one man have done so much to break the hearts of fifteen opponents as Christy Ring did through the opening 30 minutes. Munster led by twelve points at the interval – Ring's own total in the first half.'

'Ringey electrified the crowd that day and set Croke Park ablaze with three goals in the first half,' said Tony Wall. 'I particularly remember one of them when he raced out to the 21 and pulled left-handed on a ground ball which nearly broke the net behind Art Foley.'

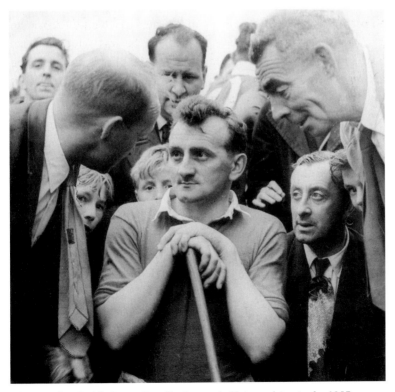

Christy offers Paddy Barry (kneeling) some half-time advice in the 1957 Munster final. On the right is Denis Conroy.

CHAPTER SIXTEEN

1958 – SITTING IT OUT

Justin Nelson's famous photograph of an injured Ring leaving the 1957 Munster championship remains the most abiding visual image of Christy departing from a game before full-time.

Almost forgotten are two instances of his premature retirement from matches the following year – one resulting from a foul stroke in an all-star exhibition game and the other a very controversial sending-off in a club match.

'Christy Ring went to the line in the Rest of Ireland v Kilkenny game in consequence of having come in contact with the more lethal part of the hurley,' reported the *Gaelic Weekly* in March and six months later Raidió Éireann announced in its Monday morning news bulletin, 'The famous hurler Christy Ring was sent off in the Cork county championship yesterday'.

'When is this kind of thing to stop?' asked Eamonn Young regarding the game in Kilkenny. 'Never,' he replied. 'Not as long as a referee has only two eyes. Mr Pádraig Ó Caoimh reports indiscretions he himself witnesses and so do some officers of my acquaintance. But, oh so often, we have referees' reports ignoring incidents seen by the public and then when we discuss the matter at a board meeting, there is a wall of silence in spite of the fact that several responsible members of the board witnessed the game.'

'Tom Sullivan of Fedamore refereed the game in which Christy was hurt and I believe he was well downfield with his back turned when the blow or blows were struck. I'm not very sure of this, but it seems the umpires weren't able to help. What then is a ref to do? He knows right well that something has happened, but can hardly spare the time for sworn affadavits from a score of people who might have seen the incident. Independent observers are needed and should, I feel, be asked to comment but the umpire, as the ref's friend and fellow official, has a definite responsibility.'

Eamonn Young was to have problems of his own around this time when he wrote his footballing memoirs in an English newspaper. Mick Mackey and Wexford's Paddy Kehoe had already written their stories in the same paper and the coverage was seen in some quarters as good promotion for hurling and football. Not so in the Cork county board, where Youngie was suspended.

As for Christy he soon recovered from his injury and was back in action the following month helping Cork to beat the All-Ireland champions. One of the biggest crowds at a league match down the Park saw Cork winning by 4-6 to 3-3. Liam Dowling and Billy Barry of Sars had a goal each, Jimmy Coughlan (St Vincent's) and Terry Kelly scored a point apiece, but it was the redoubtable Christy who dominated the scoring with two goals and four points. Kilkenny learned that day that you do not mistreat the maestro with impunity.

Suspension

Six months later, Christy lined out for the Glen in the county semi-final against Sars, the reigning champions, before 15,106 spectators. He scored five points in the first half – two from frees – and pointed a further free afterwards. Then, in remarkable circumstances, he was sent off. Christy and Mick Barry became involved in a dispute, although Christy refused to trade blows with Mick. While Ringey hardly defended himself, the matter was over in seconds, as referee Charlie Conway quickly intervened. He took both players' names and promptly sent the two men off.

One of the most respected referees in the country, Charlie had a reputation for strict discipline, no nonsense and no foul language. When it came to dispensing punishment, he was no respecter of reputations. Christy knew his form and that could explain his reluctance to get involved in fisticuffs with Charlie around.

Christy's sending off was the talk of the town for days and its inclusion on Raidió Éireann's morning news bulletin was something extremely unusual for the time, when sports items rarely made the main news.

The Glen won the match by seven points and then faced the daunting task of beating the 'Barrs without Ring or Joe Twomey, who had been sent off shortly after the Barry-Ring dismissals. Noel Lynam was drafted in at centre-forward and young Pat Healy took Christy's place in the corner. Although Tony Shaughnessy, Cyril Healy and eighteen-year-old Peter Doolan were outstanding for the 'Barrs, Glen Rovers, with Sean Kenefick, Mick McCarthy, Bernie Hackett, Frank Daly, John Lyons and Sean O'Brien in great form, achieved the 'impossible' and won their sixteenth title by 4-6 to 3-5.

Eighteen years had elapsed since the Blackpool club had won the county championship without the services of the Cloyne man. Yet here they were now on top of the Cork hurling world, and Christy a mere spectator at the county final.

Still, if it had not been for a superlative display of goalkeeping by Sean O'Brien things might have been much different. 'Young Sean O'Brien was in the form of his life,' wrote the *Examiner*. 'Several times his light body dived full length in the mud to turn certain goals around the post – ground-clipping shots, that are the bane of all goalies, he stopped with the assuredness and dexterity of Tony Reddan.'

Following his suspension Christy had to sit it out for eight weeks, but when he returned in time for a league match against Wexford, he seemed to be more devastating than ever. As for comments claiming that the Glen did not need him anymore, Christy would soon render those remarks risible.

Back Again

Itching to get back after his eight-week lay-off, Christy took just 90 seconds to score his first goal against Wexford, then got another – 'a wonderful goal', John D. Hickey called it – and added three points to make him top scorer on his fantastic return. 'Ring gave a sparkling display throughout,' said *The Irish Press*. Cork won by a point and another remarkable feature of the hour was Padge Kehoe's failure to score from three successive penalties in the dying moments. The first two were stopped, but frees were conceded before the ball could be cleared – the third went inches wide.

Christy was also good in other league matches, notably against Galway when, according to the *Examiner*, 'Ring's genius – he scored 3-2 altogether – and a very encouraging display by young Pat Fitzgerald were the cheering things from the Cork view.'

As was typical of the time, there were popular tournament and challenge games and Christy also revelled in these. He scored Cork's total of 1-6 against Tipperary at Thurles and he delighted the Buttevant crowd with another stylish display in the defeat of Kilkenny. 'The attendance, of course, gloried in Ring,' wrote the *Examiner*, 'and indeed the maestro did much to earn their admiration. He had a particularly brilliant goal in the first half when, hemmed in by defenders, he shot the ball backwards between his legs to the back of the net.'

Godfather

In the Munster championship, Ring was described as a 'fairy godfather' by the *Examiner* after his display against Clare. 'Without him Cork would have lost. There can be no doubt about that for with the hurley he favoured instead of a wand, he scored two second-half goals that deflated Clare's soaring hopes as surely as does a pin prick a balloon and he did it almost as speedily. He wore a cap and played left corner-forward. Surely it is superfluous to say his name.'

'Clare were leading by ten points at half-time,' said Mick Regan, 'and as we were lining up for the restart Christy said, "We need a point, lads". I thought if it's points we have to get, it'll take some time to catch up, not knowing what he had in mind. The ball was thrown in and he got it and pointed. That left three clear goals in it. After that he scored a goal, engineered a free and scored another goal and for the third he passed the ball to Pat Fitzgerald who scored. Finally, from the Clare puck-out by Mick Hayes, who mustn't have noticed Christy in the Cork half-back line, it reached him and he put the ball over the bar for the lead. Needless to mention Clare were deflated and easily beaten.'

'An instance of the complex Ring inspires in opposing backs is worthy of elaboration,' wrote the *Examiner*. 'It came in the first minute of the game. The ball raced along the left wing with Purcell pursued by Ring in full cry. Then Ring veered infield in anticipation of the Clareman's clearance, coolly grabbed the ball when it came his way and put it between the posts to the accompaniment of a roar of appreciation from the crowd.'

'That was the kind of score that resulted from Christy's uncanny reading of an opponent's play,' said Con Murphy. 'I remember an incident when I was refereeing a county final. There was a lobbing ball going into the goalmouth and naturally the forwards were moving in to get to that ball but, as I was moving in to observe matters, Christy started running out against me. He had read the situation so clearly that he anticipated the ball being cleared and it was cleared almost into his hand. He tapped it back over the bar and I'll always remember his remark to me, "What did ya think of that, Murphy?"'

Prior to the Munster final Christy sustained a rib injury in a

At a commemoration ceremony for IRB patriot and All-Ireland footballer, Denis O'Callaghan at Nadd graveyard in 1961 were (from left) Florence O'Donoghue, Tom Barry (auctioneer), Sean O Hegarty, Jim Hurley, Weeshie Murphy and Christy Ring.

challenge against Galway and there was some doubt that he would last the hour against Tipperary. Despite the handicap he played to the finish, scored Cork's first goal after fifteen minutes and roved out to the half-forward line when Tipp were two points ahead near the end. 'In a late effort to snatch the lead,' said the *Examiner*, 'Ring slammed in a high ball that Dowling got in his hand in front of the Tipp goal but he failed to hold it.' Tipperary won by 2-6 to 2-4 and went on to take the All-Ireland crown later. While there were no All-Star selections in those days, the *Sunday Review* picked the following line-up as the Best Hurling Team of 1958:

Ollie Walsh
(Kilkenny)

Jimmy Brohan   Michael Maher   John Maher
(Cork)   (Tipperary)   (Kilkenny)

Jimmy Finn   Tony Wall   Tom McGarry
(Tipperary)   (Tipperary)   (Limerick)

Joe Salmon   Phil Grimes
(Galway)   (Waterford)

Donie Nealon   Ned Wheeler   Jimmy Doyle
(Tipperary)   (Wexford)   (Tipperary)

Larry Keane   Christy Ring   Sean Clohessy
(Tipperary)   (Cork)   (Kilkenny)

Hurleys

'When Ring hit the ball you wouldn't see it go into the back of the net,' said Theo English (to Dermot Crowe). 'You'd watch what hurley he used and you'd model yourself on Ring. He always hurled with a heavy stick.'

Christy's choice of hurley always attracted interest and discussion. Such was his attachment to his hurley, that for many of his Shell years Christy carried it in the cab of his truck.

A fascinating insight into Christy's personal choice of hurley is revealed in the Carrigtwohill club history during an item on Mickey McCarthy, whose hurleys were also used by Paddy Barry, Tony Wall, Frank Cummins, Jimmy Barry-Murphy, Denis Murphy, Charlie McCarthy, Ray Cummins and John Fenton, right down to Brian Corcoran before Mickey died, well into his eighties, in 1995. His reputation as a hurley-maker was just beginning when word of him reached Christy and their relationship lasted most of Christy's career.

'Ring would tell you how he wanted his hurleys,' said Mick, 'and when you did your best he was quite happy. But back then he was so far ahead of his time. One morning he came into me with a four-iron golf club. He wanted the bas of the hurley angled like the face of the four-iron so he could get under the ball. That way he could hit the ball over the bar from 50 yards off the ground, no bother. He was always thinking.'

Mick said that Christy liked his hurleys lighter as he got older. 'He wanted the bas shortened, long before it was fashionable to shorten it, but he always liked the bas to be heavy. So I would insert molten lead to give it weight.'

CHAPTER SEVENTEEN

1959 – HURLER OF THE YEAR

There was widespread disbelief when the Rest of Ireland selectors named their team to play Tipperary early in 1959 – Christy Ring was dropped.

It was a decision that upset Cork followers and must certainly have hurt Christy but, as the year progressed, the Rest selectors were to be increasingly embarrassed by their action.

When the new Hogan Stand was opened in June, Christy scored four goals and five points in helping Munster to win the Railway Cup and later in the year he got a whopping 6-4 in a league game against mighty Wexford. His performances made the headlines on numerous occasions, he was the year's top scorer again and in December he was chosen as the Caltex Hurler of the Year!

What one scribe called 'the biggest bombshell in hurling history' gave Christy an extra incentive to make his mark in 1959, and he did so with such effectiveness that he was back on the Rest of Ireland team in 1960, when he was close to 40 and again the following year.

Naturally Cork people were anxious to see for themselves just how good 38-year-old Christy was in 1959 and there was a large crowd at the Churches tournament between the Glen and Sars in February, but suffering from the flu, Christy did not play. Sars won by 7-7 to 3-6 with Paddy Barry scoring 5-1 in a remarkable exhibition of hurling.

The team chosen by the Rest selectors did in fact beat the All-Ireland champions by three goals a fortnight later. Despite the victory, local pride had been hurt. The *Examiner* faithfully reported the Rest's 6-5 to 3-5 win against Tipperary, but still felt aggrieved that Christy was not playing. 'Here it is pertinent to wonder what might have happened were Christy in the left corner. The answer must surely be the humbling of the champions for, though Donal Whelan and Terry Kelly satisfied with a brace of goals each, Ring would surely have reaped a richer harvest on the chances that offered.'

Christy was back in action for the Beamish Shield final, a game played with championship fervour, with the Glen beating Sars and Joe Twomey hurling in inspired fashion. He also made his mark in the county championship opener against a youthful Na Piarsaigh. Three goals from Joe Twomey, Noel Lynam and Christy meant that the young Na Piarsaigh combination were out of their depth.

'Christy Ring Strikes Brilliant Form Again' was the *Examiner* headline after Cork beat Limerick in a tournament in April. 'Bright sunshine warmed the crowd,' went the report, 'and they were further gladdened by a Christy Ring who was back in his best form. Lining out in his customary corner-forward position, he moved at the interval to the 40 where his overhead play and, more especially, his placing of passes for Mick Quane in the right corner brought rounds of applause.'

Thus, after a few flourishes at local level, Christy was ready to return to Croke Park for the grand opening of the magnificent new Hogan Stand. The occasion would be marked by impressive ceremonials, including a pageant entitled 'They Died That Our Flag May Fly' and a fine speech by the President of Ireland, Sean T. O'Kelly, who officially opened the stand and paid tribute to Pádraig Ó Caoimh who masterminded the project.

But at the end of that glorious June afternoon, it was not the ceremonials, the speeches or the immense new stand that people were talking about. It was the magnificent hurling of Christy Ring.

Pageantry

'There was pageantry and music, reverie and remembrance – and there in all its magnitude stood the £250,000 new stand. But outshining everything else on this day in Croke Park was the splendour of a genius from Cork whose hurling wizardry crushed and humbled Connacht. Oh yes, we were truly thankful for Christy Ring from Cloyne.'

So began *The Irish Press* report under the headline 'Christy Ring humbled Connacht', while John D. Hickey in the *Independent* was equally grateful. 'I give thanks that Christy Ring was playing for the very good reason that one of the greatest hurling wizards of all time provided the only real entertainment of the hour.'

After the match as Tony Wall, the captain, led the players up the steps of the new Hogan Stand to collect their Railway Cup medals, Christy was not among them. He was already in the dressing room nursing his injuries and contemplating a personal triumph that yielded four goals and five points. His gold medal was accepted on his behalf by Jim Barry.

Christy scoring one of the four goals and five points he got for Munster in 1959 the day the last Hogan Stand was opened.

'Nobody of the 23,248 attendance,' added the *Examiner*, 'could have failed to be entranced by such classical, impudent hurling genius as was forthcoming from the Cloyne man. Almost phoenix-like arisen from the ashes of the condemnation of those who would assert that the time had come for him to fade gracefully from the hurling scene, he soared to new heights. He scored 4-5, but it was the manner, rather than the number of the scores, that will be an abiding memory to those privileged to witness the game.'

Munster led by 2-4 to 1-4 at half-time, their goals coming from Jimmy Smyth and Larry Guinan, and after Donie Nealon added a third goal early in the second half, Christy took over. His first goal was a superb first-time pull from about 30 yards to the corner of the net. His second came two minutes later.

'A high ball dropped between full-back Paddy Burke and Ring,' wrote the *Examiner*. 'Burke pulled hard and cleared, but Ring was rolling on the ground, hands to head, apparently badly injured. Then suddenly he was stumbling on his feet moving goalwards. The ball was returned to the Galway goalkeeper, Fergus Benson, but before he could clear, Ring flicked the ball over the line. He celebrated by allowing the St John's men to attend to him.'

Tipperary goalie John O'Grady regarded the third goal as one of the best he had seen: 'A high ball was coming down into the Connacht goal area. There appeared little prospect of a score even for such as Ring, for he was not only outnumbered by goalkeeper Benson and full-back Burke, but his hurley was firmly if illegally held in Burke's grasp. Fergus Benson was advancing to effect what looked like an unopposed clearance. In a flash, Ring ceased his effort to free his stick and turning like lightning, glided the falling ball past the goalie with his open palm. The score was not on for an ordinary forward, but only for one with Ring's inspired hurling brain.'

After his fourth goal, Christy eased off somewhat as Munster went on to win by 7-11 to 2-6.

Munster's scorers were Christy Ring (4-5), Jimmy Smyth (1-1), Donie Nealon (1-1), Larry Guinan (1-0), Jimmy Doyle (0-2), Seamus Power (0-1) and Tommy Casey (0-1). The victorious 1959 team was Mick Cashman (Cork), Jimmy Brohan (Cork), Mick

Maher (Tipperary), John Barron (Waterford), Tom McGarry (Limerick), Tony Wall (Tipperary) captain, Martin Óg Morrissey (Waterford), Theo English (Tipperary), Tommy Casey (Limerick), Donie Nealon (Tipperary), Seamus Power (Waterford), Jimmy Doyle (Tipperary), Jimmy Smyth (Clare), Christy Ring (Cork), Larry Guinan (Waterford) and substitute Terry Kelly (Cork).

'So often before Ring had been written off by hurling followers,' concluded *The Irish Press*, 'but never so convincingly has he given the lie to such beliefs. And of all the fifteen inter-provincial medals that the menacing maestro now possesses, none will be half so cherished as the one he received yesterday. For it is the one which stands as irrefutable evidence of the fact that this 38-year-young Corkman is still the greatest forward in hurling.'

'A lot has been written about Christy and his display,' said Munster's captain, Tony Wall. 'All I can say is that he deserves every word of praise. I've heard people say on and off over the past few years that he should retire now, but every time he comes back with that spark of genius that sets the stands ablaze. Just listen to the crowd every time Christy moves near the ball. It is not without good cause that this anticipation arises whenever the ball comes within his reach. The saying is only too true – you can bate an egg and bate a carpet but you can't bate Christy Ring.'

Dunhill

The Waterford club, Dunhill, ran a very successful inter-county club tournament in May and the Glen beat Thurles Sars and St Aidan's (Enniscorthy) to reach the final. At half-time during the opening game, Christy was presented with a set of Waterford cut glass in recognition of his immense contribution to hurling and to mark his first visit to the parish.

'We were due to play Mount Sion in the final on a Thursday evening,' said Bernie Hackett. 'They had beaten Paddy Buggy's team, Slieverue, and they had some of Waterford's best hurlers in their ranks, men like Philly Grimes, Martin Óg Morrissey, Mick Flannelly, Frankie Walsh and Seamus Power, and with Christy Ring in action for the Glen it was no surprise that a huge crowd – about 7,000 – turned up. The crowd was so big that we were delayed on the road and reached the pitch about an hour late. Naturally, the crowd got very impatient and booed us like hell when we came on the field. Gerald Mulcahy turned to me and said, "We'll give them something to boo about". Christy must have been thinking the same because he got the first goal after a few minutes and we won well.'

The Glen won the suit lengths by 4-7 to 0-4, their scores coming from Ring (1-3), Carroll (1-1), Quane (1-0), Goulding (l-0), Lynam (0-2) and Healy (0-1), with Frankie Walsh and Seamus Power sharing the Mount Sion points.

Like the Cork Churches tournament, the Dunhill competition strengthened the view that official inter-county club championships should be established. There would be difficulties, it was recognised, but eventually the Munster club championship was inaugurated in 1964. It did not get off to a propitious start – the first final had to be abandoned because of crowd trouble – but the refixture was a splendid occasion on Easter Sunday 1966. As in Dunhill, the finalists were Glen Rovers and Mount Sion and, again as in Dunhill, the man of the match was Christy Ring.

Championship

'Ring Brilliant in Rout of Clare' was the *Independent* headline after the Munster semi-final. 'Only the sheer brilliance of Christy Ring stayed most of the 10,984 attendance from leaving Thurles Sportsfield,' wrote John D. Hickey, adding that it was the worst Munster championship match he had seen. With Martin Thompson, Gerald Mulcahy, Connie Cooney, Noel O'Connell and popular Sars hurler and raconteur, Pat O'Leary, making their championship debut, Cork won by 4-15 to 1-3.

'Twenty-three score flags were waved during the game,' wrote the *Examiner*, 'and it was fitting that the score of the day should come from Ring. It was one of those points that is so typical of the man. In his do-or-die lash at a wing ball, he whipped it off the ground as he tumbled and was on his knees to see the white flag rise. In three minutes he cut over three points, all of which carried his trademark.'

Waterford had a similar victory over Tipperary in a remarkable game that saw them mount up 8-2 without reply from the reigning champions. Tipp were scoreless at half-time and their 3-4 in the second-half was of little consequence.

Waterford won a fantastic Munster final by a goal and Phil Grimes played what Michael O'Hehir used to call 'the game of his life'. 'Grimes at centre-back was as good as the very greatest who ever enchanted me in that onerous post,' wrote John D. 'He was here, there and everywhere – in short, unbeatable – and was without question the dominant figure of the game as he hurled back wave after wave of Cork onslaughts with mighty clearances and an obvious relish.'

Five minutes from time Waterford were six points in front, when Ring scored a great goal to send shockwaves through their supporters. Would he do his three-goal act of 1956 all over again, they wondered, and their thinking was not far out. 'Great credit must go to the Waterford goalie, Ned Power, who brought off several brilliant saves in the last, crucial minutes,' wrote *The Irish Times*.

Before a record attendance of 55,174 Waterford won by 3-9 to 2-9, their goals coming from John Kiely (two) and Seamus Power. Others to shine were Tom Cheasty, Frankie Walsh, Jackie Condon, Joe Harney and Austin Flynn. 'In the Cork team, whose merits surprised many,' wrote John D., 'most honours were won by the calculating John Lyons, Jimmy Brohan, Pat Fitzgerald, Martin Thompson, Paddy Barry and Noel O'Connell, even though he finished scoreless.'

As to Christy, John D. Hickey made a curious assertion: 'Although Ring had 1-5 of the Cork total – 1-1 from play – he was rarely in the picture.'

Waterford went on to the All-Ireland final, drew with Kilkenny and won the replay – a merited triumph for a truly great team.

Away from the hurling scene, a big talking point in Cork in 1959 was the opening of the Inniscarra hydro-electric dam by Post and Telegraphs Minister, Erskine Childers. Cork's first female Lord Mayor, Mrs Jenny Dowdall, attended the ceremony, and the blessing was given by Bishop John Aherne of Cloyne, who was to have the sad duty of presiding over Christy's burial twenty years later. Many people bemoaned the flooding of the beautiful river valley to facilitate the Lee Scheme, but in due course the new Inniscarra Lake and its environs gained acceptance among much of the Cork populace.

Twentieth Anniversary

Few people, apart perhaps from Christy, his brothers Willie John and Paddy Joe and some others who had followed his career very closely, could have guessed that when Cork played Kilkenny in the league in October 1959, it was a game of special significance to the Cloyne man.

Almost to the day and against the same opposition, Christy had played his first full league match for Cork in 1939, and now twenty years later, he was back in the Park again, ready to take on his old rivals from Kilkenny and test their flamboyant goalkeeper, Ollie Walsh.

'The sight of the black and amber jersey always brought out the best in Christy,' said Terry Kelly 'and the fact that the game marked the twentieth anniversary of his senior career would have added to his determination. It was no surprise that he put two goals past Ollie Walsh and gave another masterly display.'

Kilkenny, who had lost to Cork twice the same year, won this game by 5-7 to 3-9. While local followers were well pleased with another typical display by the 39-year-old maestro, Noreside supporters at the game were impressed by a wing-forward who was not even born when Christy began his senior career. Nineteen-year-old Eddie Keher made his first appearance against Cork a very memorable one and scored 3-1. 'In the former St Kieran's College star, Kilkenny had a master forward,' wrote the *Examiner*.

Eddie Keher would go on to win six All-Ireland medals, three National League awards and nine Railway Cup medals. The Rower-Inistioge stylist naturally had fond memories of his first visit to Cork and his initial outing against Ring. 'Christy had a big influence on my career,' he said, 'indeed he had a big influence on the careers of all hurling men in his day. He was the model, the ultimate. To me he was not only the greatest forward of all time, but the greatest hurler.'

Hurling Colossus

On a mild November afternoon in 1959, Cork and Wexford met in the Park, with the legendary Ring turning in a stupendous performance.

'That ageless, artful king of hurling Christy Ring turned in a hurling performance the equal of which I have never seen before,' wrote

Peadar O'Brien in *The Irish Press*, 'when he beat Wexford single-handedly and scored a personal tally of six goals and four points in the process. This was a performance to remember, a show that belied Christy's 39 years, a show that only he himself could put on. How the crowd loved it. The whole 7,000 roared him and cheered his every stroke.'

'Christy Ring was given thirteen scoring chances and he scored from ten of them,' wrote Donal Carroll in the *Independent*. 'It was Ring at his best, complete with his private bag of tricks, by his faultless positional play and devastating finish, who provided the only worthwhile memories of a game which was entertaining enough in the first half, but dishwater dull as Wexford threw in the towel.'

'Ring ended with a personal tally of 6-4,' he continued. 'Add to that the fact that the losers tried not only the original choice Ned Fenelon, but also Jim English and Willie Rackard at right corner-back in an effort to curb him and the real genius of this 39-year-old wonder man is seen in its proper perspective. The game was only a minute old when the hurling colossus pointed Cork the victory way with a goal from an almost impossible angle. He added three more before half-time at which stage Wexford, who had enjoyed wind advantage, were a point behind.'

The Wexford team, destined to regain the All-Ireland the following September, included Nick O'Donnell, Padge Kehoe, Ned Wheeler, Ned Colfer, Oliver Gough, Jim English and Billy Rackard, all household names; while Cork had newcomers like Connie Cooney, Jimmy Coughlan, Con O'Driscoll and Con Tobin, but of course Ring made all the difference.

Attempting The Impossible

'I always tried to do the impossible in hurling,' Christy used to say when questioned on his more remarkable scores. In one match he ran half the length of the field to score a winning goal, when the sides were level and his brother, Willie John, asked why he had not taken a point. 'Yerra, anyone could do that,' was the reply.

'I practise each of my shots hundreds of time each week,' he told Patrick Conn in a rare interview in *Scene* magazine in 1967. 'I like to do the unorthodox and keep defenders worried. Once I over-ran a fast pass, put a hand out behind me since I had no time to look, managed to pluck the ball and then pucked it into the net in the same movement. It looked a really great goal, but it was partly luck, partly the fact that I usually attempt what other people might think is impossible.'

'You're modest, Christy,' said Paddy Tyers, when Ring was explaining another great goal in similar fashion during the filming of *Christy Ring*. 'Yes, I am,' said Christy unabashed. 'Modesty is not saying you're no good when you are. It's knowing exactly where you stand.'

'Christy's dedication was total,' said Louis Marcus, 'and he was savage about anyone who fell short of perfection. "How could you win a game with a blind man on the wing?" he said of one celebrated hurler; and of another, "He was so yellow, it was only the palings kept him on the pitch". But he was equally hard on himself. He told us of games he had failed to win through slips that to us were human, to him unforgiveable.'

'I watched him closely when I was a referee,' said Con Murphy, 'and he was always hell-bent on getting the ball, playing the ball (not the man), performing well and winning the match for his team. The range of skills he perfected through diligent practise was absolutely wonderful. There were certain fields he'd stop at during the course of his work and he'd take his hurley and ball from the truck and practise there. I knew one field near Innishannon where he regularly practised, much to the delight and pride of the farmer who owned the field. He subsequently gave that part of the field as a direct contribution to the Ring Memorial Fund.'

'The story of Christy practising his shots is well known,' said John Horgan who, as a teenager, had the honour of marking Ring in a league match in Passage. 'I was only sixteen and Christy was getting on at the time, but I held him to a goal and four or five points! As to practising his skills, there was one occasion when he stopped his petrol truck and began striking a sliothar at it from various angles. Very soon a crowd gathered to watch and Christy, being the great showman that he was, became more and more cross with himself every time he hit the truck. "What's up, Christy," someone said, "you're hitting the back of the truck every time."

"Ah, don't mind the truck," said Christy, "I'm trying to drive the ball up the exhaust pipe!"'

Barrys

'Barry's Hotel was a mecca for GAA people throughout the 1930s, '40s and '50s,' said Seán Ó Siocháin, the footballer from Kilnamartyra 'with the right left foot' who became Secretary General at Croke Park and also a well-known ballad singer. 'Most teams stayed in Barry's Hotel on All-Ireland weekends and it was even normal for opposing teams to stay there at the same time.'

The original owner, Miss Barry, ran the hotel for six years from February 1916 to 1922 and then sold it to a Miss Farrington who was there for 43 years. When it came under new management afterwards, it retained both its Gaelic ambience and its immense popularity with the hurling and football fraternity.

'I have lots of great memories of that place during Tipp's glorious years in the '50s and '60s,' said John Doyle. 'When we were staying there you could have as many as ten to twelve people to a room.'

'Christy Ring always claimed that it was the breakfast he got at Barry's that helped him to win eight All-Ireland medals,' said hotel accountant John Deane. 'Christy would insist on staying in Room 15 because he said it was his lucky number. In his younger days he played in many different positions, but in the 1950s, Number 15 was his most familiar jersey with Cork and Munster. We always made sure Room 15 was available for him on St Patrick's Eve and, of course, if Cork were there on the first Sunday in September.'

Gaelic Sport

When Tommy McQuaid's popular magazine, *Gaelic Sport*, first appeared in the autumn of 1958 the original cover carried a picture of Christy Ring superimposed on a crowd scene at Croke Park. Inside the editorial ran:

'You know the man striding the crowd in our cover story? Yes, it's Christy Ring – dashing, daring, menacing; striding our cover as he has strode majestically across Ireland's playing fields for twenty golden years. We pay this tribute to Ring with gratitude and hope. Gratitude for all the thrilling hours he has given us in the game that he has moulded and remoulded to his own incomparable genius-cast designs. And with hope that though now in the evening – flashing, sun sparkling still – of his career, he will continue to delight the nation's hurling lovers for many seasons more.'

That was the first issue of a magazine that would last over 40 years and become required reading for generations of hurling and football fans. It would also be the first of numerous tributes to Ring. A few issues later, Des Powell wondered at the incredible longevity of Christy on the hurling pitch. Under the heading 'Portrait of the Artist' he asked:

'How does he do it, this man who scornfully defies the inroads of time; who can outhurl, outwit and at times outpace rivals scarcely more than half his age? It is impossible to tell. Perhaps even Christy himself cannot explain it for the impetus of genius is indefinable. But who wants to probe the mysteries of a legend? Who wants to analyse the magic of a man who can still captivate the crowds? Who can draw them almost from the ends of the earth to see him alone?

'Enough to sit and remember the days that are gone; the sun-splashed pitches of twenty years ago where the scores of great hurlers are but background details in the picture of one man. Green flags waving for surging goals, the tumult and the mad cheering of the crowds, joy and excitement, pride and dismay. Ring plays on the emotions like the sensitive hands of a harpist. And his memory will never die.'

Brendan MacLua served as editor for some years before emigrating to London where he took charge of the *The Irish Post*. In an editorial as *Gaeilge* entitled *Fiche Bliain ag Fás*, he wrote:

'This is the twentieth year that Christy Ring has been on the Munster hurling team. He played for the first time in 1942 when Munster beat Leinster, 4-9 to 4-5, in an excellent game. Christy was in the middle of the half-forwards that day. On his right was Willie Barron and on his left Dick Stokes. It is a long time since either of these played. It is also a long time since Mick Mackey and John Quirke played with Ring in 1950 when he won his eighth medal – no other member of that team is still playing for his county or province.

'It is now true to say that many people go to Croke Park each St

Patrick's Day to watch Christy Ring and he never disappoints them. Yes, and it is certain that he will do the same this year (1961) and with the help of God he will continue for a long time to come. Twenty years a-growing – from the young boy in 1942 to the middle-aged man who will be full-forward this year. That twenty years gathering fame and glory will last as long as our national game is played.'

Three years later (1964) Tommy McQuaid made no apologies for dedicating yet another issue of *Gaelic Sport* to the maestro, who at that stage was approaching his forty-fourth birthday and still playing top-level hurling.

'In devoting this editorial as well as the following few pages to Christy Ring, we may be accused of supporting the personality cult which so many influential GAA people are now decrying. We confess that we are believers in the cult. Without the great personalities our games would lose much of their appeal. When they emerge, how can they be submerged again? And how could a man of Ring's stature be concealed in the anonymity of the new team cult?'

Jay Brennan, in an article on the great hurlers of the day, mentioned that opponents of Kilkenny or Tipperary did not need to worry until the ball was in the grasp of their star forwards but, with Ring, the anxiety came much sooner. 'Marksman like Keher or Doyle attach no lead weight to the heart until the ball is snatched from a pass or a break or until it's already on its way for the posts, but with Ring it's a different story. Christy ties knots of apprehension in the stomachs of opposing supporters long before the ball ever reaches him.'

Wembley

'They think it's all over,' exclaimed the BBC commentator, Kenneth Wolstenholme, towards the end of the 1966 World Cup final at Wembley. 'It is now,' he added when Geoff Hurst completed his hat-trick for England that day against West Germany.

A few years earlier the famous doyen of British sports commentators had been introduced to hurling and was greatly impressed. 'A man like Christy Ring,' he wrote, 'the Uncrowned King of Cork and the Stanley Matthews of hurling, can juggle a ball on his hurley as he body-swerves his way round man after man and then finish with a 40-yard shot which no goalkeeper in the world could ever save. And some of these hurling goalkeepers are as sensational as their soccer counterparts.'

Clearly enthralled by the adroitness of Ring in actual play, Kenneth Wolstenholme also marvelled at his free-taking: 'If you have struggled with golf shots,' he said 'you would gape in wonder at the way Christy Ring can hit a dead ball with his hurley and send it screaming goalwards at something like 90 miles an hour.'

Christy had demonstrated his skills in England for the first time in 1947 when Cork and Tipperary met at Mitcham Stadium in London for the Monaghan Cup, a trophy donated by businessman, Owen Ward, who named it after his home county.

In 1950, the old rivals met again to the delight of the exiles. Special coaches from Birmingham and other centres brought people to London to join their compatriots in cheering the All-Ireland champions and the Cork challengers led by Ring. A group of New Zealand pilgrims were also there and it was the Bishop of Dunedin who threw in the ball. The match was a high-scoring affair, with Tipperary winning by 8-5 to 4-5.

Tipperary retained the trophy in 1951 and 1952 and then Cork returned, as new All-Ireland champions for the '53 clash. Great midfield work by Phil Shanahan and Mick Ryan and brilliant play by the captain Tommy Doyle saw Tipp through, although it took two late goals by Tony Wall to secure the 2-7 to 2-6 result.

The immensely popular Whitsun games were transferred to Wembley Stadium in the 1950s, but injury prevented Christy from playing there in 1959. He was bitterly disappointed at missing an opportunity to demonstrate his hurling skills in the famous soccer arena – and so too were countless exiles anxious to watch the maestro in action in Wembley.

'It was very satisfying to note that all the city papers gave the games quite a show,' wrote Paddy Mullane in May 1959. '*The Evening News*, which is the leading London evening paper, printed a special edition giving the whole front page to pictures and a story of the teams. *The Star* and the *Standard* gave the whole back page to photographs and a story. Unfortunately, their stories were all about Christy Ring, and as you know, he did not play.'

However, despite various set-backs and the injury that denied him a Wembley appearance, Christy become Hurler of the Year that December.

Christy and Tommy Doyle after the 1953 game in London.

CHAPTER EIGHTEEN

1960 – YEAR OF MIRACLES

Many religious people in 1960 believed that when the third secret of Fatima was revealed that year there would be another miracle. Some even feared that the world would come to an end. Nothing of the sort happened, of course, but 1960 did find Tipperary beating Cork in three finals – the league final in Cork, the Munster final in Thurles and the Oireachtas final in Croke Park. 'That in itself was a miracle,' said one Cork supporter, blithely ignoring the fact that Tipperary were clearly destined to become the greatest hurling force of the 1960s.

Despite the three finals, the year is best remembered for an Oireachtas match in Wexford, a game that became known as the 'The Battle of New Ross'.

'The match ended in a riot that had to be seen to be believed,' wrote John Barrett in *The Irish Press* next day. 'Entering the last quarter I was mentally preparing for the story of the downfall of the All-Ireland champions. Three minutes later the game was over as hundreds of spectators encroached on the pitch and attacked some Cork players.'

From the start of the second half things had shown signs of boiling over and referee Moss Pollard of Waterford sent off two players after a brief flare-up in the fifth minute. 'But we were totally unprepared for the sudden ending that came after Oliver McGrath was tackled as he cut through the Cork defence,' said John Barrett.

'From behind the Cork goal, hundreds of Wexford supporters promptly rushed on to the field and several Cork players were attacked. Gardaí rushed to break up the fracas but it was some minutes before the referee emerged, his jersey torn, escorted by a garda inspector. He told me he was calling off the game. He said he had been struck by a stone. But the incident was not over yet. Another five minutes elapsed before all the Cork players managed to leave the field and, even though escorted by Wexford players, they had difficulty in making their way to their cars.'

'The crowd were very aggressive and threatening,' said Denis Murphy, 'and they closed in on us as we made our way to the cars to take us to the hotel where we had togged out. However, Liam Dowling, hurley in hand, told us to form a line behind him as we headed for our car and, naturally enough, nobody was prepared to take on big Liam. As we drove to the hotel, people thumped on the roof and banged the windows and we had to stay in the hotel for about two hours before beginning the journey home. Denis Riordan, the rogue, antagonised them even more by opening an upstairs window and waving a Cork jersey at the crowd below. When we finally left the hotel they still hadn't dispersed and they followed us all the way to the river and about halfway across the bridge. It was then that Ringey added insult to injury by shouting back at them some unprintable words about their cowardly failure in 1798!'

Wexford had beaten Tipperary in the All-Ireland final just a few weeks earlier and the visit to New Ross of Christy Ring and the Cork team had been eagerly awaited. Christy had a fine game, scoring a goal and two points, but it was Mick Quane from Newmarket who created the biggest impact, scoring 3-1 off the great full-back Nick O'Donnell. Mick Mortell, future UCC president from Charleville, had the remaining point for Cork, who were leading 4-4 to 1-4 when the match was called off.

League Final

The league final in May brought 28,000 to the Athletic Grounds where Tipperary won by 2-15 to Cork's 3-8, of which 3-4 came from Ring. Jimmy Doyle had nine points for Tipperary, whose other heroes included Kieran Carey, John Doyle, Mick Burns, Tony Wall, Liam Connolly, Liam Devaney and Donie Nealon.

'The battle royal was between Ring and Mickey Byrne,' wrote the *Examiner*. 'It was a test of one power against another. Ring's total would have been enough to see a good Cork team through but this was not a good Cork team. Christy had to be satisfied with taking the glory from his own personal battle with an old rival.'

'We began filming *Christy Ring* that day,' said Louis Marcus, 'and we had the luxury of two cameras, one in the park and the other high in the showgrounds outside. Christy knew the cameras were on him and in the first half he scored two great goals and a few points. When I spoke to him at half-time he said, "I'm sorry I couldn't do anymore!"'

Munster Final

'The raw elemental rivalry of our two greatest hurling counties was laid bare at Thurles and was almost frightening in its intensity. It drove players beyond the bounds of normal endurance, it fired them with a spirit, an unrelenting fury of sustained effort which was most times heroic, but sometimes ignoble. It will be remembered as an almost unprecedented test of hurling skill in stress, of fitness and of fortitude. It will be recalled as the moment of truth and justification for a much maligned Cork team, who almost to a man, wore the red jersey with distinction.'

Thus wrote the *Examiner* of the 1960 Munster final between Cork and Tipperary. In the dressing room prior to the game, Christy Ring gave his men such a blistering tirade that even his friend, Dr Carthach McCarthy, was shocked by the tone. As the players charged out, ready to die for the cause, the priest murmured to Ring, 'You didn't find those words in the Bible, Christy.' 'No Father,' replied Ring. 'The men who wrote the Bible never played Tipperary.'

Prior to the game, Tipperary were odds-on favourites to win and win well, but – like a voice in the wilderness – a *Sunday Review* columnist saw a prospect of Cork achieving the impossible. 'Exactly twenty years ago this month a lithe flaxen-haired lad played in his first Munster final against Limerick,' he wrote. 'Today he is still hurling with the same eagerness plus a lot more skill and craft, still the keyman in the Cork attack, the chief danger man on Tipp's path to the All-Ireland final. His name? Do I have to tell you? Yes, the incomparable Christy Ring is the man to achieve the impossible this afternoon.'

Hell's kitchen.
Christy is tackled by Mickey Byrne (2) and Mick Maher as Pat Stakelum attempts to clear. Terry Kelly (left) and Florrie O'Mahony look on. On extreme left are John Doyle and Paddy Barry with Eamonn Goulding approaching in the distance.

'Christy was an inspiration once again that day,' said Terry Kelly. 'He resented all the talk about Cork being badly beaten by Tipp and he gave a fierce harangue in the dressing room. What many people expected to be a one-sided contest turned out to be a high-scoring thriller. Eight goals and 24 points were scored and we were a bit unlucky to lose by two of those points.'

'It was a game to scatter the storm clouds and illuminate this dark day just as brightly as the hot sun that shone between downpours in the first half,' wrote Mick Dunne. 'Two almost evenly matched sides recklessly threw everything into the battle and gave us 60 minutes of rugged and vigorous hurling. During the game referee Gerry Fitzgerald had to hand out warnings to Tipp's Kieran Carey and John Doyle, and Cork's Liam Dowling and

Paddy Barry but took no stricter action than name-taking.'

'There were no red cards in those days,' recalled John Doyle, 'but Paddy Barry and myself had a disagreement so we did the decent thing, dropped our hurleys and threw a few punches at one another. Gerry gave out to us, told us to cop ourselves on, took our names and that was it.'

Paddy Leahy, Phil Purcell and the other Tipperary mentors may have warned their charges of complacency before the game, but a Cork goal in the opening minute quickly alerted the Tippmen to the danger of taking Cork for granted. Paddy Barry, cutting across from the right-wing, finished a Terry Kelly ball to the net and set the pace for a swashbuckling first half which ended 3-4 to 2-4. Tipperary's goals came from Liam Connolly, Sean McLoughlin and Jimmy Doyle, with Paddy Barry getting his second goal by flicking a Ring free to the net.

A classical point by Ring after a solo had given Cork the lead just before half-time, but Jimmy Doyle gave Cashman no chance with a jet-propelled shot before tipping over the final point of the first half. So, wind-assisted Cork found themselves a goal behind at the break.

The second half, however, began in a blaze of brilliance by the underdogs. A point by Joe Twomey, two from Ring and another from Mick Quane had the Rebel supporters in fine form but no sooner had Cork regained the lead than Sean McLoughlin scored a goal and Jimmy Doyle struck a purple patch. He had four points in succession and it looked like Tipperary were on the way to their expected high-margin win.

Ring had other ideas, of course. Entering the last quarter he placed Liam Dowling for a goal, added two points himself and set up Mick Quane for Cork's fourth goal. In between these amazing scores, Tipperary somehow retained their composure with points by Doyle, Nealon and one from an 80-yards free by Tony Wall and these were enough to give them a two-point win.

On the morning of the match, Pope John XXIII noticed the uneasiness and disquiet of a certain Irish prelate in the papal apartments. The genial pontiff said nothing but offered up a silent prayer on his behalf. Later that evening he met the cleric again, this time beaming broadly. 'Ah,' said the Pope with a smile '*Tipperarius vicit.*' (Tipperary won.) 'We did surely,' whooped the priest, forgetting himself, 'now we can save the hay.'

Oireachtas

It was late October when Cork played Tipperary in the Oireachtas final and Old Timer in the *Gaelic Weekly* reflected on the player he had been watching for over twenty years. 'Christy Ring, heavier and slower I thought than in any previous Croke Park appearance since I first saw him as a crew-cropped youngster back in 1938, made his most desperate endeavours approaching half-time and Cork broke through for a succession of scores to level and even snatch a point lead just on the short whistle.'

Christy scored seven points altogether but that was not enough to help him secure the only hurling medal he was not to win.

'The Oireachtas was first played in 1939,' said Fergal McGill. 'The name of the competition was a reflection of the close ties between the GAA and the Gaelic League as the proceeds of the tournament were intended for use in the promotion of the Irish language. Originally, the competition was run between invited sides but it grew into a popular autumn precursor to the league before a burgeoning fixtures list and waning interest led to its decline in 2001.'

Limerick had won the original series in 1939 with a five-point victory over Kilkenny, who had a big win over Cork the following year, when Christy and his brother, Willie John, played together for the only time at Croke Park. The Oireachtas became a football tournament for three years after that but, when it was restored as a hurling competition, Cork's interest and success seemed minimal. The county never won the Oireachtas in Ring's long career and it was not until 1973 that John Horgan brought the trophy for the first time to Cork, where it remained in 1974 when Gerald McCarthy was captain and in 1975 when Eamonn O'Donoghue skippered the side to victory over Wexford.

'No doubt about it,' said the *Examiner* (1960), 'this game went down well with the attendance. Here were Tipp in Croke Park for the second time in a fortnight. Here, too, were Cork – always a good box-office attraction – and making a return appearance was the ageless Christy Ring. With men like Jimmy Doyle on the other side, there was a strong clash of personalities in this super-charged hurling display. From the moment Doyle sent over the first point of the game after two minutes and Ring claimed the spotlight immediately with another, everybody sat up.'

Tipperary had been beaten by Wexford in the All-Ireland and were anxious for some consolation prize, but Cork made them work hard for it. Christy and his men were a point ahead at the break, but Tipp's superior fitness told in the last quarter and they ran out winners on the scoreline 4-11 to 2-10.

Denis O'Riordan and Christy in opposition for the only time as Muskerry and the Glen line up for the 1960 championship. On Ring's right are Jerry O'Sullivan, Mick McCarthy and Mick Quane.

Denis O'Riordan

In August 1960, the Glen played Muskerry in the county semi-final and the mid-Corkmen, with Tom O'Sullivan, Dan Kelleher, Joe White, Paddy Cremin and future Cork goal-scoring hero, Colm Sheehan, in great form, seemed about to create a big upset. In an effort to retrieve the game, Ring was moved to the 40 on Muskerry's brilliant young centre-back, Denis O'Riordan. 'That move provided one of the great duels of the game,' wrote the *Examiner*, 'and it is a tribute to the Ballincollig man that Ring got only a point from play.'

A native of Ballyburden near Ballincollig, Denis O'Riordan was a Cork minor for three years and made his senior debut in 1959 when he marked Jimmy Doyle. Much admired for his hurling artistry by Christy Ring, he often travelled to matches with the maestro. 'Ring was great company and the journey was always filled with hurling talk and singing, especially when we won. I remember one day we were coming back from a Munster final and we stopped at a pub somewhere to watch the Olympics. As we entered, we saw a swimming event being shown. 'How are the Irish doing?' Christy asked. 'Great,' said a chap on a high stool, 'not one of them have drownded yet!'

Notwithstanding Denis O'Riordan's display in the county semi-final, the Glen emerged victorious and met UCC in the 1960 final. The students gave a dynamic display and led by three goals early in the second half. John Joe Browne, Mick Mortell, Noel Gallen, Stephen Long and Liam Shalloe were the college stars but, inspired by two goals from Mick Quane, the Glen staged a great rally and won 3-8 to 1-12.

'In the roll of honour first place must go to Quane by virtue of his two goals,' wrote the *Examiner*, 'but hastily it must be added that it was the old maestro Christy Ring who laid on the first one for him. True, Ring has had better games and he was caught for stamina when he moved to the 40 but let nobody think he did not leave an imprint on this final. He did much more than the three points he scored suggest.'

CHAPTER NINETEEN

UPS AND DOWNS OF 1961

Gael Linn aroused enormous interest early in 1961 when they invited people to vote for 'The Greatest Hurling Team Ever' and they received a magnificent response. It was no surprise that Christy polled the highest number of votes (10,458) and that the ultimate selection occasioned much debate and controversy.

'Picking the best hurling team of all time is absurd,' wrote John D. Hickey. 'Modern players start with a distinct advantage over the Jamesey Kellehers, the Mickey Mahers, the Jerh Norbergs, the Sim Waltons, the Jack Rochfords, the Sean Óg Hanleys and the Bob Mocklers. However, taking the poll at its face value, one is bound to conclude that Christy Ring is regarded as the greatest hurler of them all. His nomination for four positions brought him a huge total and he outclassed no less a man than Mattie Power of Kilkenny by over 5,000 for left corner.'

The Best Ever XV chosen by the sporting public in 1961 was:

Tommy Daly
(Clare)

Jimmy Brohan	Nick O'Donnell	John Doyle
(Cork)	(Wexford)	(Tipperary)

Jim English	John Keane	Paddy Phelan
(Wexford)	(Waterford)	(Kilkenny)

Lory Meagher   Mick Gill
(Kilkenny)   (Galway)

| Jim Langton | Mick Mackey | Eudie Coughlan |
| (Kilkenny) | (Limerick) | (Cork) |

| Paddy Barry | Nicky Rackard | Christy Ring |
| (Cork) | (Wexford) | (Cork) |

While the composition of the best team generated much discussion, not least in the media, Christy Ring added another accolade to his long list of credits, namely the most likeable personality ever to have graced the hurling arena.

Naturally, Christy derived great personal satisfaction from the polls and, if anything, it increased his desire to impress in every outing afterwards. As a result, he figured prominently in the score sheet after every game and by the end of 1961, he shared the top scorer of the year position with Jimmy Doyle.

Scoring Spree

In April, Christy scored 3-6 against Waterford in a tournament final at Fermoy. 'He was easily the outstanding player on view,' wrote John Joe Brosnan from Meelin. 'He showed that the passage of time had not robbed him of that superb judgement that enables him to make hurling look so easy.'

Scoring goals and points in a tournament is one thing, scoring them in the championship is another and few, if any, of the Waterford players expected Christy to repeat the 3-6 tally in the Munster semi-final. They were right, he did not. He only scored 3-4!

'We had beaten Cork in a fantastic league match in Cork a few months before that,' said Tom Cheasty, 'and we were hoping to do the same in the championship but once again Christy did the damage.' Waterford went on to the league final at Croke Park, only to lose by a goal (6-6 to 4-9) to a great Tipperary team. So, naturally, there was an air of confidence among the Decies supporters making their way to Thurles for the Munster semi-final. That confidence was soon shattered by the old-stager in the Number 14 jersey.

'Christy Ring in Devastating Form Again' was one of the headlines next day as newspapers reported on Cork's sensational 5-7 to 2-7 win.

'For ordinary mortals the passage of time extracts the inevitable toll,' wrote Mick Dunne, 'but Christy Ring in hurling is no ordinary mortal. And in proving it, this young-at-forty veteran magnificently displayed the noble hurling artistry that has made him the greatest forward the game has known.'

Christy's scoring spree, unfortunately, came at a price as his old friend, Jim Tough Barry, pointed out afterwards. 'I could have cried when I saw Christy's injured face and body after last Sunday's semi-final,' he said. 'Yet both of us were happy. And I thought that maybe he, who should be sitting in comfort on the sideline, and I, snug by a radio, understood. In this hurling madness of ours, I forgot that inside Ring's mouth was a cut which was closed later with four stitches, that his body was covered with scrapes and weals. For him it was familiar thing, this physical ordeal, the need to prove himself each time he pulls on a jersey. Ring is almost 41 and yet the burning enthusiasm for the game, which has been his life, remains as fanatical as it was when, as a nineteen-year-old, he used to call me "sir".'

In The Soup

Joe Sherwood was an Englishman who joined the *Evening Press* not long after its inception in 1954 and whose back-page column, 'In The Soup', soon became almost obligatory reading for sports fans.

Joe's knowledge of hurling and football may not have been great when he arrived in Dublin – he once referred to the start of a hurling match as kick-off 3.30pm – but he was a fast learner and his column quickly became as popular, or as exasperating, with GAA readers as it was with followers of other codes.

After Christy's remarkable 3-4 against Waterford, readers looked forward to Joe's comments, not expecting them to be acerbic after such a display. They should have known better. 'What a pity Christy got the tantrums' was the heading and the first paragraph clipped two points off Ring's total. Joe was in his usual form.

'What a pity it is that a hurling genius like Christy Ring, who again proved himself such at Thurles, would have marred his afternoon's personal triumph by giving way to tantrums like a spoiled and petted child. Instead of being happy and content with the telling blows that sent Waterford reeling to defeat, Christy seemed to resent being thwarted of not getting his own way every time and all the time. He should try and remember that, though he may be idolised by his own good folk in Cork and acclaimed by the nation as peerless in the science and art of past and present hurling, his fame does not make him untouchable any more than it does the less talented.'

The response of the readers was swift and voluminous and Joe's postman was kept busy for the next few days.

'A Kerryman living in Galway advised you to go back to England and bury yourself alive,' wrote Ringey Forever of Cork. 'But after what you wrote about Christy, our hero, if ever you come to Cork city, you'll never reach England alive. You'll be going over there in a wooden box.' ('As long as I don't have to pay the expenses, you can dump me where you like,' replied Joe.)

'You are a good judge of hurling but why did you pass those nasty remarks about Ringey?' wrote Up Cork of Kerry. 'From the moment Ringey stepped on the pitch last Sunday until the time Mick Hayes called it a day, he was subjected to some very hard tackling on the part of the Waterford defenders. Christy was fully entitled to defend himself and he did this in true Cork spirit.'

'Congratulations Joe,' wrote the Barracks of Rea, Nenagh. 'Of all the Gaelic sports writers, you were the only one who had the courage of your convictions in telling Christy just where to get off. Our so-called referees are gun-shy of him. I saw him on one occasion take the green flag from the hands of an umpire and raise it. Immediately prior to this the referee had blown the whistle. Still, he allowed Christy his goal. With Christy it is a case of being player, umpire and referee.'

'Why do you single out a particular player?' asked M.C. of Cork. 'Why have you to magnify out of all proportion the "flare ups" where Christy Ring was concerned. There is an old maxim – it takes two to make a fight. You obviously only saw one on Sunday. I saw two and my word is as good as yours. Realise my friend that if you are a man, you should apologise for the unfair comments you sent to print about Christy Ring.' ('What I've said I've said,' replied Joe. 'Sorry I had to do so but I'm standing by it.')

'I think, a Sheosaimh, your old liver must be in a bad way and needs an early overhauling,' wrote D.O.S. of Tullamore, County Offaly. 'I have no crib with you over Christy's hurling faults but why, oh why, not flavour your comments with a splash of Christian charity. As a penance for these and other sins of your past, I want you to promise faithfully to recite out loud and at the nearest cross-road three times daily for the next month the following verse:

> Don't look for the flaws
> As you go through life
> And even when you find them
> It's wise and kind to be somewhat blind
> And to seek for the virtues behind them.'

On The Wireless

Radio was still king in 1961 and sponsored programmes commanded huge audiences throughout the country. *The Kennedys of Castlerosse* and *The Dalys of Honeydew Farm* were equivalent in popularity to today's soaps on television. Leo Maguire's 'If you feel like singing …', Ian Priestly Mitchell's 'When you wish upon a star …' and Eamonn Kelly's 'Things rested so' were nationally known catch-phrases long before the term was invented, and the Sunday night play drew a captive audience comparable to any big televised event today.

There were many other unmissable programmes, although the Sunday Appeal after *Nuacht Anall, Nuacht Abhfus* at tea-time was not one of them. That is, until 25 June 1961, when the appeal on behalf of St Joseph's School for Blind Boys in Drumcondra was given by none other than Christy Ring.

'The stamp of genius finds outlets in the most unexpected ways,' wrote Gerry McCarthy in the *Press*. 'It is to Christy's great credit both as a Christian and Catholic sportsman that he has elected to do something for Irish blind boys. The superior of the school, the only establishment of its kind in Ireland, is Fr Con Cottrell, Cork's centre-field man for almost seven years and holder of five All-Ireland senior medals. When Fr Cottrell suggested making the appeal to his old friend and colleague, he was delighted with Christy's instant response.'

'Mr Christy Ring, most loved and admired of all Cork hurlers, was in a new and striking role this week,' wrote Carbery in the *Weekly Examiner*. 'That versatile and surprising genius was selected to speak on Raidió Éireann on behalf of a very worthy charity. St Joseph's is blessed in having a live-wire Head in Fr Con Cottrell, native of Upton and one of the greatest hurling midfielders of his period. An athletic youth of middle height, he was a dynamo of energy at midfield. His fielding of high balls was remarkable and he was a very true hitter of a flying sliothar. I have learnt much of Fr Cottrell's tireless work with St Joseph's – he inspires enthusiasm in his many voluntary workers. It was a happy thought of his to call the usually shy master hurler to his aid. Christy's original line of thought is always attractive.'

Christy spoke well on radio that evening and his appeal for the blind boys had the desired effect. 'Wonderful' was how Fr Cottrell described it.

Golf

One afternoon in the summer of 1961 Christy drove to Limerick to fulfil a promise and see for himself what so many people found in the game of golf. Such a leisurely pursuit seemed the very antithesis of the cut and thrust of hurling and Christy had often declined to have a go. This time, however, he had agreed to give it a try, not in Cork where he would soon be spotted and closely watched as he addressed a golf ball instead of a sliothar, but in Limerick where he believed he would have some privacy. How wrong he was.

'Christy Ring, the famed Cork hurler caused quite a stir at Limerick Golf Club last Wednesday evening,' declared the *Limerick Leader* on its front page. 'He played a round with Limerick Senior Cup players, Kevin Hayes and Percy Kennedy. It was the Glen Rovers' man's first attempt at golf and, according to Hayes, he played extremely well.'

'Christy had six bogeys in the first round,' said Kevin 'and his drive to the seventeenth was only a few yards off. Although he adopted the hurling grip – left hand below right – he was amazingly accurate.'

Not surprisingly, Christy was well pleased with his introductory round of golf that evening but little was he to know how controversial his next sporting visit to Limerick would prove to be. His initial round of golf was truly the calm before the storm.

Massive Interest

The Munster final that year probably exceeded all others, if that were possible, in interest, anticipation and excitement. The fact that Christy had scored 3-4 against Waterford, plus the fact that Paddy Barry had agreed to come out of retirement, gave Cork supporters serious hope that Tipperary could be beaten in 1961. Injury had kept Paddy out of the Waterford game, but he was ready for the final and Limerick became the Mecca of hurling followers that unforgettable weekend in July.

If there was electricity in the atmosphere as the seething masses crushed together in the crammed terraces, there was certainly no dynamism in the form of the Cork players when the game got underway. Their spiritless performance, according to Terry Kelly, stemmed from the energy-sapping manner in which they had made their own way to the pitch.

'It was the tradition of the Cork hurlers,' he said, 'to tog off at the Railway Hotel and travel by car along the Ennis Road to the pitch. On this occasion, however, we were told that there were new dressing rooms at Limerick grounds and most of us wanted to use them. Unfortunately, some of the old-timers in the party were reluctant to break with tradition and so we did the foolish thing and changed at the Railway Hotel.'

When the Cork players were ready to leave for the pitch, the road to the stadium was absolutely jam-packed with people and traffic heading for the game. As the official cars inched along, some of the impatient players decided to get out and walk, so that by the time the game was due to start only a few of the team were on the field. One by one the others gradually arrived, frustrated, tired, discomfited and agitated after their mile-long struggle to get there. The Tipperary players, for their part, had done the sensible thing and changed at the dressing room in the grounds.

Under such circumstances it was not surprising that the Corkmen gave a most lethargic display in the first half and were no match for the fresh and fit Tipperary side who, thanks to the brilliance of Donie Nealon and Jimmy Doyle, had mounted an eleven-point lead by the interval. Cork's lone score, a point by Ring, was a paltry reply to Tipp's half-time total of 3-3.

Cork's problems had begun at midfield, where Liam Devaney and Theo English were outstanding. As a result the Cork forwards were too often left just waiting for the ball and, when it did come their way, the two dangermen were well policed by the forceful Tipperary defence.

'With Ring and Barry held,' wrote the *Gaelic Weekly*, 'the rest of the forwards might as well have been trying to thatch without scollops as to score against a brilliant Donal O'Brien and his backs. Curiously, the Tipp forwards, two men excepted, had a lean day too. Donie Nealon laid the foundations of victory with his snap scores early on and Jimmy Doyle made sure of victory from the odd chance that came his way but none of the other forwards could raise a flag.'

Throughout the first half scuffles broke out among sections of the crowd and a pronounced 'needle' was also detected in the behaviour of some of the players. As the second half progressed, it became painfully clear that the slightest provocation could spark off a free-for-all on the field. Then, about twelve minutes from the end, the inevitable happened.

With few chances coming his way Christy was moved to centre-forward, a ridiculous position for a 40-year-old, and he found himself marking John Doyle. Shortly after the switch, both players went for an incoming ball, both stumbled and fell to the ground and Christy landed on his back, with Doyle falling on him and punching him repeatedly. Val Dorgan states that Ring had pulled across Doyle before they fell and when Doyle was hauled off Ring, a general mêlée broke out.

Unfortunately, Tom Moloughney, a Tipp corner-forward who had been moved to the 40, was struck on the head as he approached the scene of the trouble. He did not reach his destination and he certainly did not get near Ring, but when he was later taken off injured, many people wondered if Christy had been to blame and, without a shred of evidence, some concluded that he must have been.

Reporters on the press bench frantically tried to follow the pushing, jostling, hurley swinging and shaping-up by so many players and sought help from one another in identifying offenders. Mick Dunne was convinced Moloughney had been hit by Ring and John D. accepted his version of events, while Val Dorgan initially believed the bespectacled Matt O'Gara had been struck in the face and was in danger of a serious eye injury from shattered glass.

After order was restored and the match resumed, Doyle was struck by Ring, obviously in retaliation for the earlier punching incident on the ground. 'Christy and I got involved in each other on the ground,' said John Doyle in the *Ringy* video. 'There were a few fellas got hit the same day, but I was too busy with Christy on the ground at the time. But when I got up anyway, I got a tip from Christy's hurley in the chin and it cracked my chin-bone. That was it.'

The match ended in a 3-6 to 0-7 victory for Tipperary, with Christy scoring four points, one from play, although Donal O'Brien denied him a certain goal at one stage. As a Cork-Tipp spectacle watched by over 60,000 it was a dismal flop and yet many of the classic encounters from 1949 to 1960 would fade in memory with the passing years, while the controversial incidents of 1961 would not be forgotten.

Reports

On Sunday evening those of us who had witnessed the imbroglio were shocked to hear Seán Óg Ó Ceallacháin declare on radio that Christy had struck Moloughney. Seán Óg, who was not at the game, usually read *The Irish Press* accounts of matches he could not attend when he called to the Burgh Quay office on his way to do his broadcast. This time it was Mick Dunne's report he studied and noted that it clearly stated that Ring had been the aggressor. So, unwittingly, Seán Óg repeated the incorrect statement over the airwaves and thought little of it when he went home later.

Next morning, however, on reading *The Irish Press* he was alarmed to find that Mick's report did not contain the damning comment on Ring. On enquiry, Seán Óg discovered it had been deleted by Pádraig Puirséal, who was working as sub editor and had suggested to Oliver Weldon, the sports editor, that on legal grounds Ring's name should not be mentioned. Thus, the offending passage had been removed.

In Monday's *Independent*, however, John D. Hickey's report was innocuous enough until he got to the contentious issue. 'The exchanges were always mercilessly hard,' he wrote 'but there was only one flare-up of any consequence when John Doyle and Ring became enmeshed in a catch-as-catch-can or punch-as-punch-can on the ground eighteen minutes after the restart.'

'That was unseemly enough,' Hickey continued, 'but it was deplorable that Ring, after arising, should strike Tom Moloughney with his hurley causing the Tipperary man to be assisted from the pitch with a head injury. Numerous other players became embroiled but the incident would hardly have qualified for mention but for Ring's action.'

In the eyes of the Cork County Board losing to Tipperary in a dreadful Munster final was bad enough, but having a Cork player blamed in public for a serious offence he had not committed was too much. They rallied to Ring's side, demanded apologies and retractions and determined to take appropriate action whenever and wherever possible.

The final was over but the battle was just beginning.

Hickey Barred

Dick Cross was the *Examiner* reporter at the county football final a fortnight later and was sitting at the press bench in the back row of the Cage when John D. Hickey arrived. He was refused admission to the enclosure. 'I was sitting with my back to the fence when I got a tap on the shoulder,' said Dick. 'It was John Hickey standing outside the Cage. When I asked why he wasn't in the enclosure he told me he was barred. As a working journalist and colleague I then decided to join him and report the match from a standing position.'

At the following Tuesday's board meeting, the General Purposes Committee (GPC) brought a recommendation that Dick Cross' privileges be withdrawn 'for bringing the Association into disrepute'. Both Dick Cross and Val Dorgan, who arrived late at the meeting to support his *Examiner* colleague, found the term 'privileges' laughable. 'You reported on matches from your seat in the open air with a plank to write on,' said Dick. 'If it rained you had no shelter. I often had to compile my report using a plastic bag to keep my note-pad dry.' When the motion was put to a vote, however, the GPC recommendation was defeated.

The Dublin newspaper branch of the National Union of Journalists (NUJ) further fuelled the controversy by writing to the

County Board, asking them to withdraw the ban on John D. Hickey. 'Unless the ban is lifted,' the letter stated, 'the union will have no alternative but to advise its members not to report or take pictures of games in Cork.' Such a threat was hardly likely to go down well in Cook Street and the board treated the letter with more than a little contempt. No cessation of reports or photographs ensued.

Outcome

As for Christy himself, he was totally dismayed by the false allegations that linked his name with Moloughney. Some of his friends advised him to take legal action, a procedure that was abhorrent to Ring, yet he mulled it over and pondered on the possibility of donating to charity the proceeds of a possible court victory. That Ring would win a law-suit was never in doubt. He had been wrongly accused of striking Moloughney and his character had been vilified. Nevertheless, mindful perhaps of his friendship with Seán Óg over the years, Christy wavered on the prospect of a court action.

The County Board, on the other hand, had no compunctions about initiating legal proceedings against Raidió Éireann and the *Irish Independent*. During protracted efforts to resolve the dispute, the NUJ and the County Board held several meetings but it took months before a solution could be reached with the Irish Council of the National Union of Journalists eventually issuing a public apology.

In March 1962 a lengthy statement was read out by Seán Óg on his radio programme and printed in the *Irish Independent*. The key element stated that:

'The Council has come to the conclusion that grave doubt existed about the facts as reported and wishes to extend to Mr Christy Ring, who was mentioned widely as the player most directly concerned, its sincere regret for any distress, hardship or injury to reputation which he may have suffered as a result of his name being mentioned. He is, in fact, innocent of the offence and his name should not have been singled out.'

The statement concluded with a paragraph designed to prevent any future conflict on the matter:

'Both parties agree on full co-operation in securing the highest standards of sportsmanship on the field of play in all games. It is agreed also that the publication of the statement will ensure the withdrawal of all libel actions, the withdrawal of proposed industrial action and the withdrawal of any ban on journalists.'

Resolution

In his book, Val Dorgan gives a detailed account of how angry Christy was with him at the time, angry because he felt that one Glenman had betrayed another by supporting the journalists and, seemingly, taking sides against him. 'Renegade' was the word that rankled most with Val and relationships between the two remained chilled for some time.

Christy was not one to bear or nurse a grudge, however, and to Val's surprise and relief it was at a squash match that the old friends reunited. 'He was a spectator and I was taking a hammering,' wrote Val. 'I came out of the court between games to suffer in private. Suddenly Ring was there. He had come down from the spectator's gallery. "Why don't you drop it up the front? He's hanging back all the time," he suggested".' No mention was made of their disagreement.

At a later stage, Christy would honour Val Dorgan by attending the premiere of his play, *The Hurler*, although, as he said to Val afterwards, 'If it wasn't a Glenman who wrote it, I would have walked out!'

Similarly, when Seán Óg Ó Ceallacháin met Ring for the first time after the 1961 radio broadcast, he found Christy quite affable. Both were being driven through Hartford, Connecticut, and discussing hurling when Seán Óg casually asked what exactly happened in the 1961 Munster final. 'Christy kept looking straight ahead and said very quietly, "That's all water under the bridge. I've forgotten about it." I never asked him again.'

And what of Tom Moloughney – what had he to say about it all? At the time he admitted he did not know who struck him, as he was moving towards the mêlée, but he was certain it was not Ring. Obviously, he could see Christy in the near distance just before he was hit by a Cork defender. 'I can categorically state that Christy was not responsible,' he told Bob Honohan when they met by chance many years later.

'At the recent hurling league final in Thurles,' wrote Bob in the

Cork Independent (2006), 'Jimmy Grey, the Dublin goalie the day they were unlucky to lose to Tipperary in their last All-Ireland final, introduced me to a man named Tom Moloughney. The name immediately rang a bell and I asked him if he was the Tipperary player injured in the controversial incident of 1961. He told me that he was. I then asked him if he thought Christy Ring had been responsible, and he said he could categorically state that he was not. I asked him if I could put that on record and he told me he had many good friends in Cork – he singled out Willie John Daly for special mention – and that he would be only too glad that they would know that he had completely exonerated the man he described as the greatest hurler of them all.'

Moloughney met Ring only once afterwards. He told Val Dorgan that he was waiting for a friend outside Croke Park after the 1978 football final when Ring came towards him. Christy did not recognise him but they exchanged pleasantries as the maestro got into his car.

'Did you introduce yourself?' asked Val. 'I was too shy,' said Tom. 'I would have asked him for his autograph, but I had nothing to write on.'

CHAPTER TWENTY

1962

'Christy Ring will again get his place on the Munster team,' predicted Paul Russell in the *Sunday Review* in January 1962. 'Why am I so sure? Because Ring was top scorer in hurling last year with a huge total of 21 goals and 37 points from twelve big games. Munster can't afford to go out in defence of their title without a man of that calibre.'

As Paul predicted, Christy was back in Croke Park on St Patrick's Day, but for once he was not the focus of the greatest attention. That distinction fell on Des Foley, the fair-haired Dublin star who helped Leinster to win both Railway Cup finals that afternoon and earned himself a special place in the record books.

As for Christy, who had scored three goals against Connacht, he had a strangely subdued game at full-forward and did not seem to get much support from his Tipperary colleagues. In the end, Munster lost by two points, 1-11 to 1-9, with all their scores coming from Tipperary men – Liam Devaney (0-5), Jimmy Doyle (0-3) and Donie Nealon (1-1).

'Cork were going well in the league at that stage,' said Terry Kelly, 'and when we went down to Dungarvan to play Waterford, it was Christy's first game against them since he scored 3-4 in the championship the previous summer. There was a lot of interest in how Waterford would cope with him this time but, as it transpired, they had no answer to his brilliance.'

'Once more,' wrote Carbery, 'it was the artistry of the unending Cork star, Christy Ring, that swung the game in Cork's favour. He rattled home two goals and two points off his own ash and built up Cork's third and winning goal.'

Ring special.
*All eyes on the ball as another shot shakes the net watched by (from left)
Des Ferguson (2), Lar Foley (Dublin), Mick Quane (15) and Christy in
the 1962 league semi-final.*

The league semi-final brought Cork and Dublin together at Thurles and marked the return of Liam Dowling who gave an impressive display and scored 3-3. The match was an anti-climax, however, with Cork winning easily by 6-12 to 1-4. The other Cork scorers were Christy Ring (2-2), Mick Mortell (0-3), Patsy Harte (0-3), Mick Quane (1-0) and Jerry O'Sullivan (0-1).

Then it was on to Croke Park for the 1962 league final against Kilkenny. We did not realise it at the time, but it was to be Christy's last game for Cork at the venue he had graced so often and so magnificently since he first shone there as a minor 24 years earlier.

With outstanding hurlers like Billy Dwyer, Jim Walsh, Seamus Cleere, Mickey Walsh, Martin Coogan, Denis Heaslip, Sean Clohessy, Eddie Keher and the redoubtable Ollie Walsh, Kilkenny were fancied to win well, but one reporter saw a good reason for a possible upset.

'The years may have passed but not one iota of the Ring skill and élan has gone,' wrote the *Sunday Review*. 'On his stout shoulders may well rest the outcome of today's game. It was Ring's craft and hurling genius that saw Cork through to this league final. Indeed, were it not for him, it would be Waterford not Cork who would be opposing Kilkenny. Can Ring do it again this afternoon? It may be asking too much to expect him to do it alone, as he did against Waterford, but he should get considerable assistance from his colleagues in attack this time.'

Sadly, for Christy and for Cork, only the first part of the prediction would come true.

Last League Final

'Like a page torn from the past, a re-echo of the pulsating games that began 60 years ago when Kilkenny scored their first victory over Cork in an All-Ireland final, the counties were back in Croke Park to provide another classic,' wrote the *Kilkenny People*. 'Give us a Kilkenny-Cork hurling final at any time,' exclaimed Paddy Downey in the *Times*, while John D. Hickey described it as a contest in the classic mould and Mick Dunne went into rhapsodies: 'The game, like the song, has ended but the memory, like the melody, lingers on for this was a final containing much of the greatness of former epics between these counties.'

It was Christy's last final for Cork and, quite characteristically, he gave another marvellous display, despite his age and the atrocious weather conditions.

'Ring Wizardry Could Not Save Cork' was the *Independent* headline under which John D. Hickey wrote: 'Right up to the stage when they got their goal Kilkenny were in peril because of the presence of Ring who, even though he did not chase the ball with customary industry, did enough to cause the blood pressure of Kilkenny supporters to sky-rocket. The wonder of the game was that the hurling wizard of his age scored all but three points of his team's total and that, despite the fact that he must have wondered if he had been abandoned by his forward colleagues in the second half, so ineffective were their endeavours.'

For a while it looked as if Cork were in for a hefty defeat, as Kilkenny seemed to own the ball in the first quarter against wind and rain. Superb defensive work by Jerry O'Sullivan, Jimmy Brohan and ice-cool Mick Cashman, prevented the Noremen from getting the scores and when Cork came away at last, Christy had the ball in the Hill 16 net to give Cork the lead, very much against the run of play.

'That goal transformed Cork and for the next ten minutes they had Kilkenny on the run,' wrote the *Gaelic Weekly*, 'but three bad wides spoke badly of their attack, Ring excepted. Nevertheless, Cork led by four points at the break.'

'Although we won the toss and played against the wind, the omens were not with Kilkenny,' said Paddy Grace. 'We were in the unlucky dressing room and we broke an old tradition that Kilkenny must be the first out for the second half at Croke Park.'

For all that, Kilkenny had six unanswered points inside nine minutes of the restart and things were looking bad for Cork until, two points down, they gained a close-in free.

'You could see that Christy was going for a goal to put Cork back in the lead,' said Old Timer in the *Gaelic Weekly*, 'but his attempt to blast the ball to the net came back off a wall of defenders. Another Cork forward had an open shot from the rebound but muffed his stroke and, though Christy nipped in to cut the ball over the bar, I don't think Kilkenny were terribly worried about Cork points even when my bold Christy clipped over a beauty to equalise a minute afterwards.'

'Eddie Keher and Sean Clohessy restored our lead,' wrote the *Kilkenny People*, 'but Ring was back with another point in the forty-ninth minute. Then in the last ten minutes Kilkenny put their best endeavour into a truly amazing finish which culminated in a great Billy Dwyer goal. Just on time Billy crowned a great game with the last point after being placed by Eddie Keher. Result: Kilkenny 1-16, Cork 1-8.'

Seamus Cleere, a man of frail build who hurled with the assurance of a great ball player of huge stature, was hailed as Kilkenny's best performer with Keher, Dwyer and Heaslip also highly praised. For Cork, Mick Cashman, Jimmy Brohan, Sean Kenefick, Jerry O'Sullivan, Pat Fitzgerald and Terry Kelly earned credit. 'But in the Cork forward division,' wrote John D. Hickey, 'it was a case of Ring and Ring alone.'

Championship

True to his assertion that he took seriously all the games he played, Christy attended the opening of the Sean Treacy pitch in Tipperary town that summer and scored two goals in Cork's win over the All-Ireland champions. Jim Hurley's son, Eoin, was in goal, allowing Mick Cashman a rare return to the half-back line for the county.

Both men did well against Tipperary, but when Cork faced Waterford in the championship, Cash was back in goal although the presence among the subs of Eoin Hurley suggested to some observers that the Blackrock stalwart might move outfield again. It did not happen, despite the fact that Mick Flannelly, John Kiely and converted defender, John Barron, made life very difficult for the Cork defence.

'Waterford had sweet revenge for last year's humiliation,' said the *Examiner*, 'but Cork, weak with inexperience, gave exciting uncertainty to 31,705 people in the sunshine. Even when four minutes from the end, Waterford led by five points, the game held the attendance intent and Cork died fighting with points by Ring and Jerry Sullivan. Phil Grimes' palmed goal in the fifty-sixth minute was the score that

Waterford's Ned Power makes a spectacular and
courageous save as Tom Cunningham tackles Christy
in 1962, his last Munster championship game.

finished Cork, despite the points by Ring and Sullivan. The last thrill
for Cork supporters was when Ring put Donal Sheehan through but
Patsy Harte's shot was saved.'

Wedding Bells

'Traffic in Cork was held up for over an hour this morning when
thousands turned out to see the wedding of the famous hurler
Christy Ring and Miss Rita Taylor at Our Lady of Lourdes Church
in Ballinlough.' So reported a Raidió Éireann announcer on
Wednesday 12 September 1962 and, in so doing, marked a new
departure for the national station – the inclusion of a sports
celebrity wedding in the main news bulletin.

Christy's old friend, Bishop Cornelius Lucey, performed the ceremony, Rita's sister Bridie was bridesmaid, Christy's younger
brother Paddy Joe was best man and the wedding reception was
held at the Metropole Hotel.

A line of cars stretching over a mile along the Ballinlough Road, not to mention the hordes of well-wishers anxious to congratulate the happy couple, delayed proceedings and it was well past the scheduled time when Rita and Christy had to face another pleasant ordeal as they made their way through the crowds assembled outside the Metropole. The hotel was appropriately decorated in the Cork colours for the occasion but, observant as ever, Christy noted with sardonic humour that the wedding reception was taking place in the Leinster Room!

The fledgling Telefís Éireann filmed the wedding for its nine o'clock news telecast – another first! – but the tape, like that of the first live broadcast of a Railway Cup final the same year, was later scrubbed and used again.

The newly-weds left for their honeymoon and on return it was back to business for Christy, as he set out to achieve a new hurling record – his eleventh county senior medal.

Christy shoots for goal against UCC.

County Final

Despite Cork's failure to win the league or come out of Munster in the championship, 1962 provided pleasant memories for Christy on both a personal and sporting level. And surely nothing on the hurling scene could match the devastating manner in which he stopped the College from winning their first county title, just when it seemed victory was in sight.

At the time UCC was the sole university in Munster and undergraduates came from all over the province to study for their degrees. Many of them were fine hurlers – some were top-notch inter-county players with Waterford, Tipperary, Limerick and Cork – and in the late 1950s and early '60s, University College Cork had so many quality hurlers that a county title seemed inevitable.

Very often it had been Ringey and the Glen who had barred the students' path to glory, but in 1962 the College did not lose to the Blackpool men in the county final – they drew. With typical dexterity Christy scored 2-3 that day, but it took a late point by Tom Corbett to equalise (2-10 to 3-7).

The replay brought a huge attendance to the Park and, with Waterford's Jim Byrne having a great game, UCC seemed destined for a long-awaited triumph. The match was truly going their way, despite the brilliance of Joe Salmon, who had come to Cork with great credentials, but had never found his best Galway form with the Glen. This time, however, he gave a display reminiscent of his class in the 1953 All-Ireland but, notwithstanding his late point which clipped the lead to two, UCC were still on course.

Then four minutes from time, Bill Carroll went through for the Glen and was fouled near the goalmouth. Ring, who had been quiet for most of the hour, stepped out to take the free and the vast concourse, almost to a man, held its breath as he awaited the whistle. With a characteristic run, he approached the ball, quickly slipped the hurley under it, lifted and pushed the sliothar into the air a yard or so ahead of him and without stopping for an instant, made a mighty swing at the rising leather and sent it whizzing to the back of the net. The Glen won the match by a point.

CHAPTER TWENTY-ONE

FARRANFERRIS

'In the colleges' All-Ireland I wonder how many of the crowd recognised one of the most enthusiastic of the Farranferris mentors,'asked Moondharrig in *Gaelic Sport*. 'You are right, it was none other than Christy Ring who was appearing in Croke Park in an entirely new capacity. And I would not be at all surprised if many of the switches which brought St Finbarr's from behind to achieve a merited victory were inspired by the hurling genius from Cloyne.'

Farna's golden hour came in May 1963, as almost the entire population of Cork's diocesan seminary huddled together on the upper deck of the Hogan Stand at the Nally corner. It was their first All-Ireland colleges final, but the joy and excitement of the trip to Dublin had evaporated by half-time as Ballyfin were on level terms and had a hefty wind at their backs on the resumption. To Farna's astonishment and delight, however, some shrewd switches in the dressing room and a transformed performance by the team, resulted in a sensational win. To cap matters, the legendary Christy Ring shyly agreed to join the victorious team for the historic photograph on the Croke Park sod.

Even before that day, Christy had lent his support to the school, encouraged by his friend, Dr Carthach McCarthy, the new president. He was to be seen refereeing matches between first years, offering advice to various classes and helping to create hope of success in the Dr Harty Cup. Only a field away stood Farna's deadly rival, the North Monastery, holder of over a dozen Harty titles and nursery of countless Cork stars. When Christy won his eighth medal in 1954 there were no fewer than ten ex-Mon boys on the Cork team, a measure of the school's hurling greatness. 'Yet when the Mon played Farna,' said

Con Murphy, 'it was hell for leather with no giving up even if one side was ten goals ahead. The matches always attracted huge crowds and usually very little separated the sides at the finish.'

Christy's involvement with Farranferris was not going unnoticed in the North Mon either. 'I remember when the Mon were training,' said Bernard Allen, 'we'd be looking over the ditch at Farna training and we'd see Christy Ring in their midst. That had a terrible effect on our morale.'

'Farna rarely missed a free in all their matches,' said Brian Hurley, one of the players, 'and much of the credit for that must go to Ringey. I remember one training session when he placed twelve sliothars in a row on the 70-yard line and sent every one of them over the bar. Then he got our long-range free-takers, Connie Leary

College Champions.
Christy joins the Farranferris team and mentors after the 1963 All-Ireland victory at Croke Park. Back (from left) – Fr Denis Forde, Christy Ring, Paddy Crowley, Johnny Collins, Vincent Hodnett, Gerry Hennessy, Liam McAuliffe, Seanie Barry, John Dineen Dr Carthach McCarthy. Front – Tom McEvoy, Donal McCarthy, Frank Crowley, John Hennessy, Connie O'Leary, Mick Donegan, Kevin Collins, Denis Harrington.

and Johnny Collins, to have a go and he wasn't satisfied until they mastered the technique of scoring with every shot. He did the same with sideline cuts and other aspects of the game.'

'You must remember that a lot of young lads arrived in Farranferris from footballing areas and saw hurleys for the first time in the college,' said Connie O'Leary. 'Many of them made the Harty teams, thanks to Dr McCarthy who spent hours and hours training us. In Farna we ate, slept and drank hurling and thought nothing of getting up at 6am before Mass for training in the freezing cold. Fr Denis Forde, Fr Eddie Keohan and Fr Brian Kelly put in a lot of good work too and then, of course, we were blessed to have the maestro, Christy Ring, who was a huge influence. Christy would show us some of his own special skills, like how to take a line ball with the sliothar stuck in the mud and still put it over the crossbar from the sideline.'

'My main memory of Ringey,' said Seanie Barry, 'is of a day in the old Mon field when he gave a lot of good advice, but I think his influence was psychological in that, if he was interested in us, that meant we were good.'

'I remember as a child in Castlehaven gobbling up stories about Christy Ring from my father,' said Donal Collins. 'Then, when I went to Farranferris, Christy helped out with the Harty teams. He was a God to us. I was captain when we played Coláiste Chríost Rí in the first all-Cork Harty final in 1969. We were level at half-time and there was fierce tension in the dressing room, but Ringey was very calm. He told us we were playing well and that we'd win because we'd be playing into the scoring goal in the second half. He said we'd get a rake of goals and he was right. I scored from a 21, Tim Crowley got another and further goals by Pat Lucey, Frank O'Brien and Jimmy Hegarty put us out of sight. It was one of the greatest days of my life.'

It was no surprise that when Louis Marcus needed hurlers for the instructional sequences in the Ring film, Christy asked Dr Mac to send down Seanie Barry and other lads. Nor did it come as a surprise that when the time came, he would proudly send his son, Christy, to be educated in the imposing red-bricked college overlooking Blackpool.

Christy (in cap and raincoat) chats with Farranferris players before the 1967 Harty Cup final.

Christy continued to support the Farna teams long after Dr Mac had left the scene and the great motivators, Fr Michael O'Brien and Sean O'Riordan, had arrived. Farranferris would win five All-Ireland titles and seven Dr Harty Cup titles before the grand old college closed in 2006 after more than a century of promoting hurling.

Jekyll And Hyde

'If we take the average inter-county life of a player as six or seven years,' wrote John O'Grady in 1961, 'it will be seen that Christy Ring has already played with three distinct generations of hurlers. The names of the great men of his youth already read like ancient history.'

John was one of a string of brilliant goalies that Tipperary produced in the late 1950s and early '60s. Apart from his matches against Cork he also grew very familiar with the club scene when he played in goal

Christy signs autographs for young fans after the 1962 league semi-final.

for UCC and Blackrock. He later became a respected hurling columnist with the *Gaelic Weekly* and *Tipperary Star*.

'It is not only Christy's playing record that has set him apart,' added John, 'it is his attitude to the game that really distinguishes him from the rest. He has a dedication to victory, a single-minded concentration of energy and will-power that turns him from a quiet, retiring figure off the field into a flamboyant and demonstrative one in the tense atmosphere of a Munster or an All-Ireland final.'

'That was the most amazing thing I found about Christy,' said Billy Barry of Sars. 'He was a very quiet and shy person when you met him on the street, but on the hurling field he was a transformed man.'

Mickey Byrne agreed: 'He was a real Jekyll and Hyde. It is hard to understand that a man so fiercely determined on the field could be so quiet and unassuming off it. We had many great clashes but immediately the final whistle blew anything that happened on the field was forgotten and we were great friends long after our hurling careers were finished.'

'On the field Ring was a tornado, a flash of lightning,' said John Joe Brosnan. 'He was a perfectly built athlete and a powerful frame of a man who could take care of himself when backs surrounded him to administer some harsh treatment in trying to stop his raids on goal. But off the field he was a gentle, timid man, often seeming to lack confidence in matters other than hurling. If he paid a visit to a friend's house he would be the quietest person in the place, if there were other people there, and would normally refuse to eat or drink anything, even a bare cup of tea.'

'He had a particular fear of newspaper reporters and media people generally,' added John Joe. 'I remember being with him at the launch of *Cork's Hurling Story* and Donna O'Sullivan of RTÉ asked him to say a few words into the tape-recorder. He was terrified and turned to me, saying "I haven't read the book. What will I say?" I told him to go ahead, not to worry. Donna spotted immediately that he was as nervous as a cat. So she asked him a few easy questions about Cork-Tipp rivalry and he answered quietly. When it was over he turned to me and asked, "Was it all right?" I told him it was perfect. It was only then that he relaxed, glad that he hadn't been trapped or made a fool of himself.'

Tipperary man, Hugh O'Callaghan, son of Olympic champion Dr Pat, had a personal trainer relationship with Christy in the twilight of his career and was surprised at his strength even then. Hugh, probably the most successful American university coach in his day, was regularly billed as the strongest man in Ireland.

'The core of my various successes,' said Hugh, 'was weight training in its varied and valuable forms. Christy Ring came to me in his declining hurling years as, by his own admission, he had gained weight and lost both speed and strength. Before planning Christy's programme I evaluated him on several criteria. From his play I knew that he had to have had a reservoir of unusual strength. However, I was surprised at how strong he actually proved to be. His strength in turn nurtured his determination, aided his skills and brought him to the pinnacle of his sport – a place where he will always remain.'

'There can be no greater testimony to his greatness,' concluded John O'Grady, 'than the fact that he has immortalised those who have beaten him on particular occasions. And he has never been a specialist hurler. Midfield and each of the six forward positions have been filled by him – and in all he has been as good as the best – equal to Jack Lynch or Tim Ryan at centre-field, to Phil Cahill or Eudie Coughlan on the wing, to Mattie Power at corner-forward or to Martin Kennedy as a full-forward. If genius is the ability to do one thing supremely well, there can be little doubt that Christy Ring has a compelling claim to the title.'

'Ring and myself wouldn't shake hands at the start of a match,' said John Doyle to Raymond Smith. 'Not one word would be exchanged between us during the course of a game. The real hurlers I knew didn't indulge in idle chat. You see it was the era before the advent of television cameras. A lot of niceties like shaking hands before the ball was thrown in and swapping jerseys afterwards, even the odd embrace, are the fashion today. We lived in a far tougher and harder school. But believe me, Ring could take defeats like a man. He would be the first to congratulate you in victory even if Cork were unlucky to lose on the day. I always admired him for that. He was different from all the others in that he immediately put reverses out of his mind and began to look forward to the next day – even if it was twelve months away.'

'He was not a social being,' John added. 'Once a game was over I liked to enjoy the *craic* and a bit of banter and talk about other subjects rather than hurling. But to Ring hurling was everything, it was life itself. He was as fit in February as he was in July and that was why he helped Munster win so many Railway Cups. When we did talk hurling I found he didn't suffer fools gladly. His standards were amazingly high. If you didn't measure up to them, there was no place for you in Ring's book. He dismissed you from his mind and he could even tell you bluntly to your face if he thought you were useless.'

Val Dorgan found this when a group of All-Ireland hurlers were discussing the particular aspect of their play they would be best remembered for – Billy Murphy's long puck, Paddy Donovan's courageous high catch amid flailing hurleys and so on. One hurler, who had won top awards with the county, asked Christy what he thought he – the player – would be remembered for. Christy looked at him, thought for a moment and then said, 'Nothing.'

'Without Tipperary the GAA is only half-dressed,' said Christy when the Premier men were going through a lean period. 'The greatest hurler of all appreciated that the game of hurling could not afford to lose Tipperary from its front ranks,' wrote Seamus Leahy in *The Tipp Revival*. 'Nobody had been more often at the receiving end of Tipperary brawn – and occasionally Tipperary ash – and nobody revelled more in the peculiar fire that Tipp-Cork clashes can spark. Paradoxically, nobody had closer friends among the hurling fraternity in Tipperary than Christy.'

'Christy Ring was an enigma and a man apart,' said Owen McCrohan. 'That he was a hurling genius is beyond question. He lived for the game and dedicated himself completely to its perfection. Throughout the 1940s and 1950s when there was no TV and very little money, a whole generation grew up who never saw him in the flesh but who came to revere his name. Wherever there was a wet and dry battery radio set, the voice of Michael O'Hehir would often come crackling over the airwaves on dreamy summer days to electrify many a rural household with its descriptive terminology. Ring's skill as a hurler was matched by an unyielding determination. He was brave to the point of recklessness. When his temper was up – which was often – he would go through fire and water to win a 50/50 ball. More than any man who ever wore a red jersey he epitomised the unconquerable spirit of Cork hurling.'

Railway Cup Decline

As Christy had not played in the 1963 Munster championship, it was hardly surprising that, seven months later, his name did not appear in the Munster team to meet Connacht. 'That left myself as well as many others wondering as to whether the bould Christy had decided to bid farewell to the hurling fields,' said Old Timer, 'but we were not long left in doubt. The very next day the Glen Rovers club held their general meeting below in Cork and Christy Ring was elected captain for the coming year.'

'Well, that certainly should prove that the Old Maestro from Cloyne is coming back into the action once more this season,' he added, 'and short though the time is now between this and March 17th who will be brave enough to say even at this stage that if

Christy can whip himself back into full fitness quickly, he won't be in the Munster colours on St Patrick's Day?'

As it transpired Christy did not return to the Munster team and his departure from the inter-provincial series was to be mentioned by many as the major factor in the subsequent decline of the Railway Cup. The competition, which had commanded attendances of between 40,000 and 50,000 in the halcyon days when Ring was centre-stage, became a secondary contest that dropped alarmingly in popularity as the years went by. The arrival of television in the early 1960s and the 'live' telecast of the Railway Cup finals obviously affected attendances, but there can be little doubt that the highlight of St Patrick's Day for hurling people lost its significance, when there was no Ringey to be watched and enjoyed at Croke Park.

'For me,' said Con Houlihan in the *Sunday World* (2005), 'the Railway Cup recalls an innocence that we have lost forever and an age when people looked for tips for big races in the Mutt and Jeff cartoon in the *Evening Echo* or from bottles washed up on the seashore. It recalls the time when hurling and football finals were played on St Patrick's Day at Croke Park and when Barry's Hotel seemed the centre of the world. The attendance for the double bill was usually about 50,000. The games carried great prestige and it wasn't only the players from the "lesser" counties who looked for selection. Nobody was more committed to the inter-provincial competitions than Christy Ring, even when he was already a folk-hero and had nothing to prove.'

CHAPTER TWENTY-TWO

TWILIGHT TIME

One summer's evening in 1963, Cork and Waterford played what appeared to be a routine tournament game in Fermoy. The fixture was in aid of the new sportsfield at St Colman's College and an estimated 7,000 people attended. Nobody realised that the match would become Christy's very last appearance with the Cork team. Indeed, much of the interest that Sunday evening centred on Paddy Barry and Christy O'Shea making a comeback for championship consideration. Both did well, but Richie Browne was the outstanding forward and top scorer.

1963 Cork Senior Hurling Team.
Back (from left): Patsy Harte, Jerry O'Sullivan, Christy O'Shea, Denis O'Riordan, Tom Corbett, Jimmy Brohan, Denis Murphy, Jim Barry. Front: Pat Fitzgerald, Paddy Barry, Richie Browne, Seanie O'Brien, John Young, Noel Gallagher, Christy Ring. This was Christy's last game for Cork.

Christy himself had a quiet hour, and it looked as if Austin Flynn had finally held him scoreless. Then, in the dying moments, he gained possession, lost his hurley as he rounded Flynn, but coolly kicked the ball from ten yards to the corner of the net. It was the last goal he would ever score for Cork.

Christy had been picked as usual for the opening championship match against Clare and it came as a shock to the Cork contingent and others when it was announced by loud-speaker that he would not be playing. Paddy Downey noted how you could hear the buzz of disappointment wending its way around the stadium as spectators absorbed the dismal announcement. Instinctively he felt it marked the end of Christy's career in the Cork colours. He was not alone.

'I have a sneaking suspicion that Christy has decided to call it a day,' wrote Gerry McCarthy. 'If he has, good luck to him. He has done more than one man's part to win many matches for his club, county and province and his name and fame will never be forgotten while an ashen blade is swung in any part of Ireland. If he has retired, however, it will take us some time to get used to a Cork fifteen without the name "C. Ring" filling a position in attack.'

Changing Times

'Christy had married his charming Rita,' Eamonn Young wrote in early 1964, 'and to the great joy of all the twins arrived. God took one of them. No doubt the cross weighed heavily on the Cloyne man's stout shoulders. From the summer of last year he dropped gradually into the background and showed no real desire to play. Many of the public, myself included, were for his return. Others felt the time had come when the young men should carry the banner without the inspiration of the leader.'

Meanwhile, Christy was exercising himself in the most unlikely manner. He had taken up squash. 'Here was a game in which one pits one's brains against a smart-moving opponent, which demands quick reaction, speed over three yards and all-out effort to retrieve a fast ball and return it,' said Youngie, himself a brilliant exponent of squash. 'The game suits those with that fast murderous temperament. No wonder it appealed to Ringey.'

Christy, who had been appointed Glen captain at the start of the year, made his return for the first round of the championship against Muskerry at Ballincollig in May. People were astonished to see how slim he had become.

'I hoped and expected that Ringey would get the goals,' said Eamonn. 'Early on from a high ball that landed in the square he flicked in a lovely goal and I said to myself, "Here it comes," but from there on he seemed slow and in the second half not at all that interested. Afterwards, Dan Coughlan, a Glen selector, said to me, "He is fitter-looking than I've seen him for a long time, but he seemed weak. Maybe he knocked off the weight too quickly". And that's exactly what I thought.'

Last hurrah.
Christy in his final appearance with Cork in June 1963 – a tournament game against Waterford at Fermoy. Included are Austin Flynn on ground, Richie Browne (Castletownroche) and Ned Power.

Meanwhile public speculation was rife as to Christy's future with the Cork team. The county selectors obviously considered bringing him back when he was picked for a tournament game at the end of May 1964 and a big crowd went to Cobh, hoping to see him in action again. 'The match marked the opening of Cobh's new pitch,' said John Joe Brosnan, 'but at the outset we were subjected to a big disappointment – Christy Ring, whose selection as a corner-forward gave rise to much speculation, was not in the line-out.'

Despite all that, Cork supporters genuinely believed that Christy might be back for the championship. Rumour had it that he had let it be known that he was ready to return, but it was a bitter disappointment when the selectors named a panel of players without him. To make matters worse, Paddy Barry, with great reluctance, was called out of retirement for the third time.

Christy had been out of championship hurling for over a year and, though Jim Hurley and John Lyons had voted for his return, the three other selectors felt that, at 43 years of age, he was past it. Later in the year, however, his performance in the county final – when he scored 1-4 in the Glen's win – showed clearly that he was far from past it. He was, in fact, proclaimed Cork hurler of the year for 1964!

In Fours

'1934, 1944, 1954, 1964,' roared Christy to his jubilant followers after leading Glen Rovers to their twentieth county title and his own twelfth triumph just before his forty-fourth birthday in October 1964. It was to be his last county final and in time-honoured fashion he rose to the occasion in style.

'It was a game that thrilled the estimated 24,000 attendance,' wrote the *Examiner*. 'It was Ring's goal just on half-time which inspired the Glen to this 3-12 to 2-7 victory. With a minute to go to the interval the 'Barrs were in command, leading by six points to four. Then, when Ring swerved on to a pass from Joe Salmon and pounded it all the way, the Glen were in that split second back in the game.'

'That was my first county final,' said Charlie McCarthy, 'and in those days forwards and midfielders still lined up for the throw-in.

I was after winning an All-Ireland minor medal a few weeks earlier and just before the start of the game Christy came over to congratulate me. "You played well," he said. "Keep at it, and you'll have a good future ahead of you in hurling." I couldn't believe my ears – hearing those words of encouragement from the hurler I idolised.'

Christy's prediction would come true in time with Charlie going on to become one of the all-time great forwards, winning five All-Ireland medals and captaining Cork to the three-in-a-row in 1978. Two other victorious Cork minors shone at the Park that afternoon – Con Roche for the 'Barrs and Andrew Flynn for the Glen – but it was the oldest man on the field, an established star long before they were born, who emerged as top scorer yet again and delighted young and old with his sparkling performance.

'It was a game that left many solid memories,' said the *Examiner*, 'and Cork people of all affiliations will be glad that Christy turned in as exciting a display as is possible for any man of 44 years. He had flashes of his old brilliance all the way through and, apart from his goal, he shot across four points, all from the top drawer.'

The Glen scorers were Christy Ring (1-4), Patsy Harte (0-6), Dave Moore (1-1), Bill Carroll (0-1) and Andrew Flynn (1-0), while the 'Barrs marksmen were Mick Archer (1-2), Willie Doyle (1-0), Gerald McCarthy (0-2), Mossie Finn (0-2) and Charlie McCarthy (0-1).

County chairman, Weeshie Murphy, presented the Seán Óg Murphy Cup to Christy who, having enumerated the years of Glen glory in fours, went on to pay tribute to the 'Barrs. 'Any other team would have crumbled when the Glen went into such a big lead after half-time,' he said, 'but the 'Barrs refused to fade away. It would have been no disgrace to take second place to them today.'

Ironically, it was a 'Barrs man, Jimmy Goulding, who had proposed to the Munster Convention an inter-club championship featuring the champions of each county. That competition, when it eventually materialised, would provide Christy with the stage for his final, unforgettable achievement in hurling.

Meanwhile, Christy had something else to look forward to that week. Five days after leading his club to another county title, Christy and Rita would be guests of honour at the premiere of Louis Marcus' eagerly awaited film, *Christy Ring*, at the Savoy.

'Few of the film stars who have come to Cork got such a tremendous reception as did Christy Ring when the film *Christy Ring* had its world premiere at the Savoy cinema,' the *Examiner* would report. 'The film was directed by Louis Marcus, the commentary was written by Aran Islander, Breandán Ó hEithir and spoken by Padraig Tyers, ex-Cork county and UCC footballer and Waterford county footballer and hurler. There is also a running commentary by Michael O'Hehir and the music was specially recorded by the Artane Boys Band.'

'The Cork hurling star got a great ovation as he went into the cinema,' the report added, 'and after the film, the crowd stood in a five-minute-long tribute hailing Ireland's greatest hurler with prolonged handclapping.'

Filming Christy Ring

'The fundamental skills of football are within everyone's reach, but hurling is a different matter,' said Louis Marcus as he reflected on his two early film productions, *Peil* and *Christy Ring*. 'For speed and variety of stroke, hurling leaves football standing. Everyone knows the great skill involved but no one seems to know what it consists of. Indeed, so few counties can hurl with mastery that the rest of the country regards the game as a private mystique, a sort of closed shop – either you are born a hurler or you must remain forever on the ditch. To explode this myth was our aim in the hurling film. But to do so we needed someone who could not only demonstrate the game at its best, but who had analysed its mysteries and reduced them to basic movements that we could photograph. For this there was only one possible choice – Christy Ring.'

Getting Christy to co-operate in such a venture seemed a remote prospect, given his innate shyness and distaste for personal publicity, but when his friend Paddy Tyers, Gael Linn's manager in Cork, broached the subject, Christy's attitude softened. 'I knew that a film glorifying his achievements wouldn't interest him,' said Paddy, 'but a film that could demonstrate the skills of hurling to sporting people throughout the country was something that was close to his heart. It was his intense enthusiasm for the game and his desire to see hurling spread to the weaker counties that made

Film premiere.
At the premiere of Christy Ring (from left): Donal O Morain (Gael Linn), Alf O'Muiri (President GAA), Christy and Rita, Gus Healy (Lord Mayor), D.R. Mott (Player-Wills), Mrs Healy, Jack Lynch and Louis Marcus.

him agree to perform his skills for the camera.'

It was in Padraig Tyers' office that Louis Marcus first met Christy. 'He was sitting on the table, swinging his legs relentlessly. He was always in motion, tapping his feet, swaying his shoulders, gesturing with his hands. The first thing that struck me was his extreme shyness. He barely looked up during the small talk but as soon as the film was mentioned he came alight. He had the intensity of all committed people and he spoke in quick spurts from a tight mouth.'

Breandán Ó hEithir also recalled his first meeting with Christy: 'He came to the point quickly – how was the job going to be done? I told him that he would have to explain all the actions, emphasise what was important at each stage and that I would find the exact words to convey this to the audience. He thought about it for a time, walking around the room, changing direction frequently when emphasising a point by swivelling on his very small and shapely feet, which contrasted with the large hands and thick wrists and forearms. He knew exactly what he wanted to stress and, having discussed the filming in detail with Louis, he knew where the slow-motion and stop-action sequences occurred. In fact, when he found out later that the slow-motion filming uses twice the amount of film that usually goes through the camera, he said it was a terrible waste and added with a little smile, "If ye told me that when we were doing it, I'd have slowed everything down myself".'

The filming took place at the Mardyke pitch, close to the home of the Marcus family, and the crew arrived well prepared with new hurleys. 'Christy tried each one, bending them to test the "give",' Louis recalled. 'Finally, he sniffed his disapproval and returned to his own trusty stick. He used to keep the same hurley as long as possible, mending it if at all possible. A lot of his shooting power came from the fact that he carried the heaviest hurley in Ireland. Only his powerful wrists could swing it with such lightning speed.'

Christy insisted that all those involved in the filming, including Louis Marcus and chief cameraman, Vincent Corcoran, should try their hand at hurling during film breaks. 'My own prowess was frankly nil,' Louis admitted, 'and even after Christy's careful instruction I couldn't double on a high ball – one of the hardest strokes in hurling. Then one day a particular ball came in from out field and I made for it in the usual way. Christy was leaning against the goalpost and before I reached the ball I heard him say softly, "He has it now". Sure enough there was a sweet, sure crack and the ball went flying over the bar, right on target.'

'Working with Christy was a particularly happy experience for all of us,' said Breandán Ó hEithir. 'His humour could be very pointed, particularly where hurling was concerned. He did a very realistic imitation of a contemporary who had a habit of holding his head very low as he ran for a ground ball. Ring claimed he was almost blind and could only locate the ball by the sound it made as it came near him. He admired Joe Salmon greatly for keeping hurling alive in Connacht during the lean years, but he could also be scathing. Asked about one player's ability he replied, "He's not a hurler, he's a calamity". And I remember one crew member who

A very determined Christy Ring.

knew nothing about hurling, but thought it was dangerous, asking Christy if he was ever afraid on the field. Ring smiled the bleak smile that signalled disapproval or contempt and said, "Only when I'm playing against bad hurlers".'

'We found that even after two decades as king of his sport he had lost none of his keenness and passion for the game,' said Louis. 'He liked the idea of the film promoting hurling in weaker areas, but I also felt that, although he never said so, he welcomed the opportunity to have his skills and his ideas recorded forever on celluloid. "But," he warned us from the start, "I'm not an easy man to please. It will have to be done well." By doing it well, Christy meant planning the instructional sequence as a comprehensive and lucid demonstration of basic hurling skill. We soon discovered that his mind was rich on the subject and his talk of the game fascinating.'

The film was sponsored by the tobacco company W.D. & H.O. Wills, a rather ironic patron in view of Christy's attitude to cigarettes, and it had its premier at the Savoy in Cork on Friday 16 October 1964. It ran for several weeks in the massive cinema, much to the delight of hurling supporters some of whom, forgetting where they were, roared at the screen, 'Doubtya Ringey boy!' after every goal.

'Over the two years that we talked about and worked on the film,' Louis Marcus concluded, 'I came to realise that Ring's continuing genius was not just a gift from the gods or, as some thought even in Cork where they should have known better, some mania that gripped him on the field. It was intellect, cold and piercing. Into his late twenties Ring had depended on his natural talents. When they began to wane with age, he analysed his game and recreated it on an intellectual basis so sound that it kept him supreme through another two generations of hurlers. During the filming Christy's complete mastery of hurling revealed itself to the full. So deeply had he studied the game and so thoroughly had he disciplined his own style that whether doubling or pulling, lifting or cutting, each stroke was perfect in its economy and its effectiveness. We were privileged to witness his genius at close quarters.'

1965

'Old soldiers never die, they just fade away', went the old ballad and for much of 1965 it looked indeed as if Christy had faded quietly into retirement from the hurling scene.

Although he had shone in captaining the Glen to victory in the '64 county final, he did not play a year later when, enervated with flu, he missed the first round. The 'Barrs, with Charlie McCarthy the top scorer, won that match and went on to regain the county title after a ten-year wait. When the clubs met in the annual procession game, Ring was again an absentee.

Because he was eligible after missing the senior championship, there was much speculation that Christy would play for the Glen in the intermediate grade, a prospect that intrigued many, but dismayed many more. An Oscar-winning star ending his days in B-movies was the sad analogy drawn and, when Ring declined to play in the lower grade, there was great relief in some quarters.

With Christy again out of the scene the Munster championship was a depressing one for Cork. Having lost to Tipperary by four goals in 1964, they were hammered by even more in '65. 'Wicked' was how Babs Keating described the latter game.

'Talking about the Munster final,' said Brian Doherty in the *Gaelic Weekly*, 'could Cork not have done with Christy Ring? Veteran though he may be, he would certainly have been a great improvement on any of the Cork forwards seen in action. It strikes me that Ring was quietly forced out long before his time. His form in New York earlier this year showed that he still has plenty of hurling left in him – more than any of the Cork forwards seen in the Munster final will ever have. Not, mind you, that I would have enjoyed watching Christy sharing in so pitiful a defeat. But certainly on merit he is still entitled to a place on the Cork side – that is, if he wants it.'

The New York visit in May had been memorable for several reasons – Christy scoring 2-4 for the Cork exiles against an Offaly side dominated by Jim O'Donoghue; a proud John 'Kerry' O'Donnell announcing that $27,000 had been raised for the Peruvian mission, and the arrival at Gaelic Park of Senator Bobby Kennedy to see Ring in action.

Bobby Kennedy was captured on film and in photographs chatting with Christy and testing his hurley. It is quite possible that Ring mentioned how, like thousands of others, he had watched and welcomed his brother, President Kennedy, during his visit to Cork two years earlier, just a few months before his appalling end in Dallas.

Despite his absence from mainstream hurling, Christy's thoughts were still far from retirement. He was fascinated by the concept of a Munster club championship and the fact that Glen Rovers, as 1964 champions, had qualified as Cork's first representatives, made the competition even more alluring for him.

There were many conservative GAA people who saw no future in the club championship, just like those who scoffed at the introduction of the under-21 grade the previous year. To them, the All-Ireland, the National League and the Railway Cup were the glamour events in hurling and would remain so.

'Christy saw things differently though,' said Finbarr O'Neill, the outstanding goalkeeper and *poc fada* champion. 'Ever since the popular Churches tournament and outside tournaments in places like Dunhill and Ahane, he saw a future for Munster club hurling and I suppose, he realised that this could be his last chance of taking part. We played Kilmoyley of Kerry and Castlegar of Galway on the way to the final and Christy was all for it.'

Notwithstanding his enthusiasm, the initial competition commanded little interest outside the clubs involved. 'I have to admit,' said a hurling man from Gort, 'that Bing Crosby's first visit to Galway in 1965 to see the bay he made world famous got much more publicity than Ring and the inter-club championship.'

In time, of course, Christy's vision of a vibrant Munster club championship would materialise and expand to All-Ireland status. And the maestro himself had more than a little to do with launching the competition on its successful journey. He signalled his intention of playing in the inaugural final by lining out a week earlier at Togher in a league game against St Vincent's and putting two goals past future All-Ireland custodian, Paddy Barry. The league points were of no consequence to either side, but the match showed that the impending Munster club final meant a great deal to Christy and the Glen.

CHAPTER TWENTY-THREE

EASTER 1966

Easter Sunday 1966 set many minds thinking of the seminal events that occurred in Dublin 50 years earlier and there were appropriate celebrations to mark the anniversary of the 1916 rebellion. One of the most significant events of the day occurred in Limerick, where Glen Rovers, in their jubilee year, won the inaugural Munster club hurling championship – played albeit between the champions of 1964 – and a man born just four years after the Easter Rising was the star of the victory.

'They came to the Gaelic Grounds to see the master hurler in action,' wrote Jack Power in the *Gaelic Weekly*, 'and with that infallible sense of the big occasion, which has been a feature of his career, Christy Ring did not disappoint them. For one brief hour he enthralled them with an exhibition far beyond the power of any modern hurler to emulate. True, he was heavier and slower than in his prime. And, luckily for Mount Sion, that once devastating burst of speed was but a memory, but he was as fit as any man of 45 could possibly be. And the years had neither impaired his unerring eye for an opening nor diminished by one iota his mastery of the camán.

'When on the ball Ring was still the supreme artist. Deft touches, delicate flicks and superb control made us relive once again the glory that only the maestro possessed. Still present was the ability to weave a magic spell on the crowd and electrify them with a gem from his seemingly endless store of hurling jewels. When the final whistle sounded, he had played a major role in Glen Rovers' victory. And all present – friend, foe and neutral – paid warm tribute to a man whose mastery of the camán is sheer genius.'

'The Ennis Road ground reminded me of a place of pilgrimage,'

Jack Power concluded. 'Old and young were there from far
beyond the borders of Cork and Waterford and they had come to
see, possibly for the last time, a man whose name and fame will
forever be enshrined in the annals of Ireland.'

'It was fitting that Glen Rovers, whose green, black and gold
colours commemorate the 1916 rising, should triumph on the fiftieth anniversary of that historic occasion,' wrote Gerry McCarthy in
The Irish Press. 'Hero of the hour was undoubtedly that ageless veteran, Christy Ring, whose every stroke was greeted with wild
applause. The maestro, though much slower than in his prime, is still
the complete hurler. His deft touches had an unsettling effect on the
opposing defence, he laid on numerous scoring chances, most of
which were wasted, and he emerged from the game as his team's
most effective forward. The loudest cheer of the day greeted his goal
in the forty-sixth minute when he finished a Bill Carroll-Tom
Corbett passing movement by slapping the ball past the advancing
Michael Foley. Three minutes later the crowd acclaimed a neat point,
shot left-handed on the turn from 40 yards.'

'Where is that terrible throat-catching emotion without him,'
asked Val Dorgan in the *Examiner*. 'Truly he has been away too
long because we have almost forgotten that the aura of excitement,
which the great ones have the power to electrify, is still his. And
yesterday, with majestic disregard for logic, he held 10,000 people
in the grip of his hurling genius. What more can be said of this
ageless, dedicated man? That Ring prepared was patent in a
reduced waistline, that he no longer has the stamina of old is none
the less obvious. But only once was he beaten and in this game he
produced bursts of energy and hurling virtuosity which made the
more sustained performances of many fine hurlers look like a
laborious bit of gardening.'

'A powerful half-back line, a more than adequate midfield and
Christy Ring – that was the formula which won for Cork's Glen
Rovers the honour of being the first Munster club hurling cham-
pions,' wrote Donal Carroll in the *Independent*. 'The scenes of
jubilation at the end showed how highly the Cork public regards
Ring, even in the autumn of his glittering career.'

Inauspicious Start

And yet it might never have been. The competition, now one of the more prestigious in hurling, could hardly have got off to a more inauspicious start.

The Glen's visits to Kerry and Galway had evoked little enthusiasm, and only Mount Sion's game against Thurles Sars showed that the competition might have some possibilities. Optimistically, the *Gaelic Weekly* declared that the first final could be the making of the club championship for future years, but when that match was played in mid-winter and abandoned because of a fracas, cynics smiled their 'I told you so' smile. The club championship, they insisted, had no future.

There was an unreal feeling in Blackpool as the Glen supporters boarded the bus to Cashel on a cold Sunday morning in December 1965. They were on their way to see Christy leading the Glen against Mount Sion and hoping to make another bit of hurling history. It did not feel like a big championship occasion, let alone a Munster final,

First Munster Club Final – December 1965.
Andrew O'Flynn rises the ball as Christy and Patsy Harte approach. Glen Rovers wore Cashel jerseys that day against Mount Sion. The match was abandoned near the end and replayed the following Easter Sunday.

and when they arrived in Cashel, a few Glen clubmen anxiously asked, 'Did ye bring the jerseys?' In the excitement or lack of it, the official Glen party had set off without their gear-bag and nobody noticed. So, after hurried consultation with local clubmen, a set of Cashel jerseys was provided for the Glen team, saving them the indignity of playing in their shirts.

'A bitingly cold gale-force wind swept down the length of the pitch which cut up badly, especially around the goals,' said the *Examiner*, 'and at half-time an icy downpour must have made it a nightmare even to hold one's hurley.'

For all that, both teams served up some impressive hurling with Mick Flannelly, Larry Guinan, Freddie O'Brien, Stephen Green and the Walshes shining for Mount Sion, and the Glen's Jerry O'Sullivan, Denis O'Riordan and Sean Kenefick doing well in defence, with Ring the chief danger in attack, where Patsy Harte and John Young also shone. Flu victim Philly Grimes bravely took his place for the second half but, given the circumstances, he made little impact.

'The inhuman element of the wind ruled the game', wrote one scribe, adding that both goalkeepers found it impossible to reach the half-back line with puck-outs against the wind. Goals by Harte (two) and Ring had the Glen in front 3-6 to 2-6 ten minutes from time, a precarious position for a side facing such a wind.

Crowd trouble seemed to be brewing behind the Glen goal, as the match drew to a close and when a row developed between two players, a group of about twenty supporters rushed on to the field to take sides. That led to a general fight and, although the players did not seem involved, referee, Tommy Foran of Carrick-on-Suir, terminated the game because of the danger to the players and to his umpires.

'It was perhaps fortunate,' said the *Examiner*, 'that the heavy rain was at its height during the spectators' mêlée. It may have dampened some of their fervour.' About nine minutes remained when the match was abandoned and shortly afterwards, snow began to fall.

It looked as if the inter-county club championship was doomed to failure. Lack of interest was ominous enough, but the abandonment of the initial final because of an unseemly disturbance by rival supporters sealed its fate. Or so it seemed.

One man was to change all that in the replayed match on Easter Sunday 1966, however, and resuscitate the fledgling competition with a wonderful display that served as a fitting climax to his own lengthy and glorious career.

Triumph

'Let the story of this triumph be the story once again of Christy Ring,' wrote Paddy Downey in the *Times*. 'What a fantastic, incredible man he is. Forty-five years old and still hurling as if he were a fiery youth of twenty. He revealed his age only when the spurt for the ball was more than ten yards. Otherwise he gave us the whole gamut of his enormous skill: the dazzling stickwork, the lightning stroke, the dainty pass – all the artistry that would not have surprised us twenty years ago but enchanted with its magic every soul in the attendance at the Gaelic Grounds.

'One felt that the Cork club's following came there on a sentimental journey. Just to see Ring once more. And they were richly rewarded. Even the setting was perfect for his performance. There were white clouds in a blue sky, warm sunshine and daisies in the grass. All the trimmings that must have transported his old admirers back to the glorious years – and to Ring in his heyday.'

The game itself was an entertaining one, keenly contested by two determined teams. The early dismissal of a player from either side meant that referee Gerry Fitzgerald would brook no nonsense and consequently both clubs played to their strengths and eschewed unsavoury tactics. Glen Rovers were marginally superior throughout and only the sharpness of Foley in goal and occasional flashes of brilliance by Grimes, Power and Walsh kept Mount Sion in contention.

The Glen won by 3-7 to 1-7, their scores coming from Ring (1-1), Young (1-1), Carroll (1-0) and Corbett (0-5). As he made his way to receive the new Munster trophy, Glen supporters hoisted a banner proclaiming 'Christy (Cassius) Ring – The Greatest'.

'They gave Christy a standing ovation as he walked from the field at the end, declining to be carried off on the shoulders of his more demonstrative admirers,' wrote Paddy Downey. 'Was it a swan song?

How splendidly fitting if it was. But who can say because it is now clearer than it has been since he last appeared in his county's jersey four years ago that he is still far and away the best forward in Cork.'

Cork Comeback?

After Ring's disappointing omission from Cork's championship team of 1964 there was little talk about a possible return to the county colours the following year. In fact, it seemed to be accepted tacitly by hurling people that Christy had faded quietly into the background and, if he were to be seen playing competitively again, it would be in the Glen colours only.

Three things happened to change that perspective. Firstly, in September 1965, John Doyle won his eighth All-Ireland medal, thereby equalling Ring's seemingly unique record. Secondly, Christy's superb displays in the Munster club final and refixture showed he was still the best forward in the county and, thirdly and most significantly, Eamonn Cregan engineered Limerick's amazing victory over the almost invincible All-Ireland champions, Tipperary. For the first time in years the Munster championship was thrown wide open and Cork had as good a chance as anyone.

'Nobody appreciated the difficulties we had in picking the Cork team that year,' said Tony O'Shaughnessy, one of the selectors. 'Before the opening match with Clare we found we couldn't play the Glen players who had been innoculated for the club's American trip, and after the drawn match we lost one of our regular backs, Paddy O'Connor of Brian Dillon's, who damaged a cartilage. Christy was mentioned a few times but we weren't sure if he was interested.'

Cork were lucky to draw with a Pat Cronin-inspired Clare, thanks to a late goal by Justin McCarthy, but the replay saw Seanie Barry and Charlie McCarthy fashioning an easy win. Next came the big one – Cork against giant-killers Limerick at Killarney. With Seanie and Charlie getting the goals, Pat Fitzgerald playing one of the best games of his career and Tony Connolly subduing Cregan, Cork won by two points. Then came the real prospect of the county winning the first Munster title in a decade and, almost inevitably, the spotlight fell on Ring.

There was a vast groundswell of public opinion in favour of having him back on the team. Obviously, many followers wanted to see him regaining his foremost position in the record books, but others simply contended that he was still the best forward in the county at the time. And the players seemed to share that view.

'I was very much in favour of Ring coming back,' said Jerry O'Sullivan. 'He was a hurling genius and, even at 45, he had no equal as a snatcher of vital goals.'

Tony Connolly said he would be glad to give up his place for Ring and he believed the others would be of similar mind.

'It was a very difficult decision to make,' said Tony O'Shaughnessy. 'Christy always rose to the occasion and we knew he'd do well, even though he was approaching 46 at the time, but we had to keep in mind the effect his presence would have on the other players, especially the younger ones. Some of them might be awe-struck.'

Word finally reached the selectors that Christy was available, if chosen, and there was enormous interest in the board meeting prior to the Munster final and in the *Examiner* next day – would Ringey be back? In effect, the outcome elicited mixed feelings. Christy was back all right, but only as a substitute. The position most people hoped he would occupy went instead to another veteran, John Bennett.

'We announced our team on Tuesday evening,' said Tony O'Shaughnessy. 'The *Examiner* on Wednesday reported that Ring was back on the panel and on Thursday we read that he had withdrawn his name. Apparently, when he heard the decision to recall him was not unanimous, he lost interest in the matter.'

'Before the Munster final of 1966,' said Justin McCarthy, 'the news flashed around that Ring would be included on the panel for the game against Waterford. Some of us young players were excited at the possibility of the great man himself being part of the set-up. Sadly, it didn't happen. Some say it was not a unanimous decision to have him on and he opted out. In fact, his name was on the official programme for the final, but that's as far as it went.'

'There were several under-21 players on the team and I honestly believe that we would all have loved to have Christy there,' said Gerald McCarthy, 'not just to win his ninth All-Ireland, but because we really felt he'd have been a great asset to us. I think any one of us would have given up our place for him, but it wasn't to be. It was a decision of the selectors, a 3-2 decision to bring him back on the panel, but being the man he was, if it wasn't unanimous, he just wouldn't be part of it.'

As matters went, Cork had a good win over Waterford in the Munster final and John Bennett justified his recall by scoring two goals and a point. A Dublin reporter watching the presentation ceremony spotted Christy at the back of the crowd, listening intently and smiling as Gerald McCarthy accepted the Munster Cup which he, himself, had received in Tony Shaughnessy's absence ten years earlier. Then he turned and walked quietly out of the stand.

Final Farewell

'What promised to be one of the most exciting hurling matches of the year fizzled out as a one-sided fiasco in which the craft and experience of a Ring-inspired Glen team proved too much for a surprisingly incompetent College outfit at the Athletic Grounds on Sunday. An attendance of 9,504 turned up to see this second round game but long before the full-time whistle many patrons were heading for the exits.'

This report from the *Southern Star* in June 1967 was to record Christy Ring in championship action for the last time. There had been nothing in his display to suggest that this might be his swan song. Nobody had been surprised to see him taking the field in the distinctive Glen colours for his twenty-seventh season, nobody was surprised that even at 46, he could score 1-2 and set up another goal, and nobody was surprised that once more he gave a fine performance in helping his club to a championship victory.

UCC, with Seanie Barry, John O'Halloran, Ned Rea, Donal Clifford, Tom Field, Jim Blake, Dan Kelleher and a youthful Ray Cummins in their ranks, had wind advantage in the first half, but failed to beat brilliant goalkeeper Finbarr O'Neill and resolute full-backs, Mick Lane, Maurice Twomey and Seanie Kenefick.

'At the other end of the field stood the man whose presence had a shattering effect on the College defence and whose every move spelt disaster for the students,' went the report.

Final farewell.
46-year-old Christy (15) in his last championship game with Glen Rovers against UCC in 1967. He scored a goal and two points.

A goal by Bill Carroll left the sides level (1-2 to 0-5) at the end of a moderate first half. Then points by Harte, Carroll and Ring and a goal by John Young sent the Glen on their way and they were three goals ahead ten minutes from time. 'Then came a dropping ball which Ring, minus his hurley, dashed out to collect and, though tackled by two College backs, he palmed the sliothar to the awaiting John Young who kicked it to the net.'

Seanie Barry had a late goal for the College, but by then many spectators were on their way home, little knowing that the end of an era had come – the end of the most protracted era ever dominated by a sports star in Ireland. Remarkably, as Christy made his way up the steps of the old Cage after the game, a cameraman filmed the scene, one of the precious movie finds Joe and Tony McCarthy located for their *Ringy* video almost 40 years later.

Christy would never again play a championship match, never again walk into a dressing room togged out after a Glen victory. The video captures a proud supporter patting him on the shoulder after that last, almost mundane Glen-College encounter. 'Well done, Christy,' he is saying. Well done, indeed – after more than a quarter-century of hurling greatness and unforgettable memories. No trumpets to blare his departure, no fanfare to mark his retirement, no front page announcements to signal the end of a playing legend. Just a simple pat from a grateful fan as Christy slipped quietly away.

Ray Cummins

Remarkably, what was to be Ring's last championship game of his lengthy career was also the first senior hurling outing for Ray Cummins. In time both players would have postage stamps issued in their honour, but on that dull afternoon in 1967 it would have been difficult to find two more contrasting figures, middling-small Ring at 46 in the Glen attack and tall, gangling Cummins not yet turned nineteen in the College defence.

'I was playing right half-back marking Patsy Harte,' said Ray. 'I recall very early in the game catching a ball coming out of the Glen defence, going on a solo run, passing centre-field and hearing John O'Halloran shouting to me to take my point, which I duly did. As I struggled to get back to my position – thankfully the quick puck-out had not been invented – I recall thinking "this senior hurling is easy!" As if to teach me a lesson and no doubt recognising my lack of pace and mobility, Patsy Harte spent the rest of the game running from end to end of the pitch, and I like a terrier – a lame one at that – chasing a thoroughbred greyhound.

'I have only one other recollection of that game, which by chance involved Christy. He was taking a free about 40 yards out on the left-hand side of the College goal, city end. I was loitering in his vicinity and either took a fit of coughing or said something to him to put him off his strike. Sure, he put the ball straight between the posts and turned to me saying, "That's how it's done, son!". I felt a very small and humble boy, but Christy had taught me a lesson and put manners on me. I'm sure if I had blindfolded him, he would still have scored.'

The Glen were due to play Muskerry in the semi-final on 27 August at Bandon and Christy was expected to line out as usual. Then, almost at the last moment, came the news that he would not be playing.

'I was a selector,' said Johnny Clifford, 'and that Sunday morning I was told that there had been a phone call that Ring was doubtful. So I went down from Fair Hill to Christy's home in Ballintemple to find out what was wrong. He saw me coming into Avondale Park and he met me at the garden gate. "I cannot play," he said. That was all. I knew that if he felt he could not play, he could not play. There was no need to ask why, no need to try and persuade him. And I did not.'

The Glen won the match at Bandon and many people expected Christy to be back for the final, but he was not. The end had finally arrived. 'Christy came to us in the Glen quietly and without fuss,' said Liam Ó Tuama, 'and over a quarter of a century later he finished playing with the Glen, also quietly and without fuss.'

All-Star Glitz

During the great days of the showbands in Ireland, popular sports commentator, Jimmy Magee, came up with a novel idea of merging showbusiness and sporting names on football teams to raise funds for charity. The All-Stars played in many venues throughout the country and even travelled abroad. The games were essentially fun events and usually ended in a draw but, inevitably, a certain measure of competitiveness petered through and added extra spice to the entertainment.

Christy readily accepted the invitation to join a team of veteran hurlers and footballers, show-biz stars and other notables in raising money for good causes. He played several matches and, being the great competitor that he was, he brought his natural playing skills and unbounded determination to the forefront on each occasion.

When the All-Stars went to America in 1971, Christy was a top attraction and enjoyed another memorable visit. Galway's celebrated 'terrible twins' Frankie Stockwell and Sean Purcell, Antrim hurler Kevin Armstrong, Carlow goalkeeper John Kelly, Mayo's John Nallen and Willie Casey, Roscommon's Gerry O'Malley, Leitrim's Packey McGarty and Kerry's John Dowling and Paddy Kennedy were among the party of 26, which also included Art Supple, Frankie Carroll, Greg Hughes, Mike Murphy, Fr Michael Cleary and the captain of Louth's 1957 winning team, Dermot O'Brien, who had a No. 1 hit record with 'The Merry Ploughboy'.

'Almost certainly Ring's favourite entertainer at the time was Dermot O'Brien,' said Val Dorgan. 'Ring always went backstage to meet him at the Cork Opera House.' Christy was naturally delighted that Dermot was taking part in the 1971 tour, just as the champion accordionist and ballad singer made no secret of his eagerness to play on the same team as the maestro.

'The way the All-Stars operated meant that every player got a run,' said Jimmy Magee in his autobiography, 'but Christy hated his spells on the sidelines. It was obvious he had lost none of his competitive edge. We became close friends on that 1971 American journey. We talked a lot about the games he'd played and things he'd done. I learned to appreciate his dedicated, nearly fanatical, will to win. I learned too of his little ploys and the sometimes roguish behaviour he indulged in in an effort to swing an advantage his way.'

Ever anxious to try his hand at other sports, Christy jumped at the opportunity of playing softball in America. It happened in Hartford where a high school softball game took place before the All-Stars match. Christy watched the play intently and during the intermission some of the Irish visitors were invited to have a go. Art Supple, who had played hurling with Youghal, and Jimmy Byrne, a former Kilkenny minor, did well, but most of the party wanted to see Christy in action in the American game. Having watched the play for nearly an hour Christy felt he was ready but admitted nothing. Jimmy Magee takes up the story:

'When I suggested he might like to have a go at batting, Christy asked one of the young softball players, "Show me how to hold the bat" and then, "Now who is your best pitcher?" The best pitcher was fetched and invited to take on Christy Ring. We all hoped that Christy would acquit himself well. We need never have worried. Our hero was always one step ahead. Ring hit the first ball right on the meat of the bat, out over the fence and down the expressway towards Boston. "That'll be a home run," he announced, throwing down the bat in triumph and declining any further participation. For the umpteenth time in his remarkable career, Christy Ring had made his point.'

At the time relations between John 'Kerry' O'Donnell and Croke Park were so strained that the All-Ireland champions were not allowed to travel to New York for the Cardinal Cushing games. In their stead Seán Óg Ó Ceallacháin proposed that Jimmy Magee's All-Stars should go and John Kerry agreed on condition that Christy, Stockwell and Purcell and the other 'greats' would be included in the group. The brilliant Kerry veteran, Paddy Kennedy, was invited to travel as guest referee.

'We played a New York selection in Gaelic Park and they certainly didn't treat it as an exhibition game,' said Jimmy. 'The majority of them were ex-county players from Ireland and we had a fair few guys who couldn't play at all. No wonder Christy Ring wanted to be on the field all the time.'

The fact that it was the twentieth anniversary of his first appearance at Gaelic Park was not lost on Christy and, though football was never his favourite sport, he made the headlines again by scoring the equalising late goal.

'An attendance of 10,000 enjoyed a highly exciting game played in 80 degrees,' wrote *The Advocate*. 'Both teams were accorded a tremendous ovation by the biggest turn-out ever for the Cushing games. New York were looking all-out winners until Christy Ring blazed home the equalising goal with minutes remaining.'

Pacific Tour

'A postcard from Fiji – from Christy Ring – I couldn't believe it when the postman handed it to me,' exclaimed Jimmy Doyle.

It was the spring of 1973 and Christy was on a tour of the Pacific taking in Los Angeles, Tahiti, Fiji, New Zealand and Australia. The trip included some hurling matches, which Christy relished, and he also took part in a football game.

To mark a special occasion the New York hurling club undertook the tour and the organiser, John 'Kerry' O'Donnell suggested that Christy, Ollie Walsh, Mick O'Connell and Niall Sheehy should be distinguished guests on the three-week trip. All four were treated like royalty and found the tour a wonderful experience. Each of them was granted honorary citizenship of Los Angeles.

The football game was unique in that Christy and Kerry's iconic Mick O'Connell played together on the same team. 'My recollection is that there was a football match in New Zealand,' said Mick, 'and Christy Ring played as a defender. I was upfield myself, but can

*Christy signing autographs in Australia during
the New York GAA club's Pacific Tour of 1973.*

remember Christy coming to meet one ball dropping from the air
and he pulled on it first time up the field. No hands there but football as it should be played. Alas, it is no wonder that Christy labelled
Gaelic as a bastardised sort of game.'

New Zealand, of course, was synonymous in the minds of Cork
followers with Fr Joe Kelly and Christy made sure he renewed
acquaintance with his former hurling colleague and friend in
Christchurch. Almost 30 years had passed since both men had helped
Cork to win the four-in-a-row and there was much to be discussed.

Looking back on the Pacific tour, Mick recalled the three weeks
with a glow of pleasure. 'Overall, it was a great trip and there was no
pressure on any of the four of us to perform in any special way.
Anyway, we were all retired. But it was a very nice gesture of John
'Kerry' O'Donnell's to consider inviting a few old-timers on a holiday
trip. Usually in sport it's a case of when you're gone, you're gone.'

CHAPTER TWENTY-FOUR

THE MENTOR

As the Cork hurlers warmed up with a puck-around before the All-Ireland final of 1977, the relaxed atmosphere was suddenly shattered when a freak accident found a flying sliothar breaking Seanie Leary's nose. Amid the consternation the Youghal man was rushed back into the dressing room and Christy Ring, who had not seen the incident, dashed in after him.

'What's the matter?' he asked. 'Why aren't you out on the pitch?'

'My nose,' said Seanie. 'I think it's broken.'

'You don't play hurling with your nose,' replied Ring. 'Get some cotton wool to stop the blood and get right back out there.'

So Seanie did what he was told and, after a quick repair job, he returned to the playing field, scored a goal and two points and helped Cork to win the twenty-third All-Ireland title.

Christy had become an astute and effective mentor in the mid-1970s and had a big part to play on the sideline with both club and county. During the last four years of his life, he would help Glen Rovers to become Cork, Munster and All-Ireland club champions and, as the players acknowledged, he was instrumental in facilitating Cork's three-in-a-row from 1976 to 1978.

'I think Christy found it a little difficult at first making the transition from star player to county selector,' said Gerald McCarthy. 'He felt a bit remote from the players when he first became a selector – 1974, I think – and the following year, when five people went for four positions on the selection committee, Christy was the one who lost out. It seems hard to believe now, but that's what happened when it was put to a vote in the county board. But when he came back in 1976 he had a different way about him and I think he softened a little in his attitude towards players. He became more concerned about them and the problems they had. Before matches he would say very little, but what he said made an awful lot of sense. Overall, he was a great asset to us.'

'Selecting a team often took us hours,' said Denis Murphy, 'especially if two men went for player A and two for player B and Christy was left with the deciding vote. "None of them are any good," he'd say, and we'd go over it again and again. I think he was afraid that he'd make the wrong decision and get the blame if we lost.'

'One thing he was never wrong about, though, was the referee,' said Gerald McCarthy. 'He went to amazing lengths to study referees and get used to their form. He told me that during his own playing days, whenever he'd have a free Sunday, he would go to a match just to observe the referee and see what he would and would not allow. Then he'd know what he could get away with, when that referee was in charge of one of his own games.'

Jack Lynch and Christy with Tim Horgan at the launch of Cork's Hurling Story *in 1977.*

Jimmy Barry-Murphy and Christy chat during training for the 1978 final.

'On the Wednesday evening before the 1976 All-Ireland we had a team meeting,' said Charlie McCarthy. 'When Christy was invited to speak he said, "All I want to say is that there's a Leinster referee next Sunday and when you take three steps with the ball, take three more and he won't blow for it." And, sure enough, in the final against Wexford, Ray got the ball, took a few extra steps as Ring suggested and scored a vital goal.'

Perhaps the most notable of Christy's instructions to a player was that given to Jimmy Barry-Murphy in the 1976 final, when Mick Jacob's splendid display at centre-back was a key factor in Wexford's dominance. 'It was my first All-Ireland hurling final,' said Jimmy, 'and I was pretty much out of it at wing-forward when I saw Christy coming along the sideline, shouting at me. To be perfectly honest, I thought he was coming to take me off, but instead he told me to go in centre-forward. Mick Jacob had been brilliant up to then, but understandably he was tiring at that stage. I did what Christy told me and, being fresher and faster than Mick, I got a few points in the closing stages.'

Those scores set Cork on the road to victory and Christy wallowed in the joy of his first All-Ireland success as a mentor. Switching Jimmy to the 40 had been the decisive move and an exuberant Ring gave the young 'Barrsman a bear-hug of delight immediately afterwards.

'Ringey's presence in the dressing room was awesome,' said Johnny Crowley. 'He spoke little but what he said was dead on. He could read players, read referees, read the play like no one else and he would tell you what you were doing wrong and how to rectify it. Hurling never left his mind. I remember attending a wedding reception and somehow Ringey was there too. As soon as he saw me he came straight over and said bluntly, "I blame you for that goal". I stood there wondering what goal he had in mind but it showed that no matter where he was, hurling dominated Christy's mind.'

The 1976 final was a personal triumph for Pat Moylan of Blackrock, whose ten points from midfield were crucial after Cork's unnerving start against Wexford, who led 2-2 to nil after eight minutes. 'I said to Christy, if Wexford got another goal, we would not win,' said Jimmy Brohan, a selector. 'Then I saw the Cork points coming and I knew it was going to be Cork's year.'

It looked like being Blackrock's year too, with Ray Cummins leading the county to All-Ireland glory and then joining a star-studded 'Rockies outfit in defending their county title. But after a memorable final, it was the Glen who emerged victorious and went on to become provincial and national champions.

'Just before half-time in the county final,' recalled Michael Ellard, 'an unfortunate man collapsed in the stand and Jim Young answered the call for a doctor to attend to him. Meanwhile, on the field Denis Coughlan slipped as he caught the ball and, as he was rising in the mud, Donal Collins (Blackrock) was charging in and tried to jump over him, but his studs caught Denis in the forehead. Ring immediately took off out to remonstrate with the referee, Willie Horgan, even though it was a pure accident. Bleeding profusely, Denis was carried into the dressing room where Dr Carthach McCarthy decided to drive him immediately to the South Infirmary.

'The half-time whistle goes. Young is still up in the stand, unaware of Coughlan's injury. Ring comes into the dressing room, wants to know how Denis is and is told he's been taken to hospital. Then Young comes into the dressing room.

'How is he?' asks Ring. 'He's dead,' says Young sadly. 'Dead!' roars Christy aghast. Then, after contemplating for a few moments, he adds, 'We'd better call off the match'. 'Call off the match,' says Young. 'Sure, we don't even know who he is?' 'Don't know who he is,' Ring exclaims in astonishment, 'and he playing left-half back for the Glen!'

Victory for Glen Rovers meant that Martin O'Doherty, one of Cork's great full-backs, would captain the county the following year. An easy passage through Munster was followed by another final against Wexford and, with newcomers Tom Cashman, Dermot McCurtain and Tim Crowley excelling, Cork seemed to be coasting when the Slaney men staged a late rally. In fact, it took a magnificent save by Martin Coleman to deprive Wexford of the equalising goal. A key factor in Cork's victory was the decision, advanced by Ring, to place Gerald McCarthy at centre-forward to off-set Mick Jacob and the tactic worked.

Buoyant

Christy was unusually buoyant when I met him in town the day after Offaly had created a major surprise by beating the twice-crowned champions at St Brendan's Park, Birr, in 1978. It was the first time he had ever seen a Cork hurling team beaten by Offaly and he was not downcast, even though thirteen of the All-Ireland winning team had played. 'It's always nice to see a county like

Offaly winning,' he said, 'but, in fairness, they were very lucky to win by a point. We gave away two own-goals, which is most unusual, and I thought Ray Cummins' goal should have been allowed.'

It was after that game, in which Pat Delany, Joachim Kelly, Damian Martin and the others signalled a future for Offaly among the hurling elite, that Christy dismissed notions of a Cork decline. 'We'll be back when the cuckoo comes,' he told reporters. And he was right. Cork got over a dismal league run and went all out to complete a championship treble.

Clare were again the opponents in that year's Munster final and did so well against a gale-force wind that victory seemed theirs at half-time. Again some positional manoeuvring by Ring and a superlative display by Tom Cashman saw Cork holding out to win a game in which corner-back John Horgan was top scorer with four points!

Having beaten Wexford in 1976 and '77, Cork faced Kilkenny in the 1978 final and Christy seemed much more concerned than before. 'His own memories of narrow defeats by Kilkenny were sharp and bitter and he knew just how hard it was to beat them at Croke Park,' said Jimmy Brohan.

So, when Charlie McCarthy led out his men, Christy was unusual-ly apprehensive and his concern grew even greater watching Frank Cummins dominating at centre-field. Once more a strategic switch was needed. Tim Crowley was moved to midfield and played superbly and, with Jimmy Barry-Murphy getting a decisive goal near the end, the three-in-a-row became a reality.

Christy had been a stylish young hurler when Cork completed the treble in 1943, a living legend when they did so again in 1954, and now a three-in-a-row selector in 1978.

Playing Squash

Squash became immensely popular as an indoor sport in the late 1960s. Its success was phenomenal, considering that a decade ear-lier there had been little interest in the game in Cork, the county's only courts in use being the two at Collins Barracks. There was also a disused court at Fermoy's military barracks.

In December 1968, Lord Mayor John Bermingham opened a new squash court at the Orchard Bar in Ballinlough and the game increased in popularity to such an extent that courts were soon built at GAA clubs and other venues, while the old court at Fermoy was brought back into use.

'The Orchard entered for a team competition in 1971,' said Dave Whyte, 'and won the All-Ireland intermediate championship, the first team to bring the trophy out of Dublin. The players were Des Scannell, Peter McGrath, Kieran Madden, Tom Homan and Alec Morrough. Many of the original members of the Orchard came from the famous Collins club and some of the big names to join were Val Dorgan, Eamonn Young, Dr Jim Young, Declan Fitzgerald, Terry Hassett, Edward Hallinan, Alec Morrough and, of course, the legendary Christy Ring.'

'The game was tailor-made for Christy's particular strengths,' wrote Owen Dawson in *The Irish Times*. 'He had enormous, powerful wrists, instant acceleration over a short distance and (especially) a wonderful eye for the ball. The combination of these factors made him a potent force on the squash courts, but there was one big problem – he would not play in competitions. He would have walked on to the Munster squash team, but nothing would budge him.'

'Christy was a totally unassuming, shy man,' said Declan Hassett, 'but he loved his audience. He'd whip around on a squash court having played one of his deft drop shots and he'd have the gallery in his palm, savouring the adulation of someone who might never have seen Croke Park, but appreciated a craftsman.'

'I was living in Cork in his squash-playing days, when Christy would offer to play me once or twice a week,' added Owen Dawson.

'Those occasions were special. He could change in and out of his gear in half the time it took the rest of us. He never wore whites, but put on the first old hurling jersey that came out of his bag and then put a few more over that one. As his body warmed up during a game, the jerseys came off, one at a time, and then as you started to flag from running in circles, Christy started getting cold and put his jerseys back on. To play him was an education. Although nearing 50, he thought nothing of playing twice in a day and sometimes even three times. Most of us were merely fodder. When he hit a ball, it simply whistled past you. I doubt if I ever won a set, let alone a match.'

Terry Hassett recalled when Waterman's opened their squash courts at Glounthaune at the height of the squash boom, Pakistan's Gogi Alauddin and Australia's Cam Nancarrow, ranked in the first four in the world, gave an exhibition. 'Christy was very anxious to see them and was thrilled by their actions and stroke play. When it was over, Nancarrow thanked all who attended and asked would Christy Ring come to meet him in his dressing room. After much persuasion, Christy went to the dressing room and stayed for half an hour. He arrived back with a present from Nancarrow of the racquet which he had used in the game.'

'There are millions of great stories told about this wonderful man,' said Tony Connolly. 'One of the favourites was told to me by Val Dorgan, who had arranged to play the Irish number one, Ben Cranwell, in a squash game at Ballinlough, but had to go on some assignment on the day. He rang Christy to fill in, but introduced Cranwell by a different name, as he felt that Christy might not play if he knew who it was. Christy defeated Cranwell and gave Val an account of the game afterwards. When Val told him who he really had played, Christy went spare, but deep down he was tickled pink.'

'Gerry Murphy was the last man to play squash with Christy at the Orchard courts two days before he died,' said Terry Hassett. 'Next to go into the court was Derry O'Connor, but he had forgotten a racquet. Christy gave him a loan of one and said he would get it back when they would meet again. The racquet was later presented to the Orchard and was put in a glass case on the balcony.'

CHAPTER TWENTY-FIVE

RINGEY AND KEANO

'There will never be a hurler quite like Christy Ring or a footballer quite like Roy Keane,' wrote a reader to the *Sunday Independent* in 2005.

It was not the first time Christy's name had been coupled with that of Roy Keane in the context of sporting greatness, nor indeed is it likely to be the last, but perhaps the best appraisal of their comparative significance was provided by Dave Hannigan in the *UCC Graduate* journal the same month.

'There are so many differences between the pair that at first it seems ludicrous to talk of them in the same breath. One is a highly paid professional, hailing from a city suburb, who at one time confessed he was drinking too much. The other was a teetotaller from a village in East Cork, and the truest Corinthian eschewing countless opportunites to cash in on his fame. Over the past decade Keane has endorsed several products. Ring wouldn't allow a pub in New York to take his name in its title, rebuffed lucrative offers from newspapers and publishers to write his life story, and made do with his earnings from driving an oil truck.

'Yet, for all the disparities you'd expect between two men who played separate codes in hugely contrasting eras, there are also a wealth of similarities. Far beyond their common birthplace, and the fact that as a schoolboy soccer player, Keane's Rockmount team used to congregate outside Glen Rovers' hall in the heart of Blackpool before matches, they share pet peeves: Ring denounced hurling supporters who merely turned up for the big games; Keane's views on Old Trafford's "prawn sandwich" brigade are a matter of public record.'

For a little God is he
On the northside of the Lee …

Roy's comment on his under-performing team-mates later in 2005 – 'Talent without work-rate and pride is a waste of time' – sounds like a Ring quote from the 1950s.

Describing Keane as a man who has frequently provided an on-field example as close to the heroic as sport can accommodate, *Sunday Times* columnist Hugh McIllvanney regarded the diatribe as 'being merely another manifestation of unsubduable honesty and perfectionist values.' Shades of Ring again.

'Read the Manchester United captain's autobiography back to back with the late Val Dorgan's hugely underrated work on Christy Ring,' Dave Hannigan added, 'and it is apparent both were obsessive about their sport, fastidious about preparation, distrustful of the media, incapable of suffering fools gladly and pathological about losing. No better summation of the Cork sporting psyche than that.'

'At the end of the last millennium,' he concluded, 'Cork Corporation buried a time capsule. Amongst other things, they placed in it a Keane jersey alongside a tape of Jack Lynch's grave-side oration at the funeral of Christy Ring. What better window into the soul of a people than that? Future generations need only run their fingers along the stories of each of that trio to gain an appreciation of the place that spawned them.'

Appraising Genius

Younger hurling people today often wonder why mention of Ring dissolves those who saw him play into ecstasies of admiration, awe and nostalgia. It is difficult, almost impossible, for them to understand just what made him so extra special.

Jim McKeon (Frank O'Connor's biographer) tried to explain the phenomenon. 'If you take Pele, Carl Lewis, Babe Ruth, Lester Piggot, throw in Arkle, add the strength of an ox and the cunning of a fox, then you have Christy Ring. He played with fire in his veins and a pride and passion in his performance. He was the only player in the world I would pay to see training. He tried the impossible. What other player would practise cutting the ball over the bar from behind the corner flag?'

'More than a hundred years of competitive hurling has spawned some great artists of the game,' wrote Wexford's Billy Rackard in his autobiography. 'The sporting century is peppered with the names of magnificent players from Tyler Mackey to D.J. Carey. When it comes to selecting the greatest exponent the game has ever seen, measured opinion sees one name out of reach – above all others. That name is Christy Ring of Cork. The nearest challenger is seen to be Mick Mackey of Limerick. For almost two decades Ring's artistry brought warm sunshine to the hearts of hurling purists but to be labelled the greatest other factors had to be present and in equal abundance. Amongst many, an unquenchable competitive spirit wedded to a fiendish desire for victory are just two, but the one that stands out most in my mind was his balance. Again and again, with dancer's aplomb, he first timed chillingly accurate passes to team-mates, points between the uprights and with lethal selectivity rockets to the back of the rigging.'

'I was twenty years of age in 1922 when I saw my first senior match,' said fellow Corkonian Jim Hurley, who later won four All-Ireland medals. 'I have seen every great hurler since. I have never seen one who attained Christy's standard of excellence and maintained that standard over such a long period. You ask to what do I attribute his success? He possesses a combination of the most essential qualities in a hurler to a greater extent than any other player I have known. First there is his unbounded love and enthusiasm for the game, accentuated by an acute consciousness that it is part of our country's heritage. Next he has phenomenal strength. His speed of foot is well above average. He is a superb striker. He has what can best be described as an unbeatable spirit that brings out his greatest endeavour when the odds against him are greatest. His judgment is marvellous. It is not a case of doing the right thing instinctively. Every move of his is thought out and executed with lightning rapidity. It is no accident that on the three occasions he captained Cork in the All-Ireland final the championship came to Leeside. He was no nominal captain relying on advice from the sideline mentors. He is from head to heels a leader in the best and most effective sense – by example.'

'There is a defining moment in the *Ringy* video,' said T.P. O'Mahony. 'We're watching Eoghan Harris, serious to the point of being lugubrious, talking about Ring. "A warrior-hero," he says. "That's the way the people of Cork looked at Ring. They knew there

Manchester United manager, Frank O'Farrell (left), with Jack Lynch and Christy Ring at the Texaco Sportstar Banquet in 1971.

was a warrior-hero walking among them. D.J. Carey and the boys are good technicians but they're not warrior-heroes." Harris is right. A warrior hero can do what no technician can ever do even on his best day – overcome mighty odds, spit in the eye of the gods that rule hurling, lay waste to mighty opponents and never bow the knee to or even acknowledge the perennial and dark presence of the hobgoblin that bears the name of Defeat. Harris knows not only hurling, but his history and his mythology. And it is to the latter especially that one must look when attempting to "place" or situate the sorcerer Ring within the context of the game.'

A folk-hero was how the playwright Bryan MacMahon preferred to describe Ring: 'The folk-hero is often a difficult person to understand. He is larger than life and marches to a different drumbeat. He is often intolerant of those who do not see things his way. He is perhaps experimenting with various formulae which he is convinced will enhance life. Though at times we fail to comprehend the full measure of his methods, to those he allows to come close to his personality he is revealed as a person of immense warmth and integrity. As a great artist is in essence a great man practising his chosen branch of the arts, so also a great hurler is a great man giving his unique endorsements of mind and body to the indigenous game of hurling. To those who would follow in his footsteps he offers the challenge of once more pushing out the boundaries of achievement. Thus the folk-hero in the role of challenger is always seeking to evoke and provoke the best from those who would emulate his mighty standards.'

'Ring was hurling's Shakespeare, its Pele, its Mozart,' wrote Eamonn Sweeney in the *Pocket History of Gaelic Sports*. 'He came as close to perfection as any sportsman can. Sometimes it's difficult to think of Christy Ring as a hurler who took to the field Sunday after Sunday with 29 other players. The words "Christy Ring" seem more connected to legend than to the reality of the pitch, as if he were a figure from some heroic tale of yore whose impossible deeds exist only in the story-teller's mind. He seemed an anachronism – a re-incarnation of Cúchulainn for the modern age. But Christy Ring was real all right.'

'Christy Ring is accepted as the greatest hurler ever and it is improbable that his likes will ever be seen again,' wrote Tipperary man Seamus King in *A History Of Hurling*. 'During the height of his career no one was more feared by opposing players and supporters. He seemed to be the embodiment of skill and cunning. Nothing seemed impossible to him; no game against him was won until the final whistle was blown. He was a colossus in an era of great men, fierce rivalries and epic struggles. Allied to his incredible ability was his emphasis on preparation, his great guts and a terrific will to win.'

*Joe McCarthy's fine study of Christy in his latter days
with Cork, a league match in 1962.*

For Tipperary's Jimmy Doyle, one of the greatest forwards in hurling history, the title 'legend' is reserved for one man.

The Doyles lived just outside Semple Stadium near the railway bridge. When the Cork team would arrive in Thurles before a match, Jimmy would loiter around the Glenmorgan guesthouse, waiting for his idol.

'Nobody paid any attention to me,' Jimmy told Keith Duggan of *The Irish Times*. 'I could follow him into the hotel and then up to the field and fool my way into the ground. If Christy was playing into the Thurles end, I would stand behind the wire there and watch him in the first half. Then I would make my way around the other end for the second half. I was so small nobody took any notice. I was able to sneak down the tunnel afterwards to the dressing room and watch him tog on. Then I would go back down to the Glenmorgan and watch him eat dinner. He used to mash everything up and then spoon the food into him and so that was how I had to eat my dinner. Every chap had a favourite player and Ring was my god.'

Eddie Keher, in his delightful book, *Hurling Heroes*, mentions how Jimmy got to meet and play alongside his boyhood hero at Croke Park. 'During his illustrious career Jimmy won eight Railway Cup medals. He regarded it as a great honour to play for Munster, but it was an even greater honour to play in the same forward-line as Christy Ring.'

Jimmy was thrilled to be accepted by Ring as his travelling companion, said Eddie, 'and he remembers a Railway Cup game in Belfast when they sat together on the train journey and talked hurling all day. He also recalls another occasion when they shared a room in Barry's Hotel on St Patrick's Eve. There were three single beds in the room and Ring was in the middle bed. They went to bed early and Christy spent most of the night lying on the bed, hurl in hand hitting the ball against each wall and doubling on the return. As the ball whizzed back and forth over his head as he lay in bed, Jimmy knew that he was safe and that he wouldn't get a belt of a stray ball when the maestro was the one with the hurl'.

Another Tipperary hero, Michael 'Babs' Keating, too was deeply impressed by Christy. In his autobiography, he describes a scene in the Hibernian Hotel in Mallow, the day after the Munster final of

1968. He and Christy were discussing Babs' performance for Tipperary against Cork, and he says, Christy 'taught me one of the greatest lessons I could ever have learned in business or sport'.

'"Babs you were great yesterday," he began, "but answer me this. If you really concentrated, could you have been much better?" For a moment I just looked at him to see if he was joking. He was stoney-faced. "Well?" he probed. And I began to think and appreciate. Without much effort I picked out moments in the game where I might have held back just a fraction, relaxed when the game was clearly over and we were coasting our way to another All-Ireland final. Throughout the game I had found it relatively easy. If I had pushed myself a little harder I might have accomplished a little more. Any improvement might have been minimal but in Ring's mind the improvement was the thing, not the measurement.

'Over 20,000 Tipperary people and many neutrals had been in the Athletic Grounds the previous day and they didn't see me doing anything wrong, simply because Tipperary won. But if Tipperary had lost by a point I would have had to accept responsibility because there were one or two chances that I missed. It taught me exactly what it was that made Ring so special – he never relented in his search for perfection.'

Learning

'Christy freely acknowledged what he had learned from other hurlers, not just in his youth but even in his latter years,' said Louis Marcus. 'If Ring saw a player doing something he could not, he would study the man carefully, analyse the stroke, practise it himself and make it an instinctive part of his own game.'

'I remember sitting next to Ring one day after a Cork and Waterford league match,' said Ned Power. 'We were watching Tipperary and Limerick in the second game and at one stage Jimmy Doyle, who was new to the scene, took a free and sent the ball sweetly over the bar. "Did you see that?" said Christy giving me a nudge. He was all excited "See what?" I said. "Did you see the follow-through? I must practise that myself." I couldn't believe it. Here was Ringey with all his honours learning something new from a young hurler and planning to work on it.'

'His opponents too were subjected to the same searching enquiry that he brought to bear on his own performances,' added Louis Marcus. 'Christy told me that no man ever beat him with the same trick twice. After the first time the defeat would be analysed and – the secret once discovered – a new ruse would be needed after that.'

Strength

'From all my readings and the anecdotal evidence I have heard,' wrote Damien Irwin, in a letter to the *Examiner*, 'it seems that Ring was great because he possessed so many of the essential characteristics to be great – tremendous skills allied to Samson-like natural strength. Perhaps it is the last trait that separates him from the best of the modern players. More strength than D.J. Carey, Joe Deane, Paul Flynn, Eoin Kelly. When push comes to shove – and it often does when you are on the edge of the square – when skill has been negated by a negative defender, when speed has been nullified by an equally quick defender, strength is the final arbiter.'

In an effort to explain Ring's greatness Jimmy Smyth listed ten points:

1. the ability to leap from a standing position and befuddle any number of opponents
2. the ability to strike a ball with his feet off the ground
3. the uncanny balance displayed when he soloed and struck the ball without shortening his hurley and with the same force as if from a standing position
4. that spasm of brilliance which produced torrents of hurling power
5. the ability to play well in all positions
6. his fearlessness on the field
7. the strength of his body and the power of his stroke – the personal satisfaction displayed when a score was made
8. the total confidence in his own ability
9. the committed approach to each contest
10. his magnetism as a personality on the field

'Where was his greatness then?' Jimmy mused. 'I honestly don't know and I am doubtful if the camera could dissect his worth. Even hurlers themselves cannot pinpoint his superiority but they are unanimous he was the greatest and they do not give praise lightly.

He was a writer's hurler, a commentator's hurler, a supporter's hurler but, most of all, he was a hurler's hurler.'

'On the day of Jim Young's funeral,' said T.P. O'Mahony, 'I stood next to Tipperary's John Doyle in the Glen club and asked him why Ring was so special. I ventured, half apologetically, that it must be a question he was tired of answering. He just smiled and shook his head. "Put me on any other hurler and in ten minutes I would have them figured out in terms of strengths and weaknesses. Not with Christy. You never knew what he was going to do next and he rarely did the same thing twice. Add to that his strength and courage and the knowledge that he was one man who would go through a brick wall to get to the ball. And who didn't know the meaning of defeat. That's why we'll never see his likes again, not in my lifetime anyway."'

Mick Mackey was typically gracious in his appraisal of the man who rivalled him for pole position in the pantheon of hurling greats: 'Christy was a terrific competitor,' he said in a radio interview. 'He was very keen, very quick and he had great hurling ability, great ball control and he could come out of nowhere. He could nearly smell where the ball was going to drop. Of course, people in other counties were all saying, "If we put Ringey away, we'll put Cork away", but you could never put Ringey away. There was always the danger that he was going to break through, that he was going to get clear. You see, he was the danger. He was the inspiration. He was the man who put the world into hurling.'

***

Back in 1953, as Paddy Downey discovered, the Cork hurlers were heading to a training session in the Park. A mother was pushing her pram and baby daughter up a slope near the Atlantic Pond when two cars turned down from the road above. To her horror the second car seemed about to overtake the first and possibly crush her and her little child. Sensing the danger, the first driver pulled over to stop the following car and the accident was averted. With great relief the young woman looked through the windscreen to thank the driver and instantly recognised Christy Ring.

Twenty-six years later, Christy collapsed and died on a Cork street. Incredible though it sounds, the first to rush to his aid was Patricia Horgan, who had been the baby in the pram that Christy had saved from probable death all those years ago.

CHAPTER TWENTY-SIX

LAST DAYS

Christy spent his final Sunday in typical style at a hurling match, a Dr Harty Cup game at Buttevant between the North Monastery and St Colman's. No doubt, he was impressed by the promising hurling of future Cork stars, Tony O'Sullivan, who scored some stylish points, and Tomás Mulcahy, who got a fine goal. The Mon won the match.

The following evening the estate agents, Irish and European Holdings, held a preliminary meeting in the Imperial Hotel to select the codes to be honoured in their new sportstar awards. Christy had agreed to be one of the adjudicators and he surprised many with his knowledge of various sports. When someone suggested that hurling would have to be included, Christy took those present aback. 'I'm not so sure about that,' he said. 'If Tipperary come down the Park in June and beat Cork, we wouldn't look too clever, would we?'

Christy, who had been at a training session, arrived late for the Monday sports meeting, but soon settled to the task in hand. I had the pleasure of sitting beside him at the meal and, when proceedings were over and we went our separate ways, I bade goodnight to him in the foyer of the hotel.

Four days later, on the afternoon of Friday 2 March 1979, as Christy walked past the School of Commerce on Morrison's Island, he suffered a massive heart attack and fell to the ground. The first to rush to his aid was a young school teacher, Patricia Horgan. She used what knowledge of first aid she had, but to no avail, and then whispered an act of contrition in his ear.

On that Friday evening, when my brother dashed in home with the news, I would not believe him. Christy had been in great form on Monday, I said, it must be a mistake. 'I heard it on ERI,' he insisted. 'You can't believe the pirate stations,' I argued but, when we tuned into RTÉ immediately afterwards, the news we did not want to hear was verified.

'I was on my way home from Dublin in the train Friday evening and I hadn't heard the news,' said Terry Kelly, 'but when we got to the station I could see clusters of people talking in quiet tones. There was an eerie feeling about the place. For all the world it reminded me of the reaction in Cork when news of President Kennedy's death broke in 1963. Shock and dismay all around.'

Jack Lynch was also on his way home from Dublin that evening and he asked his driver to stop the state limousine at the Coliseum corner where he could buy an *Echo* from the popular vendor, Johnny Kelleher. As he handed Jack the paper, Johnny said, 'Did you hear the news, Mr Lynch? Ringey is dead.' Jack reeled back in his seat and, with a quiver in his voice, uttered the words 'That can't be'.

Farewell

'The heart of the city stopped beating when they carried him shoulder high through the streets for the last time,' wrote Declan Hassett. 'Men and women cried and children in their fathers' arms wondered what kind of a man would upset their own parents so much. The sun shone on the morning. It could have been June sunlight beckoning into the Ennis Road or Semple Stadium, but the turn on the road was to Cloyne not Fermoy or Mallow, and the colours fluttering in the breeze were not rampant red but sombre black. Christy Ring had died and sporting Sundays would never be the same again.'

'An estimated 50,000 to 60,000 people turned out to pay tribute to the man who, in a spectacular playing career, thrilled millions with his hurling skills,' wrote the *Echo*.' It took three hours for the cortège to complete the journey to Cloyne, normally a half-hour journey. The county of Cork and the GAA world had come to say farewell to Ringey.'

No funeral in Cork had drawn such huge numbers since the passing of Terence McSwiney. Now the descendants of those who paid tribute to the Lord Mayor lined the streets of the city to offer silent and tearful thanks to another truly great Irishman.

The great Tipperary hurlers, Tommy Doyle (left) and Mickey Byrne (right), at Christy's funeral.

Farranferris pupils formed a guard of honour as the coffin, draped in the Glen and St Nick's colours, was carried from the church in Ballinlough before the funeral procession made its way to the city centre. Then the cortège moved through St Patrick's Street and over the bridge up towards 'Paddy Barry's Corner' – the reverse journey from that seen so often when Christy and his men had come home with the cup. On to McCurtain Street and then past the railway station where Ringey had arrived home with the McCarthy Cup and his eighth All-Ireland medal. All the time and all the way thousands lined the streets and followed behind.

Many of the great Munster final men were there to honour him – Mick Mackey, Tommy Doyle, Mickey Byrne, Jackie Power, Pat Stakelum, Tony Reddan, Ned Power, John Doyle, Mick Herbert and Jimmy Doyle heading a veritable who's who of hurling greats from all over Ireland. They came from near and far, few further than his great friend, John 'Kerry' O'Donnell who, on hearing the sad news, boarded the first flight from New York.

'All day on Saturday a stream of people filed past the coffin to catch a last glimpse of their hero,' wrote the *Examiner*. 'Many wept to see the man who had thrilled them in Thurles, Limerick, Croke Park and the old Cork Athletic Grounds now lying in repose, his mighty heart stilled. A total of 30 books were filled with signatures of those who came to mourn.'

Earlier in the day Paddy Tyers had called into Forde's funeral home on the quayside. 'It was very early when I went in to say a prayer for Christy and there was only one other person there, a woman saying the rosary. As I left she turned to me and said, "Tis a sin to bury that man."'

The funeral Mass next day was presided over by Bishop Lucey who had performed Rita and Christy's marriage ceremony at the same church just sixteen years before that. The chief celebrant at the Mass was Fr Charlie Lynch (Jack's brother) and among the priests on the altar were Christy's former Cork team-mates Fr Con Cottrell, Fr Bernie Cotter and Fr. J.J. O'Brien.

On leaving the city on Sunday morning the funeral procession entered east Cork, the barony of Imokilly, bringing Christy back to his beloved Cloyne. It was a journey he had made almost every weekend of his adult life. Now he was coming home for the last time.

'The cortège, which stretched for miles, halted at Glounthaune where young boys togged out in the club colours of Erin's Own, paid their own special tribute,' wrote the *Examiner*. 'In the distance the flags of Cork and the Tri-colour could be seen flying at half-mast over the entrance to Pairc Uí Chaoimh.'

A mile outside Cloyne the procession stopped and from there to St Colman's churchyard the coffin was shouldered by renowned sporting celebrities from Cork and the other counties. 'We carried him at last,' said Paddy Barry.

Home

'A gentle breeze was blowing across the rolling hills of Kilgrellane and Knocknamadree,' wrote Pádraig Ó Loingsigh in *The Book Of Cloyne*. 'Cloyne's round tower, austere and dignified, witness to a historic past, stood as ever silent sentinel of this placid pastoral scene. Waiting by the graveside, we thought of Spit Lane, a mere

Cork three-in-a-row coach, Canon Bertie Troy with Christy at the launch of The Book of Cloyne.

puck of a sliothar to the south. We thought of the old Ring home-
stead where Nicholas Ring had fashioned the very first camán for
his son, Christy. We thought of Spillane's field, now Cloyne's hurling pitch, where Christy was to develop matchless hurling skills.
There this youngster of boundless energy had played with his
brothers, Willie John and Paddy Joe, and with Paddy and Jimmy
Motherway, Paddy Moss Ahern, John and Tommy Cahill, Sammy
and Gerry Calvert and Henry Canavan. Often it was dusk when
reluctantly the Rings came in from the playing field, and then only
in response to their mother's persistent pleading.

'The funeral procession moved slowly down Ard an Mhuilinn,
past the home of teacher Jerry Moynihan, who had purposefully
fostered young Christy's hurling potential, which years later richly
inherited the citation of author Raymond Smith that Christy Ring
was the finest artist with a camán he had ever seen, the man with
the most compelling and magnetic appeal for the crowds.'

Now the crowds were here for him again, but this time as part of
a different and more sombre gathering. And despite the packed
cemetery located in the very field where Christy had played hurling
as a youngster, only the occasional cry of a child or the stifled cough
of an adult could be heard as Jack Lynch delivered his eloquent and
emotional oration.

'Before we leave this hallowed spot let us bide just a few more
moments and cast our thoughts back over the years to which so
many of us have known the honour to know, to play with or against
Christy Ring. What more can be said of him, of his prowess, of his
competitiveness, that has not already been said, but more and more
will be said and written of him. As long as young men will match
their hurling skills against each other on Ireland's green fields; as
long as young boys swing their camáns for the sheer thrill of the feel
and the tingle in their fingers of the impact of ash on leather, as long
as hurling is played, the story of Christy Ring will be told and that
will be forever. He had consummate belief in his own ability and
that ability was consummate. Had Christy applied his talents to
another code, to another sport that had international participation, I
believe he would have achieved the same degree of perfection in it
as he did in hurling and would have won world renown.

'As a mentor, a selector, a coach, his ability was no less. He has inspired literally generations of hurlers – those of us who had the privilege of being his contemporaries on the field and the thousands of aspiring young hurlers who held him in awe and indeed in reverence. All these and so many others who he coached and trained will be inspired and continue to be inspired by him. As a hurler he had no peer. As a friend he was intensely loyal. As a man he was vibrant, intelligent and purposeful. As a father and a husband he was loving, concerned and tender and, indeed, many of you know this.

'To all of you who have come with him in this, his final journey, as he reaches his final goal – his friends, his admirers, old hurlers who played with and against him, old hurlers particularly who have come from many parts of the country – may I say on behalf of Glen Rovers hurling club and St Nicholas, and may I presume to say on behalf of the Cork County Board, and may I presume also on behalf of Rita, Christy junior and Mary, offer thanks and appreciation. May the soil of his native Cloyne rest lightly on this, its most famous and illustrious son. We'll never see his likes again.'

'As I experienced it, the funeral of Christy Ring possessed various layers of feeling and emotion,' wrote Bryan MacMahon. 'First there was the searing family grief which is neither proper nor possible to measure. There was also the sense of loss on the part of his neighbours, comrades and friends. Then there was the hurt and bewilderment experienced by a vast silent and grieving public who to a man were admirers of his consummate artistry. At every crossroads too there were bright-eyed young men – too young to have seen him play – joining the cortège as guards of honour, who had only experienced the magic of Ring at one remove and yet whose eyes betrayed the fact that his magic was contagious. There was also the admirable imaginative dimension transferred to everyone who has ever handled a hurley in the Taoiseach's phrase in his graveside oration which mentioned the tingle experienced when ash meets leather in a fiercely contested encounter. The passing of a folk-hero, whether that folk-hero be an Ó Riada, a Behan or a Ring, had shocked the people as part, it seems, of a pre-ordained plot or plan into a sense of their communal majesty and power. Here then, as it were, through the agency of the dead maestro was a renewal of the people for the people and by the people. And of this sudden renewal was born a sense of brotherhood that edged all living with prismatic hues. By the death of Christy Ring we are diminished but we are also furnished and enhanced. We do well to remember that he belongs not merely to Cloyne or Glen Rovers or Cork, not even to the Irish people but to humanity as a whole.'

The Man

In a twentieth-anniversary tribute, Aidan Stanley recalled the shock in the 'Corkabout' studios at Union Quay when news of Christy's death reached them. 'As a fledgling producer-presenter at RTÉ Cork, I was thrust with the role of recording the reactions of those who knew and loved him. I remember the details of the following (Saturday) morning going to Fitzgerald's Park, a place of quiet, away from the din of the city, to record the words of Jack Lynch, who was Taoiseach at the time.'

Jack, like so many other people, was still trying to come to terms with the news but managed to speak calmly and lucidly of his old friend. 'From the day he came on the Cork team in 1939,' he said, 'Christy was to contribute more than any man to the history of the game of hurling.' He went on to elaborate on this, but more pointedly, he spoke of an aspect of Ring's character that was not known to thousands of those who idolised him as a hurler.

'He had a very keen intellect,' said Jack. 'He was a man of great perception and he was a good judge of life and of people. I had many instances that indicated that to me. He was a very good friend and as well as that, in my capacity as a TD, he came to me often about problems, not his own problems. They were other people's problems and he pursued and persisted in ensuring that whatever problems he brought to me were either solved or came to the point where nothing else could be done about it.'

'Christy had a heart of gold,' said his brother Willie John. 'There wasn't a day when he didn't visit a patient in hospital and Mass played a great part in his life. He attended every morning if possible. He listened to the problems of people which he sorted out by taking the matter to local TDs, where he wouldn't take no for an answer. These people cried over Christy's dead body. There was no one to help them when they were in need and they appreciated this quality in Christy's character.'

'There was a very caring side to Christy Ring,' said Diarmuid O'Donovan. 'He did many things to help people in a private way. He was very willing to give of his time and he would sit and talk with people who were ill or grieving. In the early 1950s my father spent almost three months in hospital with an eye injury. He wasn't long in hospital when Ring came to visit him. Having satisfied himself that my father's eyesight was on the mend, he leaned towards my father and asked him, "Are you OK for money?"'

Christy's great friend, Dave O'Brien, worked night shifts in CIÉ. 'Christy knew this,' he said, 'and after my wife died I would be alone in the house by day. Christy would call two or three times a week for a chat. He would always have an excuse, like he was on the way to some Shell garage or whatever. Then he'd sit down and we'd chat away for half an hour or more. I was not the only one he did this for. I know of several people who can tell the same story.'

Con Murphy remembered having a disagreement with Christy over All-Ireland ticket allocation. 'I did my best to provide the number he required but he was quite annoyed that I couldn't give him the complete amount. We parted on bad terms and yet not long afterwards, when I had to go to hospital, Christy was one of the first in to see how I was. I never forgot him for that.'

'Christy was a deeply religious person,' said Seán Ó Sé, the singer. 'He used to attend Sunday Mass at the Ballinlough church and occasionally I'd find myself in a pew behind him and couldn't help noticing the scars still on his head from hurling battles of long ago.'

'I lived quite close to the Ring family,' said Owen Kirk, originally from Monaghan, 'and whenever I'd meet Christy he'd stop for a chat and we'd talk about our children's progress, never hurling! Once my mother came down to Cork to visit us and we introduced her to Christy. He made more of a fuss about her travelling alone to Cork at her age (70+), than she could ever do about his hurling. He made her feel very special.'

'Christy was a great neighbour,' added Owen. 'Once one of our near neighbours – a Mayo man – received word that his father had died. He wasn't long in Cork at the time and Christy met him on the street looking for a phone box. Christy knew by the look of him that something was wrong. Upon enquiry, the man told Christy about his father and how he needed to arrange to get a train to Mayo the following day. Christy wouldn't hear of it. He sent the man back to pack his bags and drove him straight to Mayo. When he got there, he sympathised with the family and drove straight back home.'

On the eve of the 1978 final, my own father died unexpectedly at home and my mother and the rest of the family who were in Dublin for the game had to make the sad journey back to Cork. I had planned to travel to Dublin in the 'all-in' train on Sunday morning, but instead I watched Cork winning the three-in-a-row on television. Christy, a selector, was overjoyed at the victory over Kilkenny and thousands thronged the city centre to welcome home the champions on Monday evening. Yet, as the supporters headed for the station to greet the victorious players and their mentors, Christy interrupted his celebrations by visiting O'Connor's funeral home to offer his condolences to my family. In the midst of his euphoria at the All-Ireland win and the homecoming, he still found time to pay his respects in person.

'The stories and indeed songs about Christy are the stuff of folklore, as is only natural with a great hero,' wrote Owen Dawson in *The Irish Times* in September 2004. 'There is, however, one story I know to be true. In 1979 another great multi-champion Cork hurler was seriously ill in hospital and Christy called to see him. Christy had spent the previous week in Lourdes helping disabled people and had brought back a bottle of holy water. As he was leaving, he gave some to his very sick friend. As Christy said goodbye he started to cry, the patient started to cry and the third person in the room started to cry. Christy just turned on his heel and walked out. The patient recovered and is hale and hearty to this day. Christy dropped dead in the street in Cork three days later.'

CHAPTER TWENTY-SEVEN

THE STATUES

'When I started to think of designing a memorial to Christy Ring,' said Yann Goulet, the sculptor, 'I kept in mind that the bronze statue, nine feet high, will stand in his native town for hundreds of years, an eternal and everlasting tribute to this great hurler. The Christy Ring whose memory I will perpetuate in bronze will be the perfect athlete that he was in his youth, strong but elegant like the Apollo of the Greek mythology or Michelangelo's David, men never marked by the passing of time. In Christy Ring we had the typification of an ideal Irish athlete and it is as such that he should be remembered by future generations. His determination, the pride for the game that he loved, his nobility will be the main characteristics that I will try to depict, not forgetting his great physical strength, allied with the agility and delicate balance of movement of a ballet dancer.'

Michael Sheedy, the Midleton sculptor in charge of work on the memorial, did the lettering on the base of the monument which was constructed with Kilkenny limestone. Christy's brother, Willie John, did much of the work on the building of the memorial walls which are faced with Kealkil stone.

The monument was unveiled by Jack Lynch in 1983 on the first Sunday in May, an occasion once known as 'Glenbower Sunday', when Christy won his first medal for Cloyne almost 50 years earlier.

Located on the site of Christy's old home in Spittal Street, the monument forms an imposing entrance to Cloyne's hurling pitch and was the brainchild of the Ring Memorial Committee, set up shortly after Christy's death. 'From the start one of our objects was the erection of a suitable monument,' said Dr Carthach McCarthy,

Mrs Rita Ring and Jack Lynch beneath the Ring statue in Cloyne.

'and the location was fixed for Cloyne. We felt that though Christy does not solely belong to any one place or any one county but to the whole of Ireland, nevertheless Cloyne figured so largely in his mind and heart that it had to be there and nowhere else.'

'I attended the official unveiling of the massive memorial,' wrote John Joe Brosnan in what became his final contribution to *The Corkman* before his death in 2003. 'Afterwards I retired to Garryvoe Hotel to talk with great hurlers about his deeds. But I must say that the most emotional experience I had was when I took the members of my family to visit the memorial some years later.

'I stood before the huge monument, staring up silently at the immobile figure. The children looked up too but soon lost interest and started playing around. I remained there, totally transfixed. What I found hard to cope with was the immobility and the silence. Ring was such a vibrant figure that it was hard to imagine that he was now only represented in bronze, that those powerful legs would never carry him on a goalward run again, that those magnificent wrists would never again perform such impossible feats in tight situations.

'Then the vision of the monument faded away and I was once again back to my youth, sweltering in the heat of Limerick's Gaelic Grounds with the cheering lifting the sky, or in Thurles or Killarney or Croke Park on days when all the world seemed young and Ring seemed ageless. We idolised him, we adored him because of what he did for the Cork team and we could never imagine a day when he would not be there.

'But now all that was gone forever, something only to be conjured up from memory while gazing at an inanimate object in bronze. I am not a person given to shedding tears easily, but I must confess that I got quite emotional that day. My young son came to me, he caught me brushing away a tear. "Why are you crying, Dad?" he asked.

'"You wouldn't understand, Kevin," I said, "I'll explain to you when you get older."'

Airport

'Cork airport would be an ideal location for a Christy Ring statue,' thought Barry Roche, after seeing the Cloyne monument. 'The statue in Cloyne is excellent, but many visitors to Cork would never get to see it. At the airport one of the first things the arrivals would see would be a statue of Cork's greatest sportsman.'

The airport manager's thoughts led to a two-year project to select a winning submission from one of twelve sculptors. 'The larger than life statue,' Barry insisted, 'must capture the power and movement of the hurling genius from Cloyne. It should capture the spirit and likeness of Ringey and show something of his glamour and charisma. Sean MacCarthy's magnificent work has achieved those criteria.'

The airport statue was jointly unveiled by Mrs Rita Ring and the Minister for Youth and Sport, Bernard Allen in 1995.

'The sculpture is in the classical style and is the result of hundreds of studies of the great man in action,' said Sean MacCarthy. 'I tried to keep in mind the great Italian sculptor, Donatello, but I do not delude myself as to how far I succeeded. The main thing was to create a monument worthy of such a magnificent hurler.'

Robert Ballagh

Robert Ballagh, one of Ireland's most distinguished artists, explained how he came to do a painting of Christy based on one of the best-known action shots of Ring in his latter days. 'Some years ago a publication was planned which would include poetry, art and calligraphy and was titled *Leabhar Mór na Gaeilge*. It was jointly produced in Scotland and Ireland and poets, artists and calligraphers were invited to participate. I was asked to illustrate a poem by Seán Ó Tuama on Christy Ring. I was delighted to accept because for over 30 years we have had a house in Ballycotton, only a few miles from Cloyne, and consequently I was always aware of the legend of Christy Ring. My image is derived from the excellent photograph (p. 327) which I got from the archive of the *Irish Examiner*.'

Bryan MacMahon

'We could nearly fill the book with poems about Christy Ring alone,' said Jim Cronin while he and others were compiling *Cork GAA Ballads*. In the end they settled for seventeen and, though some of the verses are masterly in their depiction of Christy, none can better Bryan MacMahon's superb paean *A Song For Christy Ring*, the penultimate stanza of which brilliantly encapsulates the magic of Ring, when all about him seems lost to Tipperary:

A Song for Christy Ring

Come gather round me boys to night and raise your glasses high
Come Rockies, 'Barrs and Rovers stars, let welcome hit the sky.
Let bonfires blaze in heroes' praise, let Shandon echoes fling
For homeward bound with hurling crown comes gallant Christy Ring.

To every man his game and sport, as every man his creed:
But where's the race that can compare with Cork's own hurling breed?
As fair and free in fierce melee the ash and leather sing
And swift among the blades outflung moves peerless Christy Ring.

So all you hurlers from the Nore, you lads from Corrib's side,
From Garryown's bright and bold, with Tipp's own men beside.
You may have hurlers straight and brave who can a camán swing
But who's the name can play the game with Cork's own Christy Ring?

When we were young we read at school that in the days of old,
The young Setanta showed his worth with shield and spear of gold,
As hurling hard on Royal sward he'd Red Branch heroes fling,
My soul, today, he'd yield the sway if he met Christy Ring.

A health to faithful Wexford, boys, to the Rackards and their team,
Should Cork surrender Ireland's crown may victory on them gleam.
John Kelly's name we hold in fame – of '98 we sing
But Slaney's plan must find a man to equal Christy Ring.

How oft I've watched him from the hill move here and there in grace,
In Cork, Killarney, Thurles Town or by the Shannon's race,
'Now Cork is bet, the hay is saved' the thousands wildly sing –
They speak too soon my sweet gorsoon, for here comes Christy Ring.

When age has claimed this warrior brave, so ended is the fight,
And o'er the hearth he hangs at last his stick and trophies bright.
Come counties all both great and small who boast a hurling king,
Can one tonight hold candlelight to Cork's own Christy Ring?

Christy Ring Bridge

In Christy's day the Cork Corporation reserved its highest honour mainly for prelates and politicians. Recent times, however, have seen more enlightened thinking on the subject and sporting figures like Con Murphy, Sonia O'Sullivan and Roy Keane are among those honoured with the Freedom of the City. In 1987, the corporation – now called Cork City Council – named an impressive new bridge over the Lee in honour of Christy.

That was a dark period in Cork's economic history, with the closure of Fords and Dunlops decimating the city's workforce and Lord Mayor, Jerry O'Sullivan, used the bridge as a metaphor for recovery. 'Christy Ring was the classic example of fighting back to win,' he said at the opening. 'Let us, as Cork men and women, unite as a team to follow his example.'

Located near the Opera House and straddling the north channel of the river, the Christy Ring Bridge links Emmet Place with Carroll's Quay.

Flower Lodge

Many eyebrows were raised in Cork when news broke in 1988 that the County Board had acquired the well-known soccer pitch Flower Lodge on the Boreenmanna Road. It was a major coup for the board officials who negotiated the purchase and extended an impressive list of playing facilities already procured at Kilbarry, Togher, Ballinlough, Douglas Road, Model Farm Road and Mayfield. To add to the surprise and delight of hurling fans, the re-developed grounds would bear the name of Christy Ring.

While the County Board had previously tried to acquire the site in the 1950s, it was to take over 30 years to purchase and £1.25 million (including the purchase price) to develop the 6.5 acre facility. Finally, on Sunday 23 May 1993, the splendid Pairc Chriostóir Uí Rinn was officially opened.

The previous day, the Cork hurlers had beaten Wexford in the league final after three hectic encounters and the young captain, Brian Corcoran, delighted the 4,000-strong attendance when he brought to the new stadium the National League Cup.

The Artane Boys Band, very appropriately, were on hand to provide the stirring music. Clearly and understandably moved by the occasion were the Ring family: Rita, Christy, Mary and their relatives. 'It's a great honour,' said Mrs Ring. 'Christy would have been delighted.'

The stadium was blessed jointly by Bishop Michael Murphy and Canon George A. Salter and a plaque was unveiled by GAA president, Peter Quinn. Among the speakers was the Lord Mayor, Micheál Martin, who described Ring as a man who personified excellence and quality. 'He was Cork's great sporting hero and a true genius of the game,' he added.

After the formalities, the first hurling match in the new stadium ended in victory for Cork over Kilkenny, with Ger Manley topping the scorers' list with 1-7 of the 1-16 total. The Cork footballers also won their game against Meath.

The mood of the occasion was fittingly captured in the souvenir programme by Frank Murphy, one of those instrumental in the purchase and development of the stadium. 'Today we celebrate the culmination of a great achievement for the Association,' he wrote, 'and we dedicate this beautiful arena to the memory of a man who, in his lifetime, contributed immeasurably to making the name of Cork GAA great – the one and only Christy Ring.'

Ringy DVD*

In 2004, Forefront Productions honoured Christy's memory with an excellent TG4 documentary called *Ringy*. 'It was the twenty-fifth anniversary of his death,' said Joe McCarthy, who, with his son Tony, produced the programme. 'TG4's commissioning editor, Micheál Ó Meallaigh, felt it was fitting that a televised tribute to Ring should be produced. The response we got from all those we asked to contribute was overwhelming and we were particularly pleased to locate some rare colour footage of Christy in action in the 1954 final and chatting with Senator Robert Kennedy in New York.'

The colour scenes from Croke Park, the day Christy won his eighth All-Ireland medal had been shot by Fr Jack Collins from Skibbereen, who was home on holidays from the African missions. Over 84,000 attended the game, but Fr Collins, with his 8mm camera and monopod, was allowed close to the action and got some splendid shots of Christy. Ironically, his films were subsequently

*While Christy was popularly known as Ringey, some sources refer to him as Ringy

lodged in the crypt of the African Missionary church, where Christy often attended mass, never knowing the only colour film of his greatest triumph was stored underneath.

'The Bobby Kennedy footage was filmed by Bill Kenneally at Gaelic Park in 1965 and given to us through a former Cork hurler, Con O'Riordan from the Charleville area,' said Tony. 'Both friends were exiles in America and we were astonished at their generosity and trust in providing the original master footage for the programme.'

Well-known actor, Niall Toibín, who provided the narration, met Christy in the Lucan Spa Hotel after the 1977 win. 'I was really chuffed when he told me he liked my work. Imagine Ringey being a fan of mine.'

The TG4 programme was highly acclaimed and inevitably a popular DVD/video followed.

Christy meets Bobby Kennedy in the States in 1965.

CHAPTER TWENTY-EIGHT

HURLER OF THE CENTURY

The advent of the new millennium prompted many people to cast their minds back and recall great names and memorable deeds. Nostalgia dominated newspaper stories as the 1990s drew to a close and, not surprisingly, the names of many of the great sports stars of the twentieth century were mentioned and compared. In hurling there were many illustrious names spoken about, but only one could be given pre-eminence. That one was Ring.

'Christy Ring – Best Hurler of the Century' was an *Irish Times* headline, similar to those in other journals where Christy's exploits were relived in print. In the *Times* Sean Moran analysed the merits of Ring, Mick Mackey, Nicky Rackard, Jimmy Doyle and Eamonn Cregan, before opting for Christy as the greatest. 'In a game as mythological as hurling, Ring's universally accepted pre-eminence is remarkable,' he wrote. 'Yet he possessed everything from talent and ferocious application to longevity and a string of records including eight All-Ireland medals. Obsessive about the game, he worked relentlessly to sustain a formidable array of techniques, complemented by a great vision and anticipation. A shamanistic sense of his own distinctness added to a reputation for eccentricity, but Ring's greatness also demoralised opponents. Physically resilient and resourceful, he played senior inter-county between 1939-63.'

'Twenty years after his death, memories of the deeds that made Ring a hurling icon are still vivid to the many fans who regard him as the greatest hurling exponent of all time,' wrote Dermot Crowe in the *Sunday Independent*. 'Ring's career straddled four decades and encompassed some epic periods in hurling history. For 23 years he was an automatic choice for Cork – people flocked to see him play, however prosaic the occasion, and he became a subject of fixation for opposing teams. Interest in Ring was intensified by his own reluctance to betray much about himself. There were reports of open cheque offers to tell his story, but he never consented. The furious pace and tempo of the modern game is unprecedented and invigorating and you wonder how Ring would fare in the current climate. Most likely he would have thrived in any era given his preoccupation with fitness, the broad arsenal of his skills which he constantly honed, and his innate confidence.'

Inevitably, various team selections were chosen and provoked much high-stool discussion. By their very nature such formations of great hurlers were subjective and often reflected almost as much on the selectors as the players they picked. Nonetheless, they provided immense fascination and heated argument, usually about the top-class hurlers who were omitted. The Cork, Munster and Ireland Teams of the Millennium were:

CORK

Ger Cunningham
(St Finbarr's)

Jamesey Kelleher	Seán Óg Murphy	Brian Corcoran
(Dungourney)	(Blackrock)	(Erin's Own)

Tom Cashman	Jim O'Regan	Denis Coughlan
(Blackrock)	(Kinsale)	(Glen Rovers)

Jack Lynch   Gerald McCarthy
(Glen Rovers)   (St Finbarr's)

Eudie Coughlan	Josie Hartnett	Christy Ring
(Blackrock)	(Glen Rovers)	(Glen Rovers)

John Quirke	Ray Cummins	Paddy Barry
(Blackrock)	(Blackrock)	(Sarsfield)

MUNSTER

Tony Reddan
(Tipperary)

John Doyle	Brian Lohan	Denis Murphy
(Tipperary)	(Clare)	(Cork)

Jimmy Finn	John Keane	Jackie Power
(Tipperary)	(Waterford)	(Limerick)

Jack Lynch   Philly Grimes
(Cork)   (Waterford)

Jimmy Doyle	Mick Mackey	Christy Ring
(Tipperary)	(Limerick)	(Cork)

Paddy Barry	Ray Cummins	Jimmy Smyth
(Cork)	(Cork)	(Clare)

IRELAND

Tony Reddan
(Tipperary)

Bobby Rackard	Nick O'Donnell	John Doyle
(Wexford)	(Wexford)	(Tipperary)

Brian Whelahan	John Keane	Paddy Phelan
(Offaly)	(Waterford)	(Kilkenny)

Lory Meagher   Jack Lynch
(Kilkenny)   (Cork)

Jim Langton	Mick Mackey	Christy Ring
(Kilkenny)	(Limerick)	(Cork)

Jimmy Doyle	Ray Cummins	Eddie Keher
(Tipperary)	(Cork)	(Kilkenny)

The players chosen by An Post were honoured with postage stamps designed by Finbarr O'Connor and during Cork's European Year of Culture (2005) postcard reproductions of selected stamps featured Michael Collins, Frank O'Connor, Roy Keane and Christy Ring. 'The Ringey cards sold out within a few weeks,' said the philatelic officer in the GPO (Cork), 'yet we still get requests for them!'

Nineteen Munster Finals

Christy Ring played a remarkable total of nineteen Munster finals, including two replays. Although he was a midfielder for some of his early years and missed the 1957 final through injury, he scored considerably more than any other forward before or since as Kieran Shannon and Leo McGough revealed in the *Sunday Tribune* (July 2007)

Pos	Total	Player	County	Score	Finals	Avg
1	106	Christy Ring	Cork	12-70	19	5.57
2	68	Jimmy Doyle	Tipperary	3-59	10	6.80
3	60	John Fenton	Cork	1-57	10	6.00
3	60	Mick Mackey	Limerick	13-21	12	5.00
5	59	Charlie McCarthy	Cork	8-35	11	5.36
6	57	Nicky English	Tipperary	6-39	11	5.18
6	57	Tony O'Sullivan	Cork	1-54	12	4.75
8	48	Joe Deane	Cork	2-42	6	8.00
9	47	Michael Cleary	Tipperary	3-38	8	5.87
10	40	Jack Lynch	Cork	6-22	12	3.33

'Old-timers tell us there has never been a hurler to match Ring and who are we to argue?' asked Vincent Hogan in the *Independent*. 'Ring's greatness is a blurred picture for all but those who lived through his time. They say he was equally good left or right. That he rarely missed frees. They say he had the fighting instincts of a shark. "Toscanini for good music, Kathy Barry for crubeens and Ringey for goals" ran the salty legend. The beauty of hurling is that it is a game made for story-telling. Rather than dull the legend of men like Ring and Mackey, time embellishes it. When Donal Óg Cusack and Diarmuid O'Sullivan, two Cloyne men, were part of this year's All-Ireland winning Cork team, every story-line about them seemed somehow stiched to Ring. It felt natural.'

'What I find beautiful,' said John Doyle, 'is that whenever you go to Cork and see young fellas pucking a ball around, if you ask them about Christy Ring, they'll know immediately who you're talking about. That's lovely and it's the way it should be. Ringey will never be forgotten.'

Better Yet To Come?

'My hurling days are over,' Christy wrote in Liam Ó Tuama's award-winning club history. 'Let no one say the best hurlers belong to the past. They are with us now and better yet to come.'

Christy was right on one point – many great hurlers have appeared on the scene since his own day – but better? Now there's the rub.

'The problem of assessing every hurler AC (After Christy),' said Enda McEvoy in the *Sunday Tribune*, 'is that Ring's shadow has become a stick not to measure his successors against, but to beat them with.'

'That he has proved himself to be the greatest hurler ever can scarcely be disputed,' wrote Jim Hurley in 1954. 'It isn't because of his eight All-Ireland medals that he is considered the greatest. It is because Sunday in, Sunday out, for fifteen years, 90 per cent of neutral spectators rated him the best man on the field. There never was anything approaching such unanimity in respect of any other player over such a long period.'

'For over twenty years, Christy Ring, often bloodied, nearly always triumphant, performed the incredible before the eyes of thousands,' said Louis Marcus. 'The crowds that tingled as he walked on to a field and that exulted at his deeds were enjoying poetry that they found nowhere else. For Ring was not simply the supreme match-winner. He was also a figure of beauty. Though thickly built and strong as a bull, he moved like a dancer. Ring in action was taut, spare, compact. He ran, lifted, swerved and struck with the economy of a lyric. For the hour they watched him on a field, the crowd were an assembly of aesthetes.'

Christy said …

'Hurling has always been a way of life with me. It was never my ambition to play the game for the sake of winning All-Ireland medals or breaking records but to perfect the art as well as possible.'

'The 1940 Munster final and replay taught me a lesson I never forgot – that hurling needs courage, heart and a firm belief in one's own ability to stand shoulder to shoulder with the best.'

'My last championship game was against the College before the county semi-final in 1967. My senior hurling career spanned close to 30 years and during that period I must have played somewhere in the region of 1,200 games. People wondered why I didn't retire sooner. The reason was that I continued to play hurling as long as I got fun out of it.'

'Never play on another man's name. Go out and play your own game. Remember, you'll never be any good unless you play the ball every time, no matter what. That's the secret of being – and remaining – a good hurler.'

'My advice to young players would be: 1. Develop the greatest possible strength in your arms; 2. Practise swift pucking and striking; and 3. Never hit the ball for the sake of hitting it – deliver it to the right place. To strengthen your arms you must play the ball on the ground – a soft ball that is hard to hit far. One day you might hit the ball ten yards, then twenty but the day will come when you'll drive it 80 yards. You'll drive it that length consistently but you can't do it without making your arms good and strong.'

'Never do anything in training that you can't do in a match – that's no use. The hardest things that you do in training will serve you well in the game because you'll never be asked to do them as hard again. The easy way happens in a game but, of course, it only seems easy because you have been doing the hard things in training.'

'Never take your eyes off the ball – even when it's in the referee's pocket.'

'I never take my opponents as individuals. I play the game for the team, for the fella alongside me. I make openings for them and do the best I can. I often played on the worst man and he was the most troublesome. Often I played on the best man and I thought he was the easy one. I tell you, when a Tipperary man or a Kilkenny man or a Limerick man goes out there, there's nothing soft about it.'

'A hurler must work hard at practice sessions. Missing them can never be excused. Dedication to training is common to all forms of sport and can never be over-emphasised.'

'I practise each of my shots hundreds of times each week. I like to do the unorthodox and keep defenders worried. Once I over-ran a fast pass, put a hand out behind me since I had no time to look, managed to pluck the ball and then pucked it into the net in the same movement. It looked a really great goal but it was partly luck, partly the fact that I usually attempt what other people might think is impossible.'

'You can call me a gambler. I try a move a hundred times in training and, when it comes off in a big match, the crowd goes wild and I say to myself – it worked.'

'You don't play hurling with your nose,' (to Seanie O'Leary after he had broken his nose in a pre-match puck-around at Croke Park. Seanie went on to play, scored 1-2 and helped Cork to win the 1977 All-Ireland.)

'I liked to play little tricks at times. One day in a match against the College I got a small nick on the forehead, no worse than a cut you'd get shaving, but I rubbed the blood all over my face until I looked like a Red Indian. Then I grabbed the next ball and headed straight for the goalie. I think he must have stepped out of the way when he saw this thing coming at him and I scored a goal.'

'My hurling days are over. Let no one say the best hurlers belong to the past. They are with us now – and better yet to come.'

Christy Ring's Roll of Honour

(St Enda's, Cloyne, Glen Rovers, St Nicholas, Cork and Munster)

All-Ireland Senior Hurling Championship Medals (8) 1941, 1942, 1943, 1944, 1946, 1952, 1953, 1954

Munster Senior Hurling Championship Medals (9) 1942, 1943, 1944, 1946, 1947, 1952, 1953, 1954, 1956

All-Ireland Minor Hurling Championships (2) 1937, 1938

Munster Minor Hurling Medal (1) 1938

National Hurling League Medals (4) 1940, 1941, 1948, 1953

Railway Cup Medals (18) 1942, 1943, 1944, 1945, 1946, 1948, 1949, 1950, 1951, 1952, 1953, 1955, 1957, 1958, 1959, 1960, 1961, 1963

Munster Club Senior Hurling Medal (1) 1966

Cork County Senior Hurling Championships (Glen Rovers) (13) 1941, 1944, 1945, 1948, 1949, 1950, 1953, 1954, 1958, 1959, 1960, 1964, 1967

Cork County Senior Football (St Nicholas) (1) 1954

Cork County Junior Hurling (Cloyne) (1) 1939

Cork County Minor Hurling (St Enda's, Midleton) (1) 1938

MAJOR MILESTONES

Captained Cork in three All-Ireland wins and became the first player to receive the McCarthy Cup three times

Played in nineteen Munster finals and remains the highest scorer ever

Won eighteen Railway Cup Medals with Munster and scored 42 goals and 105 points

Captained Cork in their 1946, 1953 and 1954 All-Ireland victories

Had already won eight All-Ireland medals when Owen McCann began compiling top scorers' records in 1955. He was the highest scorer in 1955, 1959, 1961 (with Jimmy Doyle) and 1962

Hurler of the Year 1959

Texaco Hall of Fame Award 1971

Picture Credits

The author and publishers wish to thank the following who have kindly given permission for reproduction of the photographs on the following pages. If any photographs are incorrectly attributed we apologise for this and will be glad to make corrections in any future editions.

Brian Dillons GAA Club: frontispiece
Cloyne GAA Club: page 4
Irish Examiner: pages 8, 13, 17, 20, 21, 23, 34, 36-37, 47, 52, 56, 70, 72, 79, 104, 116, 118, 119, 122, 125, 129, 133, 139, 146, 160, 172, 188, 192, 206, 210, 211, 213, 229, 255, 274, 279, 280, 283, 285, 286, 292, 294, 298, 306, 312, 320, 327, 348
Midleton GAA Club: page 14
Irish Press: pages 44, 48, 92, 111, 135, 143, 151, 165, 201, 216
Irish Independent: pages 141, 162, 184-85, 193, 218, 219, 239, 300
Justin Nelson: page 227
Private: page 234
Seamus Loughnane, Thurles: page 251
Ballinora GAA Club: page 258
Gaelic World: page 317
John G. O'Reilly: page 319
The Irish Times: page 330
Joe McCarthy: page 332
Tom Morrison: pages viii, 341
TG4: page 354

Acknowledgements

Delving into the remarkable sporting life of Christy Ring has been one of the most pleasant tasks I have ever undertaken and I wish to express my gratitude to the many people who helped in the research: those who provided cherished photographs, those who recalled names and events, those who bore with my seemingly endless questioning. All have my utmost thanks.

I am very grateful to Professor Jean Horgan (Dublin City University), Dr Robin Harte (Trinity College) and Ms Sinead Horgan (University College, Cork) for computerising the typescript.

My thanks to Examiner Newspapers, Independent Newspapers, *The Irish Times*, *The Irish Press* and the *Southern Star* for permission to use their photographs and to Justin Nelson (*Clonmel Nationalist*) for his greatly acclaimed picture of Mick Mackey and the injured Christy Ring in 1957. Thanks to Denis O'Sullivan (Ballynoe), Tom Morrison (Shanagarry) and former county chairman Jim Cronin (Millstreet) for allowing me to choose from their extensive collection of hurling photographs. I am also indebted to Aidan Stanley and Donnacha O Dulaing of RTÉ and Barry O'Mahony and Frank O'Brien of 96FM for their features on Ring.

I am indebted to the ever co-operative staff of the National Library in Dublin, Cork City Librarian, Liam Ronayne (Ballinacurra), and the staff at the Grand Parade Library, notably Ciaran Burke, Stephen O'Brien, Jamie O'Connell, Caroline Long-Nolan, Mary O'Leary and Stephen Leech, and Mary FitzGerald of the Frank O'Connor Library on the Old Youghal Road. Equally helpful and patient were Kieran Wyse, Niamh Cronin and Denis Murphy of the Cork County Library.

Notable sportswriters Diarmuid O'Flynn, Denis Walsh, Charlie Mulqueen, Peter Finnerty, Vincent Power, Martin Breheny, Tom O'Riordan, Diarmuid O'Donovan, Michael Moynihan, Damien Irwin, Dermot Crowe, Sean Moran, Kevin Cashman, Kieran Shannon, Michael Ellard, Enda McEvoy and GAA statistician Owen McCann provided valuable insights while the Ringy DVD produced by Joe and Tony McCarthy of Forefront Productions was an excellent source of information.

Special thanks to Ken Devine for his great assistance, to Nollaig O Donnabhain for his translations and to Noel and Willie Horgan for checking details. Among those who were also helpful and supportive were Jamesey Corcoran, Derry Barry-Murphy, John and Edward Newman, the Tracey and Stack families (Glen Rovers), Sean Keohane (Midleton), Michael Kilcoyne and Gerry Buckley (Westmeath), Seamus Grant (Waterford), Jim Breen (Wexford), Brendan Goggin, Ken O'Connell, Dermot McCarthy (Bath), Jim Forbes, Robert Dumigan, Paul O'Leary, Pat Galvin, Gerry Masters, Tim O'Riordan, Frank Connolly, Neil O'Donoghue, Gerry Brennan (Clare), Denis Kelleher, Mark Horgan, Fergal Walsh, Michael Aherne, Liam McAuliffe, Fr Michael Leahy OSA, Canon Michael O'Brien, Miah Aherne, Tony Bloss, Plunkett Carter, Tim O'Brien and the former Cork hurlers Mick Regan, Terry Kelly, Finbarr O'Neill, Mick Ryan and Brendan Barry.

My thanks to all at The Collins Press including Gillian Hennessy and Maria O'Donovan. And finally, my gratitude to the Ring family, Mrs Rita Ring, Christy and Mary (Kenefick) and all the relatives of this wonderful man.

Bibliography

Beecher, Sean, *A Story of Cork*, Mercier Press, 1971

Buckley, Gerry, *Fifty Years of the Hogan Cup*, Ard Chomhairle na Meanscoileanna, Westmeath, 2007

Cadogan, Tim, *Cork in Old Photographs*, Gill and MacMillan, Dublin 2003

Corr, Michael J., and O'Donoghue, Anthony, *A History of the GAA in Midleton 1884-1986*, Cumann Iomanaichta Agus Peile Mainistir na Coran, 1986

Corry, Eoghan, *God and the Referee*, Hodder Headline Ireland, Dublin 2005

Cramer, Tim, The Life of Other Days, The Collins Press, Cork 2004

Cronin, Jim, *Cork GAA – a History*, Coiste Chontae Chorcai 1986

Cronin, Jim, *A Rebel Hundred*, Coiste Chontae Chorcai 1997

Cronin, Jim, *Making Connections*, Coiste Chontae Chorcai 2006

Cronin, Jim, Barry, Brendan, Arnold, John and Smyth, Jimmy, *GAA Ballads of Rebel Cork*, Coiste Chontae Chorcai, 2001

Dorgan, Val, *Christy Ring – A Personal Portrait*, Ward River Press, Dublin 1980

Duggan, Keith, *The Lifelong Season*, Town House, Dublin 2004

Fullam, Brendan, *Hurling Giants*, Wolfhound Press, Dublin 1994

Furlong, Nicholas, The Greatest Hurling Decade, Wolfhound Press, Dublin 1996

Hassett, Declan, *All Our Yesterdays*, Mercier Press, Cork 1998

Hassett, Declan, *The Way We Were*, Mercier Press, Cork 1999

Hassett, Declan, *Passing Through*, Mercier Press, Cork 2004

Humphries, Tom, *Green Fields – Gaelic Sport in Ireland*, Weidenfeld and Nicolson, London 1996

Keating, Michael, with Donal Keenan, *Babs – A Legend In Irish Sport*, Storm Books, Dublin 1996

Keane, Colm, *Hurling's Top 20*, Mainstream Publishing, Edinburgh, 2002

Keher, Eddie, *Hurling Heroes*, Blackwater Press, Dublin 2000

King, Seamus J., *A History of Hurling*, Gill and MacMillan, Dublin 1996

Leahy, Seamus, *The Tipp Revival*, Gill and MacMillan, London 1995

Magee, Jimmy, with Sean McGoldrick, *I Remember It Well*, Blackwater Press, Dublin 2000

Mahon, Jack, *The Game Of My Life*, Blackwater Press, Dublin 1993

Morrison, Tom, *For The Record*, The Collins Press, Cork 2002

Ó Ceallachain, Sean Óg, *Sean Óg – His Own Story*, Calmac Publishing, Dublin 1988

O'Connell, Billa, *Billa*, Mercier Press, Cork 2000

Ó hEithir, Breandan, *Over The Bar*, The Collins Press, Cork 2005

O Loingsigh, Padraig, *The Book Of Cloyne*, Cloyne Historical and Archaeological Society, 1993

O'Mahony, T.P., *Jack Lynch – A Biography*, Blackwater Press, Dublin 1991

Ó Tuama, Liam, *The Spirit Of The Glen*, Fanaithe an Ghleanna, Cork 1974

Power, John P., *A Story Of Champions*, Lee Press, Cork 1945

Power, John P., *Honour To Cork*, Lee Press, Cork 1946

Power, Vincent, *Voices Of Cork*, Blackwater Press, Dublin 1997

Puirseal, Padraig, *The GAA In Its Time*, Purcell, Dublin 1982

Rackard, Billy, *No Hurling At The Dairy Door*, Blackwater Press, Dublin 1996

Redmond, Garry, *Sapient Colloquy*, Nick and Garry Redmond, Dublin 2006

Ring, William John, *History of Cloyne GAA*, Cumann Chluain Uamha 1984

Scally, John, *100 Great Sporting Moments*, Blackwater Press, Dublin 1998

Sweeney, Eamonn, *The O'Brien Pocket History Of Gaelic Sports*, O'Brien Press, Dublin 2004

Smith, Raymond, *Decades of Glory*, Little and McClean Ltd, Dublin 1966

Smith, Raymond, *Greatest Hurlers*, Sporting Books, Dublin 1971

Walsh, Denis, O'Connor, Ollie, O'Mahony, John, and Barry, Tom, *A History of Gaelic Games in Carrigtwohill*, Cork 2000

Index

Page numbers in bold indicate photos.

Abernethy, Billy 134
Aherne, Michael 'Gah' 2, 195
Aherne, Paddy 'Balty' 2, 195
Aherne, Paddy Moss 18
Allen, Norman 100, 134, 136, 145, 177, **192**, 194
Antrim 50-3
Armstrong, Kevin 51, 127, 314
Artane Boys Band 39-40, 59, 297, 352

Ballagh, Robert 350
Bannon, Seamus 65, 115, 125-7, 131, 152, 181-2
Barrett, Jack (Sean) 23-4, 40, 49-50, 68, 71
Barry, Billy 231, 287
Barry, Jim 'Tough' 77, 94, 158-9, **160**, 168, 170, 174, 204, 239
  quoted 51, 119-20, 130, 262
  summary of career 3-4
  trainer 40, 58-9, 61, 89, 140, 187, **188**
Barry, Kevin 2
Barry, Mick 201, 231
Barry, Paddy 2, 38, 86-7, 118-19, **122**, 157, 181, 228
  in All-Ireland finals 164, 217, 219
  comes out of retirement 266-7, 292, 295, 303
  in Munster final **229**, 256
  quoted 130, 131, 152, 341
  in top twenty 145
Barry, Ted 15
Barry, Tom 2, 35, 49, 191
Barry-Murphy, Dinny 2, 3, 35, 118, **172**
Barry-Murphy, Jimmy 96, **320**, 321, 323
Barry-Murphy, John 21
Barry's Hotel 59, 158-9, 168-70, 247, 291, 333
Baston, Vincent 21, 88, 91, 95, 107, 109
Bateson, Jackie 51
Beckett, Derry 21, 46
Beckett, Jerry 19
Bennett, John 215, 310, 311
Breen, Dermot 205
Brennan, Micka 23-7, 39, 85, 118
Broderick, Donal 211, 213
Brohan, Jimmy 229, 235, 243, 260, 277-8, 321, 323
Brophy, Jimmy 75, 123, 167
Brosnan, John Joe 261, 287, 295, 349

Browne, Richie 292
Buckley, Connie 34, 38, 40, 44-5
Buckley, Din Joe 13, 25-6, 41, 44-5, 54, 62, 65, 71, 82
Buckley, Jack 40
Buckley, John 26, 253
Burke, Jeremiah 35
Burke, Mick 133-4, 147, 149, 164, **165**, 166-7, 170, 174, 177, 180
Buttimer, Jim 38, 40
Byrne, Mickey 93, 152, 182, 209, 253, **255**, 287, **339**

Cahill, Niall 30
Cahill, Phil 289
Cahill, Tommy 342
Calvert, Gerry 342
Campbell, Billy 26
Campbell, Noel 51, 53
Canavan, Henry 342
Carey, Kieran 253, 255
Carlos, Bill 119-20
Carroll, Bill 281, 305, 312
Carroll, Donal 305
Carroll, Seanie 128, 176-7
Casey, Tom **210**, 240
Cashman, Mick 128, 149, 152, 181, 215, 226, 256, 277-8
Cheasty, Tom 208-9, 243, 261
Clancy, Willie 35
Clifford, Johnny 118-19, 154, 170, 179, 182, 186, 188-90, 314
Clohessy, Dave 55
Clohessy, Sean 215, 235, 276, 278
Cobbe, Vivian 201, 211
Codd, Martin 217, 220
Collins, Paddy 'Fox' 33-5, 62, 128, 130, 140, 148, **172**
Condon, Sean 38, 41, 46, 54-5, 57-62, 78, 81, 112, 115
Connolly, Dan 1
Connolly, Tony 309-10, 325
Conroy, Denis 43, 84, **229**
Corbett, Tom 281, 305, 308
Corcoran, Brian 352, 356
Corkery, Daniel 30
Corless, Colm 167, 197
Cotter, Jim 105, 128
Cottrell, Con 39, 60, 62, 75, 79, 264-5, 340

Coughlan, Dan 20, 294
Coughlan, Denis 322, 356
Coughlan, Eudie 2, 35, 89, 261, 289, 356
Creedon, Dave 60, 69, 78, 86, **172**
Cregan, Eamonn 25, 309, 355
Cregan, Peter 25, 27
Cronin, Paddy **122**
Crosby, Bing 303
Cross, Dick 269
Crotty, Anna 214
Crotty, Tom 115-16, 126
Crowley, Johnny 321
Cryan, Tom 228
Cummins, Ray 311, 313-14, 321, 323
Cummins, Willie 16
Cunningham, Tom **279**
Curran, Tom 88
Curry, John 51
Cusack, Donal Óg 359

Daly, Jackie 155, 214
Daly, Tommy 260
Daly, Willie John 88-9, 93, 105, 109, 112,
    128-9, **172**, 199, 209
    in All-Ireland Finals 164, 167, 189,
    217, **218**
    quoted 3, 14-15, 83, 115, 170, 197
    in top twenty 145
Davis, Thomas 67
Davitt, Dan 46
Dawson, Owen 346
Delea, Paddy 2, 35
Devaney, Liam 200, 267
Dineen, Bobby 13
Dixon, Tom 217, 220
Donegan, Jim 60, 81
Doolan, Peter 232
Dorgan, Val 97, 171, 267, 272, 289, 315,
    325
    book on Christy Ring 134, 271, 328
    in *Examiner* 104, 211, 269, 305
Dowling, Liam 130-2, 136, 149, 157,
    197, 235, 253, 255-6, 276
    photo **172**
Dowling, Pat (Paddy) 13
Downes, Charlie 60
Downey, Paddy 5, 81, 123, 135, 276, 293,
    308, 336
Downey, Shem 72-3
Doyle, Gerry 132, 209

Doyle, Jack 2
Doyle, Jimmy 87, 105, 253, 258, 259,
    261, 266-7, 334
    quoted 316, 333
Doyle, John 125, 152, 181-2, 255-6, 267-
    8, 309
    quoted 289, 336, 359
Doyle, Tommy 24, 66, 74, 93-4, 145, 152,
    250, **251**, **339**
Drumgoole, Noel 1
Duffy, Billy 145, 164, 166-7, 182
Duggan, Christy 68, 115
Duggan, Jimmy 164
Duggan, Neally 98
Duggan, Seanie 75, 145, 149, 164-5, 167
Duignan, Frank 90
Dunne, Mick 151-2, 154-5, 181-2, 255,
    262, 276-7
    in *Irish Press* 123-4, 157, 163, 208,
    267-8

English, Jim 186, 221, 245
English, Theo 20, 182, 235, 267

Farranferris 282-91, 340
Ferguson, Des 101-2, 106, 123, 137-40,
    215, **274-5**
Finn, Jimmy 156, 182
Fitzgerald, Pat 233, 243, 309
Flanagan, Peadar 42
Fleming, Andy 74, 107, 109
Flood, Tim 125, 189, 215, 217
Flynn, Austin 243, 293
Foley, Art 190, 215, 219-21, 223, 229
Foley, Des 106, 273
Foley, Lar **274-5**
Fouhy, Mattie 109, 112, 125, 131, 145,
    156, 161, 191
    quoted 89, 189-90
French, Sean 205
Furlong, Tom 128

Gallagher, Josie 75, 145, 165-6
Galway 132-5
Gardiner, Seamus 39
Gill, Mick 260
Glen Rovers 30-53
Goode, Jackie 127

Gordon, Hubert 133, 166-7
Goulding, Eamonn 189, 217
Goulding, Sir Basil 31
Goulding, William 30-1
Goulet, Yann 347
Grace, Paddy 23, 80-2, 86, 277
Graham, William 51
Gray, Harry 40, 46, 145
Greene, Jackie 199
Griffin, Willie 115, 136
Grimes, Phil (Philly) 131, 208, 243, 278, 307-8

Hannigan, Dave 326, 328
Harte, Patsy 79, 155, **306**, 307, 312-13
Hartnett, Josie 83, 133-4, 164, 179, 181, 190, 199, 202-3, **219**
    quoted 157, 197
Hassett, Declan 322, 338
Hayden, Pat 81, 177
Hayes, Derry 89, 157, 205
Healy, Gus, and Mrs Healy **298**
Healy, Pat (Paddy) 60, 75, 214, 232
Hearn, Seamus 186
Heffernan, Jimmy 81
Heffernan, Kevin 100, 105
Herbert, Sean 85
Herbert, Tony 137
Hickey, John D. 84, 102, 115, 124, 157, 167, 180
    on 1952 All-Ireland Final 135-7
    in 1954 183, 189-90
    in 1956 209, 211, 220
    in 1958 232
    in 1959 239, 242-3
    on fights 268-70
    on greatest hurling team ever 260
    on Ring's last final 276-7
    tribute to Ring 157
Hoare, Paddy 18
Hobbs, Danny 53, 108
Hogan, Jim 180
Hogan, Paddy 16
Hogan, Vincent 358-9
Horgan, Bobbie 70-1
Horgan, John 246, 257, 323
Horgan, Patricia 336-7
Horgan, Sean 98
Horgan, Willie 21, 322

Hough, Billy 35
Humphreys, Paul 21
Hurl, John 51
Hurley, Denis 148-9
Hurley, Jim 2, 12, 35, 278, 295, 329, 359

Jack, David 182
John XXIII, Pope 256-7

Keane, John 85, 91
Keane, Roy 326, 328, 352, 358
Keher, Eddie 244, 249, 278, 333
Kehoe, Padge 123, 125, 186, 189, 217, 231, 232
Kelleher, Jamesy 2, 33, 63-4, 191
Kelly, Dermot 200, 202, 213
Kelly, Jim 72, 130
Kelly, Joe 55, 57-8, 60-2, 66, 73-5, **79**, 80, 82-3
Kelly, Terry 168-70, 209, 217, 224, 226, 228, 231, 238, 256
    quoted 244, 255, 266, 273, 338
Kenefick, Mick 41, 46, 51, 53-4
Kennedy, Bobby 302-3, 353-4, **354**
Kennedy, Dan 81
Kennedy, Jimmy 63-4, 93-4, 112, 164
Kennedy, Martin 120, 289
Kenny, Paddy 112, 114, 131, 152, 156, 181, 186, 221, 223
Kenny, Sean 110
Kiely, Benedict 147-50
Kiely, John 125, 208-9, 243
Killeen, John 150, 167, 1133
King, Seamus 95, 331
Kirk, Owen 345-6

Langton, Jim 23-4, 83, 105, 177, 180, 186, 198
Leahy, Johnny 39, 65, 66, 94
Leahy, Terry 23-4, 73, 80-1, 82, 197
Lohan, Brian 357
Lotty, Alan 16, 62, 73, 81, 88, 93, **104**, 119
Lucey, Bishop Cornelius 99-101, 105, 176, **210**, 279, 340
Lynam, Jimmy 115-16, **135**, 152, 156
Lynam, Noel 232, 238

Lynch, Jack 27-8, 34, 38-40, 42, 79, 81, 91, 94, 103
All-Ireland medals 68
biography of 202-3
oration at Ring's funeral 328, 342-3
photos **23**, **298**, **319**, **330**, **348**
quoted 26, 32, 48, 78, 110, 117
reaction to news of Ring's death 338
tributes to 46-7, 61-2
unveils monument 347
Lyons, John 78, 105, 109, 170, 220, 295

McAuliffe, Mattie 201
McAuliffe, Owenie 196, 199
McCarthy, Carthach 100, 102, 254, 282, 284, 302, 322
McCarthy, Charlie 295-6, 302, 309, 320, 323
McCarthy, Derry **125**, 127
McCarthy, Gerald 257, 310-11, 318-19, 322
McCarthy, Gerry (journalist) 264, 293, 305
McCarthy, Joe 353
McCarthy, Justin 309-10
McCarthy, Sean 39, 43, 59, 176
MacCarthy, Sean, sculptor 350
McDonnell, Denis (Dinny) **34**, 46
McDonnell, Mossie 46
McGarry, Paddy 51
McGarry, Tom 235
McGovern, Johnny 180, 221
McGrath, Kevin 9, 16-17
McGrath, Pa 150, 176, 195
McGrath, Walter 91, 173
McInerney, Miko 149, 166
McKeon, Jim 328
Mackesy, Billy 40, 61, 96, 175, 176, 194
Mackey, John 25, 49-50, 55, 57
Mackey, Mick 26, 45, 49, 55-7, 62-3, 75, 198, 248, 329
memoirs 231
photos **56**, **227**
trainer/umpire 200, 210, 226
tribute to Ring 336
McLoughlin, Sean 256
MacMahon, Bryan 331, 343-4, 350-1
McMahon, Paddy 26
McQuaid, Tommy 101, 247, 249
McSwiney, Terence 2-3

Madden, Morgan 2, 35, 195
Magee, Jimmy 314-16
Maher, Derry 153
Maher, Jimmy 77
Maher, John 24, 65
Maher, Mick 241-2, **255**
Maher, Sonny 91, 93, 115
Mahony, Danno 2
Marcus, Louis 87, 187, 246, 301, 334-5, 359
film *Christy Ring* 246, 254, 284, 296-9, **298**
Marnell, Mark 80-1, 124-5, **125**
Matthews, Kevin 85, 136, 145, 180, 202
Mayo, Virginia 205-6
Meagher, Lory 120, 260, 357
Moloughney, Tom 267-72
Moore, Willie 191
Morey, Michael 11
Morrison, Jim 41, 55, 57, 60
Morrissey, Jim 217, 220
Morrissey, Mick 223
Mortell, Mick 253
Motherway, Jimmy 6-7, 342
Motherway, Paddy 4-5, 19-20, 342
Mott, D.R. **298**
Moylan, Christy 88
Moylan, Dan 34, 39
Moylan, Pat 321
Moynihan, Jerry 7-9, 17, 18-19, 342
Mulcahy, Jack 74, 76, 81, 82, 180
Mulcahy, Tom 41, **52**, 60, 62, **70**, 73, 85, 109, 128
Mulcahy, Tomás 337
Mulholland, Sammy 51, 53
Murphy, Bernie 90-1, 93
Murphy, Billy (Willie) 39-40, 44, **52**, 62, 65, 72, 74, 85, 89, 289
Murphy, Brian 96
Murphy, Con 62, **70**, 75, 78, 136
quoted 16, 71, 234, 246, 282-3, 345
Murphy, Connie 73, 75, 77
Murphy, Denis 236, 253, 319
Murphy, Frank 353
Murphy, Gerard 93, 130-3, 149, 152, 157-9, 162, **172**, 189, 199, 208
Murphy, James 97, 177
Murphy, Kevin 51, 153
Murphy, Michael 33, 41-2, 215, 253
Murphy, Noel 82-3

Murphy, Seamus 30
Murphy, Sean Óg 3, 22, 96, 130-1, 296
Murray, Jimmy 95
Myles, Tony 124, 130, 136-7, 150-1

Nealon, Donie 235, 240, 256, 266-7
Nelson, Justin 226, 230
Nestor, Michael 68, 83
Nugent, Matt 114

O'Brien, Dave 78, 97, 345
O'Brien, Dermot 315
O'Brien, Donal 267-8
O'Brien, Sean 23, 72, 157, 232
O'Brien, Seanie 116, 132
O'Callaghan, Denis 234
O'Callaghan, Hugh 288
O'Callaghan, Pat 2
Ó Caoimh, Pádraig 51, 100, 126, 153,
    173, 183, 230, 238
Ó Ceallacháin, Seán Óg 134, 173, 188,
    268, 271, 316
Ó Ceallaigh, Séamus 4, 78
O'Connell, Mick 35, 50, 316
O'Connell, Paddy 32-3
O'Connor, Johnny 88
O'Connor, Mossie 118, 156, 176
O'Connor, Paddy 309
O'Donnell, Billy 24, 42
O'Donnell, John 'Kerry' 81, 121, 302,
    315-17, 340
O'Donnell, Nick **125**, 189-90, **216**, 220-1,
    245, 253, 260
O'Donoghue, Bill 110, 112
O'Donovan, Con **129**
O'Donovan, Diarmuid 345
O'Donovan, Donie **104**
O'Donovan, Paddy 34, 40, 43, 62, 68-9,
    70, 75-6, 83, 87, 108-9
Ó Dulaing, Donnacha 220
O'Grady, John 126, 240, 285, 288
O'Grady, Peter 35
O'Halloran, John 313
O'Hanlon, Mick **218**
Ó hEithir, Breandán 174, 297-9
O'Leary, Dave 151
O'Leary, Pat 118, 242
O'Leary, Seanie 318, 361

Ó Loingsigh, Pádraig 341
O'Mahony, Johnny 22
O'Mahony, T.P. 202-3, 329, 336
Ó Móráin, Donal **298**
O'Muiri, Alf **298**
O'Neill, Billy 132, 144-5, 149, 167, 194,
    204
O'Neill, Jim 61, 67, 118
O'Regan, Jim 356
O'Regan, Johnny 109
O'Riordan, Denis 253, **258**, 259
O'Riordan, Jerry 72, 76, **79**, 107, 109,
    136, 156
O'Riordan, Mossie 73, 75, 77, **79**, 86, 89,
    95, 98, 107, 128
O'Riordan, Seanie 153, 285
Ó Sé, Seán 345
O'Shaughnessy, Tony 107, 128, 130, 188,
    212, 217
    quoted 129, 134-5, 148, 156, 159, 169,
    189, 309-10
    in top twenty 145
O'Shea, Brendan 203
O'Shea, Christy 210, 292
Ó Síocháin, Seán 40, 53, 247
O'Sullivan, Diarmuid 359
O'Sullivan, Eddie John 88, 89
O'Sullivan, Jerry **258**, 277-8, 310, 352
O'Sullivan, Ted 9, 15-17, 24-6, 28, 39-40
O'Sullivan, Tom 167, 175, 196, 230, 259
O'Sullivan, Tony 337
O'Toole, Mick 90
Ó Tuama, Liam 3, 61, 100, 314, 359
Ó Tuama, Seán 350

Peck, Gregory 181
Phelan, Chris 79
Phelan, Paddy 23-4, 198, 260
Philpott, Paddy 221
Porter, Ned 45-6
Powell, Tom 12
Power, Jack 304-5
Power, Jackie 25, 63, 74, 85
Power, John P. 61-3
Power, Ned 243, **279**, 334
Power, Seamus 240-3
Prendergast, Peter 79-80, 82
Prior, Jim 137
Puirséal, Pádraig 180, 198, 215-16, 225, 268

Purcell, Sean 314, 316
Purcell, Tommy 66, 91-2

Quane, Mick 38, 253, 256, **258**, 259, **274-5**
Quinlan, John 147, 150, 154
Quirke, John 23-6, 40, 45-6, 55, 57-8, 60,
   62-3, 75-6, 89, 248
   quoted 38-9, 41, 48, 71

Rackard, Billy 189, 217, **219**, 221, 328
Rackard, Bobby 105, 123-4, 127, 145,
   189-90, **216**, **218-19**, 220
Rackard, Nicky 105, 123, 125, 127, 145,
   183, 186, 189, 215-17, 219-20
   quoted 198-9, 224
   in top ten 221
Reddan, Tony 48, 91, 111, 114, 131, 145,
   152, 181, 232
Redmond, Garry 47
Regan, Mick 217, 219, 228, 233
Ring, Christy
   1938 **13**, **14**, **17**
   1939 20-5, **20**, **21**
   1940 Munster final 25-8
   1941 All-Ireland final 39-41
   1942 Cork team **44**
   1943 **47**, **48**, **52-3**
   1944 54-63
   1945 65-9
   1946 **56**, 70-7, **72**
   1947 All-Ireland final 78-82
   1948-49 matches 88-96, **92**, **104**
   1950 107-12
   1951 113-19
   1952 123-45, **125**, **129**, **133**, **135**, **141**
   1953 **143**, 147-62, **151**
   1953 All-Ireland final 160, **162**,
      163-78, **165**
   1954 179-207
   1954 All-Ireland final 183-91, **184-5**
   1955 201-7, **201**
   1956 208-21, **211**, **213**
   1956 All-Ireland final 215-21, **216**
   1957 222-9
   1958 230-6
   1959 237-51
   1960 252-9
   1961 260-72

1962 273-81, **274-5**
action photos **239**, **280**, **300**, **327**, **332**
All-Ireland medals 68, 196
assaulted 168-70
at commemoration ceremony **234**
at launch of *Cork's Hurling Story* **319**
at launch of *The Book of Cloyne* **341**
at Texaco Sportstar Banquet **330**
and Bishop Lucey **210**
and Bobby Kennedy **354**
boyhood 1-11
charity appeal on radio 264-5
charity matches 314-16
children 293
choice of hurleys 235-6
Churches Tournament 99-106
Cork against Tipperary 41-4
Cork Minor 12-29, **13**
criticism and controversy 262-4
death and funeral 336-46
and Denis O'Riordan **258**
and Farranferris team 282-91, **283**, **285**
fight and false allegations against
   267-71
film *Christy Ring* 246, 254, 284,
   296-301, **298**
first League medal 22-5
four-in-a-row 48-50, 54-64
Glen Rovers 30-53, **34**, **37**
hurler of the century 355-9
hurler of the year **113**, 221, 295
injuries **146**, 199, 203, 224, 226-7
and Jack Lynch and Jimmy Walsh **23**
and Jean Seberg during Cork Film
   Festival **206**
last games 276-8, 292-6, **292**, **294**,
   303-13, **306**, **312**
leads parade **70**
league game against Dublin **138-9**
and Liam McCarthy Cup in 1953 **160**
mentor 318-25, **320**
and Mick Mackey **56**, **227**
mother's death 157-8
and Paddy Barry **229**
and Paddy Barry and Paddy Cronin **122**
parents, brothers and sisters 2
personality 146, 262-3, 287-90, 321,
   344-5
playing football 96-8, 316
playing golf 265

playing softball 315
playing squash 293, 323-5
prior to first adult game **20**
quoted 141-4, 222, 245-7, 359-61
Ringy, TG4 documentary 353-4
signing autographs **286-7, 317**
Sportsman/Sport Star of the year **141**,
145
statues and other memorials 347-54,
348, 358
suspension 231-2
tackled **255, 279**
and throw-in **192-3**
and Tommy Doyle **251**
training 202-3
tributes to 157, 182-3, 196, 212-13,
246-50, 325, 328-36, 342-6, 355-6
trips abroad 77-8, **118**, 119-22, **119**,
195, 195-8, 314-17
voice recorded on tape 158-62
wedding to Rita Taylor 279-80
Ring, Dannix 62
Ring, Mary 1, 2, 10, 25, 157-8
Ring, Nicholas 1-2, 10, 25, 191, 342
Ring, Paddy Joe 2, 4, 6, 28, 77, 244, 279
Ring, Rita (née Taylor) 279-80, 293, 296,
340, 343, 350, 353
photos **298, 348**
Ring, Willie 9
Ring, Willie John 2-7, 18-19, 27-8, 77,
118, 244-5, 257, 344-5, 347
RTÉ 220, 288, 338, 344
Russell, Paul 273
Ryan, Mick 84, 94, 114, 115, 152, 208-9,
250
Ryan, Ned 115, 152
Ryan, Seamus 221
Ryan, Tadhg 16
Ryan, Tim 25-6, 45, 55, 63, 152, 289
Ryng, James 'Bobby' 24, 40, 42

Salmon, Joe 105, 164-7, 281, 295, 299
Scanlan, Paddy 25, 107, 141
Scannell, Andy 159, **160**, 174, 175
Seberg, Jean **206-7**
Shanahan, Phil 91, 125-7, 131, 250
Sheedy, Michael 347
Sheehan, Colm 259
Sherwood, Joe 262-4

Slattery, Tony 13
Sligo 203-4
Smyth, Jimmy 156, 199-200, 215, 240, 335
Stakelum, Pat 66-7, 91, 94, 123-4, 132,
145, 152, 198
photos **210, 255**
Stokes, Dick 26-7, 39, 55, 145, 248
Styles, Joe 95

Thornhill, Batt **20**, 21-2, 25, 41, 62, 108
Tipperary 41-4
Tisdall, Bob 2
Tóibín, Niall 354
Treacy, Tommy 42
Troy, Canon Bertie **341**
Twomey, Donie 90-1
Twomey, Joe 133, 136, 147, 149, 157,
209, 232, 238, 256
Twomey, Sean 90-1
Twomey, Vincie 128, 154, 189-90, 217
Tyers, Paddy 187, 212, 246, 297-8, 340

Wade, Ned 60
Wall, Tony 152, 182, 229, 239, 241, 250,
256
Walsh, Billy 'Bowler' 61, 68, 73, 80
Walsh, Dave 114, 125
Walsh, Frankie 228, 242
Walsh, Jimmy **23**, 53
Walsh, Maurice 30
Walsh, Ollie 244, 276, 316
Walsh, Willie 120, 145, 153, 214
Ware, Jim 89
Waterford 241-3
West, Joe 88
Wexford 123-45, 183-91
Wheeler, Ned 180, 186
Whelahan, Brian 357
White, Frank 60

Young, Eamonn 145, 173, 230-1
quoted 16-17, 68, 108, 132, 154, 156,
293
Young, Jim 24, 26, 44, 48, 62, 69, 74,
322, 336
quoted 49, 90, 104-5
Young, John 74, 307, 312

ABOUT THE AUTHOR

Tim Horgan, a retired teacher and GAA correspondent, has been a lifelong follower of hurling. He has written a number of GAA books, including *Cork's Hurling Story*.